W9-AQH-653

Military
and Strategic Policy

Also available in
Bibliographies and Indexes in Military Studies

Stress, Strain, and Vietnam: An Annotated Bibliography of Two Decades of
Psychiatric and Social Sciences Literature Reflecting the Effect of the War on
the American Soldier
Norman M. Camp, Robert H. Stretch, and William C. Marshall

Greenwood Reference Volumes on
American Public Policy Formation

These reference books deal with the development of U.S. policy in various
"single-issue" areas. Most policy areas are to be represented by three types of
sourcebooks: 1) Institutional Profiles of Leading Organizations, 2) Collection of
Documents and Policy Proposals, and 3) Bibliography.

Public Interest Law Groups: Institutional Profiles
Karen O'Connor and Lee Epstein

U.S. National Security Policy and Strategy: Documents and Policy Proposals
Sam C. Sarkesian with Robert A. Vitas

U.S. National Security Policy Groups: Institutional Profiles
Cynthia Watson

U.S. Agricultural Groups: Institutional Profiles
William P. Browne and Allan J. Cigler

MILITARY AND STRATEGIC POLICY

An Annotated Bibliography

Compiled by
Benjamin R. Beede

Bibliographies and Indexes in Military Studies, Number 2

GREENWOOD PRESS
New York • Westport, Connecticut • London

Library of Congress Cataloging-in-Publication Data

Beede, Benjamin R.
  Military and strategic policy : an annotated bibliography /
compiled by Benjamin R. Beede.
    p. cm.—(Bibliographies and indexes in military studies,
ISSN 1040-7995 ; no. 2)
  Includes bibliographical references.
  ISBN 0-313-26000-1 (lib. bdg. : alk. paper)
  1. United States—Military policy—Bibliography. 2. United
States—National security—Bibliography. I. Title. II. Series.
Z1361.D4B4   1990
[UA23]
016.355'033573—dc20   89-25616

British Library Cataloguing in Publication Data is available.

Library of Congress Catalog Card Number: 89-25616
ISBN: 0-313-26000-1
ISSN: 1040-7995

First published in 1990

Greenwood Press, 88 Post Road West, Westport, CT 06881
An imprint of Greenwood Publishing Group, Inc.

Printed in the United States of America

∞

The paper used in this book complies with the
Permanent Paper Standard issued by the National
Information Standards Organization (Z39.48-1984).

10 9 8 7 6 5 4 3 2 1

For My Mother

Virginia M. Beede

Contents

Series Foreword

Policymakers and strategists alike share a common view that in the nuclear age, issues of U.S. national security policy are increasingly complex and open to a variety of policy and strategic interpretations and options. More study is needed to define terminology, to clarify issues, and to provide a historical background for understanding concepts, varying perspectives, and the process of policy development in terms of national security.

Greenwood Press is publishing a series of Public Policy Formation reference volumes in different issue-oriented areas. The three volumes dealing with a particular issue-oriented area will include a work giving analytical profiles of public information and interest groups that have played a major role in the field, with an emphasis on the period since 1960; a collection of documents and policy proposals during that period; and an annotated bibliography. These volumes are designed for college students, teachers, researchers, and professionals in organizations, government, and the media.

While the three volumes dealing with national security policy and strategy do not claim to be all-encompassing in surveying and analyzing groups, documents, and publications in the field, they provide a real sense of history and a solid background for studying the subject. They contribute to a unique new reference series that opens up significant new lines of research in the field, and they offer guidelines for future study.

This annotated bibliography could not have been published without the generous support of the National Strategy Forum in Chicago. The Forum was organized in 1983 by a group of Chicago area civic leaders with varied views but similar concerns about the key national security issues of the day. They came together to create a forum where individuals with an interest in these important matters could learn from the experts who analyze and formulate American national security strategy-in a balanced exchange of ideas.

The National Strategy Forum sponsors educational programs and research designed to broaden citizen awareness of issues of national security. The Forum views military, diplomatic, and economic policy as critical components of national strategy.

The Forum is united by the following principles:

First, the national strategic interest of the United States consists in seeking genuine peace with freedom and justice in common cause with a community of free and independent nations.

Second, informed public opinion is essential to maintain a viable security structure and strategy in a democratic society.

Third, enduring nonpartisan consensus is crucial to establish United States strategic credibility with both allies and adversaries of the free world.

Fourth, the advancement and preservation of democracy is essential to enhance human rights, inspire principle cultural achievement and maximize economic development.

The principal officers of the National Strategy Forum include the following:

Chairman: Morris I. Liebman
Vice Chairman: Michael P. Galvin
President: Richard E. Friedman

Board of Founders:

W. Gardner Barker   Monte P. Monaster
Lester Crown   Jay A. Pritzker
William Farley   Robert A. Pritzker
Robert W. Galvin   Mr. and Mrs. Anthony J. Rudis
Charles Luckman   Patrick G. Ryan

The Forum is nonpartisan and espouses no specific political cause.

Sam C. Sarkesian
Series Editor for the three
volume set dealing with U.S.
national security policy and
strategy issues

Preface

Many of the documents reproduced in <u>Military and Strategic Issues: A Collection of Documents and Policy Proposals</u>, compiled by Sam Sarkesian, are included in this bibliography, but not all of them. Exclusions include federal statutes and materials from the years before 1953.

The internal arrangement of chapters in this bibliography follows a generally consistent plan. Absolute consistency seemed inappropriate because the salience of particular topics and issues has changed from time to time. The primary division of the bibliography into chapters covering particular presidential administrations led me to focus first in each chapter on defense and military decision-makers and then to proceed to studies of decision-making machinery in the national security sphere as it existed during that administration. Most chapters then have a section on military policy, which includes materials of a very general nature on the approach taken by the administration toward security matters. This section is followed by groups of bibliographic entries dealing with particular types of strategy, including civil defense, military assistance, and disarmament and arms control. The next section deals with military personnel, which I had difficulty conceiving of as a "strategy." Alliances generally and American security relations with countries or groups of countries in regions of the world come next. The final section in each substantive chapter, except the one on Vietnam, deals with significant crises which involved at least the serious threat of military confrontation.

Overlapping is inevitable; many items could be listed under several headings. No matter how fine the subdivisions in a bibliography, it is virtually impossible to analyze every entry through one and only one heading. Therefore, the reader should not depend solely on chapter headings and subdivisions, but should also use the subject index, which identifies each entry in terms of the major topics it covers. The separate author index will be helpful in locating references in the bibliography to writings by major policy makers and by recognized scholars in particular fields. The indexes are keyed to entry numbers; roman numerals refer to page numbers in the introduction.

Acknowledgments

It has been a pleasure working with Sam C. Sarkesian, the series editor for Greenwood reference volumes dealing with the formation of United States military and strategic policy. As with any book, there have been many questions, which Dr. Sarkesian and Mildred Vasan at Greenwood Press have answered fully and promptly. I am grateful to Dr. Sarkesian for asking me to participate in this reference project and for reproducing my manuscript on a word processor.

My wife, Anne Brugh, put a vast amount of effort into this bibliography. She checked most of the entries, saved me from several errors, and devoted a good deal of time reading the manuscript, asking questions, and noting typographical errors. My mother, Virginia M. Beede, to whom the bibliography is dedicated, also read the manuscript and checked information in detail.

I wish to express my appreciation to Emma A. Warren, Director of the Kilmer Area Library at Rutgers - The State University of New Jersey, and Dr. Joanne R. Euster, University Librarian at Rutgers, for having approved a short research leave for the purpose of working on the bibliography. Approximately a quarter of the entries in the bibliography were gathered during my leave. Having the equivalent of a month's normal working time to give to the bibliography helped greatly.

This volume could not have been prepared without the efforts and support of the National Strategy Forum. The efforts of Brenda Thompson and Debbie C. Lewis were instrumental in putting this manuscript in proper format. I am particularly grateful for their patience. I also want to express my appreciation to the principal officers of the National Strategy Forum for their support.

Although a number of people have contributed in one way or another to the completion of the project, the final responsibility for the text of the bibliography remains with me.

Introduction

There is no current general bibliography on United States national security policy, despite the continuing flood of literature on the subject. Several very fine bibliographies were produced in the early 1970's, but they are out of print.[1] Plans to update one of them never materialized.[2] This bibliography is a highly selective compilation of representative good work in the field of national security. In no sense is it comprehensive.

While the scope of the work extends back to the first Eisenhower administration, its emphasis is on the period after 1960, and, even more, on the years since the end of American involvement in the wars of Indochina. Relatively few works from the 1950's are included except those of continuing importance or of historical significance. Coverage is more extensive for the 1960's. Much of the bibliography deals with the period after the enunciation of the Nixon Doctrine in 1969.

The bibliography focuses primarily on national security policy and policy-making processes. The materials are confined to selected speeches and other policy declarations by presidents and other major figures, books, and periodical articles, most of the latter from military and political science journals. In compiling the bibliography I have utilized standard periodical indexes, including the Air University Index to Military Periodicals, bibliographic compilations such as America: History and Life, and the card catalogs and computerized catalogs of Rutgers and Princeton Universities. The cutoff for inclusion of most materials was December 31, 1987.

The bibliography provides an introduction to the processes for formulating strategies and military policies and to a number of major issues in the defense and security sphere. Decision-making structures in the United States and the efforts made to improve them, the American system of alliances, weapons technology and its impact on strategy, and American military and naval operations after 1953 receive considerable attention. Thus, a number of narrower topics and highly specialized publications have been

omitted. The bibliography focuses primarily on the executive
branch of government which was clearly dominant in decision-
making on defense matters during the period under study.
Some   monographs   and   a   few   periodical   articles   on
Congressional activism in the military and strategic sphere
are included, however.   Almost all Congressional hearings,
committee   reports   and   committee   prints,   and   General
Accounting Office and Congressional Research Service studies
were excluded.   Because of their value to those interested
in very specific research, reference is made in the first
section of this bibliography to indexes of Congressional
publications and to collections of the GAO and CRS studies.
Research   institute   reports,   which   are   usually   very
specialized, and ephemeral articles and studies of a single
budget year or other limited topics have generally been
omitted.

     Vietnam and the smaller military actions of the years
from the 1950's to the 1980's presented something of a
problem given existing bibliographies.   The section on the
Vietnam conflict was prepared with a view to avoiding too
much duplication with Louis A. Peake's The United States in
the Vietnam War 1954-1975, which should be consulted for
many additional references.[3]   The smaller scale military and
naval actions of the period may be approached bibliogra-
phically through my Intervention and Counterinsurgency: The
Small Wars of the United States, 1898-1984.[4]

     Some topics receive relatively little attention.   Most
works on   military compensation and living conditions are
excluded.   A few items are included that discuss the problem
of attracting and retaining certain types of specialists.
Affirmative action is not considered, although it has had
profound influences on the military establishment.   Defense
procurement and the "military-industrial-complex" issue are
touched upon, but are not dealt with at length.

     A special feature of this bibliography is the inclusion
of many books and a number of essays from collective works
published by the National Defense University.   Its publications appear to be among the best studies being produced at
this time.   Specialists in national security can only
welcome   the   great   increase   in   the   National   Defense
University's commitment to the production and dissemination
of research.   This development occurred during Air Force
Lieutenant   General   John   S.   Pustay's   presidency;[5]   his
policies are being continued ably by the current president,
Air Force Lieutenant General Bradley C. Hosmer.

     Many   of   the   documents   produced   in   Military and
Strategic Issues: A Collection of Documents and Policy
Proposals, compiled by Sam Sarkesian, are included in the
bibliography, but not all of them.   Exclusions include
federal statutes and materials from the years before 1953.

     A comparison of the literature on national security in
the 1950's and in the 1980's suggests the dramatic changes
that have occurred.   Relatively few books were written on
American military policy and national security thirty-five

or forty years ago, although highly valuable studies appeared in such periodicals as the <u>Military Review</u> and the <u>United States Naval Institute Proceedings</u>. These articles were written for the most part by active duty, reserve, or retired officers of the armed forces and, to a much lesser extent, by civilian governmental officials.

Military policy has been debated since the beginning of the republic by early thinkers such as Henry Knox and John C. Calhoun, but no real volume of literature developed until the United States found itself competing with other nations in the late 19th and early 20th centuries in the fields of trade and armaments. The first modern dialogue on security policy was probably the controversy over preparedness just before American involvement in World War I. Another watershed was reached in the late 1930's and early 1940's when a new preparedness campaign encountered vigorous resistance from isolationists and those who feared American militarism.

After the United States assumed superpower status in 1945, attention was given to national security, no doubt as a result of the Pearl Harbor attack and the threat of nuclear weapons. The growth in literature was gradual until the late 1950's and early 1960's. Since then, publications of all sorts: monographs, dissertations, theses, periodical articles, governmental reports, and analyses by private research organizations have multiplied rapidly. The high cost of defense and debates over defense versus domestic spending also helped make national security an attractive field for policy analysis. The development of national security studies as a special subfield can be seen as a part of the increasing concern of political scientists with a wide range of public policy issues.

Some crude figures on the increase in the number of journals in the field of military affairs demonstrate the growth of interest in defense. An examination of journal titles listed in Ulrich's <u>International Periodicals Directory</u> shows that, in terms of the years of establishment, journals were started much more frequently in the 1970's and early 1980's than during the 1950's and 1960's:

Period	Span of Years	Number of Journals
before 1950		26
1951-1960	10	15
1961-1970	10	14
1971-1980	10	37
1981-1986	5	18

Newspapers and state publications were not included in this survey; nor were journals related to defense and security but listed by <u>Ulrich's</u> in sections such as political science.

Several books should be at the reach of anyone interested in security matters. One of the most remarkable quasi-reference works is John Keegan's and Andrew Wheatcroft's <u>Zones of Conflict: An Atlas of Future Wars</u>.[6] Few books have taught me more about existing and potential areas of possible military action. Of importance also is Gerard Chaliand's and Jean-Pierre Rageau's <u>Strategic Atlas: A Comparative Geopolitics of the World's Great Powers</u>.[7] This highly informative reference work considers economic and social trends, as well as the purely military facets of national power. A fascinating study of the geopolitical perceptions of military leaders in various countries, <u>Mental Maps</u>, by Peter Gould and Rodney White also deserves to be mentioned.[8] It was based on Richard Eaton's doctoral dissertation.[9]

While it is hoped that this bibliography will contribute to debates and to research on national security policy, users of the bibliography should remember its some-what limited scope. They will need to consult the continuing reference sources cited in the first chapter and highly useful indexes such as the <u>Public Affairs Information Service</u>.

NOTES

1. John Greenwood, <u>American Defense Policy Since 1945: A Preliminary Bibliography</u>, edited by Geoffrey Kemp and others (Lawrence: University Press of Kansas, 1973); Arthur D. Larson, <u>National Security Affairs: A Guide to Information Sources</u> (Detroit: Gale Research Company, 1973).

2. Greenwood, <u>American Defense Policy</u>.

3. Louis A. Peake, <u>The United States in the Vietnam War, 1954-1975</u> (New York: Garland Publishing, Inc., 1986).

4. Benjamin R. Beede, <u>Intervention and Counterinsurgency: An Annotated Bibliography of the Small Wars of the United States, 1898-1984</u> (New York: Garland Publishing, Inc., 1985).

5. Franklin D. Margiotta, Letter, January 13, 1982. Colonel Margiotta was at that time Director, Research Directorate. Copies of this letter were enclosed with National Defense University publications.

6. John Keegan and Andrew Wheatcroft, <u>Zones of Conflict: An Atlas of Future Wars</u> (New York: Simon & Schuster, 1986).

7. Gerard Chaliand and Jean-Pierre Rageau, <u>Strategic Atlas: Comparative Geopolitics of the World's Great Powers</u> 2d rev. ed. New York: Harper & Row, Publishers, 1985).

8. Peter Gould and Rodney White, <u>Mental Maps</u>, 2d ed. (Boston: Allen & Unwin, 1986).

9. Richard Eaton, "Geopolitical Mental Maps: A Search for Synthesis," Ph.D. diss., Pennsylvania State University, 1985.

Military
and Strategic Policy

Chapter 1

Bibliographies and Other Reference Sources on Military and Strategic Policy

Only a few truly significant bibliographies and other reference sources are listed and annotated in this chapter. Most are book length, although a few are essays which lie "buried" in larger works. No effort has been made to include periodical indexes or other serial publications except for listings and analyses of federal government documents.

General Documentary Collections in Microform

Office of the Secretary of Defense

1. Public Statements by the Secretaries of Defense, 1947-1981. Frederick, Maryland: University Publications of America. Originally compiled by the Office of the Secretary of Defense for internal use. The collection includes press conferences and other materials and is organized in five parts, each with its own guide.

National Security Council

2. Documents of the National Security Council, 1947-1977. Frederick, Maryland: University Publications of America. Continuing series includes reports and other materials prepared by the National Security Council and other agencies. Topics include the Berlin crisis of 1961 and United States policies toward various countries. Later supplements include newly declassified documents from all periods of the Council.

3. Minutes of Meetings of the National Security Council; with Special Advisory Reports. 1947- Frederick, Maryland: University Publications of America. Ongoing series with many reports on American military and diplomatic policies.

General Bibliographies

4. Alcalà, Raoul H., and Douglas H. Rosenberg. "The New Politics of National Security: A Selected and Annotated Bibliography." In Military Force and American Society,

edited by Bruce M. Russett and Alfred Stepan, 196-371. New York: Harper & Row, 1973. Emphasizes political/policy aspects, utilizing both official sources and "alternative" publications critical of current policies. Entries number 2,578. This is an interesting compilation which includes bibliographies and other reference sources.

5.   Arkin, William M. Research Guide to Current Military and Strategic Affairs. Washington, D.C.: Institute for Policy Studies, 1981. 232p. Describes a great many periodicals and government documents and provides information on the agencies and institutions that generate various types of publications relating to defense issues.

6.   "Bibliography." In U.S. Congress. Senate. Committee on Government Operations. Subcommittee on National Policy Machinery. Organizing for National Security: Studies and Background Materials Submitted to the Committee on Government Operations by Its Subcommittee on National Policy Machinery (Pursuant to S. Res. 115, 86th Cong., and S. Res. 20, 87th Cong.), Volume 2, 27-111. Washington, D.C.: Government Printing Office, 1961. SOD Y4. E74/6N21se/10/v.2. Detailed bibliography of government publications, research institute reports, books, periodical articles, and other materials, including dissertations. Many items have brief annotations.

7.   Goehlert, Robert U. and Elizabeth R. Hoffmeister. The Department of State and American Diplomacy: A Bibliography. New York: Garland Publishing, Inc., 1986. 349p. II.D. "Foreign Affairs and the Military," 117-128, is most pertinent, but geographical sections and the index should also be used. Includes much material on disarmament.

8.   Greenwood, John. American Defense Policy Since 1945: A Preliminary Bibliography, edited by Geoffrey Kemp and others. Lawrence, Kansas: University Press of Kansas, 1973. 317p. Includes about three thousand unannotated listings of books, periodical articles, special reports, and government documents. Most items date from the 1960's. This is an important, well-organized compilation, which includes a section on the domestic impacts of American security policies. The well-known military historian Robin Higham served as adviser.

9.   Larson Arthur D. National Security Affairs: A Guide to Information Sources. Detroit: Gale Research Company, 1972. 411p. Stresses the years 1958 to 1972. Larson includes a good deal of theoretical material in an extensive unannotated bibliography of nearly four thousand entries. This is still a very useful compilation, much enhanced by a large key word index.

Military Policy and Foreign Policy

10. Burns, Richard Dean, editor. Guide to American Foreign Relations Since 1700. Santa Barbara, California: ABC-CLIO, Inc., 1983. 1311p. Two sections, "The Armed Forces, Strategy, and Foreign Policy," by Russell F. Weigley and others and "United States and the Soviet Union After 1953," by Thomas G. Patterson are of special importance in this annotated bibliography and guide to the literature.

11. Plischke, Elmer. U.S. Foreign Relations: A Guide to Information Sources. Detroit: Gale Research Company, 1980. 715p. Materials related to military and security policy appear in several sections. Scanning the table of contents is recommended. Of special importance are Chapters 10-12 and Chapter 18. This is a highly useful compilation because it puts military policy into the larger context of foreign relations. It lacks a subject index, but its fairly elaborate structure of sections and subsections within each chapter largely makes up for this deficiency. There is an author index, which includes both individual author's names and corporate (or agency) authors.

Military History

12. Higham, Robin, and Donald J. Mrozek, editors. A Guide to the Sources of United States Military History. Hamden, Connecticut: Archon Books, 1975. 559p. Supplement I, 1981. Supplement II, 1986. Consists of extensive bibliographic essays by authorities in each field. While the series is directed primarily to the historian, there is a great deal of material in each volume on recent and contemporary developments in the national security field. The basic volume, for example, includes a fifty-page section on "The Department of Defense, Defense Policy, and Diplomacy, 1945-1973," by Calvin L. Christman.

13. Kinnell, Susan K., editor. Military History of the United States: An Annotated Bibliography. Santa Barbara, California: ABC-CLIO, 1986. 333p. Drawing from information in America: History and Life, this bibliography presents periodical articles, dissertations, and books from the years 1974 to 1985. Section 6 deals with the period after World War II. Of interest to political scientists and national security specialists, as well as historians.

14. Lane, Jack C. America's Military Past: A Guide to Information Sources. Detroit: Gale Research Company, 1980. 280p. Chapters 7 and 8 contain small numbers of well-annotated entries pertaining to American defense after World War II and the Korean and Vietnamese conflicts. This is a helpful, well-organized bibliography.

Special Studies

Air Force and Air Warfare

15. Hoover, Robert A. The MX Controversy: A Guide to Issues & References. Claremont, California: Regina Books, 1982. 116p. About half the book consists of an essay on the MX debate; the other half is a selective bibliography dealing with all aspects of the problem. Brief introductions are included in each major division of the bibliography.

16. Miller, Samuel Duncan. An Aerospace Bibliography. Washington, D.C.: Government Printing Office, 1978. 341p. SOD D301 62/2 Ae8. Selective bibliography with brief annotations. Several sections deal with specific periods such as the Korean War. Most deal with such topics as "Aircraft Development" and "Logistics." There are sections on military policy and strategy. Miller includes a number of highly useful features such as a detailed subject index and an extensive bibliography of bibliographies.

Counterinsurgency

17. Beede, Benjamin R. Intervention and Counterinsurgency: An Annotated Bibliography of the Small Wars of the United States, 1898-1984. New York: Garland Publishing, Inc., 1985. 321p. Includes selective bibliographic chapters on most post-World War II interventions and crises from North China in 1945-1949 through the Grenada operation. Several chapters deal with the more theoretical and general works on intervention and counterinsurgency. The bibliography includes a detailed subject index.

18. Condit, D.M., and others. A Counterinsurgency Bibliography. Washington, D.C.: American University, Special Operations Research Office, 1963. 269p. Supplements through 1967. Very extensive compilation of official publications, books, periodical articles, and some research institute reports. The often detailed annotations and the indexes add much to this series. While its scope is worldwide, there are hundreds of items relating to the American experience.

Disarmament and Arms Control

Documentary Collections

19. Documents on Disarmament 1945-1982. Frederick, Maryland: University Publication of America. Published with the assistance of the United States Arms Control and Disarmament Agency. This indexed microfilm collection includes much material on specific weapons systems as well as disarmament negotiations and related items.

20. Major Studies of the Legislative Reference Service/

Congressional Research Service: 1916-1974. Frederick, Maryland: University Publications of America. Continued by supplements each year, with the current title: Major Studies and Issue Briefs of the Congressional Research Service [year] Supplement. Large numbers of defense-related reports are included. They deal with topics such as arms control, weapons transfers to other countries, and defense policies such as the Strategic Defense Initiative.

21. Nuclear Weapons, Arms Control, and the Threat of Thermonuclear War: Special Studies. Frederick, Maryland: University Publications of America. Consists of reports and analyses by consultant groups and research agencies, such as the Rand Corporation, the National Defense University, and the Strategic Studies Institute at the Army War College. The basic set covers the years 1969-1981, with supplements thereafter.

Other Sources

22. Labrie, Roger P., editor. SALT Handbook: Key Documents and Issues, 1972-1979. Washington, D.C.: American Enterprise Institute, 1979. 736p. Highly useful collection of documents, including treaties, extracts from Congressional hearings, and other materials. Also included are a glossary and bibliographies, in addition to several essays on various aspects of SALT. This remains a highly useful reference source.

Intelligence and Special Operations

23. Constantinides, George C. Intelligence and Espionage: An Analytical Bibliography. Boulder, Colorado: Westview Press, 1983. 559p. Extensive bibliography which includes coverage of much material dating from the post-World War II period. Constantinides deals with all aspects of intelligence and espionage; there is also some coverage of special warfare operations.

24. Smith, Myron J., Jr. The Secret Wars, A Guide to Sources in English: Volume II, Intelligence, Propaganda and Psychological Warfare, Covert Operations, 1945-1980. Santa Barbara, California: ABC-CLIO, 1980. Presents a large number of unannotated entries on all phases of American intelligence and psychological warfare. There are useful subsections on the U-2 incident, the Liberty and Pueblo attacks, the Bay of Pigs invasion, and the Cuban missile crisis, among other topics. Coverage is extended to books, articles, essays in books, government publications, and dissertations.

Mobilization

25. Henseler, Barbara A. "Yesterday, Today, and Tomorrow:

An Annotated Bibliography of Major Mobilization-Related Literature." In Mobilization and the National Defense, edited by Hardy L. Merritt and Luther F. Carter, 149-165. Washington, D.C.: National Defense University Press, 1985. SOD D5.402:M71/2.   Provides very detailed analyses of a small number of major books on mobilization.   There are some historical works and some items that focus on contemporary problems.

26. Mayo, Julia. Mobilization: A Bibliography. Revised and updated by Marcia Whipple and others.   Washington, D.C.: National Defense University Library, 1983. 80p. Extensive, unannotated compilation of government documents, theses, research institute reports, periodical and newspaper articles, and books.   Covers both industrial and personnel mobilization and includes references to relevant statutory and administrative authorities for mobilization-related activities.

North Atlantic Treaty Organization

27. Norton, Augustus R. and others. NATO: A Bibliography and Resource Guide.   New York: Garland Publishing, Inc., 1984. 252p. Includes more than four thousand references to NATO material under a variety of subject headings.   The bibliography contains an author index.

Navy and Naval Warfare

28. Smith, Myron J., Jr. The United States Navy and Coast Guard, 1946-1983: A Bibliography of English-Language Works and 16mm Films.   Jefferson, North Carolina: McFarland, 1984. 539p.   Includes thousands of references for the post-World War II era.   The bibliography is organized by broad categories which are further divided by more specialized topic headings and supplemented by a subject index.

Rapid Deployment Force

29. Monroe, David J. Rapid Deployment Force: A Selected Bibliography. 2d ed.   Washington, D.C: National Defense University Library, 1983. 27p. Extensive, unannotated compilation of government documents, books, periodical and newspaper articles, and reports from research institutes such as the Rand Corporation.

Terrorism

30. Lakos, Amos. A Bibliography of International Terrorism. Boulder, Colorado: Westview Press, 1986. 481p. Comprehensive bibliographic compilation of English-language materials on terrorism.   Includes books, articles, government publications, research reports, and dissertations.   The bibliography is divided into a number of topical and geographical sections.   The former include

legal aspects and efforts to counter terrorism. A subject
and an author index are also provided.

Indexes to Federal Government Publications

31. Congressional Information Service.   CIS Index to
Publications of the U.S. Congress. Washington, D.C.:
Congressional Information Service, 1970-___ . Indispensable
guide to Congressional hearings, reports and other
documents which contain extensive, unique materials on
national security affairs.   One of the most valuable
features is the summary of testimony before Congressional
committees. Indexing is quite thorough.

32. Congressional Information Service. US Congressional
Committee Hearings Index, 1833-1969. Bethesda, Maryland:
Congressional Information Service, 19__-19__ . This series
is not wholly comparable with the CIS Index to Publications
of the U.S. Congress because it lacks abstracts of the
documents.   Indexing is also less detailed, but, nevertheless, this is a useful guide to Congressional
publications.

Chapter 2

General and Comparative Studies of Military and Strategic Policy

The chapter is divided into a number of sections, ranging from decision-makers to strategy to military personnel. The word "strategy" is interpreted very broadly. An effort is made to differentiate between "military policy" and "general strategy." Materials of the broadest scope, including strategy, mobilization, decision-making, finance, and other topics, are listed under "military policy," while strategy is seen as planning in regard to specific potential adversaries. The sections on civil defense, military assistance, and disarmament and arms control refer to "strategies" outside the traditional categories of air, ground, and naval strategy.

Decision-makers

33. Bock, Joseph G. The White House Staff and the National Security Assistant: Friendship and Friction at the Water's Edge. Westport, Connecticut: Greenwood Press. 1987. 215p. Surveys the roles of national security assistants since the late 1940's, emphasizing the need for presidential control over these advisers.

34. Coletta, Paolo, editor. American Secretaries of the Navy. Annapolis, Maryland: Naval Institute Press, 1980. Volume II. Moves from Josephus Daniels (1913-1921) to John Hubbard Chafee (1969-1972). The authors of the essays, all recognized naval historians, provide biographical data nd discuss the policy issues with which the various secretaries dealt.

35. Hoxie, R. Gordon. Command Decision and the Presidency: a Study in National Security Policy Organization. New York: Reader's Digest Press, 1977. 505p. Stresses the years 1945 to 1961 in an historical study reaching back to the beginnings of the American presidency. Coverage after 1961 is less extensive. Hoxie defends the exercise of broad presidential powers in the field of national security.

36. Kinnard, Douglas. The Secretary of Defense, Lexington:

University Press of Kentucky, 1980. 252p. Reviews the
contributions and experiences of the Secretaries of Defense
from Forrestal through Schlesinger. Chapter 6 analyzes the
role of the Secretary of Defense.

37. Love, Robert William, Jr. The Chiefs of Naval
Operations. Annapolis, Maryland: Naval Institute Press,
1980. 448p. Consists of detailed biographical studies by
authorities in the field of naval history and national
security affairs. Admiral Zumwalt is the last Chief of
Naval Operations discussed. The essays put these important
naval officers into the political and military/naval
contexts of their periods.

38. Trask, Roger R. The Secretaries of Defense: A Brief
History, 1947-1985. Washington, D.C.: Historical Office,
Office of the Secretary of Defense, 1985. 75p. SOD
D1.2H62/4/947-85. "The evolution of the office and its
major activities, policies and programs are examined
through the careers of the 15 men who served as Secretary
of Defense between 1947 and 1985." There is a select list
of references; and organizational charts are appended.

Decision-making Process

Official Reports

39. Ignatius, Paul R. Department of Defense Reorganization
Study Project: Departmental Headquarters Study: a Report to
the Secretary of Defense. Washington, D.C.: Department of
Defense, 1978. 81p. SOD D1.2:R29. Recommends considerable
strengthening of the roles of the secretaries of the armed
services to avoid too much autonomy for the services and
over-management by the Office of the Secretary of Defense.
Much of the study is occupied with the functioning of the
Office of the Secretary of Defense.

40. Rice, Donald B. Defense Resource Management Study:
Final Report. Washington, D.C.: Government Printing
Office, 1979. 112p. Criticizes the Office of the Secretary
of Defense for too much interference with the individual
armed services in some areas and for failing to manage and
coordinate sufficiently in other fields. The report also
deals to a limited extent with the Joint Chiefs of Staff,
which it criticizes; it focuses on improving the
performance of the JCS, rather than recommending any
drastic structural changes.

41. Steadman, Richard C. The National Military Command
Structure: Report of a Study Requested by the President and
Conducted in the Department of Defense. Washington, D.C.:
Government Printing Office, 1978. 79p. Assails the Joint
Chiefs of Staff for failing to give the kind of military
advice needed by higher levels of decision-makers, a
deficiency stemming primarily from interservice rivalries.

The report favors strengthening the unified and specified commands and improving the Joint Staff, which supports the Joint Chiefs of Staff.

Books

42. Barrett, Archie D. Reappraising Defense Organization: An Analysis Based on the Defense Organization Study of 1977-1980. Washington, D.C.: National Defense University Press, 1983. 325p. D5.402:D36/2/977-80. Thorough study of the Department of Defense and its development since 1947. Barrett emphasizes the very powerful role of the individual services and offers some relatively conservative proposals for change.

43. Collins, John M. U.S. Defense Planning: A Critique. Boulder, Colorado: Westview Press, 1982. 337p. Comprehensive description of the elements in decision-making in the area of national defense. In addition to analyzing the institutions involved, Collins discusses the elite decision makers and their backgrounds.

44. Dixon, James H. and Associates. National Security Policy Formulation: Institutions, Processes, and Issues. Lanham, Maryland: University Press of America, Inc., 1984. 237p. Issued to support the program of the National Defense University, this is an introductory study. Most chapters deal with an institution such as the Congress or the Department of State; others examine various processes, tensions between the Congress and the executive branch, and the question of "military reform."

45. Hewes, James E. Jr., From Root to McNamara: Army Organization and Administration, 1900-1963. Washington, D.C.: Government Printing Office, 1975. 452p. SOD D114.17:or 3/900-63. Nearly half the book deals with the decade following the end of the Korean War. Individual chapters deal with the Hoelscher and Traub Committees' proposals for organizational change.

46. Kolodziej, Edward A. The Uncommon Defense and Congress, 1945-1963. Columbus: Ohio State University Press, 1966. 630p. Reviews Congressional efforts to influence military policies and discusses major Congressional decisions in detail.

47. Korb, Lawrence J. The Fall and the Rise of the Pentagon: American Defense Policies in the 1970's. Westport, Connecticut: Greenwood Press, 1979. 192p. Discusses the post-World War II nadir of the armed services at the end of the 1960's and their gradual adjustment to the post-Vietnam era. Korb emphasizes the roles of Nixon, Ford, and Carter and of McNamara, Laird, and Schlesinger. There is some consideration of the Mayaguez episode.

48. Mintz, Alex. The Politics of Resource Allocation in the U.S. Department of Defense. Boulder, Colorado: Westview Press, 1986. 149p. Suggests that economic and political factors often influence patterns of military spending. This is an analysis of how money is really spent within the Defense Department and includes various models which may help to explain what occurs.

49. Ransom, Harry Howe. Can American Democracy Survive Cold War? Garden City, New York: Doubleday & Company, 1963. 270p. Analyzes decision-making machinery in the field of defense policy, especially after World War II. Several chapters deal with governmental intelligence agencies.

50. Raymond, Jack. Power at the Pentagon. New York: Harper & Row, Publishers, 1964. 363p. Surveys American military developments since the Roosevelt administrations. Includes a chapter on McNamara's period at the Defense Department and material on the military-industrial complex issue.

Essays and Periodical Articles

51. Art, Robert J. "Congress and the Defense Budget: Enhancing Policy Oversight." Political Science Quarterly 100 (Summer 1985):227-248. Examines Congressional treatment of the defense budget from 1975 to 1984. Art believes that Congress has dealt only with each budget as it has developed and has failed to examine overall policy issues. He sets forth reforms that should restore "a better balance among the financial, programmatic, and policy oversight functions of Congress."

52. Ausland, John C. "Olive Branch and Lightning Bolts." United States Naval Institute Proceedings 95 (November 1969):67-74. Discusses the increasing cooperation between the Departments of Defense and State from the Kennedy and Johnson administrations onward. Ausland provides a number of specific examples of cooperation and coordination.

53. Destler, I.M. "National Security Advice to U.S. Presidents: Some Lessons from Thirty Years." In U.S. National Security: A Framework for Analysis, edited by Daniel J. Kaufman and others, 177-199. Lexington, Massachusetts: Lexington Books, 1985. Essay reprinted from World Politics, January 1977, discusses the various individuals and agencies that can or do provide advice. Most of the article focuses on the National Security Council and its use by the presidents.

54. Dickson, Thomas I., Jr. "American Public Opinion and American National Security." Military Review 56 (July 1976): 77-81. Stresses the importance of popular confidence in the government. If it is high, people tend to accept defense policies; during the 1960's and 1970's confidence declined. Dickson examines the findings of

public opinion polls concerning security issues and looks
at possible measures for gauging public opinion in the area
of national security.

55. Falk Stanley L. "The National Security Council Under
Truman, Eisenhower, and Kennedy." Political Science
Quarterly 79 (September 1964):403-434. Studies the
organization of the National Security Council and its role
in the formation of national security policies by three
presidents, each of whom used the Council "to satisfy his
own needs and intentions."

56. Fox, W.T.R. "The Military and United States Foreign
Policy." International Journal 38 (Winter 1982-1983): 39-
58. Suggests that military leaders in the United States
have had a greater impact on the conduct of foreign policy
in the post-World War II era than they did before 1941.

57. Gruetzner, James K. and William Caldwell. "DOD
Reorganization." United States Naval Institute Proceedings
113 (May 1987): 136-145. Brief, but highly detailed
account of post-World War II efforts at structuring an
effective defense establishment. Much of the article
discusses the most recent (1986) changes in the roles of
the Joint Chiefs of Staff and the combatant commanders.

58. Halperin, Morton H., and David Halperin. "The Key West
Key." Foreign Policy (Winter 1983-1984): 114-130.
Criticizes the Key West agreement of 1948 for discouraging
interservice cooperation on general defense problems. It
did reduce interservice friction.

59. Johnson, Robert H. "The National Security Council: The
Relevance of its Past to Its Future." Orbis 13 (Fall
1969): 709-735. Analyzes the role of the National Security
Council as it operated in four previous administrations:
Truman, Eisenhower, Kennedy, and Johnson, then looks at the
functions that the Council should perform.

60. Meyer, John C. "The Air Staff." Air University Review
21 (January-February 1970): 2-9. Reviews the performance
of the Air Staff from 1947 onward. Meyer, Vice Chief of
Staff, United States Air Force, describes some of the
changes made in the Air Staff over the years.

61. Scott, John F., and John R. Cameron. "Political Theory
and Military Groups." Military Review 45 (November, 1965):
58-64. Discusses the armed forces as interest groups
during the post-World War II period. The authors also deal
with private groups with an interest in defense issues such
as the Navy League.

62. Tatum, Lawrence B. "The Joint Chiefs of Staff and
Defense Policy Formulation." Air University Review 17
(May-June, July-August 1966): 40-45; 10-20. Focuses on

civilians and defense policy, especially McNamara's heavy use of civilian specialists. Tatum finds this development generally functional and appropriate. Part II of the series analyzes the Joint Chiefs of Staff. Tatum asserts that, until it improves its planning procedures, civilians will remain fully in control of defense policy.

63. Toole, Wycliffe D., Jr. "Military Cover and Deception vs. Freedom of Information." United States Naval Institute Proceedings 101 (December 1975): 18-23. Warns that the military services must be given leeway by the public and by the civilian element of the government to use deceptive measures and to maintain secrecy in some areas.

64. Westerfield, H. Bradford. "Congress and Closed Politics in National Security Affairs." Orbis 10 (Fall 1966): 737-753. Asserts that post-World War II decision-making in the area of defense has been the prerogative of the executive branch. The legislative branch has been virtually powerless.

Budgeting for Defense

Books

65. Hobkirk, Michael D. The Politics of Defense Budgeting: A Study of Organization and Resource Allocation in the United Kingdom and the United States. Washington D.C.: National Defense University Press, 1983. SOD D5.402:B85 167p. Describes defense organization in both countries in considerable detail. Hobkirk then offers an analysis of interservice rivalries and puts forth some very general recommendations for improving defense.

Essays and Periodical Articles

66. Clayton, James L. "The Fiscal Limits of the Warfare-Welfare State; Defense and Welfare Spending in the United States since 1900." Western Political Quarterly 29 (Spring 1976): 64-83. Discusses the definitions of defense and welfare spending. Clayton performs a number of statistical analyses which indicate the complexity of the question of how much spending there is in various categories. He argues that more is spent on welfare than defense and that welfare costs are rising faster than defense expenditures.

67. Cypher, James M. "The Basic Economics of 'Rearming America.'" Monthly Review 33 (November 1981): 11-27. Analyzes defense expenditures and general economic trends between 1950 and 1981.

68. Handberg, Robert and Robert Bledsoe. "Shifting Patterns in the American Military Budget Process: An Overview." Journal of Strategic Studies 2 (December

1979): 348-361. Traces the Congressional stance during the first Cold War to its increasingly critical approach to military budgets during the Vietnam conflict.

69. Kanter, Arnold. "Congress and the Defense Budget: 1960-1970." American Political Science Review 66 (March, 1972): 129-143. Views Congress as having been quite active in interpreting and changing defense budgets. Kanter notes, in particular, the 1960 and post-Tet (1968) budgets.

70. Kolodziej, Edward A. "Rational Consent and Defense Budgets: The Role of Congress, 1945-1962." Orbis 7 (Winter 1964):748-777. Presents a critical view of Congressional participation in budgeting for defense.

71. Korb, Lawrence J. "The Secretary of Defense and the Joint Chiefs of Staff: Conflict in the Budgetary Process, 1947-1971." Naval War College Review 24 (December 1971):21-42. Treats the problem of relations between the Secretary of Defense and the Joint Chiefs of Staff in terms of their perceptions of their respective roles. Korb feels the system has worked well, with one element being in control for long periods.

72. Lee Jong, Ryod. "Changing National Priorities of the United States: Budgets, Perceived Needs and Political Environments, 1945-1971." In Military Force and American Society, edited by Bruce M. Russett and Alfred Stepan, 61-105. New York: Harper & Row, 1973. Applies various statistical measures to post-World War II defense expenditures. Lee Jong asserts that increasing defense expenditures have brought with them heightened world tension and the greater likelihood of international incidents.

73. Moyer, Wayne. "House Voting on Defense: An Ideological Explanation." In Military Force and American Society, edited by Bruce M. Russett and Alfred Stepan, 106-141. New York: Harper & Row, Publishers, 1972. Explores the thesis that support for defense expenditures is motivated by fears of communism rather than economic considerations, such as a district's defense contracts. Moyer minimizes the influence of the military-industrial complex and suggests more lobbying against heavy defense expenditures might well be successful. Examines the defense budgets passed by the 90th and 91st Congresses.

74. Powers, Patrick W. "Butter for the Guns." Military Review 45 (December 1965):79-86. Warns that extensive military spending by the United States continues to be necessary. Careful economic management will be required.

75. Russett, Bruce M. "Making Defense Defensible." Virginia Quarterly Review 46 (Autumn 1970):529-551. Discusses the economic, political, and social consequences of the heavy American commitment to defense expenditures from the Korean

War onward. While problems do exist, they have to be balanced against the desirability of maintaining a deterrence policy.

76. Schnurr, D.V. "Military Programming and Budgeting Practices." Air University Review 21 (January-February 1970):19-27. Reviews military budgeting trends from 1950 to 1970. Schnurr sees the McNamara innovations as retaining their importance even after McNamara's departure from the Defense Department.

77. Stellini, Edward. "Force-Structure Planning: Considerations, Problems, and Issues." Air University Review 22 (May-June 1971):2-15. Reviews budgeting and defense costs in the post-Truman administrations and the political constraints on defense expenditures. Stellini examines Department of Defense decision-making on the composition of the services.

78. Tucker, Ralph M. "Cost Effectiveness-Fact and Fancy." United States Naval Institute Proceedings 90 (September 1964):74-81. Assails putting too much emphasis on assessing military problems with quantitative measures. Other standards may be more appropriate.

Military Policy

Books

79. Aliano, Richard. American Defense Policy From Eisenhower to Kennedy: the Politics of Changing Military Requirements, 1957-1961. Athens: Ohio State University Press, 1975. 309p. Stresses critics of Eisenhower's policies, especially of "massive retaliation." Aliano argues that the changes that occurred in the late 1950's and early 1960's prepared the way for American involvement in Vietnam.

80. Barnet, Richard J. The Economy of Death. New York: Antheneum Press, 1969. 201p. Sees the United States as devastating itself by its commitment to the arms race. Attention is given to the military-industrial complex.

81. Clarke, Robin. The Science of War and Peace. New York: McGraw-Hill Book Company, 1972. 335p. Critical review of the development of American military technology after World War II. Chapters include the expansion of war preparations into space and the world's oceans.

82. Coker, Christopher. US Military Power in the 1980s. London: Macmillan Press Ltd., 1983. 163p. Contrasts developments in the 1970's with those of the Reagan years. Part II consists of brief essays on American air, naval, and land forces and such topics as manpower, logistics, and economic power. These are not listed separately and

annotated in this bibliography due to their brevity.

83. Collins, John M. American and Soviet Military Trends: Since the Cuban Missile Crisis. Washington, D.C.: Center for Strategic and International Studies, Georgetown University, 1978. 496p. Presents a full discussion of military issues, analyzing both nuclear and conventional weapons and reviews the strategy of mutual assured destruction and the SALT negotiations in detail.

84. Graebner, Norman A., editor. The National Security: Its Theory and Practice, 1945-1960. New York: Oxford University Press, 1986. 316p. Essays focus primarily on Eisenhower and his administrations. This is an extremely important collection, covering many aspects of defense policy during the 1960's, including the development of the National Security Council. Much new material is presented.

85. Hadley, Arthur T. The Straw Giant: Triumph and Failure, America's Armed Forces. New York: Random House, 1986. 314p. Analyzes American military and naval performance from World War II to the early 1980's. Hadley identifies a number of problems, which he suggests might be alleviated by adopting innovations such as the funding of major defense missions rather than the services.

86. Herzog, Arthur. The War-Peace Establishment. New York: Harper & Row, Publishers, 1965. 271p. Catalogs the major trends of opinion on defense and disarmament issues. Herzog interviewed many leading figures in the course of his research.

87. Lowe, George E. The Age of Deterrence. Boston: Little, Brown & Company, 1964. 324p. Reviews defense policy from 1952 to 1963. Lowe emphasizes the continued importance of non-nuclear forces, referring to the Berlin and Cuban missile crises in this connection.

88. Rostow, Walt W. The Diffusion of Power: An Essay in Recent History. New York: Macmillian Publishing Co., 1972. 739p. Despite the title, the book is really a large collection of essays on American foreign and military policy, based in part on Rostow's experiences in government. This is an important analysis of many post-World War II events.

89. Snow, Donald M. National Security: Enduring Problems of U.S. Defense Policy. New York: St. Martin's Press, 1986. 272p. Basic survey of defense policies, including arms control issues and weapons systems. Snow also compares American and Soviet national policy since World War II.

90. Snyder, Glenn Herald. Stockpiling Strategic Materials: Politics and National Defense. San Francisco: Chandler Publishing Co., 1966. 314p. Heavily based on Congressional

hearings held in 1962, this is a survey of the entire post-World War II stockpiling process. Snyder fully covers bureaucratic conflicts in this field.

91. Steel, Ronald. Pax Americana. New York: Viking Press, 1967. 371p. Very critical account of post-World War II American foreign policy, including the military aspects of the American approach to containing the Soviets. Steel emphasizes the importance of Europe to American security, but denies that Asia is vital.

92. Weigley, Russell F. The American Way of War; A History of U.S. Military Strategy and Policy. New York: Macmillan Publishing Co., 1973. 584p. Magistral study which includes detailed analyses of American defense policies in the 1950's and 1960's. Weigley carefully correlates military and political developments and issues.

Essays and Periodical Articles

93. Alexander, Arthur J. "The Linkage Between Technology, Doctrine, and Weapons Innovation: Experimentation for Use." In Rethinking US Security Policy for the 1980s Proceedings of the Seventh National Security Affairs Conference 21-23 July 1980, 293-308. Washington, D.C.: National Defense University Press, 1980. SOD D5.412:980. Analyzes the importance of "experiments for use" as a "crucial step" between research and development and changes in doctrine and procurement policy. Alexander examines factors that obstruct changes in weapons technology; he advocates "experimental units" as a possible way to encourage innovation.

94. Kaufman, Daniel J., and others. "Appraising U.S. National Security Policy." In U.S. National Security: A Framework for Analysis, edited by Daniel J. Kaufman, and others 551-570. Lexington, Massachusetts: Lexington Books, 1985. Emphasizes the high degree of "continuity" in defense policies in a survey, administration by administration, from 1945 to nearly the end of Reagan's first term.

95. Leffler, Melvyn P. "From the Truman Doctrine to the Carter Doctrine: Lessons and Dilemmas of the Cold War." Diplomatic History 7 (Fall 1983):245-266. In part, discusses efforts of the Carter administration to base the Carter Doctrine on the Truman Doctrine. Leffler criticizes the Carter administration's unrealistic attitude toward Soviet-American relations.

96. Matloff, Maurice. "The American Quest for National Security." United States Naval Institute Proceedings 89 (May 1963):84-93. Reviews historical American isolationism and the participation of the United States in the world wars before examining post-World War II experience in

defense planning. Matloff emphasizes the strategies embraced by the individual armed services.

97. Mrozek, Donald J. "A New Look at 'Balanced Forces': Defense Continuities from Truman to Eisenhower." Military Affairs 38 (December 1974):145-151. Assails the view that there was a sharp break in defense policy from Truman to Eisenhower.

98. Osgood, Robert E. "The Post-War Strategy of Limited War: Before, During and After Vietnam." In Strategic Thought in the Nuclear Age, edited by Hassein Amirsadeghi and Laurence Martin, 93-130. Baltimore: Johns Hopkins University Press, 1979. Discusses changes in the meaning of the "limited war" concept as it came to embrace not only local wars, but also confrontations between the superpowers which might be limited in terms of technology. There are lengthy sections on limited war in Europe and the lessons of the Vietnam conflict.

99. Ward, Michael Don. "Differential Paths to Parity: A Study of the Contemporary Arms Race." American Political Science Review 78 (June 1984):297-317. Utilizes a continuous time model showing the defense expenditures and arms accumulations of the United States and the Soviet Union from 1952 through 1978. Ward asserts that the arms race is the result of reactions by the two nations both to the stocks of weapons accumulated and to the amount of money spent on defense. The consequences of parity may lead to a perception of an increased threat on the part of both countries.

100. Wells, Samuel F., Jr. "Limits on the Use of American Power." Wilson Quarterly 7 (Winter 1983):121-130. Argues that "since the early 1960's . . . America's military capabilities do not match its diplomatic commitments." The American reaction to events in Central America and the Middle East proves that the United States has no policy to determine when to use and how to use force.

101. Wells, Samuel F., Jr. "A Question of Priorities: A Comparison of the Carter and Reagan Defense Programs." Orbis 27 (Fall 1983):641-666. Describes the great differences in approach between the two administrations. Many facets of defense policy are examined.

102. Williams, Phil. "United States Defense Policy." In Contemporary Strategy: Theories and Policies, edited by John Baylis and others, 195-217. New York: Holmes & Meier Publishers, Inc., 1975. Relates defense policies to the strategy of containment. Williams emphasizes the initial reluctance of the Americans to arm heavily after World War II and the great concern of the Kennedy administration with security problems.

103. Yudkin, Richard A. "American Armed Strength and Its Influences." <u>Annals of the American Academy of Political and Social Science</u>, no. 384 (July 1969):1-13. Links policy goals and force structure and levels. Most of the military goals Yudkin cites relate to nuclear war.

General Strategy

Books

104. Brodie, Bernard. <u>War and Politics</u>. New York: Macmillan Company, 1973. 514p. Emphasizes the need to coordinate military strategy and political objectives. The first part of the book deals with these two elements in the world wars, Korea, and Vietnam; the second segment examines the problem of determining the causes of war and related matters.

105. Ginsburgh, Robert N. <u>U.S. Military Strategy in the Sixties</u>. New York: Norton, 1965. 160p. The first half of the book is an historical survey of American strategy. The other half is a statement of strategy in the McNamara era.

106. Gray, Colin S. <u>Strategic Studies and Public Policy: The American Experience</u>. Lexington: University Press of Kentucky, 1982. 230p. Reviews American strategic thinking after World War II and examines strategic analysis in the political process.

107. Huntington, Samuel P. <u>The Common Defense: Strategic Programs in National Politics</u>. New York: Columbia University Press, 1961. 500p. Reviews national strategic thinking from World War II through Eisenhower's second administration, emphasizing decisions on weapons development and on the size of the armed forces.

108. Lyons, Gene Martin and Louis Morton. <u>Schools for Strategy: Education and Research in National Security Affairs</u>. New York: Praeger Publishers, 1965. 356p. Surveys the academic commitment to security studies after World War II.

109. Power, Thomas S., with Albert A. Arnhym. <u>Designs for Survival</u>. New York: Coward-McCann, 1965. 255p. Former Strategic Air Command chief warns against disarmament in the face of an increasing Soviet challenge. Among other proposals are pleas for more civil defense preparedness and retention of a manned bomber force.

110. Rudoy, Dean William. <u>Armed and Alone; The American Security Dilemma</u>. New York: George Braziller, 1972. 96p. Presents summaries of and selections from the Citizens' Hearings on National Security, February 2-3, 1972, sponsored by the Coalition on National Priorities and Military Policy. Generally critical of the American reliance on armed forces.

111. Schwarz, Urs. American Strategy: A New Perspective; the Growth of Politico-Military Thinking in the United States. Garden City, New York: Doubleday, 1966. 170p. Emphasizes the post-World War II period. Schwarz stresses the work of Herman Kahn, Henry Kissinger, and other thinkers.

112. Snyder, Glenn Herald. Deterrence and Defense; Toward A Theory of National Security. Princeton: Princeton University Press, 1961. 294p. Employs a mathematical approach to the alternatives suggested by the title: deterrence strategy versus defense strategy.

113. Stein, Jonathan B. From H-Bomb to Star Wars; the Politics of Strategic Decision Making. Lexington, Massachusetts: Lexington Books, 1984. 118p. Focuses on Truman's decision to build the H-bomb and Reagan's Strategic Defense Initiative. Stein asserts that political considerations generally have primacy over technology in the arms field.

114. Taylor, Maxwell D. Responsibility and Response. New York: Harper & Row, Publishers, 1967. 84p. Emphasizes the change from bipolarity to a much more complex world in political and strategic terms. Includes one chapter on the lessons of Vietnam.

115. Trachtenberg, Marc. The Development of American Strategic Thought, 1945-1969. New York: Garland Publishing, 1987. 6 volumes. Important collection of documents and analyses from various sources. There are reprints of journal articles and Rand Corporation reports as well as the texts of some hitherto unpublished materials.

Essays and Periodical Articles

116. Blank, Jonas L. "The Impact of Logistics Upon Strategy." Air University Review 24 (March-April 1973): 2-21. Reviews logistics in World War II, Korea, and Vietnam to illustrate the constraints logistics puts on military operations and the opportunities it offers for innovative operations.

117. Brown, Michael L. "The Economic Dimensions of Strategy." Parameters 16 (Summer 1986):36-44. Discusses the American use of economic power in pursuing policy goals. Brown notes the Marshall Plan and the Alliance for Progress, among other efforts. He describes the conditions required for effective application of economic components in strategy.

118. Friedberg, Aaron L. "A History of the U.S. Strategic 'Doctrine'--1945 to 1960." Journal of Strategic Studies 3 (December 1980):37-71. Focuses on nuclear strategy.

Friedberg asserts that there has never been a commitment to mutual assured destruction or indeed to a single strategy at all on the part of the Americans.

119. Gray, Colin S. "National Style in Strategy: The American Example." International Security 6 (Fall 1981):21-47. American strategic thinking has not grappled with the fact that the Soviet Union does not share the American commitment to stability in the international order. This American attitude has had a great influence on American policy-making in the 1960's and 1970's, leading to a "cumulative relative decline in the American deployed strategic power."

120. Kolkowicz, Roman. "Soviet and American Approaches to the Roles of Conventional Forces in International Politics." In Nonnuclear Conflicts in the Nuclear Age, edited by Sam C. Sarkesian, 309-329. New York: Praeger Publishers, 1980. Suggests that the Soviet Union continues to develop its conventional forces significantly, while the United States still tends to underestimate their value. Kolkowicz surveys Soviet post-World War II nuclear and conventional doctrine. The essay is also, in part, an analysis of the American strategy of deterrence.

121. Lerche, Charles O. "Contrasting Strategic Styles in the Cold War." United States Naval Institute Proceedings 88 (May 1962): 22-33. Argues that Americans have responded to Soviet moves in the Cold War and have focused almost exclusively on short-run problems. In effect, American strategists play "poker" while the Soviets play "chess."

122. Lowe, George E. "Twentieth-Century Deterrents and Deterrence." Virginia Quarterly Review 46 (Winter 1970): 27-45. Discusses various weapons of the past that have been viewed as deterrents. Combat proved such weapons were somewhat less important than anticipated. Lowe advocates a strategy organized around MIRV seaborne missiles.

123. Modelski, George. "The Theory of Long Cycles and U.S. Strategic Policy." In American Security Policy and Policy-Making, edited by Robert Harkavy and Edward A. Kolodziej, 3-19. Lexington, Massachusetts: Lexington Books, 1980. Modelski's "theory of long cycles" is intended to give security policy-making a stable basis. He traces the courses of the four "world powers"--Portugal, the Netherlands, Great Britain, and the United States. An "oceanic," noninterventionist, and essentially "defensive" strategy is recommended.

124. O'Meara, Andrew P., Jr. "Strategy and the Military Professional." Military Review 60 (January, February 1980):38-45; 51-63. Presents a general history of strategy, arguing that in democratic societies, political leaders make strategy, not the military. Specifically,

military strategy derives from the politically-established national strategy. O'Meara examines various models of the relationships between political and military institutions and their leaders.

125. Ravenal, Earl C. "Perceptions of American Power." In Evolving Strategic Realities: Implications for U.S. Policy-makers, edited by Franklin D. Margiotta, 145-170. Washington, D.C.: National Defense University Press, 1980. SOD D5.402:St8. Discusses the more cautious American approach to dealing with Soviet expansionism from the Tet offensive in Vietnam through the Soviet invasion of Afghanistan. For much of the essay, Ravenal examines the strategic thinking of Edward N. Luttwak.

126. Sojka, Gary L. "The Strategic Thought of Paul H. Nitze." Naval War College Review 37 (March-April 1984):52-68. Describes the thinking and the many security-related activities of Nitze, who opposed many of Carter's initiatives and who became an important figure in the Reagan administration.

Nuclear Strategy

Books

127. Bacevich, A.J. The Pentomic Era: The U.S. Army Between Korea and Vietnam. Washington, D.C.: National Defense University Press, 1986. SOD D5.402:P38 197p. Discusses army adaptation to the potential nuclear battlefield. Bacevich examines army missiles and the army aviation in a lucid study that warns against too much emphasis on technology.

128. Betts, Richard K. Nuclear Blackmail and Nuclear Balance. Washington, D.C.:Brookings Institution, 1987. 240p. Analyzes a number of diplomatic crises which involved threats of nuclear attack. Betts sees much to criticize in American leadership, including the failure to incorporate lessons from such crises into American strategy.

129. Browning, Robert S. Two If by Sea; the Development of American Coastal Defense Policy. Westport, Connecticut: Greenwood Press, 1983. 210p. Primarily a history of coastal forts, the book has contemporary value because of its comparison between early military theory and American nuclear doctrine.

130. Herken, Gregg. Counsels of War. Expanded edition. New York: Oxford University Press, 1987. 425p. Analyzes nuclear strategy through the thinking and activities of many major civilian advisers such as Edward Teller. Herken's research included many interviews with these influential figures.

131. Jervis, Robert. The Illogic of American Nuclear Strategy. Ithaca: Cornell University Press, 1985. 204p. Applauds deterrence theory and criticizes the "countervailing strategy" which developed during the 1970's and 1980's.

132. Kahan, Jerome H. Security in the Nuclear Age; Developing U.S. Strategic Arms Policy. Washington, D.C.: Brookings Institution, 1975. 361p. Reviews policy developments between 1953 and 1974 and examines, at length, prospective problems of strategic arms policy. This is a significant contribution to the analysis of American strategy.

133. Kaplan, Fred M. The Wizards of Armageddon. New York: Simon and Schuster, 1983. 452p. Surveys American nuclear policy from the end of World War II to the 1980's. Kaplan discusses many personalities associated with defense policy. He tends to blame the United States for escalations of the arms race.

134. Midgley, John J., Jr. Deadly Illusions: Army Policy for the Nuclear Battlefield. Boulder, Colorado: Westview Press, 1986. 192p. Examines development of nuclear doctrine by the army after World War II, including various divisional configurations. Midgley believes use of tactical nuclear weapons will lead to a general war.

135. Moulton, Harland B. From Superiority to Parity: The United States and the Strategic Arms Race, 1961-1971. Westport, Connecticut: Greenwood Press, 1973. Focuses primarily on the years 1961 to 1965, but does discuss the periods 1945 to 1960 and 1966 to 1971. Moulton draws on extensive experience in the executive branch in this study of the decline of American power.

136. Rose, John P. The Evolution of U.S. Army Nuclear Doctrine, 1945-1980. Boulder, Colorado: Westview Press, 1980. 252p. Generally critical of the army for having failed to develop needed doctrine and for continuing to neglect this responsibility.

Essays and Periodical Articles

137. Abrams, Elliott. "Deterrence as Moral Response." Society 20 (September/October 1983):26-29. Deterrence strategy pursued by the United States has been the primary factor in preserving peace in the post-World War II world.

138. Alberts, D.J. "Counterforce in an Era of Essential Equivalence." Air University Review 26 (March-April 1975): 27-37. Compares discussions of counterforce doctrine in the 1970's with those of the 1960's. Alberts writes that the real problem is the meaning of "superiority" in all

spheres of military power.

139. Ball, Desmond. "The Development of the SIOP, 1960-1983." In Strategic Nuclear Targeting, edited by Desmond Ball and Jeffrey Richelson, 57-83. Ithaca: Cornell University Press, 1966. Stresses the continuity in the six versions of the Single Integrated Operational Plan (SIOP) in terms of the choice of Soviet targets.

140. Brodie, Bernard. "The Development of Nuclear Strategy." International Security 2 (Spring 1978):65-83. Reviews the course of deterrence theory in the United States. At the conclusion, Brodie focuses on former Secretary of Defense Schlesinger's proposals for the gradual utilization of strategic nuclear weapons.

141. Brown, William D. "Whatever Happened to...Tactical Nuclear Warfare?" Military Review 60 (January 1980):46-53. Criticizes the army for having failed to plan for nuclear warfare. The authors compare American and Soviet responses to this type of conflict.

142. Carlin, Robert J. "A 400-Megaton Misunderstanding." Military Review 54 (November 1974):3-12. Examines relationships between SALT I, American deterrence theory, and the ability to wage nuclear war effectively without unleashing strategic weapons on a completely devastating level. Carlin argues "that there is no way of knowing with certainty what will deter a potential aggressor." Much of the article deals with assertions about deterrence made by former Secretary of Defense McNamara.

143. Clark, Melvin D. and Richard C. Orphan. "Army Nuclear Doctrine: Is It Out of Date?" Military Review 49 (March 1969):3-9. The authors believe that army nuclear doctrine does take into account the many technological and other changes that have occurred. This doctrine includes such principles as the need to contain the vast destructive power of nuclear weapons when used in battle.

144. Coffey, Joseph I. "Nuclear Guarantees and Nonproliferation." International Organization 25 (Autumn 1971):836-844. Surveys American policies on nonproliferation and recommends modifications. Coffey examines the role of the Peoples Republic of China and France as nuclear powers and Japan and West Germany as potential ones.

145. Hinterhoff, Eugene. "The Delicate Balance." Military Review 48 (December 1968):78-85. Warns that MIRV may alter the balance between the two superpowers, making the concept of a stalemate obsolete.

146. Hollier, Louis S. "Nuclear Policy and Military Strategy." Military Review 48 (December 1968):73-77. Discusses the doctrine of "flexible response" in the

context of general American military policy. Various
levels of force may be applied in a critical situation
involving American interests.

147. "Is there a Strategic Arms Race?" Foreign Policy, no.
16 (Fall 1974):48-92. Albert Wohlstetter, Paul H. Nitze,
Joseph Alsop, Morton H. Halperin, and Jeremy J. Stone
discuss such issues as the American tendency to over-
estimate Soviet capabilities.

148. Jenson, John W. "Nuclear Strategy: Differences in
Soviet and American Thinking." Air University Review 30
(March-April 1979):2-17. Discusses the flexible response
strategy and its relationship to force levels. Jenson sees
military doctrine as developing very differently in the
United States and the USSR. American doctrine is highly
subject to change and is more openly discussed.

149. Kahan, Jerome H. "Strategic Armaments." In The Next
Phase in Foreign Policy, edited by Henry Owen, 225-246.
Washington, D.C.: Brookings Institution, 1973. Discusses
deterrence in the new environment created by increasing
Soviet strength and by the SALT negotiations. Kahan
examines the American deployment of strategic weapons
systems.

150. Kerr, James W. "Military Support of Civil Authority."
Military Review 50 (July 1970):77-82. Considers civil
government needs for military assistance in the wake of a
nuclear attack on the United States.

151. Meyer, John C. "The Synergy of the Triad." Air
University Review 22 (September-October 1971):17-25. Shows
the importance of the Triad, using the Cuban missile crisis
as an example. Meyer asserts that the Triad gives the
United States assurance that a surprise Soviet attack could
not be completely successful.

152. O'Malley, Jerome F. "JSTPS: The Link between Strategy
and Execution." Air University Review 28 (May-June 1977):
38-46. Examines the role of the Joint Strategic Target
Planning Staff and its part in preparing for possible
nuclear war. O'Malley also studies changes in the SIOP
plan as targeting philosophies have changed.

153. Richelson, Jeffrey. "Population Targeting and U.S.
Strategic Doctrine." In Strategic Nuclear Targeting, edited
by Desmond Ball and Jeffrey Richelson, 234-249. Ithaca:
Cornell University Press, 1986. Reviews American nuclear
targeting from 1945 to the 1980's. The initial emphasis on
hitting cities changed as the weapons became more sophisticated. American planners still want the capacity to attack
populations. Richelson emphasizes the complexity of distinguishing between counterforce strategy and population
targeting.

154. Rosenberg, David Alan. "U.S. Nuclear War Planning, 1945-1960." In Strategic Nuclear Targeting, edited by Desmond Ball and Jeffrey Richelson, 35-56. Ithaca: Cornell University Press, 1986. Emphasizes the process of nuclear war planning in the United States, focusing primarily on the Eisenhower administration.

155. Rumble, Greville. "US and Soviet Nuclear Policy." Chap. 3 in The Politics of Nuclear Defense: A Comprehensive Introduction, 42-77. Cambridge, England: Polity Press, 1985. The first half of the chapter deals with American policy from Truman through Reagan. It is a brief summary of policies adopted administration by administration and of conflicts over policies.

156. Sagan, Scott D. "Nuclear Alerts and Crisis Management," International Security 9 (Spring 1985):99-139. Reviews alerts in 1960, 1962, and 1973 for Laos, Cuba and the Yom Kippur war. Such alerts can be utilized in diplomatic negotiations, but carry heavy risks.

157. Schilling, Warner R. "U.S. Strategic Nuclear Concepts in the 1970s: The Search for Sufficiently Equivalent Countervailing Parity." International Security 6 (Fall 1981):48-79. Reviews American reactions to increasing Soviet nuclear capability since the early 1960's and discusses the current military balance between the superpowers.

158. Seybold, Calvin C. "Mutual Destruction: A Deterrent to Nuclear War?" Military Review 59 (September 1979):22-28. Asserts that the Soviets are not deterred by American nuclear weapons. They perceive the United States as less resolute than it professes to be and to be unable to decide to use its weapons in crises. Seybold theorizes that the Soviets are, in fact, deterred by the "economic strength" of the United States and its allies.

159. Snow, Donald M. "Strategic Implications of Enhanced Radiation Weapons: A Preliminary Analysis." Air University Review 30 (July-August 1979):2-16. Examines enhanced radiation weapons such as the neutron warheads on Lance missiles. Snow gives a technical review of these devices. Several pages discuss ER weapons and cruise missiles.

160. York, Herbert. "Thirty-Seven Years of Nuclear Weapons: Vertical Proliferation." Bulletin of the Atomic Scientists 38 (December 1982):47-50. Discusses Soviet-American nuclear weapons competition during the post-World War II period.

Air Strategy

General

161. Goldsworthy, Harry E. "Aircraft Development: Its Role

in Flexible Military Response." Air University Review 20
(January-February 1969):20-31. Discusses the F-111 and C-5A
as examples of new aircraft. There is a need for airplanes
to serve both general and limited war needs.

162. Haid, Donald J. "How to Shoot a Duck." Military Review
45 (September 1965):3-12. Discusses armed helicopters and
their use in various conflicts after World War II. Haid's
particular concern is the development of doctrine for
helicopters to fight other helicopters.

163. Hutcheson, Rufus D. "The Dilemma of Air Force Technology." Air University Review 22 (November-December
1970):26-34. Discusses problems the air force faces in
maintaining its superiority over the Soviets and notes some
of the air force's achievements.

164. McConnell, John P. "Some Reflections on a Tour of
Duty." Air University Review 20 (September-October 1969):2-
11. A former United States Air Force Chief of Staff
discusses his experiences and the challenges ahead for the
air force.

165. Macmillan, David T. "Technology: The Catalyst for
Doctrinal Change." Air University Review 29 (November-
December 1977):16-22. Emphasizes the impact of technological change on tactical air warfare and examines many
current developments in air technology.

Missiles

Books

166. Beard, Edmund. Developing the ICBM; a Study in Bureaucratic Politics. New York: Columbia University Press, 1976.
273p. Traces American missile development from the end of
World War II to the advent of Sputnik, which focused
attention on the ICBM issue.

167. Yanarella, Ernest. The Missile Defense Controversy:
Strategy, Technology, and Politics, 1955-1972. Lexington:
University Press of Kentucky, 1977. 236p. Focuses on the
ballistic defense missile (BDM). Yanarella denies that
McNamara made the great impact on defense policy that he is
generally credited with or attacked for.

Periodical Articles

168. Dick, James C. "The Strategic Arms Race, 1957-61: Who
Opened a Missile Gap?" Journal of Politics 34 (November
1972):1062-1110. Asserts that there was never a missile
gap. Dick analyzes the myth of the missile gap and the
1960 election.

169. Hammes, Thomas X. "Rethinking Air Interdiction" United

States Naval Institute Proceedings 113 (December 1987):50-
55. Describes failure in air interdiction from World War
II, the Korean War and Vietnam. Despite the enhanced power
of tactical air forces, ground observers in communication
with aircraft are vitally necessary.

170. Lewis, Kevin N. "Balance and Counterbalance: Technology and the Arms Race." Orbis 29 (Summer 1985):259-268.
Discusses the development of strategic missiles between
1962 and 1972 and changes in the Soviet and American air
forces during the same period.

Space Operations

171. Downey, Arthur J. The Emerging Role of the US Army in
Space. Washington, D.C.: National Defense University Press,
1985. 92p. SOD D5.409:sp1. Documents the cautious approach
of the army to space operations. Downey briefly describes
the advances made by the navy and air force in space.

172. Stares, Paul B. The Militarization of Space: U.S.
Policy, 1945-1984. Ithaca: Cornell University Press, 1985.
352p. Detailed historical account of American military
policy concerning outer space. Stares links this topic with
disarmament and arms control considerations. He is skeptical of the claims made by many specialists about the long-
range impact of the militarization of space, seeing it as
just another element in the Soviet-American rivalry.

Counterinsurgency

Books

173. Blaufarb, Douglas S. The Counterinsurgency Era: U.S.
Doctrine and Performance, 1950 to the Present. New York:
Free Press, 1977. 356p. One of the more important surveys
of the American experience with counterinsurgency. Written
from the perspective of the CIA, the book devotes considerable attention to CIA and army developments and gives
coverage to the other services.

174. Cable, Larry E. Conflict of Myths: The Development of
American Counterinsurgency Doctrine and the Vietnam War.
New York: New York University Press, 1986. 288p. Examines
post-World War II counterinsurgency campaigns and compares
American doctrine with pre-World War II marine doctrine.
Cable ends his study with large-scale American commitments
of troops in Vietnam.

175. Sarkesian, Sam C., editor. Revolutionary Guerrilla
Warfare. Chicago: Precedent Publishing, Inc., 1975. Large
collection of essays by authorities in the field. Chapter 7
deals with counterinsurgency.

Periodical Articles

176. Alnwick, Kenneth J. "Perspectives on Air Power at the Low End of the Conflict Spectrum." Air University Review 35 (March-April, 1984):17-28. Reviews the use of air power in American and British small wars from 1916 onward. Alnwick emphasizes the great variety of ways in which air power can be used in such conflicts. The last few pages discuss Vietnam and refer to air force doctrine for special operations.

177. Child, Jack. "US Policies Toward Insurgencies in Latin America." In Latin American Insurgencies, edited by George Fauriol, 131-160. Washington, D.C.: National Defense University Press, 1984. SOD D5.402:In7 Provides an historical review, 1961-1980, analyzes the Reagan administration's responses, and discusses various possible policy options.

178. Lobe, Thomas. "The Rise and Demise of the Office of Public Safety." Armed Forces & Society 9 (Winter, 1983): 187-213. Views police assistance through the Agency for International Development as a significant element in the American effort to fight Third World insurgency. Such aid was prohibited by Congress in 1975.

Naval Strategy

Books

179. Ryan, Paul B. First Line of Defense; the U.S. Navy Since 1945. Stanford, California: Hoover Institution Press, 1981. 224p. Pursues what Ryan views as the decline in American seapower. His portrayal weaves together naval developments and political events in the United States.

Essays and Periodical Articles

180. Crowe, William J., Jr. "Strategic Applications of Seapower." In Military Strategy, edited by Anthony W. Gray, Jr. and Eston T. White. Washington, D.C.: National Defense University Press, 1983. SOD D5.410:St 8. After reviewing World War II experience, Crowe turns to maritime issues that arose after 1945. He points to the increasing amount of cargo shipped by sea and the continuing American dependence upon the sea.

181. Friedman, Norman. "The Sixth Fleet at Forty." United States Naval Institute Proceedings 113 (May 1987) 150-161. Surveys the history of the Sixth Fleet since its formation at the very beginning of the Cold War. Friedman emphasizes the strategic aspects of the fleet, although some attention is given to the fleet's ships and weapons.

182. Hayes, John D. "The Influence of Modern Sea Power, 1945-1970." United States Naval Institute Proceedings 97

(May 1971):274-284. Focuses on Soviet naval cruises in the Caribbean in 1969-1970. Hayes also makes predictions about the importance of sea power during the rest of the 20th century.

183. Hayes, John D. "Patterns of American Sea Power, 1945-1956: Their Portents for the Future." United States Naval Institute Proceedings 96 (May 1970):337-353. Examines the failure of the United States to use its naval strength in Korea and the subsequent decline of the navy. Hayes devotes much attention to the merchant marine and its problems.

184. McGruther, Kenneth R. "The Dilemma of the U.S. Pacific Fleet." United States Naval Institute Proceedings 104 (June 1978):26-33. Predicts further reductions in the strength of the Pacific Fleet in favor of the Atlantic Fleet. McGruther sees the Pacific Fleet's role as primarily force projection. He also reviews the history of the post-World War II Pacific Fleet.

Civil Defense

185. Vale, Lawrence J. The Limits of Civil Defense in the USA, Switzerland, Britain and the Soviet Union: The Evolution of Policies Since 1945. New York: St. Martin's Press, 1987. Detailed study which emphasizes the problems of creating an effective civil defense program. Vale deals with both the political and technological facets of civil defense. The book includes an important bibliography.

Intelligence Agencies

Books

186. Blum, William. The CIA: a Forgotten History: US Global Interventions since World War 2. Atlantic Highlands, New Jersey: Zed Books, 1986. 428p. Discusses forty-nine instances of CIA involvement outside the United States. Some episodes pre-date the formal establishment of the CIA, for example, intervention in the Chinese Civil War of the 1940's. Blum is highly critical of the CIA, but also of the American press for having served as an instrument of the government.

187. Breckinridge, Scott D. The CIA and the U.S. Intelligence System. Boulder, Colorado: Westview Press, 1986. 364p. Examines all phases of intelligence operations and presents a brief history of the CIA. Its major duties are analyzed. There is an extensive treatment of intelligence operations in terms of both American and international law.

188. Prouty, L. Fletcher. The Secret Team: The CIA and Its Allies in Control of the United States and the World. Englewood Cliffs, New Jersey: Prentice-Hall, Inc., 1973.

496p. Highly critical account of CIA operations by a former liaison officer between the air force and the CIA. Despite the muckraking tone of the book and the fact that much of the narrative does not seem to be based on Prouty's personal experiences, this remains a useful source.

189. Treverton, Gregory F. Covert Action: The Limits of Intervention in the Postwar World. New York: Basic Books, Inc., Publisher, 1987. Examines a number of examples of American covert action from Guatemala in 1954 through the Iran-Contra affair. Treverton emphasizes the problems in executing such operations and discusses the impact of increased Congressional assertiveness.

Periodical Articles

190. Cooper, Chester L. "The CIA and Decision-Making." Foreign Affairs 50 (January 1972):223-236. Studies the impact of CIA "estimates" on high-level decision-making during the 1950's and 1960's. Cooper argues that these estimates are generally correct.

191. Kirkpatrick, Lyman B. "United States Intelligence." Military Review 41 (April 1961):18-22. Describes intelligence as "our first line of defense" and reviews American experiences with intelligence from the OSS onward. Kirkpatrick briefly discusses the components of the American intelligence community and notes Soviet campaigns against it.

Military Assistance

Books

192. Graves, Ernest, and Steven A. Hildreth, editors. U.S. Security Assistance: The Political Process. Lexington, Massachusetts: Lexington Books, 1985. 208p. Contains five essays on facets of the mutual security program, including an historical survey and an analysis, administration by administration, up to 1984, of major debates over American policies and public opinion concerning aid.

193. Hovey, Harold A. United States Military Assistance: A Study of Policies and Practices. New York: Frederick A. Praeger, Publishers, 1965. 306p. Detailed description of American military assistance, both by types of assistance, such as repair work and by country or region. One chapter deals with general policy. One very brief chapter discusses critics of military assistance.

194. Wolpin, Miles D. Military Aid and Counterrevolution in the Third World. Lexington, Massachusetts: Lexington Books, 1972. 327p. Focuses on American training of foreign military personnel overseas and in the United States, especially the political indoctrination associated with

such training. Wolpin presents a detailed picture of all aspects of the military assistance program.

Periodical Articles

195. Stein Robert M. and others. "The Fiscal Impact of the U.S. Military Assistance Program, 1967-1976." Western Political Quarterly 38 (March 1985):27-43. Focuses on countries receiving American aid. Such assistance does not appear to allow these countries to use more of their resources for fruitful, nonmilitary development programs as had been intended.

Disarmament and Arms Control

Books

196. Barnet, Richard Joseph. Who Wants Disarmament? Boston: Beacon Press, 1961. 141p. Reviews both Soviet and American approaches to disarmament after World War II. One section assesses current disarmament prospects.

197. Bechhoefer, Bernard G. Postwar Negotiations for Arms Control. Washington, D.C.:Brookings Institution, 1961. 641p. Reviews disarmament negotiations from World War II to the failed conference at Geneva in 1960. This is a highly detailed analysis of the studies and discussions of the disarmament problem.

198. Blacker, Coit D. Reluctant Warriors: the United States, the Soviet Union, and Arms Control. New York: W. H. Freeman, 1987. 193p. Discusses Soviet-United States conflicts, primarily in terms of American policies and experiences. Blacker emphasizes the interplay of weapons technology and political relations between the superpowers.

199. Carnesale, Albert and Richard N. Haass, eds. Superpower Arms Control: Setting the Record Straight. Cambridge, Massachusetts: Ballinger Publishing Co., 1987. 300p. Emphasizes relations between public opinion and disarmament. The essays discuss various efforts to control armaments and present some generalizations about arms control negotiations.

200. Clarke, Duncan L. Politics of Arms Control: The Role and Effectiveness of the U.S. Arms Control and Disarmament Agency. New York: Free Press, 1979. 297p. Sympathetic account of the agency, in which Clarke argues that a pressure group committed to disarmament must develop in order to battle elements favorable to larger and larger armaments.

201. Diehl, Paul F. and Loch K. Johnson Through the Straits of Armageddon: Arms Control Issues and Prospects. Athens: University of Georgia Press, 1987. 279p. Deals with nuclear

and conventional arms and with the Strategic Defense Initiative. The authors include both historical treatments and analyses of contemporary problems.

202. Forbes, Henry W. The Strategy of Disarmament. Washington, D.C.: Public Affairs Press, 1962. 158p. Surveys the history of disarmament negotiations and analyzes the principal proposals advanced. Forbes argues that disarmament cannot be achieved without basic changes in world political relationships.

203. Gilpin, Robert George. American Scientists and Nuclear Weapons Policy. Princeton: Princeton University Press, 1962. 352p. Stressing the debate over an end to nuclear testing, Gilpin reviews scientists' involvement in military decision-making from late in World War II up to the 1960's.

204. Lens, Sidney. The Day Before Doomsday; an Anatomy of the Nuclear Arms Race. Garden City, New York: Doubleday, 1977. 274p. Presents the story of American nuclear policies from a radical perspective. Lens assails the assumption, apparently current in American defense circles, that a nuclear war can be "won" and discusses limited wars to some extent.

205. Wallop, Malcolm and Angelo Codevilla. The Arms Control Delusion. Washington, D.C.: Institute for Contemporary Studies, 1987. 220p. Vigorous criticism of American commitments to arms control. The authors defend the Strategic Defense Initiative and assail Reagan's efforts at arms control negotiations.

Essays and Periodical Articles

206. Blechman, Barry. "Is There a Future for Negotiated Arms Limitation?" In Defense Planning and Arms Control: Proceedings of a Special NSAI Conference 12-14 June 1980 National Defense University, 69-85. Washington, D.C.: National Security Affairs Institute, 1980. SOD D5.402:D36. Discusses the arms control failures of the Carter administration. The inability of the United States to maintain appropriate conventional deterrence forces increases American reliance on nuclear weapons. Blechman feels that arms control should be pursued because it does work to a limited degree.

207. Bloomfield, Lincoln P. "American Approaches to Military Strategy, Arms Control, and Disarmament: A Critique of the Postwar Experience." In American Security Policy and Policy-Making, edited by Robert Harkavy and Edward A. Kolodziej, 225-238. Lexington, Massachusetts: Lexington Books, 1980. Discusses United States nuclear strategy generally, especially deterrence. Bloomfield also surveys disarmament negotiations.

208. Bobrow, Davis B. "Arms Control through Communication and Information Regimes." In American Security Policy and Policy-Making, edited by Robert Harkavy and Edward A. Kolodziej, 115-128. Lexington, Massachusetts: Lexington Books, 1980. Argues that conventional efforts at arms control and reduction probably do not further the objective. Instead, the focus should be on using information and communication to encourage and implement arms control.

209. Greb, G. Allen, and Gerald W. Johnson. "A History of Strategic Arms Limitations." Bulletin of the Atomic Scientists 40 (January 1984):30-37. Puts SALT and START into historical perspective by examining the course of negotiations to limit arms.

210. Jensen, Lloyd, "Negotiating Strategic Arms Control, 1969-1979." Journal of Conflict Resolution 28 (September 1984):535-559. Reviews SALT I and SALT II and discusses the negotiating stances of the superpowers.

211. Kruzel, Joseph J. "Arms Control and American Defense Policy: New Alternatives and Old Realities." In Military Strategy, edited by Anthony W. Gray, Jr., and Eston T. White, 272-292. Washington, D.C.: National Defense University Press, 1983. SOD 5.410:St8. Analyzes the efforts made by the United States and the Soviet Union to achieve effective arms control, with emphasis on SALT in the 1970's. Kruzel stresses that failure to achieve an arms control program should not conceal the contributions to international security that have resulted from these efforts.

212. Miller, Steven E. "Politics over Promise: Domestic Impediments to Arms Control." International Security 8 (Spring 1984):67-90. Argues that internal politics must be taken into account in pursuing disarmament. Miller discusses relations between internal politics and American arms control policy from the 1950's through Reagan's first term.

213. Morgan, Patrick M. "Arms Control: A Theoretical Perspective." In American Security Policy and Policy-Making, edited by Robert Harkavy and Edward A. Kolodziej, 209-224. Lexington, Massachusetts: Lexington Books, 1980. Describes the objectives of arms control and sharply distinguishes between arms control and disarmament. Morgan emphasizes the various conditions conducive to arms control. His final observations are, nevertheless, far from optimistic.

214. Morrison, Philip. "The Spiral of Peril: A Narrative of the Nuclear Arms Race." Bulletin of the Atomic Scientists 39 (January 1983):10-17. Reviews nuclear weapons competition from its inception. Morrison includes a discussion of proliferation.

215. Payne, Keith B., and others. "Strategic Force Development and Arms Control Success: Two Sides of the Same Coin." Air University Review 36 (November-December 1984):16-25. Reviews 20th century disarmament and arms control efforts, deducing the principle that armaments are often needed to foster agreements. The last few pages deal with SALT II.

Military Personnel

Books

216. Berryman, Sue E. Who Serves? The Persistent Myth of the Underclass Army. Boulder, Colorado: Westview Press, 1986. 120p. Examines, on a comparative basis, the social and economic composition of the army. Moving as far back as the 19th century, Berryman provides an important picture of the enlisted force and thereby destroys many misconceptions.

217. Cohen, Eliot A. Citizens and Soldiers: The Dilemmas of Military Service. Ithaca: Cornell University Press, 1985. 227p. Stresses the use of economic criteria in making the decision to move to an all-volunteer force. Cohen provides a long critique of the Gates Commission report and argues that the volunteer concept has not worked well.

218. Flynn, George Q. Lewis B. Hershey, Mr. Selective Service. Chapel Hill: University of North Carolina Press, 1985. 385p. Nearly half the biography deals with the years encompassed by this bibliography. Flynn focuses almost exclusively on Hershey's administrative role, but for the policy specialist, James M. Gerhardt's The Draft and Public Policy remains the most important study.

219. Gerhardt, James M. The Draft and Public Policy: Issues in Military Manpower Procurement 1945-1970. Columbus: Ohio State University Press, 1971. 425p. Thorough survey of personnel procurement during the post-World War II draft era. The study includes many statistics on force levels and the operations of selective service. This is an important study of personnel procurement as it existed on the eve of the all-volunteer force.

Periodical Articles

220. Dunn, Joe P. "UMT: A Historical Perspective." Military Review 61 (January 1981):11-18. Examines the debate over universal military training and summarizes relevant legislation, noting the role of interest groups opposed to the concept.

221. Goldlich, Robert L. "Historical Continuity in the U.S. Miliary Reserve System." Armed Forces and Society 7 (Fall 1980):88-112. Provides an extensive exposition of reserve

policies from their English beginnings. Goldlich argues
that an understanding of this history is important.

Alliances

222. Deibel, Terry L. "Alliances and Security Relationships: A Dialogue with Kennan and His Critics." In Containment: Concept and Policy, edited by Terry L. Deibel and
John Lewis Gaddis, 189-215. Washington, D.C.: National
Defense University Press, 1986. SOD D5.402:C76/2 v. 1.
Analyzes the nature of American post-World War II alliances
and Kennan's skeptical view of them. Deibel takes a
generally positive view of the alliance system. He examines
its development, administration by administration.

Latin America

Books

223. Child, John. Unequal Alliance: The Inter-American
Military System, 1938-1978. Boulder, Colorado: Westview
Press, 1980. 253p. Deals primarily with the post-World War
II period, discussing several approaches to hemispheric
defense. American military assistance programs and counter-
insurgency strategies are considered in depth.

Periodical Articles

224. Guntharp, Walter A. and Covey T. Oliver. "The Concept
of Hemispheric Defense." Current History 56 (June 1969):
355-361, 366-367. Western Hemisphere countries have
cooperated well in the area of mutual defense. This
principle has materialized in American military assistance
and the Inter-American Defense Board, as well as in the
Inter-American Peace Force that served in the Dominican
Republic in 1965-1966.

225. Rabe, Stephen G. "The Johnson (Eisenhower?) Doctrine
for Latin America." Diplomatic History 9 (Winter 1985):95-
100. Sees continuity between Eisenhower's Latin American
policy and Johnson's Dominican Republic intervention.

226. Weiland, Francis H. "The Inter-American Defense
Board." Air University Review 23 (November-December
1971):21-31. Describes the history and functions of the
Board, which has existed since 1942. Weiland, to some
extent, compares the IADB and NATO and examines the IADB's
efforts to plan for counterinsurgency.

North Atlantic Treaty Organization

Books

227. Cyr, Arthur. U.S. Foreign Policy and European Security. New York: St. Martin's Press, 1987. 156p. Surveys

American relations with the NATO partners, administration
by administration. Cyr deals in some detail with the
evolution of NATO and its various crises.

228. Duke, Simon, US Defence Bases in the United Kingdom: a
Matter for Joint Decision. New York: St. Martin's Press,
1987. 261p. Useful review of basing agreements between the
United States and Great Britain since World War II. These
agreements have many implications for American strategy.
Duke notes that Great Britain has been the most cooperative
of the European allies.

229. Huston, James A. One for All: NATO Strategy and
Logistics Through the Formative Period (1949-1969).
Wilmington: University of Delaware Press, 1984. 336p.
Stresses the logistics of NATO strategy. This is an
extremely detailed account in the form of an historical
narrative rather than an analysis of the decisions taken
during the period studied.

230. Jackson, Robert J. Continuity of Discord: Crises and
Responses in the Atlantic Community. New York: Praeger
Publishers, 1985. 288p. Analyzes major disputes within
NATO, emphasizing the problems of the 1980's.

231. Nelson, Daniel J. A History of U.S. Military Forces in
Germany. Boulder, Colorado: Westview Press, 1986. 259p.
Survey of the American military presence in the Federal
Republic of Germany from 1945 to 1985. Nelson predicts a
continued American military commitment to the Federal
Republic and assesses both accomplishments and problems in
the German-American relationship.

232. Park, William H. Defending the West: A History of
NATO. Boulder, Colorado: Westview Press, 1986. 242p. Criticizes the European members of NATO for having failed to
respond adequately to American efforts to move toward more
emphasis on conventional defense and away from so much
dependence on nuclear weapons.

233. Williams, Phil. The Senate and US Troops in Europe.
New York: St. Martin's Press, 1985. 244p. Reviews American
commitments in Europe from 1951 through the mid-1970's. Of
particular note is the gradual shifting of the Republicans
and Democrats on major issues.

Periodical Articles

234. Tow, William T. "NATO's Out-of-Region Challenges and
Extended Containment." Orbis 28 (Winter 1985):829-855.
Provides an historical perspective on the general NATO
policy of refusing to extend the alliance outside Europe.
Tow examines some problems relating to NATO that have
arisen outside Europe.

Asia

235. Chadda, Maya. <u>Paradox of Power: The United States in Southwest Asia, 1973-1984</u>. Santa Barbara, California: ABC-CLIO, 1986. 272p. Deals with the area from Israel to Pakistan and Afghanistan. One chapter is devoted to American military policies regarding the Persian Gulf.

Crises and Force Projection

Books

236. Betts, Richard K. <u>Soldiers, Statesmen, and Cold War Crises</u>. Cambridge: Harvard University Press, 1977. 292p. Draws upon a considerable number of crises, beginning with the Korean War, to generalize about the contribution of military leaders to decision-making.

237. Blechman, Barry and others. <u>Force Without War: U.S. Armed Forces as a Political Instrument</u>. Washington, D.C.: Brookings Institution, 1978. 584p. Ambitious examination of American interventions, "shows of force," and other employment of military force to support diplomatic efforts. This is a very complete record and analysis of post-World War II events.

238. George, Alexander L. and Richard Smoke. <u>Deterrence in American Foreign Policy: Theory and Practice</u>. New York: Columbia University Press, 1974. 666p. Presents many case histories of the use of deterrence from the Berlin blockade in 1949 to the Cuban missile crisis of 1962. Highly sophisticated analysis.

239. Girling, John L.S. <u>American and the Third World: Revolution and Intervention</u>. London: Routledge & Kegan Paul, 1980. 276p. Important theoretical analysis of American counterrevoluntary policies and activities. Girling argues that intervention must be used only in certain cases.

240. Payne, James L. <u>The American Threat: The Fear of War as an Instrument of Foreign Policy</u>. Chicago: Markham Publishing Company, 1970. 241p. Not a denunciation of American foreign policy, but rather an analysis of the American use of military deterrence in crisis situations.

241. Tillema, Herbert K. <u>Appeal to Force: American Intervention in the Era of Containment</u>. New York: Thomas Y. Crowell Company, 1973. 260p. Comparative study of American interventions in Korea, Lebanon (1958), South Vietnam, and the Dominican Republic. Primarily focusing on diplomatic aspects of these episodes, Tillema's study does include some material on the military side.

242. Young, Oran R. <u>The Politics of Force: Bargaining</u>

<u>During International Crises</u>.   Princeton, New Jersey:
Princeton University Press, 1968. 438p. Examines a number
of crises involving the United States and the Soviet Union.

Essays and Periodical Articles

243. Atkeson, Edward B. "International Crises and the
Evolution of Strategy and Forces." <u>Military Review</u> 55
(October, November 1975):80-94; 47-55. Focuses on post-
World War II American experiences in crisis management.
Atkeson analyzes the relationships between general strategy
and the course of various crises. The last several pages
deal with possible reactions to the challenge posed by
OPEC.

244. Bauer, Charles J. "Military Crisis Management at the
National Level." <u>Military Review</u> 55 (August 1975):3-15.
Analyzes the ways in which armed services respond to
crises. The system is constantly being changed as a result
of further crisis experience. Threat analysis, operational
planning, and other phases are examined. Several pages are
concerned with the use of computers.

245. Endicott, John E. "Flexible Military Containment:
Forward Deployed Expeditionary Forces." In <u>Containment:
Concept and Policy</u>, edited by Terry L. Deibel and John
Lewis Gaddis, 1, 239-254.   Washington, D.C.: National
Defense University Press, 1986. SOD D5.402:C76/2 v.1.
Discusses changes in the world that make older concepts of
containment obsolete and forecasts further economic and
social changes likely to alter the military postures of the
major powers. Endicott wants greater flexibility in Europe
to provide more American forces for Third World contingencies.

246. Furlong, Raymond B. "The Utility of Military Forces."
<u>Air University Review</u> 33 (November-December 1981):29-33.
Discusses the importance of military presence as an aid to
diplomacy, using the United States Army's Berlin Brigade
and Perry's voyages to Japan in the 1850's as examples.
Furlong thoroughly discusses the limitations to effective
use of military forces in non-war or near-war situations.

247. Grindle, Merilee. "Armed Intervention and U.S.-Latin
American Relations." <u>Latin American Research Review</u> 16, no.
1 (1981):207-217. Discusses a number of studies of United
States intervention in Latin America. Grindle emphasizes
the importance of intervention and potential intervention
in American-Latin American relations, especially since
1945.

248. Harlow, Bruce. "The Legal Use of Force...Short of
War." <u>United States Naval Institute Proceedings</u> 92
(November 1966):88-98. Analyzes intervention, reprisals,
and retorsion. This is a legal study which refers very

briefly to a number of actions by the United States in the
19th and 20th centuries.

249. Krasner, Stephen.   "The Protection of Investments
after 1950: The Use of Force." In Defending the National
Interest: Raw Materials Investments and U.S. Foreign
Policy, 274-326.   Princeton: Princeton University Press,
1978.   Analyzes American involvement in Guatemala, Cuba,
the Dominican Republic, and Chile. The whole volume is of
interest to national security specialists.   Scattered
throughout the book are observations on the Vietnam war.

250. Stokes, William M. "Power Projection 1990: The Role of
US Military Power." Military Review 55 (May 1975):3-11.
Presents a relatively accurate survey of world political
relationships in the 1990's.   Stokes believes that nonmilitary elements of national power will assume more
importance and advocates better integration of economic,
political, and military policies.

251. Young, Leilyn M. "'Win': Its Meaning in Crisis Resolution." Military Review 46 (January 1966):30-39. Compares
the degree of military success in the Korean war, Lebanon
(1958), the Thailand crisis of 1962, and the Cuban missile
crisis.

Chapter 3

Eisenhower and "The New Look"

The coming of the Eisenhower administration is commonly viewed as having brought with it various new defense policies, notably a strong commitment to air power, nuclear weapons, and even the beginnings of an advance into space. Ground forces were reduced, and the army came to be seen as the least important of the armed services.

Weapons were to become deadlier and their use decisive in deterring any Soviet bloc expansion. While the emphasis became "more bang for the buck," other forms of defense expenditures were reduced. The use of nuclear weapons was even considered in the limited wars of Korea and Indochina.

As the 1950's progressed, there was increasing dissatisfaction with the perceived shortcomings of "massive retaliation." Secretary of State John Foster Dulles, and by indirection, President Dwight D. Eisenhower, were criticized for "brinksmanship." Interest was rekindled in limited war.

Despite the emphasis on new weapons, such as the intercontinental ballistic missile, and ventures into space, special military operations received some attention. Field manuals were produced on anti-guerrilla tactics, and some military exercises were conducted to test American capability in this field. The Central Intelligence Agency and the armed forces showed interest in using guerrilla forces against the Soviets in case of a general war.

Europe was of primary concern to the United States. Most crises of the period, however, occurred in Asia, notably the Indochina defeat in 1954 and the recurring problem of the Nationalist Chinese islands in the Formosa Strait. Military assistance was an area of concern, and at the end of the decade it underwent major study.

Decision-makers

President Eisenhower

252. Eisenhower, Dwight D. "A New Look at America's Defenses." In The White House Years: Mandate for Change 1953-1956, 445-458. New York: Doubleday & Company, Inc., 1963. Eisenhower's retrospective account of changes in defense policy initiated early in his first administration. Eisenhower stresses the need for economy in national security budgeting and the vastly changed environment in which large-scale war is likely to occur.

253. Kinnard, Douglas. President Eisenhower and Strategy Management: A Study in Defense Politics. Lexington: University Press of Kentucky, 1977. 169p. Stresses Eisenhower's activist role in setting defense policy during his two terms. Kinnard analyzes the ways Eisenhower used governmental structures and processes while retaining freedom to make the ultimate decisions.

254. Kinnard, Douglas, "President Eisenhower and the Defense Budget." Journal of Politics 39 (August 1977):596-623. Discusses Eisenhower's effort to achieve an adequate defense establishment at a level of expenditure supportive of a healthy civilian economy. The article examines Eisenhower's skillful pursuit of this goal and his battle to continue the strategy during his second administration.

255. Krone, Robert. "Eisenhower at the Naval War College." United States Naval Institute Proceedings 97 (June 1971): 18-24. Consists primarily of Eisenhower's answers to student and faculty questions at the Naval War College in 1961. Among the topics discussed was Eisenhower's conception of the military-industrial complex.

256. Nelson, Anna Kasten. "The 'Top of Policy Hill': President Eisenhower and the National Security Council." Diplomatic History 7 (Fall 1983):307-326. Argues that Eisenhower used the National Security Council for general planning, but made decisions on specific diplomatic moves with a smaller group, including the Secretary of State. The role of the National Security Council changed under Kennedy, who was critical of what he thought had been its role in the Eisenhower administrations.

257. Rourke, John T. "Marshall, Eisenhower and the Military Mind." Military Review 61 (February 1961):26-32. Analyzes the role of military experiences on the political/governmental careers of the two former generals. Rourke finds that both leaders were cautious and moderate in their approaches to the Soviet challenge.

258. Saunders, Richard M. "Military Force in the Foreign Policy of the Eisenhower Presidency." Political Science

Quarterly 100 (January 1985):97-116.   Discusses Eisenhower's cautious use of military power and his emphasis on
the need for a consensus to support its application.

Other Decision Makers

259. Geelhoed, E. Bruce. <u>Charles E. Wilson and Controversy</u>
<u>at the Pentagon, 1953 to 1957</u>.   Detroit: Wayne State
University Press, 1979.   216p. Suggests that Wilson functioned well in administering Eisenhower's defense policy,
which emphasized economy as well as security.   Wilson
opposed the "flexible response" theory and provided stability in the Department of Defense.   One chapter deals with
the "new look."

260. Radford, Arthur W. <u>From Pearl Harbor to Vietnam: The</u>
<u>Memoirs of Admiral Arthur W. Radford</u>, edited by Stephen
Jurika, Jr.   Stanford, California: Hoover Institution
Press, 1980. 476p. As Chairman of the Joint Chiefs of
Staff, Radford was one of the primary administration
advocates of the "new look."   Later, in 1954, he was a
leading proponent of going to the aid of the French in
Indochina.

Decision-making

Official Policy Statements

261. Eisenhower, Dwight D. "White House Statement Concerning Steps Taken to Strengthen and Improve the Operation of
the National Security Council. March 23, 1953." In <u>Public</u>
<u>Papers of the Presidents of the United States: Dwight D.</u>
<u>Eisenhower 1953</u>, 120-122.   Washington, D.C.: Government
Printing Office, 1960.   Outlines changes in the National
Security Council.   The statement discusses the membership,
which will now include some "qualified civilians" outside
government, and the formation of a National Security
Council Planning Staff.

262. Eisenhower, Dwight D. "Special Message to the Congress
on Reorganization of the Defense Establishment. April 3,
1958."   In <u>Public Papers of the Presidents of the United</u>
<u>States: Dwight D. Eisenhower 1958</u>, 274-290.   Washington,
D.C.: Government Printing Office, 1959.   Discusses the
centralization of military planning, the establishment of
"unified commands," and the strengthening of the Office of
the Secretary of Defense.   One primary purpose of the
proposed legislation is to reduce interservice rivalry and
thereby improve America's defense posture.

Bibliography

263. "A Selected Bibliography on Defense Reorganization."
<u>Air University Quarterly Review</u> 12 (Summer 1960):131-134.
Very   brief,   unannotated   bibliography   which   emphasizes

government documents, war college theses, contractors' reports, and other materials. It also includes some books and periodical articles.

Books

264. Millis, Walter and others. Arms and the State; Civil-Military Elements in National Policy. New York: Twentieth Century Fund, 1958. 436p. Examines relations between civilian leaders and the military from the end of World War II through the Korean armistice. The authors stress the need to integrate military and political policies.

Periodical Articles

265. Baldridge, Elward F. "Politico-Military Policy in Today's Navy." United States Naval Institute Proceedings 85 (March 1959):30-35. Uses the provision of humanitarian assistance to Ceylon in 1957 as an example of politico-military decision-making. Baldridge examines the process by which it was decided to send the aircraft carrier Princeton to the Indian Ocean from Japan. He devotes much of the article to a description of the Politico-Military Policy Division of the Office of the Chief of Naval Operations.

266. Bentley, Jack L. "Civilian-Military Balance in the Defense Establishment." Air University Quarterly Review 12 (Summer 1960):91-94. Discusses the problems of implementing civilian control over the military in the 1960's. Service disunity is giving the civilians more and more power; Bentley suggests strengthening the unified commands, the Joint Chiefs of Staff, and the service departments.

267. Bergren, Orville V. "The New Look in Defense Organization." Marine Corps Gazette 42 (December 1958):40-48. Surveys the impact of the Defense Reorganization Act of 1958 on the Department of Defense and the armed services.

268. Brannen, Philip Barry. "A Single Service: Perennial Issue in National Defense." United States Naval Institute Proceedings 83 (December 1957):1280-1287. Discusses repeated efforts after World War II to bring about radical centralization of the armed services. Brannen argues that the continued existence of the separate services does not waste money and provides substantial benefits in improved decision-making.

269. Chen, Arthur Si Y. "A Survey of Selected Reorganizational Proposals." Air University Quarterly Review 12 (Summer 1960):123-130. Examines five categories of proposals for change, going from complete unification of the services to restructuring planning systems and procedures. This is a useful survey of thinking about reorganization on the eve of McNamara's arrival at the Department of Defense.

270. Cutler, Robert. "The Development of the National
Security Council." Foreign Affairs 34 (April 1956):441-458.
Summarizes the functions, operations, and techniques used
by the National Security Council. Cutler emphasizes its
policy planning function and its support staff function.
He comments on some changes in the membership of the
Council and the composition of its permanent staff.

271. Dow, Leonard F. "The Case for Genuine National
Military Planning." Air University Quarterly Review 12
(Summer 1960):95-101. Asserts that interservice planning
is not being achieved despite the responsibility that has
been given to the Joint Chiefs of Staff. Dow wants to
emphasize the unified commands and establish a National
Military Staff to prepare plans and a National Military
Evaluation Board. He also proposes "a single chief of
staff."

272. Eliot, George Fielding. "The Uncertain Trumpet."
United States Naval Institute Proceedings 84 (May 1958):36-
48. Discusses the principle of vesting ultimate responsibility for military policy and strategy in civilian
leaders. The problem is that the services are not given
clear policies to follow or definite objectives. Eliot
praises the services and the Joint Chiefs of Staff for
opposing structural reorganizations based on missions. He
is generally critical of various proposals advanced by
Henry Kissinger.

273. Fox, William T.R. "Civilians, Soldiers, and American
Military Policy." World Politics 7 (April 1955):402-418.
Discusses the problems of integrating civilian and military
elements within a national security policy. Fox argues
that the military is properly assuming a larger role in
major policy decisions, citing the National Security
Council as an example.

274. Gilman, Seymour I. "A New Concept for Military
Organization." Military Review 39 (April 1959):35-42.
Assails the Department of Defense Reorganization Act of
1958 for having failed to unify the services further.
Weapons technology is breaking down the roles of the
services; and this development needs to be recognized in
the terms of organization.

275. Gumz, Donald G. "The Bureau of the Budget and Defense
Fiscal Policy." United States Naval Institute Proceedings
85 (April 1959):80-89. Explains the functions of the
Bureau of the Budget in respect to defense expenditures and
reviews relationships between it and the Department of
Defense during the late 1940's and 1950's. Gumz is
concerned that the armed services are not able to articu-
late their needs more specifically and proposes structural
changes to permit this.

276. Hammond, Paul Y. "The National Security Council as a Device for Interdepartmental Coordination: An Interpretation and Appraisal." _American Political Science Review_ 54 (December 1960):899-910. Describes the Council's origin and structure and presents a detailed study of its operations.

277. Healey, John C. "Some Reflections on the General Staff." _Air University Quarterly Review_ 12 (July 1960): 115-122. Asserts that many objections to a unified staff arise from ignorance or prejudice, specifically identifying the concept with Prussian militarism. There is little reason to fear that such a staff could not be kept within its proper sphere in the United States.

278. Hensel, H. Struve. "Changes Inside the Pentagon." _Military Review_ 34 (April 1954):36-50. Describes changes in the wake of the Rockefeller Committee's report. Hensel emphasizes the importance of increasing the civilian upper echelon staff to ensure effective civilian control.

279. Hittle, J.D. "Military Planning at the Seat of Government." _United States Naval Institute Proceedings_ 83 (July 1957):713-721. Deals with the question of whether to replace the Joint Chiefs of Staff with a general staff and a single chief of staff. Hittle marshals a great deal of historical evidence to refute the case for the general staff.

280. Kintner, William R. "Organizing for Conflict: A Proposal." _Orbis_ 2 (Summer 1958):155-174. Stresses that the United States must restructure its method for making national security decisions, in order to counter the very powerful, highly integrated Soviet system. Kintner argues that the National Security Council must become an active instrument of the president for transcending the compromises imposed by bargaining between service departments and committees.

281. Knight, Archie J. and Allen F. Herzberg. "A Proposal for the Next Step in Defense Reorganization." _Air University Quarterly Review_ 12 (Summer 1960):53-90. Reviews various post-World War II studies of the defense establishment. The authors discuss the proposals these studies made and, very usefully, highlight the changes that were not made, even though suggested. Knight and Herzberg present extensive proposals of their own for changes in the structure and responsibilities of the services.

282. Kugel, Richard C. "Arguments for Unified Combat and Support Commands." _Air University Quarterly Review_ 12 (Summer 1960):102-114. Asserts that these commands should become the critical elements of the defense establishment, primarily because of technological change, the cost of weapons systems, and the need to adapt quickly to the

advent of new weapons.

283. Orem, Howard E. "Shall We Junk the Joint Chiefs of Staff." United States Naval Institute Proceedings 84 (February 1958):57-60. Strong defense of the Joint Chiefs. Orem praises them for the relative unanimity of their advice, and he assails proposals for further centralization in the defense sphere.

284. Palfrey, Campbell, Jr. and James W. Rothwell. "Command and Organization of Aerospace Offense and Defense." Air University Quarterly Review 12 (Winter-Spring 1960-1961): 135-147. Discusses shortcomings in coordination between the services and argues that there should be a single strategic force command, including navy aviation, Polaris submarines, and the Strategic Air Command.

285. Probert, John R. "Pentagon Reorganization: Phase Three." United States Naval Institute Proceedings 81 (January 1955):51-62. Analyzes Reorganization Plan 6, which was proposed in 1954. It focuses on the Office of the Secretary of Defense. Probert examines the controversy over the plan and summarizes major testimony.

286. Sights, Albert P., Jr. "Major Tasks and Military Reorganization." Air University Quarterly Review 9 (Winter 1956-1957):3-26. Criticizes joint commands, which, in the author's view, do not provide effective unified fighting forces. Sights warns, too, that nuclear deterrence is not appropriate for stopping gradual enemy advances. He favors movement toward a single, integrated service headed by a Chief of Military Operations to replace the Joint Chiefs of Staff.

287. Wermuth, Anthony L. "A General Staff for America in the Sixties." Military Review 39 (February 1960):11-20. After a short historical survey of interservice planning in the United States, Wermuth discusses current problems of the Joint Chiefs of Staff. Wermuth also believes the Department of Defense has been over-civilianized.

288. Wylie, J.C. "Why a Sailor Thinks Like a Sailor." United States Naval Institute Proceedings 83 (August 1957):811-817. Praises the contribution to national defense of "inter-service rivalries" and discusses the maritime approach to national strategy. Wylie examines possible Western naval responses to a Soviet attack in Europe. He argues that "the maritime strategies are the one field in which the United States has an inherent advantage over any enemy."

General Strategy

Official Policy Statements

289. Dulles, John Foster. "Policy for Security and Peace."
Foreign Affairs 32 (April 1954):353-364.   Reviews the
nature of the communist threat, discusses the American
alliance system, and puts forth a strategy for coping with
possible attacks.   Dulles emphasizes flexibility and the
ability to promote uncertainty about the nature of American
responses to communist moves.

290. Eisenhower, Dwight D. "Radio Address to the American
People on the National Security and Its Costs. May 19,
1953."   In Public Papers of the Presidents of the United
States: Dwight D. Eisenhower 1953, 306-316.   Washington,
D.C.: Government Printing Office, 1960.   Warns that the
Soviets plan to bankrupt the United States by forcing it to
expend vast sums on defense.   Eisenhower emphasizes the
need to maintain economic strength and to avoid converting
the United States into a "garrison state." He announces
that the 1954 defense budget will heavily emphasize
aviation.

291. Eisenhower, Dwight D. "The President's News Conference. March 17, 1954."   In Public Papers of the Presidents of the United States: Dwight D. Eisenhower 1954, 320-
322.   Washington, D.C.: Government Printing Office, 1960.
Criticizes the more extreme interpretations given to John
Foster Dulles' reference to "massive retaliation" and then
describes the "new look" in defense policy.   Eisenhower
somewhat downplays the novelty of the "new look," describing it as "an attempt by intelligent people to keep
abreast of the times."

Books

292. Gavin, James Maurice. War and Peace in the Space Age.
New York: Harper & Row, Publishers, 1959. 304p. Stresses
the need to prepare for limited war and describes a considerable variety of weapons and weapons systems.   Gavin
seems pessimistic about the ability of the United States to
meet new challenges in the field of defense.

293. Morgenstern, Oskar.   Question of National Defense.
New York: Random House, 1959. 306p. Emphasizes the need for
a retaliatory force that can elude attack.   He finds this
in the Polaris submarines.   Morgenstern also discusses many
other facets of defense policy, including civil defense.

294. Reinhardt, George Cooper. American Strategy in the
Atomic Age.   Norman: University of Oklahoma Press, 1955.
236p. Warns of the danger of inadvertent war.   Reinhardt
advocates developing the non-communist world both militarily and economically and advocates promoting anti-

communism within the Soviet bloc.

295. Smith, Dale O. <u>U.S. Military Doctrine; a Study and Appraisal</u>. New York: Duell, Sloan and Pearce, 1955. 256p. Puts current strategic thinking into historical perspective by reviewing American military doctrine since the Revolutionary War. Smith stresses the recent impact of air power.

296. Taylor, Maxwell Davenport. <u>Uncertain Trumpet</u>. New York: Harper & Row, Publishers, 1960. 203p. This critique of the Eisenhower administration's emphasis on "massive retaliation" helped bring Taylor into the Kennedy circle as chairman of the Joint Chiefs of Staff after Kennedy defeated Nixon for the presidency in 1960. Taylor advocated strengthening the role of the chairman of the Joint Chiefs among other changes.

Periodical Articles

297. Church, Albert T. "The Three Wars That Face Us." <u>United States Naval Institute Proceedings</u> 82 (February 1956):144-151. Discusses the problems of military and naval planning. There must be a middle ground between being tied to a single plan and developing a confusing array of plans. Church distinguishes between general nuclear war, general conventional war, and "peripheral" or "limited war."

298. Donnelly, Charles H. "Evolution of United States Military Strategic Thought." <u>Military Review</u> 39 (October 1959):12-24. Discusses the nature of strategy and reviews American strategic thinking from 1945 to 1958. About half the article deals with the Eisenhower administration, especially the years 1957 and 1958.

299. Eliot, George Fielding. "Bolt from the Blue." <u>United States Naval Institute Proceedings</u> 85 (July 1959):22-33. Compares the position of the United States today with that of Great Britain before World War I in the sense that both possessed strategic resources (the Royal Navy and nuclear weapons capability), the loss of which would bring immediate defeat. Mobility was the key to protecting the British Grand Fleet in 1914-1918, and it is mobility through sea power that must be used to protect the American nuclear striking forces.

300. Eliot, George Fielding. "The Fatal Virus of a Static Strategy." <u>United States Naval Institute Proceedings</u> 86 (February 1960):22-30. Argues that "collective security" and "a defense strategy" contradict one another. Eliot's analysis is critical of the "new look." In particular, tying itself to a missile system to deter Soviet nuclear attack is an inappropriate strategy for the United States.

301. Eliot, George Fielding. "Strategic Mobility is a National State of Mind." <u>Military Review</u> 40 (October 1960): 43-53. After reviewing the role of mobility in American wars, Eliot warns against fixed defenses such as some missile systems. Our deterrence must be mobile; this principle requires more attention to airlift and sealift capacity.

302. Hessler, William H. "There's no Substitute for Diplomacy--or for Power." <u>United States Naval Institute Proceedings</u> 83 (July 1957):691-697. Discusses the importance of military power as an aid to diplomacy. Hessler sees a considerable role for the United Nations in world politics, but contends that diplomacy and associated military strength remains the primary method for conducting relations among the major powers.

303. Hopwood, Lloyd P. "A Formula for Strategic Planning." <u>Air University Quarterly Review</u> 8 (Spring 1956):21-33. Analyzes the various levels of conflict, confusion about which Hopwood sees as obscuring the basic concept of war. Hopwood examines Soviet strategy and offers some guidelines for a counter strategy.

304. Huntington, Samuel P. "To Choose Peace or War." <u>United States Naval Institute Proceedings</u> 83 (April 1957):359-369. Asserting that neither "massive retaliation" nor "limited war theories" adequately deal with the military challenges facing the United States, Huntington discusses the theory of "preventive war." He views limited preventive war as a possible, legitimate American strategy.

305. McGarr, Lionel C. "Keeping Pace with the Future--The Power of Thought--New Horizons." <u>Military Review</u> 39 (September 1959):3-19. Analyzes the development of new ideas (doctrine) about national security. McGarr emphasizes the need for flexibility and discusses the interplay of technology and doctrine.

306. Maney, John R. "The Support of Strategy." <u>Air University Quarterly Review</u> 6 (Fall 1953):42-51. Faults the relatively unassertive posture of the United States in the Cold War. Maney attributes this to a continuing focus on strategy from the perspective of the ground forces.

307. Meyer, John C. "Evaluating Military Strategy." <u>Air University Quarterly Review</u> 10 (Winter 1958-1959):21-30. Intercontinental ballistic missiles will accentuate the primacy of the super powers. Meyer sees military strategy as the offspring of national objectives and national power and suggests ways to assess the validity of American strategy.

308. Reinhardt, George C. "Technology and National Survival." <u>Orbis</u> 2 (Winter 1959):413-424. Cautions against

too much emphasis on military technology, important as it is, when developing national strategy. Reinhardt reviews Soviet military technological advances during the post-World War II years and suggests American policies to meet the prospect of further Soviet breakthroughs.

309. Richardson, Robert C. III. "The Stalemate in Concepts." Air University Quarterly Review 12 (Summer 1960): 2-13. Argues that American defense planning has reached a plateau at which interservice conflicts are increasing. Richardson emphasizes the influence of more and more expensive weapons systems on the development of strategy.

310. "The Search for the Shape of Atomic War." Air University Quarterly Review 8 (Summer 1955):63-82. Emphasizes the enhanced importance of maneuvers in a world where, should war come again, there will not be time for the United States to develop its forces as in the two world wars. The article charges the army had not adjusted to the prospect of nuclear war as had the air force.

311. Strausz-Hupé, Robert. "Back to Sanity." United States Naval Institute Proceedings 84 (May 1958):22-31. Discusses American loss of confidence after the successful Soviet launching of artificial satellites. Strausz-Hupe argues that often Americans have indulged in wishful thinking and have failed to develop plans for eliminating deficiencies. He views concentrating on preparation for limited wars as dangerous; the major threat is the Soviets' ability to improve their military technology.

312. Wells, Samuel F., Jr. "The Origin of Massive Retalia-tion." Political Science Quarterly 96 (Spring 1981):31-52. Argues that the Eisenhower administration, in developing the "New Look," built heavily on weapons and military planning that originated in the Truman administration. Wells discusses the roles of Eisenhower, Dulles, and Nixon in defense decisions during 1953 and 1954.

Nuclear Strategy

Books

313. Kissinger, Henry A. Nuclear Weapons and Foreign Policy. New York: Harper & Row, Publishers, 1957. 455p. Constitutes one of the most important critiques of Eisen-hower's "New Look." Kissinger surveys interrelations between strategy, nuclear weapons, and diplomacy.

314. Knorr, Klaus, Eugene and Thornton Read, editors. Limited Strategic War. New York: Praeger Publishers, 1962. Essays examine the feasibility of limited nuclear war between the superpowers, and the negotiations that would parallel the fighting of such a war.

Periodical Articles

315. "Accidental War: Dangers in the 1960's." Military Review 41 (January 1961):73-86. Mershon National Security Program Study discusses the nature of such risks and recommends steps to be taken to avoid them. Several pages deal with the possibility of a limited war escalating to a nuclear exchange.

316. Acheson, Dean. "Acheson Speaks Out Against 'Retaliation' Policy." US News & World Report 36 (April 9, 1954):81-84. Advocates the "strengthening of our coalition of free nations." He stresses that this coalition must be defensive, not aggressive, as he suggests Dulles' policy of "massive retaliation" is. The article includes comments by Adlai Stevenson and Canada's Foreign Minister, Lester B. Pearson.

317. Alexander, R.G. "Making Atomic Strategy." United States Naval Institute Proceedings 81 (October 1955):1081-1083. Views the "new look" as a decision to use nuclear arms virtually to the exclusion of other weapons. Alexander assails a "war policy" of nuclear weapons which seems to him to lose any connection with political goals. Moreover, such weapons are unlikely to be used in many crisis situations because of their very power.

318. Andrews, Andrew E. "Tactical Nuclear Doctrine." Military Review 60 (October 1960):13-19. Argues against the concept that a particular point ("firebreak") distinguishes between "nuclear" and "tactical" nuclear weapons. Andrews feels that the army has been consistently slow to develop doctrine for newer nuclear weapons. He posits a number of problems that need to be examined, including the level at which decisions are made on the employment of nuclear arms.

319. Backus, P.H. "Finite Deterrence, Controlled Retaliation." United States Naval Institute Proceedings 85 (March 1959):22-29. Discusses the defensive reactions to the development of Soviet intercontinental ballistic missiles. Backus describes two possible approaches to preserving our strategic aircraft from enemy attack. They may be dispersed or defended at their normal bases by fortification.

320. Brodie, Bernard. "Nuclear Weapons: Strategic or Tactical?" Foreign Affairs 32 (January 1954):217-229. Discusses the American and Soviet nuclear weapons programs, noting the limited knowledge available. Brodie asserts that there is a need to plan to apply nuclear weapons without unleashing total destruction, that is, to use nuclear weapons tactically.

321. Freed, De Bow. "Using Our Nuclear Weapons." Military

Review 38 (March 1958):60-67.   Argues that army planning
needs to be more responsive to the availability of nuclear
weapons. Freed outlines procedures for target analysis and
selection.

322. Green, Laurence B. and John H. Burt. "Massive Retaliation: Salvation or ----?" United States Naval Institute
Proceedings 84 (October 1958):22-28.   Advises against
relying on strategic nuclear weapons when Soviet nuclear
attacks may not be the primary danger to American security.
The authors point to the Soviet Union's balanced forces and
assert that the United States needs balanced forces to
fulfill our "containment" policy.

323. Kintner, William R. "American Responsibilities in the
Nuclear Age." United States Naval Institute Proceedings 82
(March 1956):242-254.   Asserts that the Soviets are gaining
in nuclear weapons and outlines possible Soviet nuclear
strategies.   The United States must develop a plan for
coping with an environment of nuclear "parity" between the
superpowers.   More emphasis will necessarily be put on
conventional forces, including tactical nuclear weapons.

324. Kissinger, Henry A. "Force and Diplomacy in the
Nuclear Age." Foreign Affairs 34 (April 1956):349-366.
Another critique of "massive retaliation." Kissinger
believes Americans lack flexibility and overemphasize
military factors in assessing the Soviet threat. He argues
for a policy of "graduated employment of force."

325. Kissinger, Henry A. "Military Policy and Defense of
the 'Grey Areas.'" Foreign Affairs 33 (April 1955):416-
428.   Important attack on the Eisenhower administration's
"New Look". Kissinger argues that American nuclear forces
are declining in relation to those of the Soviets, giving
the Soviets more incentive to intervene in "grey areas," a
strategy which cannot be stopped by "massive retaliation."

326. Murphy, Robert. "The Interrelationship of Military
Power and Foreign Policy." Department of State Bulletin 31
(August 30, 1954):291-294.   States that the United States
is far superior to its possible enemies in terms of
military power.   Its great power has created uneasiness at
home and among our allies.   The Soviet Union has played on
these fears and has refused to share in efforts to control
nuclear weapons.   This has forced the United States to
develop the strategy of "massive retaliation".

327. Nitze, Paul H. "Atoms, Strategy and Policy." Foreign
Affairs 34 (January 1956):187-198.   Asserts that any use of
nuclear weapons by the United States and its allies is
likely to be limited or "graduated," not "massive retaliation." Nitze suggests that "massive retaliation" is not a
functional strategy and proposes an alternative "action
policy."

328. Oppenheimer, J. Robert. "Atomic Weapons and American Policy." Foreign Affairs 31 (July 1953):525-535. Warns that while the United States is well ahead of the USSR in nuclear technology, the general development of nuclear arms is growing rapidly more threatening. More information on these arms needs to be made public. There should also be more collaboration between the United States and its allies and more attention given to developing an active defense against nuclear attacks.

329. Parrish, Noel F. "Effective Aerospace Power 1. Deterrence: The Hard Question." Air University Quarterly Review 12 (Winter-Spring 1960-1961):148-152. Examines various concepts of deterrence advanced in the West during the late 1940's and early 1950's and criticizes much of this theorizing for its timidity. Parrish worries that nuclear weapons will not be used in limited wars when appropriate.

330. Richardson, Robert C. III. "The Fallacy of the Concept of Minimum Deterrence." Air University Quarterly Review 12 (Spring 1960):108-117. Argues that the theory which down-plays the need for a counterforce and maximizes threats to civilian populations leaves the Soviets free to pursue aggression through limited wars. Richardson feels the United States should emphasize defeating the enemy, not simply doing a great deal of damage.

331. Rosencrance, R.N. "Can we Limit Nuclear War?" Military Review 38 (March 1959):51-59. Argues that "massive retalia-tion" is no longer a relevant strategy because of the increase in Soviet power. Rosencrance advocates devoting more attention to limited war, especially limited conven-tional war. A limited nuclear war is so uncertain that a variety of other strategies need to be pursued by the United States.

332. Sokol, Anthony E. "Sword and Shield in Our Power Structure." United States Naval Institute Proceedings 85 (April 1959):44-53. Traces the development of a defense policy in the West that puts its trust in American nuclear weapons, while reducing conventional forces. Sokol believes the European members of NATO could contribute more to the alliance and proposes a multilateral rapid deploy-ment force to supplement NATO's nuclear capability.

333. Wermuth, Anthony L. "Dollars and Sons." United States Naval Institute Proceedings 85 (August 1959):72-80. Argues that "massive retaliation" has been a failure, citing the rise to power of the communists in China as an example. This article is a powerful critique of over-dependence on nuclear weapons. Wermuth believes that adequate conven-tional forces may keep war at a conventional level. Without conventional military resources, atomic war will be

the only alternative to submitting to Soviet advances.

334. Williams, Ralph E. "America's Moment of Trust." United States Naval Institute Proceedings 81 (March 1955):245-255. Reflects on the fact that the superpowers can destroy one another. Williams asserts that air power is important primarily because it can deter general war and maintain the "limits" of any limited war. He endorses coexistence and hopes, much as Kennan did in his "X" article, for changes in the Soviet Union.

335. Williams, Ralph E. "The Great Debate: 1954." United States Naval Institute Proceedings 80 (March 1954):247-255. Discusses the controversy over what Williams calls the "air-atomic concept" and the "balanced force concept" and examines the nature of limited war as exemplified by the Korean conflict. Williams is clearly an adherent of balanced forces. This is an early criticism of nuclear "overkill".

Air Strategy

General

336. Friedman, Robert J. "Budgeting for the Aerospace Force." Air University Quarterly Review 12 (Winter-Spring 1960-1961): 222-226. Argues that a significant increase in defense spending could be undertaken without damaging the economy. Friedman admits that funds alone cannot build an adequate aerospace force; long-range planning is essential.

337. Griffin, S.F. "Relationships Among Military Forces." Air University Quarterly Review 9 (Winter 1957-1958):31-45. Discusses air power utilized by the navy and army, as well as by the air force. Griffin seems to support the "new look" and optimistically asserts that deterrence prevents limited as well as general war. He favors development of nuclear capability by the powers allied to the United States.

338. Hampton, Ephraim M. "Air Power, Global Force in a Global Struggle." Air University Quarterly Review 7 (Spring 1955):68-77. Denies that air power is only applicable in a general, nuclear war. Hampton feels that the air forces cannot be tied too closely to ground forces, frequently citing the Korean experience.

339. Hessler, William H. "America's Merchant Marine of the Air: A Vital National Asset." United States Naval Institute Proceedings 85 (May 1959):48-63. Describes the valuable military airlift capacity represented by the American airlines. Hessler examines the structure of the civil air fleet and American governmental policies that encourage or hinder the development of strong airlines. Several pages deal with the Civil Reserve Air Fleet, the 295 airliners

specifically earmarked for emergency military use.

340. Holloway, Bruce K. "Requirement for Aerospace Weapons
Systems." Air University Quarterly Review 12 (Winter-Spring
1960-1961):213-221. Discusses long-range requirements, the
role of strategy in respect to weapons development, and the
effect of budgetary restraints.

341. Kuter, Laurence S. "An Air Perspective in the Jetomic
Age." Air University Quarterly Review 8 (Spring 1956): 3-
17, 108-123. Provides an historical view of the development of air power. Kuter notes the divergence of opinion
about the proper employment of aviation and propounds some
basic air doctrine.

342. LeMay, Curtis. "The Present Pattern." Air University
Quarterly Review 12 (Winter-Spring 1960-1961):25-39. Forecasts the structure and posture of the air force in the
first half of the 1960's. LeMay seems to believe that
changing weapons systems will not require much modification
of air force doctrine.

343. "North American Air Defense Command." Military Review
38 (April, 1958):43-50. Early description of NORAD. Much
of the illustrated article describes NORAD weapons such as
the Nike-Zeus antimissile missile.

344. Page, Jerry D. "Total Air Power and the Public." Air
University Quarterly Review 8 (Spring, 1956):18-29.
Asserts the need to explain the totality of the air force
missions to the public. The flexibility of air power must
be emphasized. The article includes some references to the
Quemoy-Matsu problem.

345. Richardson, Robert C. "In the Looking Glass." Air
University Quarterly Review 9 (Winter 1957):46-54.
Condemns the over-centralization of the air force.
Richardson also contends that too many people are in staff
and too few in line positions.

346. Smith, B.J. "Is Air Power Indivisible?" Air University
Quarterly Review 8 (Fall 1956):79-85. Analyzes the air
power concept and discusses the problem of developing
doctrine that reflects the unity of air power. Air power
is dispersed among the several armed services and among
various air force commands, thereby limiting its conceptual
development.

347. Smith, Dale O. "The Role of Air Power Since World War
II." Military Affairs 19 (Summer 1955):71-76. Examines the
future of air power and the weapons that may be used in
coming air wars.

348. Strother, Dean C. "Aerospace Forces and the Range of
Situations." Air University Quarterly Review 12 (Winter-

Spring 1960-1961):53-58. Discusses the many categories of conflict between complete peace and total nuclear war. Strother examines deterrence, limited war, and cold war situations.

349. Todd, Walter E. "Evolution of Aerospace Power." Air University Quarterly Review 12 (Winter-Spring 1960-1961):9-24. Reviews the World War II experience and briefly examines air operations in Korea. Todd concludes with a discussion of trends in the late 1950's such as the advent of missiles.

350. Tunner, William H. "Strategic Airlift" Air University Quarterly Review 12 (Winter-Spring 1960-1961):104-119. Discusses relationships between airlift and offensive forces and describes the Military Air Transport Service (MATS).

351. White, Thomas D. "The Aerospace and Military Operations." Air University Quarterly Review 12 (Winter-Spring 1960-1961):4-6. Introduces a special issue on aerospace power, emphasizing its complete flexibility. White briefly reviews the many applications of aerospace power in a general war, local conflicts and "small wars," force projection, and humanitarian relief.

352. White, Thomas, D. "The Current Concept of American Military Strength: Its Meaning and Challenge to the U.S. Air Force." Air University Quarterly Review 7 (Spring 1954):3-14. Discusses the impact of national air strength on diplomacy. The primary role of the air force is deterrence. White favors highly centralized control of the air force to avoid "piecemeal" deployment.

Missiles and Bombers

353. Agan, Arthur C., Jr. "Aerospace Defense." Air University Quarterly Review 12 (Winter-Spring 1960-1961):89-103. Analyzes the changes in American air defense strategy necessitated by Soviet deployment of ICBMs. Agan also reviews earlier American defense efforts against manned bombers.

354. Bowers, Robert D. "Fundamental Equations of Force Survival." Air University Quarterly Review 10 (Spring 1958):82-92. Presents a detailed and very early statistical analysis of chances that a "retaliatory force" would survive at a level at which it would remain a deterrent.

355. Brooks, Robert O. "Surprise in the Missile Era." Air University Quarterly Review 11 (Spring 1959):76-83. Discusses the challenge of intercontinental ballistic missiles in the hands of an enemy who may use them first. Brooks examines intelligence and air defense against surprise attack, technical limitations of the ICBMs and

other factors that make one fatal raid on American targets unlikely and unfeasible.

356. Ferguson, James, "Manned Craft and the Ballistic Missile." Air University Quarterly Review 12 (Winter-Spring 1960-1961):251-256.   Argues that manned aircraft, even manned bombers, retain their importance. Ferguson points to various kinds of limited war in which missiles would have little or no value.

357. Ferguson, Roy L., Jr. "The Ballistic Missile and Operational Capability." Air University Quarterly Review 9 (Winter 1957-1958):55-61.   Discusses the deployment of ballistic missiles in field forces. Ferguson examines such topics as training and logistics.

358. Hall, Edward N. "Air Force Missile Experience." Air University Quarterly Review 9 (Summer 1957):22-33. Reviews the development of missiles, stressing pioneers such as Robert Goddard. Hall includes a brief description of air force missiles, including highly experimental types.

359. Martin, Donald F. "Effective Aerospace Power. 2. Counterforce." Air University Quarterly Review 12 (Winter-Spring 1960-1961):152-158. Describes counterforce strategy and the factors that make a single, massive nuclear exchange unlikely. Martin distinguishes between "deterrence through terror" and "deterrence through strength," regarding the latter as the capacity to destroy enemy forces.

360. Power, Thomas S. "SAC and the Ballistic Missile." Air University Quarterly Review 9 (Winter 1957-1958):2-30. Discusses the advantages to the Strategic Air Command of the ballistic missile for fulfilling its missions.

361. Putnam, Claud E. "Missiles in Perspective." Air University Quarterly Review 10 (Spring 1958):3-10. Traces the origin of missiles to efforts pioneered by the air force. Putnam sees missiles as being phased in gradually to supplement aircraft.

362. Schriever, Bernard A. "The USAF Ballistic Missile Program." Air University Quarterly Review 9 (Summer 1957):5-21. Describes the history of the ballistic missile program in detail, including its organizational and managerial facets. Schriever also considers the role of contractors at some length.

363. "The Strategic Bomber." Air University Quarterly Review 8 (Summer 1955):88-137. Reviews the development of strategic air bombardment doctrine in the air force and describes major bombers.

364. Wheless, Hewitt T. "The Deterrent Offensive Force." Air University Quarterly Review 12 (Winter-Spring 1960-

1961):59-73. Examines the development of SAC and projects trends through 1970. Wheless describes manned bombers and looks at the tactics of strategic air strikes.

365. White, Thomas D. "The Ballistic Missile: An Instrument of National Policy." Air University Quarterly Review 9 (Summer 1957):2-4. Discusses ballistic missiles as the next step in deterring enemy attack. White sees them as a supplement to the bomber force for the purpose of attacking especially difficult targets.

366. Wilson, Roscoe C. "Tomorrow in Aerospace Power." Air University Quarterly Review 12 (Winter-Spring 1960-1961): 40-50. Emphasizes the importance of counterforce capability, and discusses possible strategy alternatives to preserve deterrence.

Space Operations

367. Hopwood, Lloyd P. "The Military Impact of Space Operations." Air University Quarterly Review 10 (Summer 1958):142-146. Warns that space is as open as the oceans and that territorial limits are unlikely to be maintained. Hopwood reviews the history of air defense and applies the principles of war to space.

368. Rigg, Robert B. "Outer Space and National Defense." Military Review 39 (May 1959):21-26. Focuses on the potential military significance of the moon. Rigg describes a possible lunar base and discusses other topics such as spy satellites.

369. No entry.

Tactical Air Support

370. Brotherton, Robert G. "Close Air Support in the Nuclear Age." Military Review 39 (April 1959):30-35. Describes the mission of tactical air support and the contemporary system for applying it. Brotherton specifically reviews Joint Air-Ground Operations, issued by the air force and the army in 1957. After further experience, the two services should issue a joint directive.

371. Donovan, Stanley J. "Tactical Aerospace Forces." Air University Quarterly Review 12 (Winter-Spring 1960-1961): 74-88. Discusses the role of the Tactical Air Command in general wars and limited wars and describes the aircraft it employs.

372. Ferguson, James. "The Role of Tactical Air Forces." Air University Quarterly Review 7 (Summer 1954):29-41. Discusses the "new look" and the important place it gives military aviation. Ferguson reviews tactical air employment in World War II and uses its lessons to analyze current

problems.   Finally, he discusses newer equipment and its
impact on tactical air operations.

Ground Strategy

General

373. Krause, Frederick C. "Airborne Operations." Military
Review 39 (November 1959):65-78. Reviews the development of
airborne forces, examines their use in general and limited
war, and discusses the various types of airborne attacks.

374. McMahon, Robert E. "Airmobility Operations." Military
Review 39 (June 1959):28-35. Ties the need for airmobility,
in part, to the revolutionary nature of the nuclear battlefield. McMahon argues that there can be a clear division of
labor between the army and air force.

375. Ogorkiewicz, Richard M. "Armor in the Nuclear Age."
Military Review 38 (September 1958):3-9. Suggests that the
United States has lagged in armor development because it
does not see that tanks need to be fully integrated with
other arms.   Ogorkiewicz comments on post-World War II armored vehicle development, including armored personnel carriers.

376. Wermuth, Anthony L. "Can't Live without Them." Military
Review 38 (February 1959):52-54. Warns against misguided
attempts   to   save   military   resources   by   reducing   or
eliminating nondivisional military organizations.

Limited War

Books

377. Osgood, Robert Endicott. Limited War; the Challenge to
American Strategy. Chicago: University of Chicago Press,
1957. 315p. One of the most significant studies of limited
war.   Osgood examines the difficulty Americans face in
grappling with limited war and warns that political leaders
have to explain the nature of limited conflicts to the
American people.

Periodical Articles

378. Bashore, Boyd T. "Dual Strategy for Limited War." Military Review 40 (May 1960):46-62.   Describes Raymond
Magsaysay's successful campaign against the Huk guerrillas
in the Phillipines. Bashore says relatively little about
American participation, but feels that this campaign is influencing American military thinking.

379. Fisher, Thomas L., II. "'Limited War'--What is it?"
Air University Quarterly Review 9 (Winter 1957-1958):127-
142. Warns that the air force must prepare for limited and-
small wars. Fisher examines the nature of these conflicts
in considerable detail in terms of "objectives," "methods,"

and "area." He asserts there are many varieties of limited war.

380. Hampton, Ephraim M. "Unlimited Confusion over Limited War." Air University Quarterly Review 9 (Spring 1957):28-47. Warns that war is difficult to keep at the "limited" level and that, therefore, theorizing about limited war can be dangerous. Hampton analyzes the elements such as objectives and weapons used which can be employed to "limit" a war.

381. Reid, William M. "Tactical Air in Limited War." Air University Quarterly Review 8 (Spring 1956):40-48. Describes the serious organizational problems that beset aviation during the initial deployment in Korea. The army and the air force were not ready to use tactical air effectively. Reid also criticizes French use of aviation in Indochina.

382. Smith, Frederic H. "Nuclear Weapons and Limited War." Air University Quarterly Review 12 (Spring 1960):3-27. Argues that tactical nuclear weapons can be used effectively in limited wars without the risk of escalation. Smith discusses instances in World War II and Korea where nuclear weapons could have been helpful and analyzes their possible employment in various locales such as rain forests and mountain defiles.

Unconventional Warfare

383. Bjelajac, Slavko N. "Strategy of Protracted Defense." Military Review 40 (June 1960):63-69. Applies the lessons of the Nazi blitzkrieg to Asian nations, which often lack resources for developing an adequate defense. Bjelajac recommends that in the event of an attack, such countries should be prepared to use unconventional strategy and tactics to supplement their conventional military response.

384. Gleason, Frank A. "Unconventional Forces--The Commander's Untapped Resources." Military Review 39 (October 1959):25-33. Discusses the strength of guerrilla movements as demonstrated in Algeria, Malaya, and the Philippines. Gleason then examines possible United States employment of guerillas in operational areas.

385. Miller, George H. "Not for the Timid." United States Naval Institute Proceedings 85 (May 1959):34-42. Argues that the Soviets are advancing toward world domination despite the American policy of "massive retaliation" and that the United States must concentrate more attention on dealing with nonnuclear confrontations. It must be resourceful in planning for constantly changing conditions and new contingencies.

386. Van de Velde, R.W. "The Neglected Deterrent." Military

Review 38 (August 1958):3-10. Warns that the United States is virtually ignoring the usefulness of guerilla warfare. The author focuses on possible American-supported guerilla campaigns in Europe during a general war. He advocates more support for Special Forces, which can be a real part of our deterrence strategy.

387. Wilkins, Frederick. "Guerilla Warfare." United States Naval Institute Proceedings 80 (March 1954):311-318. Historical examination of guerilla warfare which also includes much analysis. Wilkins asserts that counterinsurgency in Asia will be a greater challenge than the post-World War II campaign in Greece.

Naval Strategy

388. Andersen, A.E. "Flexible Response and the Marine Corps." Marine Corps Gazette 56 (January 1972):40-44. Traces marine responses to the increasing American concern with limited war theory during the 1950's.

389. Asprey, Robert B. "The New Fleet Marine Force." United States Naval Institute Proceedings 85 (August 1959):40-48. Discusses marine use of helicopters to make attacks by "vertical envelopment" instead of by beach assaults that could easily be destroyed by nuclear weapons. Doctrine on vertical envelopment had been formulated by the end of 1955.

390. Beavers, Roy L. "Seapower and Geopolitics in the Missile Age." United States Naval Institute Proceedings 85 (June 1959):40-46. Strongly advocates development of a seaborne missile capability instead of land-based missiles to offset Soviet intercontinental ballistic missiles. The feasibility of such seaborn missiles make sea control more important than ever.

391. Cagle, Malcolm W. "The Neglected Ocean." United States Naval Institute Proceedings 84 (November 1958):54-61. Examines the geography of the Indian Ocean in some detail and reviews its naval history. Cagle advocates a significant American naval presence in the Indian Ocean and describes quite specifically what forces are needed.

392. Cagle. Malcolm W. "A Philosophy for Naval Atomic Warfare." United States Naval Institute Proceedings 83 (March 1957):249-258. Argues that after long experimentation, it is incumbent on the navy to develop doctrine for the use of nuclear weapons at sea. Cagle asserts that limited use can be made of nuclear weapons without a nuclear holocaust.

393. Canzona, Nicholas A. "Is Amphibious War Dead?" United States Naval Institute Proceedings 81 (September 1955):986-

991. Warns that war is possible despite the great destructive power of nuclear weapons and that amphibious capability should be maintained. Canzona examines the arguments
against amphibious operations in the nuclear age and points
to their usefulness in limited wars, noting the Inchon
invasion in Korea.

394. Carney, Robert B. "Always the Sea." United States
Naval Institute Proceedings 81 (May 1955):497-503. Discusses the inherent strength and the success of a maritime
as opposed to a continental strategy. Carney examines the
loss of sea control by the Japanese during World War II and
the application of sea power in the years after 1945.
Carney argues that the Soviets' ability to expand is
limited by their weakness at sea.

395. Carney, Robert B. "Principles of Sea Power." United
States Naval Institute Proceedings 81 (September 1955):967-
985. Emphasizes the importance of a deterrent force to
maintain peace. Carney examines the significance of sea
power to NATO and other American-supported alliances. By
implication, at least, this article is critical of the "new
look", which may be an example of "ephermal solutions to
ephermal problems."

396. Collins, John J. "The American Merchant Marine in
World War III." United States Naval Institute Proceedings
82 (April 1956):406-415. Reviews the record of the merchant
marine in World War II and discusses its contemporary problems, including discriminatory tactics by other countries.
Collins offers a number of specific and rather drastic
means to strengthen the American merchant marine.

397. Dissette, Edward F. "Overseas Bases--How Long for This
World?" United States Naval Institute Proceedings 86 (July
1960):22-30. Discusses the problems of retaining bases in
the face of increasing nationalism abroad, the financial
drain of maintaining the bases, and Soviet efforts to drive
the United States out of its overseas bases. With the
advent of intercontinental ballistic missiles, some bases
may lose their importance, and carrier groups may take up
some of the slack for bases that are lost.

398. Fiore, Louis R. "MSTS-The Navy's Fourth Arm." United
States Naval Institute Proceedings 83 (August 1957):868-
890. Examines the role of the Military Sea Transportation
Service (MSTS) in supporting the armed services and giving
them a fleet ready for immediate deployment in a crisis.

399. Ford, Walter C. "The U.S. Merchant Marine and National
Defense." United States Naval Institute Proceedings 83
(November 1957):1178-1187. Describes the neglect of the
American merchant marine and the current problems of
obsolescence that threaten it. Ford also discusses efforts
to modernize World War II ships to promote a competitive

American merchant marine.

400. Garrison, Daniel J. "The Role of the Navy in Cold War." United States Naval Institute Proceedings 85 (June 1959):57-63. Describes the increasing power that naval forces have over land masses and details the various roles that they can and should play in the rivalry of communist and non-communist blocs. Garrison discusses the deterrent value of seaborne missiles and then analyzes the use of sea power in limited wars and low-intensity conflicts.

401. Harrigan, Anthony. "Sea Power: Bulwark Against Chinese Communist Imperialism." United States Naval Institute Proceedings 86 (June 1960):68-74. Discusses the menace of China's revolutionary communism and the emerging division between the Soviet Union and the Peoples Republic of China. Harrigan stresses the significance of Formosa in the American effort to stem Chinese expansionism and asserts that a "floating barrier of U.S. naval vessels can prevent the Communist hordes from overrunning Southeast Asia and Australia."

402. Hellner, Maurice H. "America's Growing Dependence on the Sea." United States Naval Institute Proceedings 83 (October 1957):1082-1091. This increased "dependence" arises from the American need to import more and more raw materials from overseas and from the American leadership role of the non-communist world. Hellner describes maritime contributions to both the "massive retaliation" and "graduated deterrence" strategies.

403. Hellner Maurice H. "Sea Power and the Struggle for Asia." United States Naval Institute Proceedings 82 (April 1956):352-361. Downplays the impact of nuclear weapons on international relations, pointing to conventional wars in Greece and Korea. Fear of nuclear war has encouraged many Asian nations to seek nonalignment in the cold war. Hellner discusses strategic relationships in the Pacific and Soviet initiatives in Indonesia and elsewhere.

404. Hessler, William H. "Sixth Fleet: Beefed Up for a Bigger Job." United States Naval Institute Proceedings 84 (August 1958):22-30. Discusses the problems facing the United States in the Mediterranean and the Middle East, necessitating a stronger fleet to support American poli- cies. The "great resurgence of Islamic nationalism" is the primary motive force in the Middle East and is directed in part against the United States. Hessler also examines the structure and weapons of the Sixth Fleet.

405. Huntington, Samuel P. "National Policy and the Trans- oceanic Navy." United States Naval Institute Proceedings 80 (May 1954):483-493. Asserts that to be effective, a military force must have a "strategic concept" for achiev- ing national goals. Huntington suggests that the navy

developed such a concept after World War II, but that it needs to be fully accepted within the navy and then used to implement changes in its organization and deployment. Huntington sees the navy as projecting force landward rather than seeking to dominate the oceans.

406. Lewis, D.D. "The Problems of Obsolescence." United States Naval Institute Proceedings 85 (October 1959):26-31. Warns that the navy is growing older and that many ships will be obsolete soon. New ships are not being built fast enough to make up for the approaching obsolescence of so many World War II ships. Constructing more nuclear-powered ships will cost more and reduce the number of vessels that will become available.

407. Mataxis, Theodore C. "The Marines' New Look." Military Review 38 (February 1959):10-17. Compares marine corps division structure with army pentomic divisions. The marines now emphasize helicopter-borne landings instead of beach assaults.

408. McNevin, Michael T. "An Atomic-Age Navy." United States Naval Institute Proceedings 85 (October 1959):40-49. Defends the role of the navy as an element in deterring aggressors and suggests utilizing the principles of "dispersal" and "mobility" in enhancing the ability of the navy to function even in a nuclear war. "Dispersal" would include such steps as putting limited fixed and floating naval facilities in smaller ports.

409. Rand, H.P. "A United States Counteraggression Force." Military Review 39 (July 1959):50-55. Very early call for what would now be termed a rapid deployment force. Rand asserts that the United States should shift more attention and resources to limited war as part of the deterrence policy. He praises the STRAC concept, but says air force and navy forces need to be added to STRAC.

410. Smith, James H. "Mobile Sea Base Systems in Nuclear Warfare." United States Naval Institute Proceedings 81 (February 1955):131-135. Discusses the need for a seaborne nuclear deterrence force. Smith argues that long-range missiles cannot be used effectively against submarines, aircraft carriers, and other ships armed with nuclear weapons.

411. Utgoff, Vadym V. "The Future of the Navy." United States Naval Institute Proceedings 84 (August 1958):73-81. Forecasts trends for the next ten to forty years. Utgoff predicts far greater use of nuclear propulsion for navy ships and changes in air mobility. Much of the article discusses the projection of seapower into land areas by naval aircraft.

412. Williams, Ralph E. "Task for Today: Security Through

Seapower." United States Naval Institute Proceedings 84
(March 1958):23-30. Notes the rapidly escalating costs of
new weapons which put more and more emphasis on nuclear
warfare. Williams suggests that the United States need put
only a limited investment in its deterrent forces and
reemphasize conventional warfare.

Civil Defense

413. Eisenhower, Dwight D. "Letter to Val Peterson,
Administrator of Civil Defense, on the Occasion of Operation Alert 1956. July 17, 1956." In Public Papers of the
Presidents of the United States: Dwight D. Eisenhower 1956,
598-601. Washington, D.C.: Government Printing Office,
1958. Describes progress in civil defense during Peterson's
tenure in office and emphasizes the need for greater
efforts. While Eisenhower had favored as little federal
guidance as possible, he now advocates "vesting in the
Federal Government a larger responsibility in our national
plan of civil defense." Much of the letter discusses action
taken to strengthen the role of the Administrator of Civil
Defense.

Intelligence Agencies

414. Ransom, Harry Howe. Central Intelligence and National
Security. Cambridge: Harvard University Press, 1958. 287p.
Examines military intelligence services, the CIA, and other
intelligence agencies in the executive branch. This very
early study of the American intelligence community grew out
of research at the Graduate School of Public Administration
at Harvard.

Military Assistance

Official Policy Statements

415. Eisenhower, Dwight D. "Radio and Television Address to
the American People on the Need for Mutual Security in
Waging the Peace. May 21, 1957." In Public Papers of the
Presidents of the United States: Dwight D. Eisenhower 1957,
385-396. Washington, D.C.: Government Printing Office,
1958. Vigorously defends the mutual security program as a
nonpartisan strategy which began with the Truman Doctrine.
Eisenhower asserts that it is vital to prevent the United
States from being "gradually encircled" by communist
countries and uses South Vietnam as an example of how the
mutual security program works successfully.

416. Eisenhower, Dwight D. "Special Message to the Congress
on the Mutual Security Program. February 11, 1960." In
Public Papers of the Presidents of the United States:
Dwight D. Eisenhower 1960-61, 177-188. Washington, D.C.:
Government Printing Office, 1961. Stresses the vital need
for the mutual security program in the face of increasing

Sino-Soviet military strength. Eisenhower describes the program for fiscal year 1961 and refers to his expectation that the NATO countries will assist by providing more assistance to developing nations.

Periodical Articles

417. Jordan, Amos, Jr. "Military Assistance and National Policy." Orbis 2 (Summer 1958):236-253. Presents a generally favorable picture of the mutual security program, but highlights several problems such as the cumbersome processes which create excessive time lags in providing aid.

418. Pickell, Clyde V. and Thomas C. Musgrave. "Investment in Security." Military Review 40 (December 1960):50-59. Surveys the development of post-World War II American military assistance programs and describes the organizational structure used to administer such aid and training.

419. Reday, Joseph Z. "Is U.S. Aid to the Orient Working?" United States Naval Institute Proceedings 83 (November 1957):1149-1157. Discusses the problems presented by Asian suspicions of the West and the friction between American servicemen in Asia and local nationals. Americans must not be seen as controlling development in Asian countries; Reday therefore advocates reducing the size of military advisory missions and training foreigners in the United States rather than in their own countries.

420. Shiffrin, Benjamin H. "MDAP Air Training." Air University Quarterly Review 6 (Fall 1953):63-73. Early description of the air force contribution to the Mutual Defense Assistance Program. Shiffrin stresses the importance of training foreign personnel to use and maintain American equipment properly.

421. Smith, C. Alphonso. "Military Assistance in the Far East." United States Naval Institute Proceedings 86 (December 1960):40-47. Examines the economic, social, and political challenges facing the non-communist states of the Far East, other than Japan, and the impact of the Military Assistance Program (MAP). Smith sees the Peoples Republic of China as the primary threat. MAP operations in each Asian country are briefly surveyed.

422. Stewart, William R., Jr. "Allied Air Power Has Outgrown Our MAAG's." Air University Quarterly Review 8 (Spring 1956):79-88. Discusses the contribution of Military Assistance Advisory Groups to the strengthening of American allies. This effort has declined in importance, primarily because many allied air forces have reached maturity and need less guidance.

Disarmament and Arms Control

Official Policy Statements

423. Eisenhower, Dwight D. "Statement by the President Reviewing the Government's Policies and Actions With Respect to the Development and Testing of Nuclear Weapons. October 24, 1956." In Public Papers of the Presidents of the United States: Dwight D. Eisenhower 1956, 997-1002. Washington, D.C.: Government Printing Office, 1958. Asserts that the United States must seek disarmament and, until effective controls are established, must maintain an adequate defense capability. The statement is highly critical of the USSR for rejecting American proposals, including provision for mutual inspections.

424. Eisenhower, Dwight D. "Letter to Nikita Khrushchev, Chairman, Council of Ministers, U.S.S.R., on the Discontinuance of Nuclear Weapons Tests. April 20, 1959." In Public Papers of the Presidents of the United States: Dwight D. Eisenhower 1959, 331-332. Washington, D.C.: Government Printing Office, 1960. States that the "United States strongly seeks a lasting agreement for the discontinuance of nuclear weapons tests" and proposes an immediate end to above ground testing. Eisenhower suggests various interim steps toward reaching a total agreement.

Books

425. Rostow, W.W. Open Skies: Eisenhower's Proposal of July 21, 1955. Austin: University of Texas Press, 1982. 226p. Highly detailed analysis of Eisenhower's most important arms control initiative. Half the book consists of appendices, which contain documents. Rostow supplements his extensive research with his recollections of the episode.

Essays and Periodical Articles

426. Kelly, George A. "Arms Control and the Military Establishment." Military Review 41 (January 1961):62-72. Argues that arms control theory should be an integral part of defense planning and that military leaders should devote more attention to the subject. The alternative may be for public opinion to force dangerous forms of disarmament on the nation.

427. Matteson, Robert E. "The Disarmament Dilemma." Orbis 2 (Fall 1958):285-299. Observes that some progress has been made on disarmament through the London negotiations of 1957. Even greater efforts must be made.

428. Soapes, Thomas F. "A Cold Warrior Seeks Peace: Eisenhower's Strategy for Nuclear Disarmament." Diplomatic History 4 (Winter 1980):57-71. Interprets Eisenhower as genuinely seeking nuclear disarmament and reviews his

efforts and those of his associates during the 1950's. His
inherent hostility toward the Soviet Union is said to have
hindered progress in this field.

429. Strausz-Hupe, Robert. "The Disarmament Delusion."
United States Naval Institute Proceedings 86 (February
1960):41-47. Presents a critique of Khrushchev's proposal
for complete disarmament at the United Nations on September
18, 1959, comparing it with Soviet initiatives in the
1920's, 1930's and 1950's. Strausz-Hupe questions the
feasibility of total disarmament, especially in view of the
communist ability to conduct low-intensity revolutionary
warfare.

430. Strong, Robert A. "Eisenhower and Arms Control." In
Reevaluating Eisenhower: American Foreign Policy in the
1950's, edited by Richard A. Melanson and David Mayers,
241-266. Urbana: University of Illinois Press, 1987.
Emphasizes the profound impact of nuclear weapons on
military and arms control policy. Eisenhower is seen by
Strong as making some increases in nuclear military
capability and taking cautious steps towards arms control,
recognizing the acute need for the latter.

Military Personnel

Official Policy Statements

431. Eisenhower, Dwight D. "Special Message to the Congress
on National Security Requirements. January 13, 1955." In
Public Papers of the Presidents of the United States:
Dwight D. Eisenhower 1955, 72-78. Washington D.C.: Government Printing Office, 1959. Recommends continuance of the
draft for four years and the medical draft for two years.
Much of the address deals with reserve forces and especially the new system of short-term training and long-term
reserve obligations. Eisenhower recommends various legislation to improve manpower procurement and the reserve
forces.

432. Eisenhower, Dwight D. "Statement by the President upon
Signing the Reserve Forces Act of 1955. August 9, 1955." In
Public Papers of the Presidents of the United States:
Dwight D. Eisenhower 1955, 775-776. Washington, D.C.:
Government Printing Office, 1959. Describes the major
provisions of the statute and generally praises the
legislation even though it does not meet all of
Eisenhower's requirements. Reserve forces are to be
expanded substantially, although Eisenhower expresses
"serious doubts" that the National Guard will reach its
established strength or the proper level of training and
preparation.

433. Eisenhower, Dwight D. "Statement by the President on
the Need for Maintaining the Draft. October 7, 1956." In

Public Papers of the Presidents of the United States:
Dwight D. Eisenhower 1956, 867-870. Washington, D.C.:
Government Printing Office, 1958. Asserts that the continuing communist threat makes the draft essential; it will be
necessary for some time to come. Eisenhower also discusses
efforts his administration is making to reduce the number
of military personnel by greater use of technology.

Periodical Articles

434. Garrison, D.J. "Reserves--What Kind?" United States
Naval Institute Proceedings 81 (May 1955):528-533. Discusses current reports of serious deficiencies in the
training and readiness of reserve forces.   Garrison
examines various aspects of the reserve problem, including
the special need of the navy and air force for personnel to
serve for long period, in order to be trained as technicians.   He notes the effects of the Korean War reserve
callup of reservists on the desire for "equity" in requiring military service.

Alliances

Official Policy Statement

435. Eisenhower, Dwight D. "Address at the American Legion
Convention. August 30, 1954." In Public Papers of the
Presidents of the United States: Dwight D. Eisenhower 1954,
779-787.   Washington, D.C.: Government Printing Office,
1960.   Several pages explain the American concern with
developing anti-communist alliances in various parts of the
world.   A kind of "falling domino" theory is put forth,
although the phrase is not used; Eisenhower says that this
administration "tirelessly seeks to solidify partnerships
with the free world."

Periodical Articles

436. Barber, Hollis W. "United States Alliance Policy."
United States Naval Institute Proceedings 84 (September
1958):74-82. Reflects on the novelty of American participation in alliances.   Barber briefly examines George Washington's thoughts on alliances and discusses their current
significance to the United States. Barber favors more
economic aid, citing the pattern of Soviet assistance.

437. Hargreaves, Reginald. "The Chain of Defense." Military
Review 38 (October 1958):11-17. After a pessimistic review
of non-communist military prospects in Asia, Hargreaves
recommends that a general strategy for NATO, SEATO, and the
Middle East be developed to avoid piecemeal defeats.

438. Trask, David F. "Political-Military Consultation Among
Allies." Military Review 39 (September 1959):20-28.
Analyzes the challenges posed by the need to work with

allies in maintaining American security. Much of the
article is an historical survey of the American experience
in the world wars.

Latin America

439. Lieuwen, Edwin. <u>Arms and Politics in Latin America</u>.
Rev. ed. New York: Praeger Publishers, 1961. 335p. Detailed
analysis of the role of the military in Latin American
political systems and American policy toward the Latin
American armed forces. Lieuwen is highly critical of the
American government for providing Latin American armed
forces with weapons that may be used for domestic
repression rather than for the defense of the Western
Hemisphere.

North Atlantic Treaty Organization

440. Baum, Keith W. "Treating the Allies Properly: The
Eisenhower Administration, NATO, and the Multilateral
Force." <u>Presidential Studies Quarterly</u> 13 (Winter 1983):85-
97. Examines European opposition to American control of
nuclear weapons and negative Congressional views of the
multilateral force concept.

441. Boone, W.F. "NATO--Keystone of Defense." <u>United States
Naval Institute Proceedings</u> 85 (April 1959):22-43. Includes
very detailed information on the organization of NATO. On
the eve of its tenth anniversary Boone praises its success.

442. Collins, J. Lawton. "NATO: Still Vital for Peace."
<u>Foreign Affairs</u> 34 (April 1956):367-379. Reviews the
history of NATO and examines its role in an era of reduced
tension. There are limitations to NATO, but none of its
members should be enticed by the attractions of
"neutralism."

443. Crowther, Geoffrey. "Reconstruction of an Alliance."
<u>Foreign Affairs</u> 35 (January 1957):173-183. Discusses the
tensions between the United States and its British and
French allies in the aftermath of Suez. Crowther argues
vigorously that while the United States should respect
differences of opinion within the alliance, the European
countries must follow American leadership.

444. Jackson, Bennett L. "Limited Defense is Not Enough."
<u>Military Review</u> 38 (October 1958):55-58. Argues that an
attack on NATO forces should not automatically be treated
as a limited war situation. In effect, Jackson questions
the distinction between "limited" and "general" war.

445. Jackson, Bennett L. "Nuclear Weapons and NATO."
<u>Military Review</u> 39 (April 1959):16-21. Stresses the vital
role nuclear deterrence plays in the NATO alliance. Jackson
also asserts that an intermediate range missile is badly

needed, in order to make best use of NATO's geographical position.

446. Miksche, Ferdinand Otto. "Defense Organization for Western Europe." Military Review 41 (January 1961):52-61. Faults NATO for its political and military rigidity, in particular, its inability to deal with problems existing outside Europe. Miksche also argues for using smaller tactical units to provide more flexibility.

447. Strausz-Hupé, Robert. "Is NATO Expendable?" United States Naval Institute Proceedings 83 (September 1957):923-930. Asserts that current Soviet disarmament proposals are designed to destroy NATO. Strausz-Hupe summarizes the arguments for accepting the Soviet initiatives, and then analyzes their implications. He argues that both strategic and conventional deterrent forces continue to be needed in Europe and that NATO is indispensible.

The Middle East

448. Baldwin, Hanson W. "Strategy of the Middle East." Foreign Affairs 35 (July 1957):654-665. Recommends the establishment of a Middle Eastern-Indian Ocean American defense command. Baldwin examines the nature of communist infiltration in this area.

449. Howard, Harry N. "The Regional Pacts and the Eisenhower Doctrine." Annals of the American Academy of Political & Social Science, no 401 (May 1972):85-94. Assesses the Central Treaty Organization (Baghdad Pact) and asserts that the Eisenhower administration pursued a more balanced Middle Eastern policy than most other post-World War II administrations.

Asia

Official Policy Statements

450. Eisenhower, Dwight D. "Letter to the President of the Council of Ministers of Viet-Nam Regarding Assistance for That Country. October 25, 1954. In Public Papers of the Presidents of the United States: Dwight D. Eisenhower 1954, 948-949. Washington, D.C.: Government Printing Office, 1960. Expresses the desire of the United States to aid the Republic of Vietnam, but specifically notes the need for "reforms." Eisenhower mentions his concern for the security of South Vietnam and hints that the Vietnamese government must be "responsive" to the Vietnamese people.

451. Eisenhower, Dwight D. "Special Message to the Senate Transmitting the Southeast Asia Collective Defense Treaty and Protocol Thereof. November 10, 1954" In Public Papers of the Presidents of the United States: Dwight D. Eisenhower 1954, 1041-1042. Washington, D.C.: Government

Printing Office, 1960. Describes the documents, including the Pacific Charter, being sent to the Senate. Eisenhower notes the deterrent nature of the alliance and the states that it is aimed at "both open armed attack and internal subversion."

Periodical Articles

452. Barber, Hollis W. "United States Alliances East of Suez." United States Naval Institute Proceedings 85 (July 1959):66-76. Examines treaty arrangements in Asia that involve the United States. The Asian treaty organizations are much weaker than NATO militarily and rather frail politically. Barber sees a need for the United States to increase economic assistance to many Asian nations, which will make them stronger militarily and therefore more useful as alliance partners.

453. Brannen, Phillip Barry. "Strength and Weakness in the Asian Littorial." United States Naval Institute Proceedings 84 (December 1958):68-84. Examines social, economic, and military affairs in Japan, South Korea, Taiwan, Hong Kong, and Indonesia. The article is intended to inform planners about these nations in anticipation of possible conflicts in the Far East.

454. Miller, August C., Jr. "SEATO--Segment of Collective Security." United States Naval Institute Proceedings 86 (February 1960):50-62. Discusses the origins of SEATO and its development during the 1950's. Miller examines the agreements that constituted the Manila Pact of 1954 and the organizational structure of SEATO. He also notes the military and political limitations of the alliance.

455. Padelford, Norman J. "Collective Security in the Pacific: Nine Years of the ANZUS Pact." United States Naval Institute Proceedings 86 (September 1960):38-47. Traces the background of ANZUS and the alliance's development during the 1950's. ANZUS is a more limited alliance than NATO, and, for a number of reasons, it is unlikely to become a larger grouping, embracing many Pacific nations.

Crises and Force Projection

Indochina, 1954

Official Policy Statements

456. Eisenhower, Dwight D. "The President's News Conference. April 7, 1954." In Public Papers of the Presidents of the United States: Dwight D. Eisenhower 1954, 381-390. Washington, D.C.: Government Printing Office, 1960. In response to a question, Eisenhower discusses "the strategic importance of Indochina to the free world." He advances the "'falling domino' principle" and notes the

large population and rich resources of Southeast Asia. To Eisenhower, the Indochina situation is "of the utmost moment."

Books

457. Fall, Bernard. Hell in a Very Small Place: The Siege of Dien Bien Phu. Philadelphia: J.B. Lippincott Company, 1966. Thorough study of the battle of Dien Bien Phu and the negotiations over possible American intervention in Vietnam. Fall provides much information on the military aspects of the proposed intervention.

458. Gurtov, Melvin. The First Vietnam Crisis: Chinese Communist Strategy and United States Involvement, 1953-54. New York: Columbia University Press, 1967. 228p. Probably the most important single study of the controversy over intervention. Fears for the security of Southeast Asia overwhelmed earlier American misgivings during the Dien Bien Phu crisis about French colonialism.

Essays and Periodical Articles

459. Eisenhower, Dwight D. "Indochina Crisis of 1954." In The White House Years: Mandate for Change 1953-1956, 332-375. Garden City, New York: Doubleday & Company, Inc., 1963. Discusses the challenge confronting France and the United States in Indochina and Eisenhower's views of the crisis. While he was extremely concerned about the effect that a defeat in Indochina would have on the rest of Southeast Asia, Eisenhower agreed with Congressional leaders that the United States should not intervene alone or just with France.

460. Herring, George C., and Richard H. Immerman. "Eisenhower, Dulles, and Dienbienphu: 'The Day We Didn't Go to War' Revisited." Journal of American History 71 (September 1984):343-363. Discusses the debate over American intervention in Indochina in 1954, using new material from declassified documents. The authors emphasize friction between the French and the Americans.

461. Immerman, Richard H. "Between the Unattainable and the Unacceptable: Eisenhower and Dienbienphu." In Reevaluating Eisenhower: American Foreign Policy in the 1950s, edited by Richard A. Melanson and David Mayers, 120-154. Urbana: University of Illinois Press, 1987. Emphasizes Eisenhower's great distaste for and apprehensions about an American land war in Indochina. Nevertheless, Eisenhower was deeply concerned about a possible communist success and allowed contingency plans to be developed for greater American military involvement.

462. Ridgway, Matthew B. "Indo-China, Quemoy, and Matsu." In Soldier: The Memoirs of Matthew B. Ridgway, As Told to

Harold H. Martin, Chapter 32. New York: Harper & Brothers, 1956. Summarizes the analysis that Ridgway prepared during the controversy over intervention in 1954. Ridgway's recommendation was that the United States should not undertake a land war in Southeast Asia.

463. Roberts, Chalmers. "The Day We Didn't Go to War." Reporter 11 (September 14, 1954):31-32, 34-35. Celebrated analysis of discussions between Secretary of State Dulles and Congressional leaders on April 3, 1954, regarding an active American commitment in Indochina. Roberts argues that Eisenhower could have received Congressional support for intervention if he had been insistent.

Formosa Strait Crises

Official Policy Statements

464. Eisenhower, Dwight D. "Special Message to the Congress Regarding United States Policy for the Defense of Formosa. January 24, 1955." In Public Papers of the Presidents of the United States: Dwight D. Eisenhower 1955, 207-211. Washington, D.C.: Government Printing Office, 1959. Warns that the Formosa Strait crisis "seriously imperils the peace and our security." Eisenhower reviews American commitments to the defense of Formosa and the actions of the communists against the offshore islands held by the Nationalist Chinese. He asks the Congress for a resolution supporting his position on the Formosa Strait issue.

465. Dulles, John Foster. "Authorized Statement by the Secretary of State Following His Review With the President of the Situation in the Formosa Straits Area. September 4, 1958." In Public Papers of the Presidents of the United States: Dwight D. Eisenhower 1958, 687-689. Washington, D.C.: Government Printing Office, 1959. Notes American commitments to Nationalist China and the attacks made by the Chinese communists on Quemoy and its supply routes. Dulles expresses some skepticism about the communist desire to launch an all-out attack. He urges the communists to refrain from the use of military force, although they need not drop their claims to the offshore islands.

466. Eisenhower, Dwight D. "Radio and Television Report to the American People Regarding the Situation in the Formosa Straits. September 11, 1958." In Public Papers of the Presidents of the United States: Dwight D. Eisenhower 1958, 694-700. Washington, D.C.: Government Printing Office, 1959. Discusses communist actions in the Far East and refers to the futility of appeasement before World War II. Eisenhower contends that, if not stopped, the Chinese communists and their Soviet allies will endeavor to "dominate at least the Western half of the now friendly Pacific Ocean." He emphasizes the need to settle the island problem through negotiation.

Essays and Periodical Articles

467. Eisenhower, Dwight D.   "Formosa Doctrine." In The White House Years: Mandate for Change 1953-1956, 459-483. Garden City, New York: Doubleday & Co., Inc., 1963. Discusses the wide variety of policy options that were available in the Formosa Strait crisis. Eisenhower agreed with the Nationalists about the political significance of the islands, but would have preferred a reduction of Nationalist forces committed to the offshore islands.

468. Eisenhower, Dwight D.   "The Troubled Islands Again-- Quemoy and Matsu, 1958." In The White House Years: Waging Peace 1956-1961, 292-304.   Garden City, New York: Double- day & Co., Inc., 1965.   Reviews American-Nationalist Chinese negotiations concerning the islands and American naval support for Quemoy and Matsu.

469. Halperin, Morton H. and Tang Tsou.   "United States Policy Toward the Offshore Islands." In National Security Decision-Making: Analyses, Cases, and Proposals, edited by Morton H. Halperin, 31-46.   Lexington, Massachusetts: Lexington Books, 1975.   Traces changing American views of the offshore islands and their strategic significance and political importance.

Lebanon

Official Policy Statements

470. Eisenhower, Dwight D. "Special Message to the Congress on the Situation in the Middle East.   January 5, 1957." In Public Papers of the Presidents of the United States: Dwight D. Eisenhower 1957, 6-16.   Washington, D.C.: Government Printing Office, 1958.   Warns that the newly independent nations of the Middle East need assistance against Soviet imperialism.   Eisenhower asks for a joint resolution to authorize assistance to Middle Eastern countries and, if need be, to use American military forces "to secure and protect the territorial integrity and political independence" of nations threatened by communist activity.

471. Eisenhower, Dwight D.   "Special Message to the Congress on the Sending of United States Forces to Lebanon. July 15, 1958." In Public Papers of the Presidents of the United States: Dwight D. Eisenhower 1958, 550-552. Washington, D.C.: Government Printing Office, 1959. Describes Lebanon's plea for assistance from the United States.   Eisenhower praises the involvement of the United Nations, but asserts that Lebanon's security was endangered by the coup in Iraq on July 14, 1958.   He states that "the events which have been occurring in Lebanon represent indirect aggression from without."

Books

472. Murphy, Robert. <u>Diplomat Among Warriors</u>. Garden City, New York: Doubleday & Company, Inc., 1964. Reviews the events of the Lebanon crisis and the deployment of American forces. Murphy devoted himself to quieting the Middle East by assuring various countries in the area about American aims in Lebanon.

473. Shulimson, Jack. <u>Marines in Lebanon 1958</u>. Washington, D.C.: Headquarters, U.S. Marine Corps, Historical Branch, G-3 Division, 1966. SOD 214.14/2:L49 Detailed examination of marine operations in Lebanon, including the successful effort to avoid combat and to pacify the country.

474. Spiller, Roger J. <u>"Not War But Like War": The American Interventiion in Lebanon</u>. Fort Leavenworth, Kansas: Combat Studies Institute, U.S. Army Command and General Staff College, 1981. 56p. SOD D110.9:3 While focusing on army operations, this detailed study provides valuable material on the other services.

Periodical Articles

475. Calhoun, Christopher S. "Lebanon: That was Then." <u>United States Naval Institute Proceedings</u> 111 (September 1985):74-80. Reviews all aspects of the 1958 Lebanon landing. Calhoun believes the episode was generally a success, showing that the United States could deal quickly and effectively with emergencies in the Middle East.

476. Sights, Albert P., Jr. "Lessons of Lebanon: A Study in Air Strategy." <u>Air University Review</u> 16 (July-August 1965): 28-43. Focuses on the airlift that supported the intervention, but Sights does not ignore the broader facets of the Lebanon crisis or the contributions of the other services.

Chapter 4

Kennedy and Johnson: Balanced Forces, Flexible Response, and Counterinsurgency

Kennedy seems to have won the 1960 election in part because of his charge that the Republicans had allowed the Soviets to outdistance the United States in missile development. After the election, the "missile gap" was found to be much narrower than thought. Kennedy also argued that the Eisenhower administration had done nothing about the communist stronghold Cuba had become. Eisenhower, in fact, authorized support for a Cuban exile venture to overthrow Castro. The plan was enlarged after the change in administrations.

In terms of defense policy, Kennedy is perhaps best known for his emphasis on ground forces, especially a considerable increase in American capability for counterinsurgency. Certainly, the armed services, the Central Intelligence Agency, the Agency for International Development, and other offices devoted considerable effort to developing and improving programs for coping with the "wars of national liberation" waged in the Third World with Soviet encouragement.

The Kennedy and Johnson administrations were subjected to a number of challenges, from the Bay of Pigs and the Berlin crises of 1961 to the seizure of the _Pueblo_ in 1968. It seems natural, therefore, that the two administrations moved away from detente. The Communist bloc continued to be viewed as a monolith; the United States faced two major powers with the assistance of many smaller allies. A significant strategic change was the adoption of a "flexible response" in the potential use of nuclear weapons in Europe. For example, "massive retaliation" would not necessarily occur if the Soviets advanced into Western Europe.

Concern over the Middle East continued, but except for the _Liberty_ attack in 1967, American forces were not involved directly.

Decision-makers

President Kennedy

477. Leach, W. Barton. "The Professor and the Candidate." Aerospace Historian 13 (Summer 1966):51-59. Discusses Leach's interaction with Kennedy and Ted Sorensen on defense issues during the 1960 campaign.

478. Lessard, Suzannah. "A New Look at John Kennedy." Washington Monthly 3 (October 1971):8-18. Criticizes Kennedy for his handling of foreign policy crises such as Cuba and Vietnam. Lessard views his approach as superficial, too concerned with appearances and not enough with substance.

479. Smith, Jean Edward. "Kennedy and Defense." Air University Review 18 (March-April 1967):38-54. Traces Kennedy's views on national security from his days at Harvard through his Congressional experience. Kennedy's anticommunism grew stronger, and he became more critical of European colonialism.

Robert S. McNamara

Books

480. McNamara, Robert S. The Essence of Security; Reflections in Office. New York: Harper & Row, 1968. 176p. Reviews McNamara's revolutionary changes in the Defense Department and puts forth his views on security. This is primarily a collection of speeches and papers from 1963 on. It includes very little about Vietnam.

481. Murdock, Clark A. Defense Policy Formation; A Comparative Analysis of the McNamara Era. Albany: State University of New York Press, 1974. High-level study of centralization and the use of statistical anlaysis by McNamara and his staff. "Comparative" in the title refers to the use of many examples from the McNamara era, not to comparisons between American and foreign situations.

482. Roherty, James M. Decisions of Robert S. McNamara: A Study of the Role of the Secretary of Defense. Coral Gables, Florida: University of Miami Press, 1970. 222p. Discusses earlier Secretaries of Defense, the McNamara team's approach and controversies such as the bomber program and the construction of nuclear aircraft carriers.

Periodical Articles

483. Baldwin, Hanson W. "Slow-Down in the Pentagon." Foreign Affairs 43 (January 1965):262-280. Criticizes what Baldwin regards as too much centralization and over-planning in the Department of Defense under McNamara.

484. Barnes, Stanley M. "Defense Planning Policies." United States Naval Institute Proceedings 90 (June 1964):26-39. Criticizes the lack of coordination within the government regarding defense policies. Barnes generally applauds the efforts of McNamara and the civilian defense analysts.

485. Brodie, Bernard. "The McNamara Phenomenon." World Politics 17 (July 1965):672-686. Brodie stresses McNamara's independence and self-confidence in the face of considerable controversy over his policies and approaches.

486. Kintner, William R. "The McNamara Era in the Defense Department." Naval Review 1962/63, 104-121. Examines the impact of McNamara's first year as Secretary of Defense. Kintner suggests that while McNamara may be a very eminent Secretary of Defense, he needs to take into account personnel as well as facts and figures.

487. Korb, Lawrence J. "Robert McNamara's Impact on the Budgeting Strategies of the Joint Chiefs of Staff." Aerospace Historian 17 (Winter, December 1970):132-136. Describes McNamara's success in curbing the tendency of the Joint Chiefs of Staff to follow its own priorities. Korb suggests that greater cooperation eventually developed between the Joint Chiefs and the Secretary of Defense.

488. Longley, Charles H. "McNamara and Military Behavior." American Journal of Political Science 18 (February 1974): 1-21. Despite the title, Longley examines both the Eisenhower and Kennedy administrations. Longley used content analysis and budgetary information to plumb the nature and extent of civil control over the armed forces.

Decision-making Process

Official Studies

489. U.S. Congress. Senate. Committee on Government Operations. Subcommittee on National Policy Machinery. Organizing for National Security: Hearings before the Subcommittee on National Policy Machinery of the Senate Committee on Government Operations, 87th Cong., 1st Sess. 3 volumes. Washington, D.C.: Government Printing Office, 1961. SOD Y4. G75\46: N21 se/10 v 1-3. Exhaustive study of decision-making on defense matters. The National Security Council and the State and Defense Departments are studied extensively, as are the roles of science and technology and the budget process.

Books

490. Clark, Keith C. and Laurence J. Legere, editors. The President and the Management of National Security; a Report. New York: Praeger Publishers, 1969. 274 p. Surveys national security decision-making from the Eisenhower to the Nixon administrations. The research included many interviews with participants in the process.

491. Hitch, Charles J. Decision-Making for Defense. Berkeley: University of California Press, 1965. 83p. Leading authority and former Assistant Secretary of Defense under McNamara analyzes defense decisions from 1789 to 1960 and examines the use of quantitative measures for aiding in making national security decisions.

492. Schlesinger, Arthur M. A Thousand Days: John F. Kennedy in the White House. Boston: Houghton Mifflin Company, 1965. Highly detailed account of top level planning related to Cuba, Vietnam, and other crisis areas during the Kennedy administration. Of particular importance is Schlesinger's discussion of decision-making during the Bay of Pigs episode.

Periodical Articles

493. Baldwin, Hanson W. "CNO--Past, Present, and--Future?" United States Naval Institute Proceedings 89 (August 1963): 32-43. Reviews the post of Chief of Naval Operations since 1915, describing changes in legal authority and analyzing the duties of the position. Baldwin also examines the place of the Chief of Naval Operations on the Joint Chiefs of Staff. He emphasizes that the ideal Chief of Naval Operations must have considerable independence, rising above the needs of the navy, if need be.

494. Barrett, Raymond J. "Politico-Military Expertise: A Practical Program." Military Review 46 (November 1966):44-52. Strongly urges greater cooperation between the Department of Defense and the armed services with the Department of State. Cross-fertilization of ideas and personnel is a necessity.

495. Bigley, Thomas J. "The Office of International Security Affairs." United States Naval Institute Proceedings 92 (April 1966):61-72. Discusses the development and the organization of the Office of International Security Affairs of the Department of Defense. Its responsibilities include military assistance.

496. Church, Albert J., and Lloyd R. Vasey. "Defense Organization Issues." United States Naval Institute Proceedings 87 (February 1961):22-31. Reviews current bills on reorganizing the Department of Defense and the services. The authors summarize post-World War II legisla-

tion in this field and then analyze each of the issues in dispute. Several pages deal with the part Unified Commanders should play.

497. Colbert, Richard G., and Robert N. Ginsburgh. "The Policy Planning Council." United States Naval Institute Proceedings 92 (April 1966):73-81. Among the functions of the Policy Planning Council of the Department of State is studying problems with both political and military ramifications.

498. Edinger, Lewis J. "Military Leaders and Foreign Policy-Making." American Political Science Review 57 (June 1963): 392-405. Examines the problems of analyzing relations between the civilian and military elites. This is primarily a theoretical study with some information on civil-military relations in Japan and several major Western nations, including the United States.

499. Glennon, Alan N. "The Perennial Fallacy." United States Naval Institute Proceedings 86 (December (1960): 55-61. Reviews the debate over unification of the services in the 1940's and asserts that current proponents of a "single service" are not offering anything new to substantiate their views. Civilian control would be weakened, decision-making would not be improved, and greater economies would not be produced by unification.

500. Gray, Colin S. "The Rise and Fall of Academic Strategy." Journal of the Royal United Services Institute for Defence Studies 116 (June 1971): 54-57. Discusses the participation of academics in strategy formation during the 1950's and 1960's. Gray emphasizes role conflicts among such strategists.

501. Hagerman, George M. "The Navy's Politico-Military Program: Where Pen Meets Sword." United States Naval Institute Proceedings 89 (November 1963):44-51. Recommends that service officers receive much more training in political and administrative matters. Hagerman notes the many officers assigned to posts which involve political as well as military duties such as working with NATO and SEATO.

502. Hays, S.H., and Thomas A. Rehn. "The Military in a Free Society." United States Naval Institute Proceedings 95 (February 1969):26-36. Analyzes differences between civilian and military goals. The authors see civilians as working for their own goals, while military personnel are oriented toward group and organization attainments.

503. Ingram, Samuel P. "Civilian Command or Civilian Control?" United States Naval Institute Proceedings 94 (May 1968):26-31. Attributes increasing civilian direction of military efforts to the possibility that incidents can

escalate to serious crises. Ingram deplores civilian decision-making in specialized areas in which they necessarily
have limited knowledge and is critical of what seems to be
overuse of systems analysis under McNamara.

504. Kolodziej, Edward A. "Strategic Policy and American
Government; Structural Constants and Variables." Review of
Politics 27 (October 1965):465-490. Discusses the problem
of developing strategy within American government. Relations between the civilian and military elites will improve
if the legislative and executive branches engage effectively in strategy making.

505. Lerche, Charles O., Jr. "The Professional Officer and
Foreign Policy." United States Naval Institute Proceedings
90 (July 1964):68-74. Praises the contribution of the
services' officer corps to decision-making in the area of
foreign affairs.

506. Massey, Robert J. "The First Hundred Days of the New
Frontier." United States Naval Institute Proceedings 87
(August 1961):26-39. Examines what Massey regards as the
revolutionary changes effected early in the Kennedy administration. Massey refers to major policy statements and
reviews the decisions made on such issues as military space
ventures.

507. Paone, Rocco M. "Foreign Policy and Military Power."
Military Review 44 (November 1964):9-13. Discusses efforts
to promote coordinated operations by civilian and military
elements of the federal government. Paone examines the
Cuban missile crisis in this regard.

508. Selton, Robert W. "Rational Victory." United States
Naval Institute Proceedings 94 (February 1968):26-32.
Discusses relationships between various levels of military
power and their connection to diplomacy. Selton emphasizes
the need for the United States to establish reasonable
goals and to apply the appropriate degree of force to reach
the objectives decided upon.

509. Stillman, Richard J. "The Pentagon's Whiz Kids."
United States Naval Institute Proceedings 92 (April
1966):52-60. Asserts that failures on the part of the
military led to extensive control of national security by
civilian officials. There are both advantages and disadvantages to the new division of labor in the Department of
Defense.

The Role of Public Opinion

510. Abt, Clark C. "National Opinion and Military Security: Research Problems." Journal of Conflict Resolution 9
(September 1965):334-344. Analyzes the problems of assessing opinion on defense issues. Abt proposes ways to plumb

the views of opinion leaders and other persons.

511. Bobrow, Davis B. "Organization of American National Security Opinions." Public Opinion Quarterly 33 (Summer 1969):223-239. Describes public opinion on various defense issues in 1963 and 1964. Bobrow notes the lack of integration of popular attitudes on these issues.

512. Hamilton, Richard F. "A Research Note on the Mass Support for 'Tough' Military Initiatives." American Sociological Review 33 (June 1968):439-445. Asserts that high socio-economic status and attention to the media are linked with support for assertive military action. The Korean and Vietnam conflicts are discussed.

Military Policy

Official Policy Statements

513. Kennedy, John F. "Inaugural Address. January 20, 1961." In Public Papers of the Presidents of the United States: John F. Kennedy 1961, 1-3. Washington, D.C.: Government Printing Office, 1962. Devotes much of the speech to promises of American aid to the Third World and a plea for renewed efforts at disarmament.

514. Kennedy, John F. "Special Message to the Congress on Urgent National Needs. May 25, 1961." In Public Papers of the Presidents of the United States: John F. Kennedy 1961, 396-406. Washington, D.C.: Government Printing Office, 1962. Deals in part with domestic programs. Kennedy also discusses various defense programs, including an increased commitment to unconventional warfare. Large sections refer to civil defense and space policy.

515. Kennedy, John F. "Annual Budget Message to the Congress, Fiscal Year 1963. January 18, 1962." In Public Papers of the Presidents of the United States: John F. Kennedy 1962, 25-39. Washington, D.C.: Government Printing Office, 1963. Stresses the need to improve American conventional military capabilities and notes progress in civil defense.

516. Johnson, Lyndon B. "Remarks to the Joint Chiefs of Staff and to Officials of the Department of Defense. December 11, 1963." In Public Papers of the Presidents of the United States: Lyndon B. Johnson 1963-64, I, 43-45. Washington, D.C.: Government Printing Office, 1965. Warns the audience that there must be savings in defense. Johnson praises Secretary of Defense McNamara very highly. He asserts that "the United States need[s] unity across the board in the execution of . . . national security policies" and pledges vigorous action against communism in Vietnam and in Latin America.

517. Johnson, Lyndon B.   "Special Message to the Congress on the State of the Nation's Defenses. January 18, 1965." In <u>Public Papers of the Presidents of the United States: Lyndon B. Johnson 1965</u>, I, 62-71.   Washington, D.C.: Government Printing Office, 1966.   Stresses the continuity between administrations in terms of defense policy. Johnson discusses the "balanced forces" available for deployment and describes changes in defense planning and budgeting.   He also outlines "basic defense policies" in some detail, with specific references to various weapons systems.   A large section of the Message deals with "Principles of Defense Management."

Resource Collections

518. <u>The John F.   Kennedy Presidential Oral History Collection</u>.   Frederick, Maryland: University Publications of America, Inc..   Includes a massive amount of information relevant not only to the Laotian crisis and the increasing commitment in Vietnam, but also regarding the Bay of Pigs, Berlin, and the Cuban missile crises of 1961-1962.   W. Averell Harriman, Richard Helms, Lyman Lemnitzer, John McCone, Maxwell Taylor, and Roger Hilsman are among the contributors of oral history material.

519. <u>Oral Histories of the Johnson Administration</u>. Frederick, Maryland: University Publications of America, Inc.   Microfiche collection includes a great deal of material pertinent to the Vietnam conflict and other military topics.   Generals Taylor and Westmoreland, William Colby, and others provided oral history material.

Periodical Articles

520. Amme, Carl H., Jr.   "Crisis of Confidence." <u>United States Naval Institute Proceedings</u> 90 (March 1964):26-35. Expresses the view that the various services do not respect one another enough to develop general military doctrine.

521. Baldwin, Hanson W.   "The Critical Tomorrows." <u>United States Naval Institute Proceedings</u> 88 (December 1962):22-31.   Emphasizes the need to define national goals in both the economic and military spheres.   Baldwin discusses various weaknesses in American society that make it less able to compete effectively with the Soviets and the increased strength of the Soviets in terms of industrial development.

522. Baldwin, Hanson W.   "Stalemate--Or?"   <u>United States Naval Institute Proceedings</u> 90 (April 1964):48-55.   Recommends that the United States devote more attention to its non-nuclear forces.   The superpowers already have a surplus of nuclear weapons. Baldwin describes the horrors of a nuclear war and warns that the United States must maintain its technological advantage.

523. Barnett, Frank R. "A Proposal for Political Warfare." Military Review 41 (March 1961):2-10. Points to the need for a strategy of political warfare, beginning with a much more sustained effort to inform the American people about communist aggression. Barnett also discusses educational programs sponsored by the Institute for American Strategy, the National War College, and other institutions.

524. Enthoven, Alain C. "Choosing Strategies and Selecting Weapon Systems." United States Naval Institute Proceedings 90 (January 1964):150-158. Address at the National War College by Deputy Assistant Secretary of Defense Enthoven reviews and defends the use of systems analysis in making national security decisions.

525. Fergusson, Charles M., Jr. "Statecraft and Military Force: An Analytical Concept." Military Review 46 (February 1966):69-79. Analyzes "statecraft" in detail. Strategy develops from policy objectives pursued by a given nation-state.

526. Harrigan, Anthony. "Creativeness in Total Defense." Military Review 48 (July 1968):10-16. Presents very detailed prescriptions for keeping the United States well defended. These involve not only technological, but also moral considerations.

527. Hessler, William H. "Patience: Bedrock of Strategy." United States Naval Institute Proceedings 91 (February 1965):26-33. Warns that the military forces are closely linked with diplomacy. Victory in conflict between the superpowers is not possible. Hessler assails critics who demand more vigorous action against the Soviets and applauds the caution of American decision makers.

528. Hoag, Malcolm W. "What New Look in Defense?" World Politics 22 (October 1969):1-28. Proposes a new defense policy which is compared with Eisenhower's and McNamara's approaches. Hoag emphasizes flexibility, but wants to limit defense expenditures to no more than 7% of the gross national product.

529. Hodgson, Gordon S. "Of Hawks and Doves." United States Naval Institute Proceedings 93 (May 1967):30-37. Criticizes the "doves" and suggests a "hawk" plan for curtailing communist bloc expansion. Hodgson expresses optimism about the outcome in Vietnam.

530. Huglin, Henry C. "Our Strategic Superiority--Why We Continue to Have It." Air University Review 18 (September-October 1967):42-49. Describes the elements of "strategic power" such as technology. Huglin emphasizes that the United States bases its actions in world politics on its strategic position.

531. Kessler, Herman E., Jr. "What Price Strategy?" Military Review 51 (February 1971):56-66. Examines strategy and defense funding. Kessler states that these concerns can be brought together through "resource management" and describes McNamara's approach to balancing defense needs with funding that was available.

532. McConnell, J.P. "Strategy and Analysis." Air University Review 17 (January-February 1966):2-6. Discusses the value of "analysis," such as operations research and computerized wargaming as contributions to effective strategy. McConnell emerges as a vigorous advocate of such techniques.

533. Moulton, Harland B. "The McNamara General War Strategy." Orbis 8 (Summer 1964):238-254. Outlines United States strategy with emphasis on deterrence theory. Moulton also argues for maintaining limited war fighting capacity.

534. Posvar, Wesley W. "National Security Policy: The Realm of Obscurity." Orbis 9 (Fall 1965):694-713. Surveys all facets of decision-making in the field of security. Posvar warns that "subjectivity" is always present.

535. Smith, Dale O. "Flexible Response vs. Determined Retaliation." Air University Review 16 (January-February 1965):69-71. Analyzes the "flexible response" strategy, which Smith sees as similar to the United States' relatively slow response and initial failures in World War II and Korea. Smith offers, instead, a strategy "to persuade" adversaries to defer to American policies and objectives.

536. Strausz-Hupe, Robert. "New Weapons and National Strategy." Military Review 41 (May 1961):70-76. Discusses the communist use of revolutionary techniques and the ability of the communists to mold difficult situations to suit their ends. The United States is in for a long period of struggle with the communists and must put more effort into combatting communism.

Defense Costs

Books

537. Duscha, Julius. Arms, Money, and Politics. New York: I. Washburn, 1965. 218p. Analyzes relationships between American economic problems and defense spending, focusing on waste. Duscha makes general proposals for reducing military expenditures and alleviating those problems.

Periodical Articles

538. Carlisle, Howard M. "Incentive Contracts: Management Strategy of the Department of Defense." Public Administration Review 24 (January 1964):21-28. Surveys post-World War II practices in defense contracting. Carlisle advocates various changes to promote effective cost-benefit analysis.

539. Cobb, Stephen A. "Defense Spending and Foreign Policy in the House of Representatives." Journal of Conflict Resolution 13 (September 1969):358-369. Analyzes relationships between the level of defense contracts in a representative's district and his/her voting on foreign relations issues. Cobb found no real correlation between these factors.

540. Held, Virginia. "PPBS Comes to Washington." Public Interest, no. 4 (Summer 1966):102-115. Focuses on Department of Defense use of the Planning-Programming-Budgeting System. This technique was employed thereafter by other federal agencies.

General Strategy

Books

541. Abshire, David M. and Richard V. Allen, editors. National Security: Political, Military, and Economic Strategies in the Decade Ahead. New York: Praeger Publishers, 1963. 1039p. Papers presented at a conference held by the Center for Strategic Studies, Georgetown University. This is a comprehensive examination of American, Soviet, and Peoples Republic of China military strategies and the relationship between American strategy and the free market economy.

542. Kissinger, Henry A., editor. Problems of National Strategy; a Book of Readings. New York: Praeger Publishers, 1965. 477p. Important collection of materials. Kissinger includes a number of items that criticized then current conceptions of defense policy.

Essays and Periodical Articles

543. Beinke, Walter. "Flexible Response in Perspective." Military Review 48 (November 1968):47-52. Emphasizes the need to change military strategy in response to different situations. Beinke discusses the need to develop principles for deciding on the use of American forces in a given set of circumstances.

544. Beloff, Max. "Reflections on Intervention." Journal of International Affairs 22 (1968):198-207. Argues that

Americans should generate a policy for intervention in the
Third World. Beloff examines Soviet and American interventions, warning that such events will continue to occur.

545. Bowman, Richard C.   "National Policy in the War of
Wills." United States Naval Institute Proceedings 91 (April
1965):46-53.   Emphasizes the importance of constancy of
purpose as well as sheer military power in dealing with
foreign affairs problems and military challenges. Bowman
notes that foreign aid will encourage weak, developing
nations to resist communist thrusts.

546. Bull, Hedley N.   "Strategic Studies and Its Critics."
World Politics 20 (July 1968):593-605.   Generally defends
the usefulness of concepts generated by civilian strategists.   Bull conceeds that mistakes have been made, but the
contributions of the strategists outweigh the problems.

547. Carpenter, John W.   "Alternatives and Optimum
Strategy." Air University Review 17 (July-August 1966):2-9.
Argues that absolute deterrence strategies have worked for
brief historical periods, but fairly quickly lost their
omnipotence.   Carpenter deals in good part with changes in
handling service budgets under McNamara and the impact of
systems analysis.   He feels the services must adapt to this
new environment.

548. Coffey, Joseph I.   "The Human Factor in Deterrence."
United States Naval Institute Proceedings 90 (December
1964):44-51.   Discusses the nature of deterrence, citing
statements by American leaders of the early 1960's.   Coffey
admits the usefulness of formal (mathematical) analysis in
defense planning, but argues that other factors, including
psychological elements, need to be considered.

549. Coffey, Joseph I. "Strategies and Realities." United
States Naval Institute Proceedings 92 (February 1966):34-
41.   Argues that better strategic thought is needed.
Coffey discusses the effects of existing deterrent forces
of the superpowers on strategy formulation.

550. Davis, William O.   "The Ordering of Technological
Warfare." Air University Quarterly Review 12 (Spring
1960):66-73.   Sees war as embracing initially nonviolent
advances in technology.   Davis examines the political
aspects of technology, asserting that superiority is not
enough.   Technology needs to be used to achieve goals by
impacting on hostile countries.

551. Kintner, William R.   "The Politicalization of
Strategy." Marine Corps Gazette 49 (April, May 1965):20-26;
51-55.   Surveys the development of American strategic
thinking from World War II to the mid-1960's.

552. Kintner, William R. and Stefan Thomas Possony.

"Strategic Asymmetries." <u>Orbis</u> 9 (Fall 1965):23-48. Analyzes some of the differences in power and capability between the United States and the Soviet Union. Kintner ranges widely, from food stocks to propaganda and information.

553. Kissinger, Henry A. "American Strategic Doctrine and Diplomacy." In <u>Theory and Practice of War: Essays Presented to Captain B.H. Liddell Hart on His Seventieth Birthday</u>. edited by Michael Howard, 271-292. London: Cassel & Company Ltd. 1965. Reviews post-World War II American strategic theory. Kissinger describes the American role in a system of bipolarity.

554. Larsen, Larry J. "The Delusion of Strategic Parity." <u>United States Naval Institute Proceedings</u> 91 (October 1965): 46-53. Outlines the problems associated with the pursuit of parity, which cannot be the basis of enduring peace. Larsen deals with factors that are not subject to quantitative analysis in assessing military power.

Nuclear Strategy

Books

555. Brodie Bernard. <u>Escalation and the Nuclear Option</u>. Princeton: Princeton University Press, 1966. 151p. Recommends commitment to the possible use of both strategic and tactical nuclear weapons. Brodie asserts that limited nuclear warfare is possible.

556. Chayes, Abram, and Jerome B. Wiesner. <u>ABM; Evaluation of the Decision to Deploy an Anti-Ballistic Missile System</u>. New York: Harper & Row, Publishers, 1969. 282p. Essays present the arguments against ABM (Safeguard), along with discussions of deterrence theory and much technical information.

557. Englebardt, Stanley L. <u>Strategic Defenses</u>. New York: Crowell, 1966. 168p. Describes various weapons systems and early warning devices. Useful introduction to a highly technical area.

558. Laird, Melvin R. <u>A House Divided; America's Strategy Gap</u>. Chicago: Regnery 1962. 179p. Advances many military and foreign policy proposals for strengthening American defenses. Laird emphasizes the importance of nuclear deterrence.

559. Mallan, Lloyd. <u>Peace is a Three-Edged Sword</u>. Englewood Cliffs, New Jersey: Prentice-Hall, 1964. 253p. Discusses the means by which the United States pursues its policy of nuclear deterrence. Mallan asserts that, because of the excellence of the American defense system, there is little chance of an accidental war.

560. Waslow, Arthur I. The Limits of Defense. Garden City, New York: Doubleday & Company, 1962. Analyzes American deterrence strategy extensively. Waslow also puts forth a radical scheme of total world disarmament and international government.

Essays and Periodical Articles

561. Agan, Arthur C., Jr. "Aerospace Defense in a Counterforce Strategy." Air University Quarterly Review 13 (Summer 1961):35-43. Vigorously defends the counterforce strategy and describes air defense capability to supplement attacks on enemy bases. Agan generally discusses the role and structure of the air force's Air Defense Command.

562. Bader, W.B. "Nuclear Weapons Sharing and 'the German Problem.'" Foreign Affairs 44 (July 1966):693-700. Suggests ways for dealing with the German desire for nuclear weapons. Even the potential of nuclear weapons in German hands might induce more serious negotiations on reunifying Germany.

563. Dillon, John G. "The Real Meaning of Nuclear Stalemate." Military Review 41 (January 1961):25-28. Discusses the effects of increasing Soviet nuclear strength and Soviet efforts at political warfare. A nuclear stalemate gives the Soviets a significant advantage because of their superiority in conventional forces.

564. Dunham, Jack V. "Nuclear Chess." Military Review 41 (March 1963):73-79. Criticizes current American thinking about nuclear target selection and methods for selecting particular weapons to be used. Dunham offers methods for vastly simplifying the use of tactical nuclear weapons.

565. Forsythe, Forrest. "Flexible Response vs. Determined Retaliation: A Critique." Air University Review 17 (November-December 1965):80-83. Replies to Dale O. Smith's article [entry 535]. Forsythe feels Smith misrepresented the nature of flexible response; so he proceeds to elucidate this concept and expresses skepticism about the ability of any nation to follow the kind of intellectual strategy proposed by Smith.

566. Hartsook, E.H. "'Overkill': Theories and Implications." Orbis 7 (Winter 1964):709-718. Writes in favor of more flexibility in responding to enemy attack.

567. Hitchens, Harold L. "Objectives in Future Strategic War: National Military Policy Goals and Controlled Conflict." Air University Review 17 (November-December 1965): 43-51. Warns that a strategy is needed for conflict between a general nuclear exchange and "conventional war." Hitchens believes that technological change will bring even

greater refinements in the use of nuclear weapons.

568. Hoeber, Amoretta M.   "Strategic Stability."   Air University Review 19 (July-August 1968):67-73. Emphasizes that a strategy of deterrence requires that constant attention be given to weapons and tactics, in order to preserve deterrence capability and credibility.

569. Kahn, Herman. "United States Central War Policy." In Beyond the Cold War: Essays on American Foreign Policy in a Changing World Environment, edited by Robert A. Goldwin, 45-76. Chicago: Rand McNally & Company, 1965. Analyzes deterrence and the interaction of military and political assumptions in developing war policy. Kahn offers various crisis scenarios and nuclear targeting strategies.

570. Kaysen, Carl.   "Keeping the Strategic Balance." Foreign Affairs 46 (July, 1968):665-675.   Discusses changing emphases in American strategic weapons policy as various planners demand movement from deterrence to superiority for the United States. Kaysen argues that an arms control pact between the superpowers is imperative.

571. Lowe, George E. "Balanced Forces or Counterforce-Does It Make a Difference?" United States Naval Institute Proceedings 88 (April 1962):22-33. Criticizes exclusive reliance on the counterforce strategy and writes strongly in favor of a "balanced forces" approach to defense. Lowe discusses differences and continuities in the defense policies of the Eisenhower and Kennedy administrations at some length.

572. Lowe, George E. "Neither Humiliation Nor Holocaust." United States Naval Institute Proceedings 89 (June 1963): 56-65. Regards "massive retaliation" as a failed policy. The new competing strategies are "balanced forces" and "counterforce." Under Kennedy they became complementary, although emphasis gradually passed to "counterforce."

573. Lynch, Hugh F.   "Presidential Control of Nuclear Weapons in Limited War Situations." Naval War College Review 23 (February 1971):71-88. Describes the many facets of the problem of when and if to use nuclear weapons in limited warfare. This is a highly detailed analysis.

574. Martin, Donald F.   "The Pro and Con of Military Force." Air University Quarterly Review 14 (Summer 1963):11-24. Discusses the capacity for attacking military targets as opposed to cities. Martin argues against proposals to put missile forces in American cities and demolishes arguments against a strategy for winning a general war.

575. Possony, Stefan T. "U.S. Intelligence at the Cross-roads." Orbis 9 (Fall 1965):587-610. Probes the in-

fluences of intelligence studies concerning Soviet goals and identifies two major theories about their objectives. Possony warns that the United States must remain alert to the possibility of nuclear war, which might well occur.

576. Richstein, A.R. "Legal Rules in Nuclear Weapons Employment." Military Review 41 (July 1961):91-98. Presents a hypothetical problem to illustrate the possible application of international law to the use of tactical nuclear weapons. Richstein notes, in particular, the impact of the Geneva Convention of 1949.

577. Sights, Albert P. "We Can Win a Nuclear War." Air University Review 14 (September-October 1963):37-45. Argues that the military must plan to win any war in prospect, even if political leaders decide to stop short of victory. The key is to gain control of the air at once. Sights presents innovative proposals for aircraft dispersal as part of his plan.

578. Van Cleave, William R. "The Nuclear Weapons Debate." United States Naval Institute Proceedings 92 (May 1966): 26-38. Examines a variety of approaches to the problems nuclear weapons present. Van Cleave rejects extreme views professed by pacifists or adherents of a possible preventive war.

579. Williams, Benjamin H. "American Security in the Nuclear Age." Social Science 41 (June 1966):147-152. Expresses the view that nuclear weapons have caused a decline in American security and that the national government is using approaches that are outdated in the nuclear age.

580. Willrich, Mason. "No First Use of Nuclear Weapons: An Assessment." Orbis 9 (Summer 1965):299-315. Adopting a "no first use" policy could weaken the United States. Willrich reviews other aspects of nuclear disarmament and advises against major changes in current American policies.

Air Strategy

General

581. Ascani, Fred J. "Innovations Within AFLC." Air University Review 20 (July-August 1969):37-47. Examines Air Force Logistics Command advances in supporting changing weapons systems and commitments. Includes a little materal on Vietnam.

582. Bergerson, Frederic A. The Army Gets an Air Force: Tactics of Insurgent Bureaucratic Politics. Baltimore: Johns Hopkins University Press, 1980. While emphasizing inter- and intraservice conflict, Bergeson sheds much light on the way in which the Vietnam War came to be fought.

583. Clay, Lucius D., Jr. "Shaping the Air Force Contribution to National Strategy." <u>Air University Review</u> 21 (March-April 1970):2-9. Analyzes the air force's part in developing deterrence theory. About half the article deals with air force planning structures and processes.

584. Collins, David C. "Doctrine Development for the Employment of Tactical Air Forces." <u>Air University Review</u> 19 (November-December 1967):44-49. Asserts that there needs to be more consultation between the air force and the army, despite the outstanding success of interservice cooperation in Vietnam. Collins examines doctrinal development in the early 1960's, including airlift.

585. Cooke, Gerald E., and Raymond C. Preston, Jr. "The Air Force Decision Process." <u>Air University Review</u> 26 (January-February 1975):40-48. Compares decision-making in the air force with that of major private corporations. The formal chain of command and committee/board structure of the air force is described.

586. Ginsburgh, Robert N., and Edd D. Wheeler. "The Evolution of Air Warfare." <u>Air University Review</u> 23 (March-April 1972):2-9. Reviews all facets of the impact of air power on strategy and emphasizes the role of technology in altering strategic concepts.

587. Long, Gordon A. "Tactical Air Forces in a Period of Uncertainty." <u>Air University Review</u> 27 (November-December 1975):72-87. Examines the rationale for tactical air when air force resources are becoming more restricted. Long discusses the problems facing tactical air specialists at length, including the challenge of long-range planning.

588. McLaughlin, John J. "Organization of the Air Force." <u>Air University Quarterly Review</u> 13 (Spring 1962):3-13. Examines the mixed system of civilian centralization and military decentralization in the air force. McLaughlin reviews development of the air force's structure and management practice after World War II generally, but focuses on the 1950's.

589. Martin, Donald F. "Views on Aerospace Power." <u>Air University Review</u> 19 (March-April 1968):30-39. Discusses the application of air power in counterinsurgency, limited war, and general war. Martin suggests that the American contribution to a given conflict should rise as the level of fighting intensifies. His argument anticipates what became the Nixon Doctrine.

590. Merrell, Jack G. "Air Force Logistics Command." <u>Air University Review</u> 20 (July-August 1969):2-13. Presents an overview of the operations of the Logistics Command and discusses relationships between logistics and combat.

591. Nazzaro, Joseph J. "SAC: Instrument of National Policy." Air University Review 19 (January-February 1968): 2-9.
Discusses all aspects of SAC's role, including its
relationship with unconventional warfare. Nazzaro also describes SAC aircraft and missile firepower.

592. Stillie, Edward O. "Tactical Air Employment--Current
       Status and Future Objectives." Air University Review
19 (November-December 1967):50-61. Outlines the impact of
Vietnam on air force thinking about the utilization of tactical air.

593. Sturm, Thomas A. "Organizational Evolution." Air Force
and Space Digest 53 (September 1970):58-64. Discusses
changes in air force organization in the post-World War II
period. The basic patterns had been achieved by the time of
the Korean War.

594. Watts, Barry D., and James O. Hale. "Doctrine: Mere
Words, or a Key to War-Fighting Competence?" Air University
Review 35 (September-October 1964):4-15. Asserts that there
has been little development in air force doctrine since the
1940's. The authors emphasize that usable doctrine must be
based on war experience and should avoid too much abstrac-
tion.

Missiles

595. Crosby, H. Ashton. "The Case for Anti-Ballistic
Missiles." United States Naval Institute Proceedings 93
(July 1967):26-31. Presents a systematic defense of the use
of anti-ballistic missiles.

596. Davis, W.A. "Ballistic Systems: A New Order of
Weaponry for a New Dimension of Defense." Air University
Quarterly Review 14 (Winter-Spring 1962-1963):126-144. Reviews the development of American ballistic missiles. The
article also describes management of the program and the
"activation" of missile firing sites.

597. Johnston, Douglas M., Jr. "ABM: The High Cost of Living." United States Naval Institute Proceedings 93 (October
1967):26-38. Argues for the establishment of an ABM system
to protect the United States and to enhance deterrence of
Soviet military actions.

598. Morton, Louis. "The Anti-Ballistic Missile: Some Political and Strategic Considerations." Virginia Quarterly
Review 42 (Winter 1966):28-42. Compares American and Soviet
attitudes toward the anti-Ballistic missile. Morton favors
a Soviet-American agreement.

599. Russell, Kendall. "Strategic Missiles and Basing Concepts." Air University Quarterly Review 13 (Summer 1962):
69-82. Relates several aspects of missiles, "survivabili-
ty," their "capability to destroy targets," and the

"credibility of their employment" to basing strategy. Russell also briefly compares missiles based on land and aboard
submarines.

600. Steel, Ronald. "Fortress America." Commentary 36
(August, 1963):119-124. Sees the counterforce doctrine as
leading to total dependence on missiles, thereby weakening
the American alliance system.

601. Sweitzer, H.B.   "Sovereignty and the SLBM." United
States Naval Institute Proceedings 92 (September,1966):
32-41. Advocates increasing the "three mile limit" to promote defense against Soviet submarines, which would be
barred from these waters.

Missile Gap Controversy

Official Policy Statements

602. Kennedy, John F. "The Missile Gap." In The Strategy of
Peace, 33-45. New York: Harper & Row, Publishers, 1960.
This speech to the United States Senate on August 14, 1958,
was an early expression of Kennedy's view that the
Eisenhower administration had failed to develop American
missile forces enough to maintain a lead over the Soviets.

603. Kennedy, John F.   "The President's News Conference of
February 8, 1961." In Public Papers of the Presidents of the
United States: John F. Kennedy 1961, 66-77. Washington,
D.C.: Government Printing Office, 1962. Discusses the current perception of the missile gap. Kennedy asserts that no
adequate study has been completed, when asked by a reporter
about Secretary of Defense McNamara's statement that there
is no gap in missile capability between the United States
and the Soviet Union.

604. Kennedy, John F.   "The President's News Conference of
March 8, 1961." In Public Papers of the Presidents of the
United States: John F. Kennedy 1961, 152-160. Washington,
D.C.: Government Printing Office, 1962. Kennedy assures
reporters that there will soon be a definitive report on the
alleged missile gap and that the results will be sent to
Congress.

Books

605. Ball, Desmond.   Politics and Force Levels: The
Strategic Missile Program of the Kennedy Administration.
Berkeley: University of California Press, 1980. 322p.
Highly detailed comparison of the Eisenhower and Kennedy
administrations' approach to missiles. Also discusses
strategy and technology during the Kennedy years. Ball

examines the impact of Kennedy, McNamara, and others on particular decisions.

Periodical Articles

606. Licklider, Roy E. "The Missile Gap Controversy." Political Science Quarterly 85 (December 1970):600-615. Discusses the controversy during the Eisenhower and Kennedy administrations. Licklider feels that Eisenhower made a conscious decision to run some risks in relations with the Soviet Union, in order to keep defense spending within strict limits.

607. Schratz, Paul R. "The Caesars, the Sieges, and the Anti-Ballistic Missile." United States Naval Institute Proceedings 94 (March 1968):24-32. Argues that seaborne anti-missile defenses may be the best answer to the problem of preserving the United States from nuclear attack. Schratz briefly discusses Soviet efforts to build an anti-missile system and examines McNamara's opposition to a similar American commitment.

Space Operations

608. Agan, Arthur C. "Aerospace Defense and National Security." Air University Review 20 (November-December 1968):78-83. Warns that the United States must develop space warfare capability in the face of Soviet military preparations for space operations.

609. Cagle, Malcolm W. "The Navy's Future Role in Space." United States Naval Institute Proceedings 89 (January 1963):86-93. Examines all aspects of navy activities in space, both current and projected. Cagle predicts that the navy's entrance into space will have more impact than earlier revolutionary changes such as the move from sail to steam or the advent of naval aviation.

610. Freitag, Robert F. "The Effects of Space Operations on Naval Warfare." Naval Review 1962/63, 172-195. Discusses navy space programs, which the author describes as severely practical in nature. Freitag emphasizes the increasing "speed" in military operations, which makes utilization of space age techniques imperative.

611. Funk, Ben I. "The Spectrum of Space: A Military Appraisal." Air University Review 15 (March-April 1964): 2-19. Emphasizes the special needs of the military in space and why these often differ from civilian requirements. Funk also puts much stress on management of space programs.

612. Hanes, Horace A. "Satellites, Sensors, and Space Specialists." Air University Review 16 (January-February 1965):2-12. Notes the development of intelligence

satellites by the air force, emphasizing the technical aspects of satellites, cameras, and sensors.

613. Johnson, Oris B. "Space: Today's Front Line of Defense." Air University Review 20 (November-December 1968): 95-102. Relates the evolution of space weapons. Johnson sees space warfare as a natural development from air warfare and emphasizes that the United States must provide itself with a "space defense system."

614. Puckett, Robert H. "American Space Policy: Civilian/ Military Dichotomy." Air University Review 16 (March-April 1965):45-50. Criticizes overemphasis by the United States on nonmilitary space operations and civilian direction of the space effort. This tendency began in the Eisenhower administration and continued with some changes during the Kennedy administration.

615. Winter, Thomas C., Jr. "The Army's Role in Space." Military Review 48 (July 1968):82-86. Presents a general space strategy for the United States. Winter also outlines some ways in which the army may participate in space defense.

Military Airlift

616. Albertson, James J. "The C-5A." Military Review 48 (May 1968):3-10. Discusses the impact of the C-5A transport in terms of making American forces much more mobile. Now, this aircraft has to be utilized effectively.

617. Estes, Howell M., Jr. "The Revolution in Airlift." Air University Review 17 (March-April 1966):2-15. Reviews the contributions of military airlift after World War II and discusses the limited support MATS received in the 1950's. Estes examines MATS aircraft such as the C-124 and C-130. Development of the C-5 holds great promise for expanding airlift capacity and improving its cost effectiveness.

618. Jones, Lowell W., and Don A. Lindbo. "Tactical Airlift." Air University Review 18 (September-October 1967):6-19. Examines tactical airlift generally, but there is some emphasis on operations in Vietnam.

619. Oden, Delk M. "The Army and Air Mobility." Military Review 42 (October 1962):57-63. Describes army aviation as an integral part of ground operations; Oden carefully distinguishes its role from the functions of the air force. He also explains why many army aircraft are armed despite the apparent duplication of effort with the air force.

Ground Strategy

Limited War

620. Ferguson, James. "Tactics and Technology--The Unlimited War on Limited War." Air University Review 19 (November-December 1967):8-18. Reviews logistical and technical problems associated with the limited war concept.

621. Gormley, Robert H. "Limited War and the Striking Fleets." United States Naval Institute Proceedings 89 (February 1963):52-59. Examines the problems of modernization in the Third World that are being used by the communists. Gormley advocates developing "limited war striking forces" organized around aircraft carriers. They would be oriented toward limited war contingencies, not toward fighting a strategic nuclear war.

622. Lofgren, Charles A. "How New Is Limited War?" Military Review 47 (July 1967):16-23. Suggests that Vietnam is a truly limited war in contrast to the Korean conflict. Lofgren explores the limited war concept in detail.

623. Monroe, Robert E. "Limited War and Political Conflict." Military Review 42 (October 1962):2-12. Analyzes limited war in terms of domestic politics in the United States. Those concerned with national security seem to have accepted the concept of limited war, but when the United States actually engages in a limited war, there is great danger that partisanship in the United States may provoke a crisis.

624. Ponturo, John. "The Deterrence of Limited Aggression: Strategic and Non-Strategic Interactions." Orbis 6 (Winter 1963):593-622. Views nuclear weapons as highly effective means for discouraging limited wars of aggression.

625. Shane, Robert A. "Incremental Phasing of Mobile Air Strike Forces for Limited War." Air University Quarterly Review 14 (Summer 1963):49-69. Examines the logistical problems of limited war. This is a detailed operations research approach.

626. Shane, Robert A. "Limited-War Research Needs in Lower-Level Crisis Management." Air University Review 15 (March-April 1964):20-25. Focuses on the problems of combat commanders who are faced with crises. Shane identifies psychological elements influencing individuals in such situations. He also contrasts attitudes and approaches to crises at various command levels.

627. Sights, Albert P. "Limited War for Unlimited Goals." Air University Quarterly Review 13 (Spring 1962):38-48. Discusses the opposing strategies of mutual assured

destruction and winning a nuclear war, then proposes
graduated use of air power to deter aggressors without
necessarily employing nuclear weapons.

Counterinsurgency

Official Policy Statements

628. Kennedy, John F. "Remarks at West Point to the
Graduating Class of the Military Academy. June 6, 1962."
In Public Papers of the Presidents of the United States:
John F. Kennedy 1962, 452-455. Washington, D.C.: Government Printing Office, 1963. Emphasizes the importance of
unconventional warfare and discusses the nature of the
"wars of liberation" waged by the communists. Kennedy also
reviews many politico-military tasks such as peacemaking
and arms control that are the responsibility of the armed
services.

Books

629. Eckstein, Harry, editor. Internal War: Problems and
Approaches. New York: Free Press of Glencoe, 1964. 339p.
Important study of insurgency in the Third World from an
American perspective. There is not too much directly
pertinent to counterinsurgency, but there are significant
implications.

Periodical Articles

630. Barrett, Raymond J. "The Problem of Lower Spectrum
Violence." Military Review 46 (February 1966):90-93.
Discusses a variety of guerrilla, terrorist, and other
activities designed to bring about change. Important
American countermeasures include military and economic
assistance.

631. Boatner, Mark M. III. "The Unheeded History of
Counterinsurgency." Army 16 (September 1, 1966):31-36. A
powerful argument that there is nothing really new about
counterinsurgency, which is the American military tradi-
tion. Boatner emphasizes the need for personnel who can
operate effectively in foreign environments.

632. Bobrow, Davis B. "The Civil Role of the Military:
Some Critical Hypotheses." Western Political Quarterly 19
(March 1966):101-111. Discusses counterinsurgency and the
changes in the American military establishment that a
counterinsurgency strategy requires. Bobrow also examines
the limitations of many Third World governments and their
armed forces is a factor which limits the effectiveness of
counterinsurgency efforts.

633. Harrigan, Anthony. "A New Dimension in Special Opera-

tions." Military Review 41 (September 1961):4-9. Discusses
the potential use of nuclear submarines for landing raiding
parties and guerrilla forces in communistheld territory.
They might even be used to move troops through the Arctic
to the Soviet homeland.

634. Hilsman, Roger.   "Internal War--The New Communist
Tactic." Military Review 42 (April 1962):11-22. Describes
the Soviet strategy of "wars of liberation," which Hilsman
feels is a response to the success of the American nuclear
deterrence strategy and the stalemate in Korea.   Hilsman
examines American historical experience with insurgency and
counterinsurgency.   He asserts that the United States must
relearn and then practice the art of internal war.

635. Holliday, Sam C. "An Offensive Response." Military
Review 41 (April 1963):16-23. Argues that it is essential
that western nations employ irregular (guerrilla) warfare
in conflicts with communist countries.   Holliday points to
some French operations in Indochina as possible models.

636. Hughes, David R. "Contingency Planning: "A New
Perspective." United States Naval Institute Proceedings 94
(November 1968):26-37.   Discusses the various types of
"conflict" which may face the United States.   Hughes
stresses that for analytical purpose "conflict" should be
the governing concept, not "war," because many problems may
well not be "war" as it has generally been understood.

637. Kent, Irvin M.   "Soldier's Mission." Military Review
46 (February 1966):80-85.   Discusses counterinsurgency
doctrine in the context of army roles and missions.
Counterinsurgency should be taught to every soldier.

638. Kent, Irvin M., and Ruth A. Caldwell. "A Stitch in
Time." Military Review 48 (June 1968):69-74.   Presents a
plan to aid Third World nations wage counterinsurgency.
The authors stress the importance of intelligence in this
kind of warfare.

639. Lindsay, Franklin A.   "Unconventional Warfare."
Military Review 42 (June 1962):53-62.   Asserts that the
anti-communist alliance must develop the capacity to defeat
communist insurgencies, which often succeed and which are
extremely expensive to combat.   Lindsay also discusses the
great challenges presented by efforts to conduct guerrilla
warfare in communist-held countries.

640. Methin, Eugene H.   "Ideology and Organization in
Counterinsurgency." Orbis 8 (Spring 1964):106-124.   Recommends that the United States put more effort into
studying and using the psychological aspects of counterinsurgency.

641. Miller, Roger J.   "Internal Defense and Development--

'Idealism' or 'Realism'?" <u>Air University Review</u> 19
(January-February 1968):51-56. Examines and defends
American efforts to promote defensive capabilities in
various Third World countries through military assistance.

642. Taylor, Maxwell D. "Post-Vietnam Role of the Military
in Foreign Policy." <u>Air University Review</u> 19 (July-August
1968):50-58. Discusses the armed services as a force in
being that supports foreign policy goals. Taylor sketches
changes in international relations, such as the Sino-Soviet
split, and domestic trends, such as slowing support for
intervention, that influence military roles.

643. Wood, John S., Jr. "Counterinsurgency Coordination at
the National and Regional Level." <u>Military Review</u> 46 (March
1966):80-85. Examines intelligence challenges facing the
United States in fighting insurgencies. Wood stresses the
need for personnel equipped to cope with counterinsurgency
assignments.

Other Topics

644. Box, Clyde. "United States Strike Command-Stateside
and Global." <u>Air University Review</u> 15 (September-October
1964): 2-14. Describes the origins and development of
Strike Command as a response to limited war dangers. Box
also examines major Strike Command exercises.

645. Locksley, Norman. "From the Ocean to the Drop Zone."
<u>Military Review</u> 39 (February 1960):21-26. Presents a
highly imaginative plan for deploying airborne forces from
aircraft carriers. Locksley sees such operations as
especially important for limited and small wars, but also
useful in general conflicts.

646. "United States Army, Pacific." <u>Military Review</u> 39
(October 1959):38-56. Discusses the structure and mission
of United States Army, Pacific and its major components.

Naval Strategy

647. Amme, Carl H., Jr. "The Changing Nature of Power."
<u>United States Naval Institute Proceedings</u> 89 (March 1963):
26-35. Criticizes old conceptions of power and offers
proposals for developing new theories. Amme also discusses
the need for naval and marine readiness for low-intensity
challenges such as the 1958 Lebanon landings.

648. Amme, Carl H., Jr. "Developments and Problems in
Naval Weapons." <u>Naval Review 1962/1963</u>, 196-215. Examines
naval weapons development in considerable detail. Amme
discusses the need to provide better monitoring of weapons
programs.

649. Amme, Carl H., Jr. "Naval Strategy and the New

Frontier." United States Naval Institute Proceedings 88 (March 1962):22-33.   Examines changes in the 1962 defense budget made by the Kennedy administration.   While there are, of course, differences between the Kennedy and Eisenhower administrations' approaches to national strate- gy, Amme argues that they have not been too extensive. He seems to believe that the navy needs to maintain its strategic capabilities and not put all its emphasis on responding to small-scale crises and guerrilla warfare.

650. Amme, Carl H., Jr. "Seapower and the Superpowers." United States Naval Institute Proceedings 94 (October 1968): 26-35.   Discusses basic changes in international relations that require modifications in Alfred Thayer Mahan's theories.   Amme briefly reviews the role of seapower in the Korean and Vietnam conflicts and asserts that the "true mission of the Navy is to provide a base for projecting our national power on and over the land over- seas."

651. Beach, Edward L. "U.S. Nuclear-Powered Submarines." United States Naval Institute Proceedings 93 (August 1967):87-101.   Reviews the American nuclear submarine program. Various classes of ships are discussed.

652. Beresford, Spencer M.   "Preface to Naval Strategy in Outer Space." United States Naval Institute Proceedings 87 (March 1961):33-41.   Discusses the various reconnaissance and bombardment missions that can be conducted from space. Beresford sees space vehicles as a natural extension of naval weaponry.

653. Brandenburg, Robert L.   "USS Bainbridge Is Not the Answer." United States Naval Institute Proceedings 90 (January 1964):36-43.   Advocates construction of many, relatively small destroyers rather than very costly vessels such as the Bainbridge.

654. Chase, John D. "South of Thirty." United States Naval Institute Proceedings 93 (April 1967):30-39.   Analyzes world politics in terms of a North-South division, the South being countries below thirty degrees North Latitude. Chase states that this area is also "the ocean hemisphere" with ample opportunities for the employment of sea power. He also discusses the naval role in counterinsurgency, especially through blockades.

655. Clark, John J.,and Francis A. Lees. "The Economics of Sea Power." United States Naval Institute Proceedings 92 (August 1966):40-49.   Discusses relationships between domestic economic growth and the assurance of adequate defenses, especially naval power. The authors examine the economics of warfare from the 1600's into the 20th century.

656. Connolly, Thomas W.   "The Ballistic Missile Surface

Force." <u>United States Naval Institute Proceedings</u> 90 (June 1964):40-47. Advocates NATO use of merchant ships as bases for ballistic missiles. Connolly had participated in a study of the feasibility of such a move.

657. Crenshaw, Russell S., Jr. "The Fleet Versus the Ballistic Missile." <u>United States Naval Institute Proceedings</u> 89 (April 1963):34-39. Warns that sea control can be maintained by the United States only if it succeeds in protecting its fleets from missiles.

658. Eliot, George Fielding. "Our Far-Flung Ramparts." <u>United States Naval Institute Proceedings</u> 90 (October 1964):26-34. Discusses the defense aspects of the waters adjacent to North America. Eliot emphasizes that sea control is of great importance in limited wars and force projection.

659. Glennon, Allan N. "An Approach to ASW." <u>United States Naval Institute Proceedings</u> 90 (September 1964):48-55. Analyzes the nature of antisubmarine warfare, using the World War II experience as a point of reference. Glennon argues that the technology for detecting submarines is lagging seriously.

660. Graven, John P. "Sea Power and the Sea Bed." <u>United States Naval Institute Proceedings</u> 92 (April 1966):36-51. Examines American capabilities for exploiting the sea bed for military and other purposes. Graven relates Mahan's principles to this field and very briefly describes some of the technology used beneath the sea.

661. Grenfell, Elton W. "The Growing Role of the Submarine." <u>United States Naval Institute Proceedings</u> 89 (January 1963):48-55. Briefly reviews the development of submarines and submarine warfare, including their new capability for fighting other submarines. Grenfell warns that the submarine is less effective in this respect than surface ships.

662. Hayes, John D. "Sea Power and Sea Law." <u>United States Naval Institute Proceedings</u> 90 (May 1964):60-67. Discusses legal aspects of international conflict at sea. Hayes wants the United States to be more assertive in this sphere.

663. Hayes, John D. "Sine Qua Non of U.S. Sea Power: The Merchant Ship." <u>United States Naval Institute Proceedings</u> 91 (March 1965):26-33. Emphasizes the importance of the merchant marine to American sea control. Hayes advocates establishing a federal department that would deal with both the navy and the merchant marine.

664. Holmquist, Carl O. "Developments and Problems in Carrier-Based Attack Aircraft." <u>Naval Review 1969</u>, 194-215.

Offers guidelines for selecting carrier aircraft, but observes that there are increasing problems in following these principles because of changing technology. This historical article moves from the beginnings of carrier aviation through the 1960's.

665. Holmquist, Carl O. "United States Naval Aviation Today." Naval Review 1962/63, 216-241. Presents a profile of naval aviation as it existed in 1961. Holmquist warned that despite American strength, further development of naval air weapons had to be pursued vigorously.

666. Hughes, Wayne, Jr. "Missiles and Missions." United States Naval Institute Proceedings 90 (December 1964):38-43. Discusses the views of Samuel P. Huntington and others who asserted that the current mission of the navy was to use the sea as a kind of base from which to attack land targets. Hughes criticizes this theory, arguing that decisive victories have been and can still be gained at sea.

667. Lowe, George E. "The Case for the Oceanic Strategy." United States Naval Institute Proceedings 94 (June 1968): 26-34. Advocates further development of the nuclear submarine force with antimissile capability. An oceanic strategy might reduce defense spending with benefits for American society.

668. McCain, John S., Jr. "Amphibious Warfare During the Next Decade." United States Naval Institute Proceedings 89 (January 1963):104-111. Focuses on the new technology that needs to be developed in order to maintain appropriate amphibious capability.

669. McCleave, Robert E., Jr. "The National Defense Requirement for a U.S.-Flag Merchant Marine." Naval War College Review 21 (October 1969):64-79. Offers many suggestions for strengthening the American merchant marine, which can, in turn, contribute to national defense and improve the American economy.

670. McDonald, David L. "Carrier Employment Since 1950." United States Naval Institute Proceedings 90 (November 1964):26-33. Examines the use of carriers in various crises from Korean War through the Cuban missile crisis. Carriers have continued to prove their worth in many varied situations.

671. McNeil, W.J. "The Economic Importance of a U.S.-Flag Merchant Marine." Naval Review 1968, 148-165. Despite the title, McNeil discusses defense aspects of the merchant marine. He argues that, relatively, the merchant marine receives less governmental assistance than many other industries.

672. Madouse, Richard L.   "The FDL Surfaces Again." United States Naval Institute Proceedings 94 (June 1968):54-66. Detailed description of proposed Fast Rapid Deloggistics Ships which Congress rejected in 1967. These ships are, in part, helicopter carriers which have various novel features. Madouse discusses the need for such ships to enhance the crisis capability of American forces.

673. Marshall, S.L.A.   "Naval Power as Understood by a Soldier." Naval Review 1962/63, 2-19. Emphasizes the role of the navy in projecting American power and supporting land forces overseas. The Strategic Air Command, while a powerful weapon, does not and cannot replace a strong navy.

674. Noel, J.V.   "The Navy and the Department of Defense." United States Naval Institute Proceedings 87 (November 1961):23-31. Describes the continuous expansion of the Department of Defense and its increasing control over the navy. Noel cites a number of instances which show the Office of the Secretary of Defense often fails to differentiate between the services when their respective organizations and problems warrant distinct policies.

675. Oliver, J.D., Jr. and A.W. Slifer.   "Evaluating the DDG." United States Naval Institute Proceedings 91 (July 1965):78-86. Reviews the advent and the worth of the navy's first destroyers mounting missiles. The authors discuss modifications in the ships that became necessary.

676. Outlaw, E.C. "V/STOL in the Navy of the Future." Naval Review 1968, 184-201. Reviews the vertical/short takeoff and landing airplane program. Such aircraft have been slow in coming, but are valuable and will increase in importance.

677. Packard, W.H.   "Intelligence and the Navy." Naval Review 1968, 202-217. Discusses current problems in gathering naval intelligence. Packard believes that the navy must have a more elaborate intelligence structure of its own. He is critical of what seems to be too much dependence on the Defense Intelligence Agency.

678. Perry, E.B.   "Do We Realy Need a U.S. Merchant Marine." United States Naval Institute Proceedings 91 (November 1965):59-63. Asserts that the United States should abandon its half-hearted policy and either support the merchant marine effectively or eliminate support.

679. Raring, George L.   "The Atom, the Navy, and Limited War."   United States Naval Institute Proceedings 88 (February 1962):50-57. Recommends that the United States develop plans for and the capability for using nuclear weapons in limited conlicts, although clearly their employment weakens the "limited" character of such wars. Raring also discusses the   continued usefulness of   amphibious

operations under varying conditions.

680. Rebentisch, J.A., Jr.   "MATS' Role in Naval
Logistics."   United States Naval Institute Proceedings 90
(June 1964): 76-87. Discusses the disadvantages of tying
the Military Air Transport Service (MATS) so closely to the
air force that naval requirements suffer.   Rebentisch
examines the structure and functioning of MATS and speci-
fies the problems.

681. Ricketts, Claude.   "Naval Power--Present and Future."
United States Naval Institute Proceedings 89 (January
1963): 32-39.   Focuses on the need for a counterforce
strategy and to the navy's role in force projection.
Ricketts emphasizes the flexibility of naval power, an
advantage that has increased greatly through the development of submarine-based missiles.

682. Simpson, Howard R. "Offshore Guerilla War." Naval War
College Review 22 (October 1969):17-20. Discusses various
types of possible unconventional attacks on American and
perhaps allied shipping.   Simpson concentrates on small
Soviet motor vessels which can carry missiles.

683. Smith, Robert H., Jr.   "The Submarine's Long Shadow."
United States Naval Institute Proceedings 92 (March 1966):
30-39.   Describes the increasing strength and power of the
submarine.   Smith argues that the United States must devote
much more attention to antisubmarine warfare.

684. Smith, Robert H.   "A United States Navy for the
Future."   United States Naval Institute Proceedings 97
(March 1971):18-25. Criticizes the navy generally for its
performance and for its apparent inability to meet new
challenges.   As a result of these conditions, popular
support for the navy has declined.

685. Thach, John W.   "The ASW Navy of the Seventies."
United States Naval Institute Proceedings 89 (January
1963): 56-65.   Forecasts the development of antisubmarine
warfare for the next decade.   Thach suggests that there
will be an increasing role for submarines in antisubmarine
operations and discusses new ships and new weapons.

686. Trout, B. Thomas. "NAVAL STRATEGY AND NAVAL POLITICS:
Peacetime Uses of a Wartime Naval Force."   Naval War
College Review 27 (July-August 1974):3-16. Both the Soviet
and American navies are following parallel lines in
developing roles for themselves in short of war situations.
In this area, the Soviets seem to be following American
patterns.

687. Turner, Stansfield.   "Missions of the Navy." United
States Naval Institute Proceedings 100 (February 1974):18-
25.   Emphasizes that the missions outlined by the Chief of

Naval Operations in 1970 are interwoven and not entirely separable. Turner advocates continued analysis of the navy's objectives by its officers.

688. Whidden, W.V. "The Future of the 'Second Segment.'" United States Naval Institute Proceedings 90 (November 1964):76-81. Examines the current role of aircraft carriers in antisubmarine warfare after a review of their service during World War II. Whidden briefly discusses antisubmarine warfare aircraft and possible changes in American strategy when the Essex class carriers become obsolete.

689. Williams, Ralph E. "The Navy in the Cold War: A Year in Retrospect." Naval Review 1962/63, 20-37. Focuses on developments in 1961, which Williams considers a critical year. Polaris submarines were introduced and other important steps taken.

Civil Defense

Official Policy Statements

690. Johnson, Lyndon B. "Statements by the President on the Need for Federal, State, and Local Cooperation in Civil Defense and Emergency Preparedness. April 13, 1968." In Public Papers of the Presidents of the United States: Lyndon B. Johnson 1968-69, I, 510-511. Washington, D.C.: Government Printing Office, 1970. Recommends more "fallout protection" and other civil defense measures in support of the American military posture. Johnson refers briefly to the work of the National Civil Defense Advisory Council.

Periodical Articles

691. Huebner, Clarence R. "What Is Civil Defense?" Military Review 42 (February 1962):65-72. Deals with the many problems of civil defense against nuclear attack. These include protection of the civilian population, capability for continuing support of the armed forces, and emergency government.

Military Assistance

692. Farrington, Robert F. "Military Assistance at the Crossroads." United States Naval Institute Proceedings 92 (June 1966):68-76. Decries reductions in military assistance appropriations. Farrington argues that improvements are needed for various reasons, including the unfavorable balance of payments situation. There needs to be more emphasis on arms sales, but aid for many poorer countries is still justified.

693. Gailer, Frank L., Jr. "Air Force Missions in Latin America." Air University Quarterly Review 13 (Fall 1961): 45-58. Describes air force missions overseas and contrasts

them with military assistance advisory groups and air at-
taches.   The   missions   emphasize   training   and   promote
technical standardization and cooperation with the United
States.

694. Hanks, Lucien M.   "American Aid is Damaging Thai Society." Trans-action 5 (October 1968):29-34.   Charges that
the American emphasis on military assistance is giving the
Thai military too much power.   Changes in Thai society are
occurring too rapidly and may be political destabilizing.

695. Jones, Douglas N.   "Economic Aspects of Military Assistance."   Air University Review 16 (November-December
1964):42-46.   Suggests that military aid has nonmilitary
benefits.   Jones also discusses the American strategy of
foreign aid, both military and nonmilitary.

696. Lynch, John E.   "ANALYSIS for Military Assistance."
Military Review 48 (May 1968):41-49. Examines the political
and diplomatic facets of military assistance and the evaluation it is undergoing in the United States.

697. Porter, Robert W.   "Look South to Latin America."
Military Review 48 (June 1968):82-90.   Proposes more aid to
Latin American armed forces and stresses their importance in
fighting communism.

698. Williams, Samuel T. "The Practical Demands of MAAG."
Miltary Review 41 (July 1961):2-14.   Describes the structure
and functioning of military assistance advisory groups, using examples from Williams' service in Vietnam, 1955-1960,
as a Chief of the Military Assistance Advisory Group, Vietnam.

699. Zook, David H., Jr.   "United States Military Assistance
to Latin America."   Air University Review 14 (September-
October 1963):82-85.   Discusses efforts to assist Latin
American nations against internal subversion, especially
since the beginning of the Kennedy administration.   Zook
discounts fears that military assistance encourages military
dictators.

Disarmament and Arms Control

Official Policy Statements

700. Kennedy, John F.   "Radio and Television Address to the
American People on the Nuclear Test Ban Treaty.   July 26,
1963." In Public Papers of the Presidents of the United
States: John F. Kennedy 1963, 601-606. Washington, D.C.:
Government Printing Ofice, 1964.   Kennedy emphasizes the
limited nature of the agreement.   It prohibits above ground

testing, but he asserts that it may lead to other agreements and to better, if not perfect, East-West relations.
The speech includes the assurance that the United States
has, and under the terms of the agreement, "will continue
to have, the nuclear strength that we need."

701. Johnson, Lyndon B. "Letter to Chairman Khrushchev on
the Eve of the Reopening of the Geneva Disarmament
Conference. January 20, 1964." In Public Papers of the
Presidents of the United States: Lyndon B. Johnson 1963-64,
I, 153-155. Washington, D.C.: Government Printing Office,
1965. Reviews areas where a common approach is needed.
Johnson concurs with Khrushchev's assertion that questions
involving "territorial disputes" should not be allowed to
lead to war. He also stresses the importance of the United
Nations in American policy.

702. Johnson, Lyndon B. "Letter in Response to Report of
the Committee on the Economic Impact of Defense and
Disarmament. September 5, 1965. In "Public Papers of the
Presidents of the United States: Lyndon B. Johnson 1965, II
976-977. Washington, D.C.: Government Printing Office,
1966. Summarizes the Report as saying that defense
expenditures will not conflict with disarmament; the United
States economy can easily adjust to sharp reductions in
defense expenditures.

703. Johnson, Lyndon B. "Remarks Before the U.N. General
Assembly Following Its Endorsement of the Nuclear Nonproliferation Treaty. June 12, 1968." In Public Papers of
the Presidents of the United States: Lyndon B. Johnson
1968-69, I, 712-715. Washington, D.C.: Government Printing
Office, 1970. Notes that the nonproliferation talks lasted
for four and a half years and asserts that the treaty
should be implemented quickly. Johnson pledges full
adherence to the Treaty by the United States and promises
that various other steps will be taken to achieve disarmament and enhance the peaceful use of atomic energy.

Books

704. Benoit, Emile, editor. Disarmament and the Economy.
New York: Harper & Row, Publishers, 1963. 310p. Plan
prepared by fifteen economists for disarmament to be
implemented over twelve years to avoid dislocations in the
American economy.

705. Brennan, Donald G., editor. Arms Control, Disarmament,
and National Security. New York: George Braziller, 1961.
475p. Important collection of essays, presented in
somewhat modified form from the Fall 1960 issue of
Daedalus. A great variety of viewpoints is presented.

706. Hadley, Arthur Twining. The Nation's Safety and Arms

<u>Control.</u> New York: Viking Press, 1961. 160p. Comments on the 1960 Arms Control Summer Study's deliberations and propounds Hadley's own view on the structure of an effective arms control system.

707. Lang, Daniel. <u>An Inquiry Into Enoughness; of Bombs and Men and Staying Alive</u>. New York: McGraw-Hill Book Co., 1965. 216p. Reprints Lang's articles from <u>The New Yorker</u>. He interviewed various public figures, including McNamara, and visited disarmament meetings and marches and other events related to the nuclear arms race.

708. Levine, Robert A. <u>The Arms Debate</u>. Cambridge: Harvard University Press, 1963. 347p. Analyzes what Levine believes are five theories relating to military policy and disarmament which he fleshes out with quotations from leading adherents of these theories.

709. Lilienthal, David Eli. <u>Change, Hope and the Bomb</u>. Princeton: Princeton University Press, 1963. 168p. Scores efforts at total solutions to the problems of disarmament. Lilienthal favors a very gradual approach, which he considers is more realistic and, at the same time, denies the claims of those who assert there must be immediate disarmament or nuclear disaster.

710. Spanier, John W. and Joseph L. Nogee. <u>The Politics of Disarmament; a Study in Soviet-American Gamesmanship</u>. New York: Praeger Publishers, 1963. 226p. As the title suggests, the authors emphasize the tactical and "political" aspects of Soviet-American disarmament negotiations. They find that these negotiations are used simply for propaganda purposes.

711. Teller, Edward, with Allen Brown. <u>The Legacy of Hiroshima</u>. Garden City, New York: Doubleday & Company, 1962. 325p. Strongly advocates continued testing of nuclear weapons, and the implementation of an extensive civil defense program. This is an important statment by a major participant in the continued debates over nuclear strategy and nuclear weapons.

712. Twining, Nathan F. <u>Neither Liberty Nor Safety; a Hard Look at U.S. Military Policy and Strategy</u>. New York: Holt, Rinehart & Winston, 1966. 320p. Deprecates disarmament, but suggests changes in the USSR that would advance the cause of peace. This is an early statement of the need to develop space weapons.

Essays and Periodical Articles

713. Coffey, Joseph I. "Strategy, Strategic Forces, and Arms Control." <u>Orbis</u> 9 (Spring 1965):98-115. Focuses on Soviet and American perceptions of nuclear strategy. Coffey reviews major disarmament proposals and discusses the

factors that have obstructed agreement.

714. Dean, Fred M.   "The Bird's-Eye View of Arms Control and Disarmament."   Air University Review 17 (May-June 1966):2-11.   Discusses the views of "hawks" and "doves" toward military power and international relations.   Dean speaks for the "eagles" who are more concerned with defense than are the "doves", but who see some utility in arms control.

715. Dwan, John E. II.   "The Anatomy of Disengagement." Military Review 42 (February 1962):2-15.   Surveys the many plans for troop reduction and lessening tensions in Europe, emphasizing the Polish Rapacki plan.   Dwan argues that disengagement is unrealistic, given Soviet-American competition, and would, if consummated, tend to destabilize, rather than stabilize, Europe.

716. Gasteyger, Curt.   "The Problems of International Disarmament."   Military Review 46 (January 1966):23-29. Discusses conflicting pressures on the United States from the USSR and the American allies.   Gasteyger notes that there can be arms control without formal agreements or structures.

717. Horn, Herbert O. and John Ponturo. "Stable Deterrence Proposals: Some Questions."   Orbis 7 (Winter 1964): 821-832.   Argues that many proposals for controlling nuclear weapons made by nonmilitary figures relect ignorance of basic military and technological factors.

718. Jensen, Lloyd. "Military Capabilities and Bargaining Behavior." Journal of Conflict Resolution 9 (June 1965):155-163. Denies that the superpowers "negotiate from strength" in disarmament talks. Superiority reduces the incentive a superpower has to negotiate.

719. Maddox, John. "At the Brink of a Test Ban." Commentary 35 (June 1963):461-466. Strongly advocates negotiation of a test ban.   Maddox examines the various arguments against such an agreement.

720. Osgood, Robert E.   "The Place of Disarmament in American Policy." In Beyond the Cold War: Essays on American Foreign Policy in a Changing World Environment, 18-43.   Chicago: Rand McNally & Company, 1965.   Discusses arms races theoretically and historically and relates them to disarmament efforts.   The second half of the essay assesses the advantages of disarmament and analyzes the types of arms control.

721. Paolucci, Dominic A. "POSEIDON and Minuteman: Either, or; Neither, Nor?" United States Naval Institute Proceedings 94 (August 1968):46-58.   Extols the virtues of the submarine-launched Poseidon and advocates the replacement

of Minuteman by Poseidon missiles.

722. Raser, John R. "Weapons Design and Arms Control: The Polaris Example." Journal of Conflict Resolution 9 (December 1965):450-462. Thorough discussion of POLARIS weapons and their advantages and their limitations.

723. Robison, David. "Self-Restrictions in the American Military Use of Space." Orbis 9 (Spring 1965):116-139. Decries the failure of the United States to invest more resources in the military utilization of space. Robison proposes a merger of the civilian and military space programs and their associated governmental agencies.

724. Rubinstein, Alvin A. "Political Barriers to Disarmament." Orbis 9 (Spring 1965):140-154. These barriers include such factors as the influence of Marxism-Leninism on Soviet views and policies and the interplay of technological developments and disarmament policies.

Economic Warfare

725. Clark, John J. "Economic Warfare: A Positive Conception." Military Review 46 (March 1966):64-75. Emphasizes economic programs of the United States and the Soviet Union. Clark also discusses economic warfare in more general terms.

726. Geneste, M.E. "U.S. 'Strategies' and Continental Europe." United States Naval Institute Proceedings 90 (October 1964):35-41. Advocates fighting the eastern bloc through an economic offensive and psychological warfare.

Military Personnel

Official Policy Statements

727. U.S. Congress. House. Committee on Armed Services. Civilian Advisory Panel on Military Manpower Procurement. Report. 90th Cong., 1st sess., 1967. SOD Y4. Ar5/2:M31. Commonly known as the Clark Panel report, this study criticizes many aspects of manpower procurement, but recommends retention of student and occupational deferments.

728. U.S. National Advisory Commission on Selective Service. In Pursuit of Equity: Who Serves When Not All Serve? Report of the Commission. Washington, D.C.: Government Printing Office, 1967. SOD Pr. 36.8:Se4/Eq5 Commonly known as the Marshall Commission report, this analysis examines the incidence of military service and recommends against continuance of student and occupational deferments. It recommends a draft lottery that the Clark panel had opposed. The role of reserve forces is criticized.

Periodical Articles

729. Alden, John. "National Strength Through National Service." United States Naval Institute Proceedings 95 (July 1969):68-78. Proposes a kind of mixed system with various alternatives to military service. The military option would be improved by upgrading benefits and salaries for servicemen.

730. Altman, Stuart H., and Alan E. Fechter. "The Supply of Military Personnel in the Absence of a Draft." American Economic Review 57 (May 1967):19-31. Presents an economic analysis of the problems of maintaining appropriate force levels without conscription. Reserve forces and active duty medical specialists are omitted from the study.

731. Baxter, Robert J. "Progress is Our Most Important Problem." Naval Review 1962/1963, 160-171. Warns that shortcomings in naval personnel may limit the usefulness of higher level weapons and other equipment. Improved training and more emphasis on retention of skilled navy personnel should be priorities for the navy.

732. Brooks, Leon Preston. "Vital Interests and Volunteer Forces." United States Naval Institute Proceedings 97 (January 1971):18-23. Warns that drastic force reductions will undermine American defense efforts. Brooks discusses the all-volunteer force and proposes many changes in the structure of the defense establishment to save money.

733. Chatterjee, Pranab, and Barbara F. Chatterjee. "Some Structural Dilemmas of Selective Service Boards." Human Organization 29 (Winter 1970):288-293. Studying Ohio draft boards, the authors analyze some of the problems in the status and operations of boards. Accountability is unclear, and the boards are composed of a relatively narrow social strata.

734. Curtis, Gilbert L. "A New Era for MAC's Reserve Forces." Air University Review 20 (September-October 1969): 26-34. Discusses new training programs which bring reservists of the Military Airlift Command into contact with state-of-the-art technology.

735. Hanks, R.J. "The Thin Blue Line." United States Naval Institute Proceedings 90 (October 1964):60-65. Examines the problems of attracting and retaining the personnel to meet the navy's needs. Hanks proposes a strategy to provide fuller personnel complements and to improve recruiting.

736. Janowitz, Morris. "The Case for a National Service System." Public Interest, no. 5. (Fall 1966):90-109. Recommends universal national service, including military and nonmilitary assignments, in lieu of a draft lottery.

737. Levantrosser, William F. "The Army Reserve Merger Proposal." Military Affairs 30 (Fall 1966):135-147. Focuses on Congress' part in the debate over Secretary of Defense McNamara's proposal for combining these forces.

738. Mundy, C. E., Jr. "Enlisted Recruiting Update." Marine Corps Gazette 68 (July 1968):30-38. After the end of conscription, the marines encountered difficulties in recruiting appropriate personnel and had to work harder to maintain both their force level and personnel.

739. Oi, Walter. "The Economic Cost of the Draft." American Economic Review 57 (May 1967):39-62. Discusses possible economic incentives for volunteer armed forces. Oi also examines the economic impact on the draftee.

740. Rilling, Alexander W. "The Question of Universal Military Training." United States Naval Institute Proceedings 93 (August 1967):65-75. Argues for truly universal military training. Rilling analyzes the selective service system and various other possible approaches to providing personnel for the armed services.

741. Rucker, Colby G. "The Fifth Man." United States Naval Institute Proceedings 92 (January 1966):86-92. Recommends that more attention be given to the twenty percent of the enlisted men who stay in the navy. Rucker expresses considerable alarm about the loss of so many men, especially those trained in electronics and other specialized fields.

742. Shepard, Taxewell and Allan Slaff. "The People Factor." United States Naval Institute Proceedings 93 (March 1967):76-88. Describes efforts made by Secretary of the Navy Paul Nitze to improve retention rates and to deal with other personnel problems. The authors examine the work of the task force Nitze appointed and provide a great deal of specific information on the retention problem.

743. Shupper, B.H. "Manning the Fleet in the Nuclear Age." Naval Review 1967, 66-83. Examines navy efforts to maintain a high grade of officer and enlisted personnel. Shupper expresses optimism about the effectiveness of the navy personnel system.

744. Smedberg, William R. "Manning the Future Fleets." United States Naval Institute Proceedings 89 (January 1963): 120-129. Emphasizes the effects rapid technological change has on personnel requirements of the navy. Recommends taking people into consideration when designing new technology.

745. Smith, Lynn D. "'Those are Regulars, By God!'," Military Review 41 (May 1961):82-90. Discusses the role and status of reserve forces. Many reserve units are

prepared for immediate service despite deficiencies in
equipment. Smith emphasizes that for the first time in
American history there is a large, reasonably well-
supported reserve component as a part of the military
establishment.

746. Thompson, William. "The Selected Reserve." United
States Naval Institute Proceedings 88 (January 1962):69-77.
Emphasizes that, while in an emergency, reservists would be
required very quickly, the selected reserve would meet the
challenge. Thompson describes preparations for utilizing
reservists at once in a mobilization and explains the
efforts that are needed to maintain appropriate reserve
force levels.

747. Wyckoff, Theodore. "Required ROTC: The New Look."
Military Review 44 (November 1964):24-28. Argues that
requiring ROTC training will influence more men to accept
commissions.

Alliances

748. Findley, Paul. "Does American Foreign Policy Entail
Frequent Wars?" Annals of the American Academy of Political
and Social Science, no. 384 (July 1969):45-52. Sees a
significant contradiction between American detente policy
and the maintenance of an alliance system. Findley argues,
too, that American policy toward the Peoples Republic of
China should be modified.

749. McGovern, George S. "Are Our Military Alliances
Meaningful?" Annals of the American Academy of Political
and Social Science, no. 384 (July 1969):14-20. Advocates
examining our obligations and commitments under alliances
such as NATO and SEATO. McGovern favors putting less
reliance on armaments and alliances.

750. Stambuk, George. "Foreign Policy and Stationing of
American Forces Abroad." Journal of Politics 25 (August
1963):472-488. Discusses the United States alliance system
and the military cooperation associated with it. Stambuk
questions the continuing importance of national states.

North Atlantic Treaty Organization

Official Policy Statements

751. Johnson, Lyndon B. "Remarks on the 15th Anniversary of
the Signing of the North Atlantic Treaty. April 3, 1964."
In Public Papers of the Presidents of the United States:
Lyndon B. Johnson 1963-64, I, 433-436. Washington, D.C.:
Government Printing Office, 1965. Notes the continued
strengthening of NATO military power and its lasting
deterrence value. Johnson warns that further development

of NATO is necessary, although efforts toward the reduction of tensions in Europe should also be made.

752. North Atlantic Treaty Organization. Report of the NATO Committee of the Atlantic Council of the United States. "NATO--Crisis or Opportunity?" Atlantic Community Quarterly 3 (Winter 1966):419-441. Consists of a "Policy Statement" and a description of the "Non-Military Functions of NATO." The report recommends that NATO be broadened into more of an Atlantic community rather than simply being a military alliance. A concrete American commitment to this concept is needed, however, for it to be widely accepted.

Documentary Collections

753. Western Europe: National Security Files, 1961-1969. Frederick, Maryland: University Publications of America, Inc. Microfilm collection contains among other items many studies of De Gaulle's policies regarding the NATO alliance and of the impact of the Vietnam conflict in Europe. Berlin and other crisis areas are included. There are many documents relating to the defense policies of European countries.

Periodical Articles

754. Amme, Carl H., Jr. "NATO Strategy and Flexible Response." United States Naval Institute Proceedings 93 (May 1967):58-69. Describes the strategy of "flexible response" and the anxiety it has created among the European members of NATO. Amme thoroughly explores possible nuclear strategies for Europe, especially those involving the use of tactical nuclear weapons. Amme seems to believe that tactical nuclear weapons can be used without there being an inevitable move to general nuclear war.

755. Amme, Carl H., Jr. "Nuclear Control and the Multilateral Force." United States Naval Institute Proceedings 91 (April 1965):24-35. Discusses the advantages and disadvantages of a multilateral force. The proposal is very difficult to evaluate and certainly difficult to implement because of the differing perspectives of the major NATO nations.

756. Church, Frank. "Toward a More Perfect Union." Atlantic Community Quarterly 3 (Fall 1965):285-292. Argues that NATO's role should be expanded. Church recommends a presidential commission to explore the possibility of developing a genuine Atlantic community.

757. Cordier, Sherwood S. "The Atlantic Alliance: Problems and Prospects." United States Naval Institute Proceedings 92 (December 1966):38-49. Traces the development of NATO. Success has paradoxically reduced the momentum of the alliance. There should be more cooperation and less

American dominance.

758. Cottrell, Alvin J., and Stanley L. Harrison. "Alliances: The Ties That Bind." United States Naval Institute Proceedings 94 (September 1968):26-35. Surveys the American alliance system. The authors are generally critical of the alliances other than NATO and suggest alternative approaches for achieving American goals.

759. Dabros, Walter J. "The Credibility of the Deterrent and Its Implications for NATO." United States Naval Institute Proceedings 91 (July 1965):26-35. Speaks in favor of the multilateral force (MLF), which will strengthen NATO greatly in terms of deterrence.

760. Emmet, Christopher. "The U.S. Plan for a NATO Nuclear Deterrent." Orbis 7 (Summer 1963):265-277. Discusses the theory of a multilateral nuclear force for defending Europe. Emmet feels American proposals are a reasonable compromise.

761. No entry.

762. Goodman, Elliot R. "Five Nuclear Options for the West." Atlantic Community Quarterly 2 (Winter 1964-1965):571-587. Describes five possible approaches to nuclear weapons and their advantages and disadvantages. The focus of the article is on European-American relations and nuclear weapons.

763. Halstead, John G.H. "The Atlantic: The Linchpin." United States Naval Institute Proceedings 110 (December 1984 Supplement):18-25. Discusses the continuing relationship of the defense of the Atlantic to the NATO alliance and to the United States.

764. Hanks, Robert J. "The High Price of Success." United States Naval Institute Proceedings 94 (April 1968):26-33. Suggests that NATO has been so effective that it has persuaded the Soviets to move toward at least the appearance of detente. This development, however, tends to undermine support for NATO in Europe.

765. Hartley, Livingston. "Atlantic Partnership--How?" Orbis 8 (Spring 1964):141-152. Recommends expanding NATO's role in order to develop a genuine Atlantic community. Hartley examines the means that could be used to unify the members of the projected Atlantic community.

766. Hoffmann, Stanley. "De Gaulle, Europe, and the Atlantic Alliance." International Organization 18 (Winter 1964): 1-28. Discusses the disadvantages of De Gaulle's independent nuclear force initiative and the reaction of the French to American proposals.

767. Holmes, John W. "Fearful Symmetry: The Dilemmas of Consultation and Coordination in the North Atlantic Treaty

Organization." _International Organization_ 22 (Autumn 1968):
821-840.   Analyzes disunity in Europe and the United
States. Despite problems, Holmes values NATO, especially
for its consultative role.

768. Kenny, Edward T. "MLF: The New NATO Sword?" _United
States Naval Institute Proceedings_ 90 (February 1964):24-
35. Examines possibilities for developing a multinational
naval force for NATO, which would help consolidate the
alliance.

769. Kissinger, Henry A. "Coalition Diplomacy in a Nuclear
Age." _Atlantic Community Quarterly_ 2 (Fall 1964):430-449.
Discusses the need for balancing cooperation within NATO
with the need for the United States to give more respect to
the European members of NATO. Kissinger provides a
thorough analysis of the influence of nuclear weapons on
the NATO alliance.

770. Kohl, Wilfrid L. "Nuclear Sharing in NATO and the
Multilateral Force." _Political Science Quarterly_ 80 (March
1965):88-109. Discusses all aspects of the MLF and the
broader issue of the European allies' role in controlling
nuclear weapons.

771. Locksley, Norman. "NATO's Southern Exposure." _United
States Naval Institute Proceedings_ 88 (November 1962):40-
54.   Examines the Allied Forces Southern Command, consist-
ing of Italy, Greece, and Turkey. Locksley describes the
structure of the Command and some of the exercises that
have been carried out recently.

772. Norstad, Lauris.   "NATO, Its Problems and Its
Continuing Promise." _Proceedings of the Academy of Political Science_ 27 (May 1963):102-114.   Examines the need to
meet increasing demands by European members of NATO for a
voice in nuclear weapons policy.

773. Possony, Stefan T. "Toward Nuclear Isolationism?"
Orbis 6 (Winter 1963):623-644. Asserts that, by failing to
arm its European allies with nuclear weapons, the United
States is undermining NATO. Possony is strongly supportive
of the alliance.

774. Schelling, Thomas C. "The Atlantic Alliance." _Virginia
Quarterly Review_ 43 (Winter 1967):20-35.   Differentiates
NATO and the concept of the Atlantic community. Schelling
offers several prescriptions for improving American relations with Europe and for strengthening the alliance.

775. Schelling, Thomas   C. "The Future of NATO." _Air
University Review_ 19 (March-April 1968):40-47.   Examines
the origins of NATO and its development through the 1960's.
Schelling concludes that stagnation in NATO reflects its
success; it will only be strengthened if there are new
crises in Europe.

776. Stanley, Timothy W. "Decentralizing Nuclear Control in NATO." Orbis 7 (Spring 1963):41-48. Proposes various schemes for giving the European allies of the United States a greater role in making decisions on the deployment and use of nuclear weapons.

777. Van devanter, E., Jr. "Nuclear Forces and the Future of NATO." Air University Review 15 (July-August 1964):2-8. Discusses the multinational nuclear force (MLF), but argues that this use of submarines for bases is not the only approach to giving the European allies a greater role in nuclear weapons decision-making. Van devanter makes specific suggestions for providing this participation.

Asia

778. Bell, Coral. "Security in Asia: Reappraisals After Vietnam." International Journal 24 (Winter 1968-1969):1-12. Even though an American retreat from Vietnam is almost inevitable, the United States may be able to keep forces in those Southeast Asian nations that still fear the Peoples Republic of China.

779. Butler, Olva B., and others. "A Committee Report of the Strategic Planning Study on U.S. Alternatives for an Indian Ocean Area Policy." Naval War College Review 21 (June 1969):160-174. Discusses American options in the face of the coming British withdrawal from Southwest Asia. The Naval War College's committee report asserts that a maritime strategy would be very effective in this area.

780. Hessler, William H. "India as a Prospective Partner." United States Naval Institute Proceedings 90 (February 1964):72-83. Asserts that India may well become an American ally as a result of India's continuing tensions with the Peoples Republic of China. Hessler discusses the Indian response to the Chinese conflict in 1962.

781. Kennan, George F. "Japanese Security and American Policy." Foreign Affairs 43 (October 1964):14-28. Reviews various courses of action Japan may take toward the Soviet Union and the Peoples Republic of China. Kennan also examines American perceptions of Japan's problems.

782. Millar, Thomas B. "Australia and the American Alliance." Pacific Affairs 37 (Summer 1964):148-160. Reviews the development of the ANZUS Pact. Millar notes Australian concern about possible Indonesian threats.

783. Miller, Roger J. "Is SEATO Obsolete?" United States Naval Institute Proceedings 94 (November 1968):56-63. Analyzes the weaknesses of SEATO, including, at least initially, the limited power of the United States in terms of conventional military power. There have been some gains,

but efforts must be made to change the alliance, to include a greater commitment to economic development.

784. Nairn, Ronald C. "SEATO: A Critique." Pacific Affairs 41 (Spring 1968):5-18.   Assails maintenance of the SEATO pact and explores the many problems associated with what seems to be an unnatural alliance.

785. Salans, Carl F. "U.S. Alliances in the Pacific." United States Naval Institute Proceedings 92 (July 1966):62-71.   Critizes SEATO and other alliances for not dealing effectively with the insurgency challenge.   Salans warns that American military intervention alone cannot defeat insurgents.

786. Withrow, John E., Jr. "Needed: A Credible Presence." United States Naval Institute Proceedings 92 (March 1966): 52-61.   Analyzes the allied military posture in the Indian Ocean, noting British commitments that still existed in the 1960's.   Withrow asserts that a maritime strategy is the best approach to the maintenance of security in the area. The author deemphasizes air power.

Foreign Bases

787. Black, Edwin F. "The Quest for Common Ground." United States Naval Institute Proceedings 94 (January 1968):28-36. Recommends taking a broadly political approach in acquiring foreign bases.   The security of such bases depends upon the local inhabitants and the local government.   Black proposes a plan for negotiating for bases.

788. Calhoun, C.R. "How Powerful are Overseas Bases?" Naval Review 1968, 166-183.   Assesses the value of major American overseas bases.   In addition to their important function in supporting American forces, they are, in a sense, a force in being to deter Soviet advances in many parts of the world.

Crises and Force Projection

Documentary Collections

789. Africa: National Security Files, 1961-1969. Frederick, Maryland: University Publications of America, Inc. Microfilm collection includes items related to the crises of the period and military and economic assistance programs of the United States in regard to African countries.   Some information on African attitudes toward the Vietnam conflict is provided.

790. Asia and the Pacific: National Security Files, 1961-1969.   Frederick, Maryland: University Publications of America, Inc. Microfilm collection includes much material on Laos, Cambodia, and Thailand that is related to the

Vietnam conflict.   Items dealing with the movement of
United States marines to Thailand in 1962 and contemplated
American troop movements to Laos, for example, are part of
the file.

791. Crises in Panama and the Dominican Republic: National
Security Files and NSC Histories (1963-1969).   Frederick,
Maryland: University Publications of America, Inc. Microfilm collection contains many documents dealing with the
conflict between Panama and the United States in 1964 and
the occupation of the Dominican Republic by American and
Latin American Forces in 1965-1966.

792. Latin America: National Security Files, 1961-1969.
Frederick, Maryland: University Publications of America,
Inc.   Microfilm collection includes material on the Cuban
missile crisis, the occupation of the Dominican Republic,
insurgency and counterinsurgency in Latin America, and the
movement of American warships to support American policies,
among other topics.

793. The Middle East: National Security Files, 1961-1969.
Frederick, Maryland: University Publications of America,
Inc.   Microfilm collection includes material on the many
crises and conflicts of the period, including the wars
between Israel and the Arab states and between India and
Pakistan.   American military and economic assistance to a
number of countries is also considered in this collection,
which embraces India, Pakistan, and Afghanistan as well as
the traditional Middle East.

794. The United Nations: National Security Files, 1963-
1969.   Frederick, Maryland: University Publications of
America, Inc. Microfilm collection includes materials on a
great variety of topics related to American security and
American foreign policy.   Many documents on the Dominican
crisis of 1965 and the Vietnam conflict are contained in
the collection.

795. U.S.S.R. and Eastern Europe: National Security Files,
1961-1969.   Frederick, Maryland: University Publications of
America, Inc.   Microfilm collection includes a considerable
variety of materials on topics related to American security.   Many items refer to the Vietnamese conflict and naval
movements by both the Soviet Union and its allies and the
United States and its allies.

Books

796. Draper, Theodore. Abuse of Power.   New York: Viking
Press, 1967. 244p. Criticizes what the author sees as the
American tendencies to emphasize military solutions to
foreign relations problems and to support anti-communist
regimes abroad that neither merit American aid nor can
govern effectively.   Draper emphasizes Vietnam, but also

discusses Cuba and the Dominican Republic.

Periodical Articles

797. Adams, Paul D. "Strike Command." Military Review 42 (May 1962):2-10. Describes the functions, organization, and training of STRICOM, a joint army-air force command which is designed to meet all types of contingencies, from reinforcing other joint commands under general war conditions to counterinsurgency and disaster assistance.

798. Granger, Clinton E., Jr. "Global Deployments." Military Review 44 (October 1964):9-14. Examines the question of whether to concentrate on a strategic reserve or on the deployment of most forces in contested or perhaps to be contested areas of the world.

799. Wheeler, Earle G. "The Design of Military Power." Military Review 43 (February 1963):16-25. Reviews the components of national power and surveys the application of American power in the Laotian, Berlin, and Cuban crises of the early 1960's.

Berlin Crisis, 1961

Official Policy Statements

800. Kennedy, John F. "Radio and Television Report to the American People on the Berlin Crisis. July 25, 1961." In Public Papers of the Presidents of the United States: John F. Kennedy 1961, 533-540. Washington, D.C.: Government Printing Office, 1962. Notes Khruschev's threats and recites Allied rights in Berlin. Kennedy also reviews his defense program and his new requests for increases in personnel and additional conventional weapons.

801. Kennedy, John F. "Remarks in the Rudolph Wilde Platz, Berlin. June 26, 1963." In Public Papers of the Presidents of the United States: John F. Kennedy 1963, 524-525. Washington, D.C.: Government Printing Office, 1964. Contrasts the freedom and tyranny represented by East and West Berlin. Kennedy seems to attack the existence of the German Democratic Republic.

Periodical Articles

802. Schick, Jack M. "The Berlin Crisis of 1961 and U.S. Military Strategy." Orbis 8 (Winter 1965):816-831. Analyzes the Kennedy administration's responses. Schick criticizes the United States for "going it alone" in the face of concerns expressed by its major European allies.

803. Smith, Jean Edward. "Berlin Confrontation." Virginia Quarterly Review 42 (Summer 1966):349-365. Provides a thorough analysis of the Berlin crisis of 1961, which Smith

compares to the Berlin blockade of 1948-1949.

804. Viotti, Paul R. "Berlin and Conflict Management with
the USSR." Orbis 28 (Fall 1984):575-591. Reviews American
involvement with Berlin, including the 1961 crisis, and the
relatively successful efforts to stablize the Berlin situation.

Bay of Pigs

Official Policy Statements

805. Eisenhower, Dwight D. "Statement by the President
Restating United States Policy Toward Cuba. January 26,
1960." In Public Papers of the Presidents of the United
States: Dwight D. Eisenhower 1960-61, 134-136. Washington,
D.C.: Government Printing Office, 1961. Reviews Eisenhower's discussions with Secretary of State Herter and
Ambassador Bonsal on Cuban-American relations. Eisenhower
affirms that the United States "adheres strictly to the
policy of nonintervention" and works to "prevent illegal
acts... directed against other governments."

806. Eisenhower, Dwight D. "Statement by the President on
Terminating Diplomatic Relations with Cuba. January 3,
1961." In Public Papers of the Presidents of the United
States: Dwight D. Eisenhower 1960-61, 891. Washington,
D.C.: Government Printing Office, 1961. Explains that the
United States is ending relations with Cuba because of the
demand that the United States Embassy staff be limited to
eleven persons. This action, however, is "only the latest
of a long series of harassments, baseless accusations, and
vilification."

807. Kennedy, John F. "The President's News Conference of
April 12, 1961." In Public Papers of the Presidents of the
United States: John F. Kennedy 1961, 258-265. Washington,
D.C.: Government Printing Office, 1962. Discusses
Kennedy's views of the Castro regime. Kennedy stated his
opposition to American military intervention in Cuba or
basing an anti-Castro attack in the United States.

808. Kennedy, John F. "Message to Chairman Khruschev
Concerning the Meaning of Events in Cuba. April 18, 1961."
In Public Papers of the Presidents of the United States:
John F. Kennedy 1961, 286-287. Washington, D.C.: Government Printing Office, 1962. Reaffirms the determination of
the United States not to intervene in Cuba. Kennedy
states, however, that Americans admire the anti-Castro
Cubans and that the "United States can take no action to
stifle the spirit of liberty."

Reports

809. Operation Zapata: The "Ultrasensitive" Report and Testimony of the Board of Inquiry on the Bay of Pigs. Frederick, Maryland: University Publications of America, Inc. 1981. 267p. Includes testimony taken during the spring of 1961, immediately following the unsuccessful invasion. Although, for security reasons the record is far from complete, this volume is an essential source.

Books

810. Higgins, Trumbull. The Perfect Failure: Kennedy, Eisenhower, and the CIA at the Bay of Pigs. New York: W.W. Norton, 1987. 224p. Focuses primarily on Kennedy's role in the planning and implementation of the invasion. Higgins stresses deficiencies in the CIA's performance and criticizes Kennedy for having followed its recommendations too readily.

811. Wyden, Peter. Bay of Pigs: The Untold Story. New York: Simon & Schuster, 1979. 352p. Probably the definitive account, pending the release of new documentation. Wyden succeeded in interviewing Fidel Castro, among many other participants in the events of the invasion and its defeat.

Periodical Articles

812. Sandman, Joshua H. "Analyzing Foreign Policy Crisis Situations: The Bay of Pigs." Presidential Studies Quarterly 16 (Spring 1986):310-316. Examines decision-making before and during the Bay of Pigs invasion, focusing on Kennedy's role. Sandman argues that Kennedy learned a great deal from this episode, in which he did not participate as actively as he might have.

813. Vandenbroucke, Lucien S. "Anatomy of a Failure: The Decision to Land at the Bay of Pigs." Political Science Quarterly 99 (Fall 1984):471-491. Assesses various approaches to analyzing the decision to intervene in Cuba. Vandenbroucke utilizes methodology from Graham T. Allison's Essence of Decision: Explaining the Cuban Missile Crisis.

814. Wilcox, Arthur W. "Cuba's Place in U.S. Naval Strategy." United States Naval Institute Proceedings 88 (December 1962):38-47. Examines American naval and strategic thinking about Cuba from the early 19th century onward, emphasizing Mahan's views. Wilcox makes reference to current concerns, notably the Cuban adherence to the Soviet bloc in 1961, and stresses the need to retain Guantánamo Bay.

Cuban Missile Crisis

Official Policy Statements

815. Kennedy, John F. "Radio and Television Report to the American People on the Soviet Arms Buildup in Cuba. October 22, 1962." In Public Papers of the Presidents of the United States: John F. Kennedy 1962, 806-809. Washington, D.C.: Government Printing Office, 1963. Announces the discovery of Soviet missile installations under construction in Cuba. Kennedy briefly describes the missiles and mentions the presence of Soviet bombers in Cuba. He proclaims a blockade of Cuba and lists six other steps being taken to deal with the crisis.

816. Kennedy, John F.   "Message to Chairman Khruschev Calling for Removal of Soviet Missiles from Cuba. October 27, 1962."   In Public Papers of the Presidents of the United States: John F. Kennedy 1962, 813-814. Washington, D.C.: Government Printing Office, 1963.   Welcomes Khruschev's response to Kennedy's message to U Thant, Acting Secretary-General of the United Nations, concerning the crisis. He pledges that no American invasion of Cuba will be made. Kennedy closes with an expression of his desire to pursue disarmament.

817. Kennedy, John F. "Message in Reply to a Broadcast by Chairman Khruschev on the Cuban Crisis. October 28, 1962." In Public Papers of the Presidents of the United States: John F. Kennedy 1962, 814-815. Washington, D.C.: Government Printing Office, 1963. Notes progress on resolving the missile crisis and indicates further that Kennedy is interested in disarmament and especially in halting the "proliferation of nuclear weapons" and an end to nuclear weapons tests.

Bibliography

818. Brune, Lester H. The Missile Crisis of October 1962: A Review of Issues and References. Claremont, California: Regina Books, 1985. Consists of a summary of the crisis, several more detailed chapters on the confrontation, and a bibliographic essay. Relatively extensive annotations are provided for the entries, which refer to various types of materials, including books, articles and government publications.

Books

819. Allison, Graham T. Essence of Decision: Explaining the Cuban Missile Crisis. Boston: Little, Brown & Company, 1971. 338p. Remains the best known study of the crisis. Allison deals with all phases of the missile problem in a readable, but sophisticated manner.

820. Leighton, Richard M. The Cuban Missile Crisis of 1962-
-A Case in National Security Crisis Management. 55p.
Washington, D.C.: National Defense University, 1978. SOD
D5.410:C89. Focuses on Kennedy's decisions and the ways in
which they were reached. Includes a lengthy chronology of
the missile affair.

Periodical Articles

821. Hampson, Fen Osler.   "The Divided Decision-Maker:
American Domestic Politics and the Cuban Crises." International Security 9 (Winter 1984-1985):130-165.   Discusses
the interaction of American internal politics and American
policies toward Cuba during crises in 1962, 1970, and 1979.

822. Pocalyko, Michael N. "25 Years After the Blink."
United States Naval Institute Proceedings 113 (September
1987):41-47.   Examines the influence of the Cuban missile
crisis on subsequent East-West confrontations, focusing on
the naval "quarantine" of Cuba. Pocalyko praises Kennedy's
leadership, but warns that another president might not act
as effectively as he did.

823. Sugden, G. Scott. "Public Diplomacy and the Missiles
of October." Naval War College Review 24 (October 1971):28-
43. Discusses the Kennedy administration's successful
influence on the media. Sugden discusses several phases of
Kennedy's media strategy which provided support for his
foreign policies.

824. Trachtenberg, Marc. "The Influence of Nuclear Weapons
in the Cuban Missile Crisis." International Security 10
(Summer 1985):137-163.   Argues that the Soviets were
deterred from extreme measures by the United States'
nuclear weapons superiority.

The Dominican Republic Intervention, 1965-1966

Official Policy Statements

825. Johnson, Lyndon B. "Statement by the President Upon
Ordering Troops Into Dominican Republic. April 28, 1965."
In Public Papers of the Presidents of the United States:
Lyndon B. Johnson 1965, I, 461. Washington, D.C.: Government Printing Office, 1966.   Asserts that American forces
entered the Dominican Republic to protect American and
other foreign nationals. Johnson expresses a desire for a
cease-fire in the civil war in the Dominican Republic.

826. Johnson, Lyndon B. "Statement by the President on the
Situation in the Dominican Republic. April 30, 1965." In
Public Papers of the Presidents of the United States:
Lyndon B. Johnson 1965, I, 465-466. Washington, D.C.:
Government Printing Office, 1966. Describes American rescue
efforts in the Dominican Republic and states that "violence

and disorder have increased" owing to the involvement of revolutionaries "trained outside the Dominican Republic." Johnson discusses the need for swift action by the Organization of American States and pledges American support for OAS decisions.

Books

827. Georgetown University. Center for Strategic Studies. Dominican Action--1965:   Intervention or Cooperation? Washington, D.C.: Georgetown University, 1966. 85p. Constitutes a reference book on the intervention. The volume provides a chronological outline of the crisis and supplies other types of factual material.

828. Gleijeses, Piero.   The Dominican Crisis: The 1965 Constitutionalist Revolt and American Intervention. Baltimore: Johns Hopkins University Press, 1978. 460p. Vigorously defends Juan Bosch's role in the episode and is generally critical of American actions preceding and during the intervention.

829. Lowenthal, Abraham F. The Dominican Intervention. Cambridge: Harvard University Press, 1972. 246p. Deals primarily with decision-making by the Johnson administration in the crisis.

830. Martin, John Barlow. Overtaken by Events: The Dominican Crisis-From the Fall of Trujillo to the Civil War. Garden City, New York: Doubleday & Company, Inc., 1966. 821p. Probably the most detailed defense of the Johnson administration's actions in the crisis.   Martin takes the view that, without American involvement, the communists would have taken control of the Bosch movement.

Chapter 5

Vietnam and Its Impact on National Security

The Vietnam conflict constituted a profound political and military challenge to American thinking about war and world politics. The Vietnam experience still heavily colors elite and public opinion about current military-political problems facing the United States, as shown by the continuing debate over American involvement with Central America.

Initially, South Vietnamese and American planners feared an invasion of South Vietnam by North Vietnam similar to the North Korean invasion of South Korea in 1950. Only gradually did their attention turn to the problem of internal subversion. For too long, militia units were neglected, giving communist insurgents the opportunity to weaken government control of the countryside.

New forms of weaponry and new tactics such as defoliation were employed with often disputed results. A very large American support effort sometimes seemed to dwarf American combat forces, while for much of the 1960's South Vietnamese mobilization left something to be desired. From an advisory effort, American commitment moved to air bombardment and, finally, to the use of American ground forces. Political factors forced a reversion to military assistance and advice, that is, Vietnamization. Ultimately, Vietnamization failed when South Vietnam fought in 1975 without sufficient assistance and without American air support.

In many respects, Vietnam was a replay of the American experience in the Caribbean between 1910 and 1933. In several countries, American forces were deployed, civic action programs undertaken, elections held, and as domestic American support dwindled, a hurried process of "Haitianization" or "Nicaraguanization" occurred. Finally, American military commitments were ended unilaterally.

Reference Sources

Bibliographies

831. Burns, Richard Dean, and Milton Leitenberg. The Wars in Vietnam, Cambodia and Laos, 1945-1982: A Bibliographic

Guide. Santa Barbara, California: ABC-CLIO, 1984. 290p.
The most complete bibliography to date on the Indochina
wars. It is divided by hundreds of headings, and many
entries are annotated.

832. Peake, Louis A. The United States in the Vietnam War
1954-1975: A Selected, Annotated Bibliography. New York:
Garland Publishing, Inc., 1986. 600p. Very well organized
compilation with rather extensive annotations. The
bibliography is usefully divided into a large number of
topics and subtopics, and there is a relatively detailed
subject index. All aspects of the wars are dealt with.

833. Petitmermet, Jane. The Vietnam Experience: A Selected
Bibliography. Washington, D.C.: National Defense
University Library, 1986. 65p. Unannotated bibliography
covering government documents, research institute reports,
periodical articles, and even fiction and media. It is
usefully organized into ten sections such as "Military
Strategy" and the "Role of the Media."

834. Sugnet, Christopher L., and John T. Hickey, with
Robert Crispino. Vietnam War Bibliography. Lexington,
Massachusetts: Lexington Books, 1983. 592p. Based solely on
the extensive John M. Echols collection at Cornell
University, this work provides broad coverage of the
American effort in Vietnam. The bibliography is very
thoroughly indexed.

Documentary Sources

835. United States. Department of Defense. United States-
Vietnam Relations, 1945-67. Washington, D.C.: Government
Printing Office, 1971. 12 volumes. SOD Y4.Ar5/2:v67/3/945-
67 Bk 1-12. Official text of the "Pentagon papers," which
contains much material not in other editions.

836. United States. Department of Defense. The Pentagon
Papers: The Defense Department History of United States
Decision-Making on Vietnam. The Senator Gravel Edition. 5
volumes. Boston: Beacon Press, 1971-1972. Contains only a
portion of the text issued by the government, but includes
some documents not in the official version. The relations
between the editions is explained in the last volume, which
also contains a number of essays by prominent critics of
the American commitment in Vietnam such as Noam Chomsky and
Howard Zinn.

837. Vietnam: National Security Files, November 1963-June
1965. Frederick, Maryland: University Publications of
America, Inc. Huge collection of materials from the
National Security Council dealing with the critical period
from the fall of Diem regime through the commitment of
ground troops to Vietnam. The documents go far beyond the
National Security Council files, embracing items prepared
by American agencies in Vietnam, the Joint Chiefs of Staff

and other organizations.

838.   The War in Vietnam: Classified Histories by the
National Security Council. Frederick, Maryland: University
Publications of America, Inc. Somewhat similar to the
Pentagon Papers, but much more extensive, this microfilm
collection consists of analyses prepared between 1964 and
1968. Included are reports from General Westmoreland and
the United States Embassy in Saigon.

Other Reference Sources

839.   Summers, Harry G., Jr. Vietnam War Almanac. New York:
Facts on File, 1985. 400p. An encyclopedic treatment of the
Vietnam conflict. Summers includes a lengthy chronology
and a narrative section on Vietnam and its history.

General Studies

840.   Baritz, Loren. Backfire: A History of How American
Culture Led Us into Vietnam and Made Us Fight the Way We
Did. New York: William Morrow and Company, Inc., 1985.
Three parts discuss American messianism and expansion, the
gradual American commitment to Vietnam, and Americans at
war in Vietnam. The last section surveys the many
criticisms made of American performance.

841.   Chodes, John J. The Myth of America's Military Power.
Boston: Branden Press, 1972. 224p. Attacks the overreliance
on air power during and after World War II and other flawed
approaches to combat which helped, over time, to bring on
the American failure in Vietnam.

842.   Ellsberg, Daniel. Papers on the War. New York:
Simon & Schuster, 1972. 309p. Consists of papers, articles,
and book reviews Ellsberg wrote in the 1960's and 1970's.
They cover various topics related to the Vietnam conflict.
Ellsberg is best known for his disclosure of the "Pentagon
Papers."

843.   Fitzgerald, Frances. Fire in the Lake; the
Vietnamese and the Americans in Vietnam. Boston: Little,
Brown and Company, 1972. Criticizes American military
operations and pacification activities in Vietnam. Much
acclaimed in the 1970's, this remains an important study of
the war.

844.   Kolko, Gabriel. Anatomy of A War; Vietnam, the
United States, and the Modern Historical Experience. New
York: Pantheon Books, 1985. 491p. Presents an analysis
that is highly critical of the United States and the
Republic of Vietnam and very sympathetic to the National
Liberation Front and the Democratic Republic of Vietnam.
Kolko made much use of materials from North Vietnam and
emphasizes the development of communism in Vietnam.

845. Lewy, Guenter. America in Vietnam. New York: Oxford University Press, 1978. 540p. Perhaps the most important of those studies that are supportive of the American policies in Vietnam. Lewy defends American conduct, although he criticizes some aspects of the military side of the war.

846. Lomperis, Timothy J. The War Everyone Lost--and Won: America's Intervention in Viet Nam's Twin Struggles. Baton Rouge: Louisiana State University Press, 1984. 216p. Focuses on the battle for popular support between the communists and the non-communist Vietnamese and the latter's American allies. Ultimately, neither side achieved "legitimacy," Lomperis argues.

847. Nixon, Richard M. No More Vietnams. New York: Arbor House, 1985. Reviews the history of American involvement, especially Nixon's Vietnam policies. Nixon asserts that the Republic of Vietnam fell in 1975 because Congress ignored American commitments to its ally. The book concludes with Nixon's recommendation that the United States increase, signficantly, its assistance to Third World countries in order to forestall the Soviets.

848. Schlight, John, editor. The Second Indochina War: Proceedings of a Symposium Held at Airlie, Virginia 7-9 November 1984. Washington, D.C.: Government Printing Office, 1986. 276p. SOD D114.2:In2 Exceptionally important papers from a symposium sponsored by the United States Army Center of Military History. Major students of the Vietnam conflict such as Douglas Pike, George C. Herring, and Ronald H. Spector presented papers; commentaries were provided by Richard D. Challener, Robert W. Komer, and others. The studies deal with the decisions leading to intervention, American prosecution of the war, and the impact of the conflict on the United States and its allies.

849. Thayer, Thomas C. War Without Fronts: The American Experience in Vietnam. Boulder, Colorado: Westview Press, 1985. 276p. Deals with ground combat in its various forms, pacification and internal security, and civic action. There is a brief section on the impact of air power. This is an important study of how the land war was actually fought and how well it was conducted.

850. Trooboff, Peter, editor. Law and Responsibility in Warfare: the Vietnam Experience. Chapel Hill: University of North Carolina Press, 1975. 280p. An important collection of essays on the conduct of the Vietnam war by American forces. Authors include Paul Warnke, Robert W. Komer, and others.

Decision-making Process

Books

851. Baral, Jaya Krishna. The Pentagon and the Making of US Foreign Policy; a Case Study of Vietnam, 1960-1968. Atlantic Highlands, New Jersey: Humanities Press, 1978. 333p. Examines the role of the Department of Defense in decision-making on Vietnam policy. Baral also considers Congressional involvement in the decisions he studies.

852. Gelb, Leslie H. with Richard K. Betts. The Irony of Vietnam; the System Worked. Washington, D.C.: Brookings Institution, 1979, 387p. Asserts that the advisory machinery of government, i.e., the career civil service, produced policies for the Vietnam problem and that, in this sense, "the system worked." The authors carry their analysis up to 1968, when Johnson decided to pursue negotiations with the communists.

853. Graff, Henry F. The Tuesday Cabinet: Deliberation and Decision on Peace and War under Lyndon B. Johnson. Englewood Cliffs, New Jersey: Prentice-Hall, Inc., 1970. 200p. Reviews discussions between Johnson and his closest advisers on strategic issues related to the American commitment in Vietnam. Graff deals with the period from early 1965 to late 1968 when Johnson ended the bombing of North Vietnam.

854. Kinnard, Douglas. The War Managers. Hanover, New Hampshire: Published for the University of Vermont by the University Press of New England, 1977. 216p. Provides an invaluable perspective on the views of general grade officers who served in Vietnam. Perhaps the most striking finding from Kinnard's survey was the generals' emphasis on the lack of clear American objectives. A large minority expressed concern about large-scale operations and overuse of firepower in the conflict.

855. Palmer, Bruce, Jr. The 25-Year War: America's Military Role in Vietnam. New York: Simon & Schuster, Inc., 1984. 248p. Praises many aspects of American performance in Vietnam, but faults many decisions made in Washington, for example, not mobilizing reserve and national guard forces. Palmer believes that North Vietnam could have been put under pressure by activating an amphibious threat and that United States forces should have been concentrated on the borders of South Vietnam.

856. Sullivan, Michael P. The Vietnam War: A Study in the Making of American Policy. Lexington: University Press of Kentucky, 1985. 208p. Sophisticated analysis of American decision-making in regard to Vietnam. Sullivan uses content analysis of presidential documents and public opinion polls, among other sources, to explore the impact of world politics on decisions made within one nation.

Essays and Periodical Articles

857.   Beavers, Roy L. "An Absence of Accountability."
United States Naval Institute Proceedings 102 (January
1970):18-23. Analyzes the United States political system
to determine reasons for the American failure in Vietnam.
Beavers attributes most problems to political leaders and
the media.

858.   Burdick, Frank A. "Vietnam Revisioned: The Military
Campaign Against Civilian Control." Democracy 2 (January
1982):36-52.   Assails the view that civilian political
leaders prevented an effective strategy in Vietnam. Burdick focuses on General Westmoreland's arguments along this
line.

859.   Chamberland, Dennis.   "Interview: Westmoreland."
United States Naval Institute Proceedings 112 (July 1986):
45-48. Former commander of United States forces in Vietnam
recalls the navy's part in the conflict.   Westmoreland
describes the various types of support rendered by naval
forces and briefly refers to the general strategy of the
war.

860.   Davidson, Michael W. "Senior Officers and Vietnam
Policymaking." Parameters 16 (Spring 1986):55-62. Compares
presidential relations with key military leaders during
World War II, in the 1950's under Eisenhower, and in the
1960's under Kennedy and Johnson. During the Vietnam war,
military leaders had a much lesser role than they had
enjoyed earlier.

861.   Gelb, Leslie H. "The Essential Domino: American
Politics and Vietnam." Foreign Affairs 50 (April 1972):
459-475.   Focuses on the vital role that American public
opinion played in the war. Gelb discusses the political
and military planning by the United States and the Democratic Republic of Vietnam and the problems faced by the
Kennedy, Johnson, and Nixon administrations in dealing with
the Vietnam situation.

862.   Hoopes, Townsend. "Legacy of the Cold War in
Indochina." Foreign Affairs 48 (April 1970):601-616.
Analyzes the attitudes and policies that brought about
large-scale American intervention. Hoopes enthusiastically
supports complete withdrawal from Indochina.

863.   Huglin, Henry C. "Our Gains from Success in
Vietnam." Air University Review 20 (January-February
1969):71-78. Discusses advantages to the United States of
successes in Vietnam. The United States has been faithful
to its allies and has promoted stability in Indonesia.

864.   Lansdale, Edward G. "Viet Nam: Still the Search for
Goals." Foreign Affairs 47 (January 1968):92-98. Lansdale
views the American objective as the defense of democracy.

865.   Lewy, Guenter.   "Some Political-Military Lessons of the Vietnam War." Parameters 14 (January 1984):2-14. Presents a general critique of American methods of war in Vietnam.   Republic of Vietnam armed forces followed American precepts, but were not prepared to fight American-style campaigns without massive support.

866.   Nardin, Terry, and Jerome Slater.   "Vietnam Revisited." World Politics 33 (March 1981):436-448. Seeks to refute various analyses of the Vietnam conflict that view the war favorably.   The authors argue that the revisionist works overlook many of the moral and legal problems associated with the war.

867.   Payne, Don H.   "What Happens After Vietnam?" Military Review 48 (September 1968):42-48. Asserts that American goals need to be reassessed and that the answers should be applied in Vietnam.

868.   Pelz, Stephen.   "John F. Kennedy's 1961 Vietnam War Decisions." Journal of Strategic Studies 4 (December 1981): 356-385. Asserts that Kennedy always had a significant commitment to the Republic of Vietnam and never contemplated withdrawal of American forces.   Pelz criticizes Kennedy's Vietnam strategy.

869.   Powe, Marc B.   "The US Army After the Fall of Vietnam: A Contemporary Dilemma." Military Review 56 (February 1976): 3-17.   Focuses on organizational and technological shortcomings of the army during the Vietnam war.

870.   Race, Jeffrey. "Vietnam Intervention: Systematic Distortion in Policy-Making." Armed Forces and Society 2 (Spring 1976):377-396.   Focuses on American counter-insurgency and intervention theory during the Vietnam conflict.

871.   Schandler, Herbert Y.   "JCS Strategic Planning and Vietnam: The Search for An Objective." In Military Planning in the Twentieth Century: Proceedings of the Eleventh Military History Symposium 10-12 October 1984, edited by Harry R. Borowski. Washington, D.C.: Government Printing Office, 1984.   SOD D305.12:68. Uses the Vietnam conflict to test the accuracy of criticisms commonly made of the Joint Chiefs of Staff.   A serious communications gap between Johnson and the JCS developed, which resulted in a lack of direction for the war.

872.   Silverman, Jerry Mark.   "The Domino Theory: Alternatives to a Self-Fulfilling Prophecy." Asian Survey 15 (November 1975):915-939. Examines the domino theory during the Vietnam war.

873.   Stuckey, John D., and Joseph H. Pistorios. "Mobiliza-

tion for the Vietnam War: A Political and Military Catastrophe." Parameters 15 (Spring 1985):26-38. Details the serious effects that not having the trained personnel in the National Guard and reserve forces available for service in Vietnam had on the armed services during the Vietnam conflict.

874.   Summers, Harry G., Jr.   "Lessons: A Soldier's View." Wilson Quarterly 7 (Summer 1983):125-135. Asserts that the failure of Congress to support the American effort in Vietnam prevented employment of an effective strategy. Summers also points to the lack of clear American objectives in Vietnam.

875.   Twining, David T.   "Vietnam and the Six Criteria for the Use of Military Force." Parameters 15 (April 1985):10-18. Analyzes Secretary of Defense Weinberger's speech of November 28, 1984, and compares the principles Weinberger articulated with the policies the United States followed during the Vietnam conflict.

876.   Westmoreland, William C.   "Vietnam in Perpsective." Military Review 59 (January 1979):34-43. Places the blame for failure in Vietnam on nonmilitary factors such as poor leadership by political figures and media hostility toward the war.

877.   Williams, R.E., Jr.   "After Vietnam." United States Naval Institute Proceedings 96 (April 1970):18-25. Argues that naval forces can and should uphold American defense commitments in Asia after United States forces leave Vietnam. Williams also asserts that nuclear weapons should all be based at sea.

Comparative Studies

Books

878.   Donovan, Robert J.   Nemesis: Truman and Johnson in the Coils of War in Asia. New York: St. Martin's Press/Marek, 1984. 256p. Compares Truman and the Korean War with Johnson and the Vietnam conflict. Donovan puts more emphasis on the political aspects than military facets.

879.   Reston, James.   Sherman's March and Vietnam. New York: Macmillan, 1984. 304p. Compares Sherman's "March to the sea" in 1864 with American handling of the Vietnam war. Reston asserts that many tactics used in Vietnam had their origins in Sherman's ruthless campaign.

880.   Sarkesian, Sam C. America's Forgotten Wars: The Counterrevolutionary Past and Lessons for the Future. Westport, Connecticut: Greenwood Press, 1984. 265p. Compares the United States commitment in Vietnam (1965-1970) to similar conflicts with the Seminole Indians (1835-1842), the Philippine Insurrection (1899-1902), and Mexican

irregulars (1916).

Periodical Articles

881. Drummond, Stuart. "Korea and Vietnam: Some Specula-
tions About the Possible Influence of the Korean War on
American Policy in Vietnam." Army Quarterly and Defence
Journal 97 (October 1968):65-71. Suggests that the Korean
War experience influenced American decision makers to put
too much faith in air power; Vietnam turned out to be very
different from the war in Korea.

882. Long, William F. "The Spectre of Dien Bien Phu."
Military Review 46 (October 1966):35-39. Discusses the
reasons why the French lost Indochina. The current (1966)
situation is far different from the 1950's. The
differences include the greater military power of the
United States as compared to France.

883. McMahon, John F., Jr. "Vietnam: Our World War II
Legacy." Air University Review 19 (July-August 1968):59-66.
Discusses the deepening American commitment to Vietnam
during the post-World War II years. McMahon links this
with what he sees as the American emphasis in the late
1950's on limited war.

The Advisor War

Books

884. Hooper, Edwin Bickford and others. The United States
Navy and the Vietnam Conflict: Volume I--The Setting of the
Stage to 1959. Washington, D.C.: Government Printing
Office, 1976. 460p. SOD:D207.10/3:1 Concentrates on early
United States Navy advisory activities in Vietnam after the
departure of the French, but a lengthy section deals with
the Dien Bien Phu crisis and American discussions of large-
scale intervention.

885. Spector, Ronald H. The United States Army in Vietnam
Advice and Support: The Early Years 1941-1960. Washington,
D.C.: Center of Military History, United States Army, 1983.
Detailed study portrays tensions between the Americans and
Vietnamese and among American agencies and individuals in
Vietnam. This was the first period of "Vietnamization" in
a sense.

Periodical Articles

886. Black, Edwin F. "Advisory Warfare vs. Sanctuary
Warfare." United States Naval Institute Proceedings 91
(February 1965):34-42. Uses the Vietnam experience to
generalize about the two types of warfare. Black discusses
the changing nature of sanctuaries, which are now usually
nations protected by the Soviet Union. The article

includes an extensive examination of counterinsurgency.

887. Denno, Bryce F. "New War in Vietnam." United States
Naval Institute Proceedings 92 (March 1966):70-79. Details
the gradual involvement of the United States in Vietnam and
counsels Americans to adjust to a long war. Denno
describes military operations and pacification programs in
Vietnam. American advisers to Vietnamese forces remain an
important factor despite the deployment of American combat
units.

888. Ray, James F. "The District Advisor." Military Review
45 (May 1965):3-8. Analyzes the problems facing district
advisers in Vietnam. Ray recommends that special training
be given officers assigned in this capacity.

889. Slaff, Allan P. "Naval Advisor Vietnam." United
States Naval Institute Proceedings 95 (April 1969):38-44.
Praises the work of the many American naval advisers in the
Republic of Vietnam. Slaff feels that they succeeded in
operating effectively with their Vietnamese counterparts.

The Commitment of Ground Forces

Official Policy Statements

890. Johnson, Lyndon B. "Statement by the President on
Viet-Nam.   March 25, 1965," In Public Papers of the
Presidents of the United States: Lyndon B. Johnson 1965, I,
319. Washington, D.C.: Government Printing Office, 1966.
Assails communist aggression against the Republic of
Vietnam and implies that the conflict in Vietnam is not a
colonial war. Johnson also expresses great interest in
negotiations to end the war.

891.   Johnson, Lyndon B.   "Address at Johns Hopkins
University: 'Peace Without Conquest.' April 7, 1965" In
Public Papers of the Presidents of the United States:
Lyndon B. Johnson 1965, I, 394-399. Washington, D.C.:
Government Printing Office, 1966. Explains the reasons for
the United States commitment to Vietnam and pledges
continuance of American efforts. He decries the use of
force and paints a picture of a "cooperative effort for
development" in Southeast Asia.

892. Johnson, Lyndon B. "Remarks to Committee Members on
the Need for Additional Appropriations for Military
Purposes in Viet-Nam and the Dominican Republic. May 4,
1965." In Public Papers of the Presidents of the United
States: Lyndon B. Johnson 1965, I, 484-492. Washington,
D.C.: Government Printing Office, 1966. Asserts that
special funds are needed "to halt communist aggression."
The statement explains at length the American policies in
Vietnam, including the bombing offensive against North
Vietnam. About half the address deals with the emergency

in the Dominican Republic.

893. Johnson, Lyndon B.   "The President's News Conference
of July 28, 1965." In Public Papers of the Presidents of
the United States: Lyndon B. Johnson 1965, II, 794-798.
Washington, D.C.: Government Printing Office, 1966.
Annonnces that the "Air Mobile Division" and other military
forces have been ordered to Vietnam, that draft calls have
been doubled, and that no reserve forces have been put on
active duty. Johnson summarizes current American policies
in Southeast Asia.

Books

894. Austin, Anthony. The President's War; the Story of
the Tonkin Gulf Resolution and How the Nation was Trapped
in Vietnam. Philadelphia: Lippincott, 1971. 368p. Austin
reconstructs the events of the Tonkin Gulf crisis and the
resulting Congressional endorsement of Johnson's policies.
The study is based on New York Times stories and interviews.

895. Gallucci, Robert L.   Neither Peace Nor Honor: the
Politics of American Military Policy in Viet-Nam.
Baltimore: Johns Hopkins University Press, 1975.   187p.
Focuses on specific decisions concerning the Vietnam
intervention. After delineating the bureaucratic struggles
over Vietnam decisions, Gallucci asserts that the State
Department should have taken a more activist course.

General Strategy

Books

896. Schandler, Herbert Y.   The Unmaking of a President;
Lyndon Johnson and Vietnam. Princeton: Princeton University Press, 1977. 419p. Discusses American strategy after
the Tet offensive and the early efforts to reach a
settlement. Schandler examines the reasons for changes in
policy in 1968 and the problems of assuring that
alternative policies are properly evaluated within the
executive branch.

897. Summers, Harry G. On Strategy; A Critical Analysis of
the Vietnam War. Novato, California: Presidio Press, 1982.
240p. Presents one of the most significant critiques of
American strategy in Vietnam. Summers blames decision
makers for not having rallied public opinion behind the war
and for not having acted more aggressively against North
Vietnam.

898. Westmoreland, William C. A Soldier Reports. Garden
City, New York: Doubleday & Company, 1976. 466p. Defends
Westmoreland's role as commanding general of American
forces during much of the war. Westmoreland places much of
the blame for failures on less than adequate support from

the government.

Essays and Periodical Articles

899.   Brown, Michael L.   "Vietnam: Learning From the
Debate."   Military Review 67 (February 1987):48-55.
Discusses the "debate" over the question of whether Vietnam
was a "war" or an "insurgency situation." Brown believes
some lessons can be learned from the fact that such a
debate continues.

900.   Geneste, Marc E.   "Vietnam...A New Type of War?"
United States Naval Institute Proceedings 94 (May 1968):66-
77.   French officer and Indochina veteran compares his
country's and the American experiences in Vietnam. Geneste
stresses that technology cannot win primitive wars; either
the counterinsurgents have to learn guerrilla tactics or
have to use extreme measures such as nuclear weapons.
Geneste speculates that, eventually, small nuclear devices
may end warfare.

901.   Grinter, Lawrence E.   "How They Lost: Doctrines,
Strategies, and Outcomes of the Vietnam War." Asian Survey
15 (December 1975):1114-1132.   Covers the entire period of
the second Indochina war in an effort to identify the
causes of the demise of the Republic of Vietnam.   Grinter
deals in part with Department of State and CIA involvement
in military affairs.

902.   Hackworth, David H.   "Target Acquisition: Vietnam
Style." Military Review 48 (April 1968):73-79.   Discusses
the problem of locating enemy troop concentrations and
bases.   Hackworth advocates use of a number of expedients
to eliminate this problem.

903.   Heilbrunn, Otto. "How Many Men to Vietnam?" Military
Review 45 (December 1965):27-33.   Proposes that forces in
Vietnam be developed to about five hundred and fifty
thousand, an interesting prophecy since American troop
strength peaked at not too much more.   Heilbrunn compares
manpower requirements in Vietnam with those in Malaya and
in East Africa during the Mau Mau uprising.

904.   Herring, George C.   "American Strategy in Vietnam:
The Post War Debate." Military Affairs 46 (February
1982):57-63.   Reviews various theoretical approaches to the
Vietnam war. Three general concepts of the conflict appear
to have emerged.

905.   Hoffmann, Stanley and others.   "Vietnam Reappraised."
International Security 6 (Summer 1981):3-26.   Puts the
Vietnam conflict into the context of United States rela-
tions with Third World nations.

906.   Hughes, Wayne P., Jr.   "Vietnam: Winnable War?"
United States Naval Institute Proceedings 103 (July

1977):60-65. Argues that the United States limited its
efforts in Vietnam to an excessive degree. Hughes believes
that vigorous air attacks in 1965 and 1966 against North
Vietnam similar to those launched in 1972 could have won
the war.

907. Kinnard, Douglas. "The 'Strategy' of the War in
South Vietnam." In Vietnam in Remission, edited by James F.
Veninga and Harry A. Wilmer, 19-32. College Station: Texas
A&M University Press, 1985. Suggests that various
approaches to the war were developed by American decision
makers, but no overall strategy emerged. Kinnard devotes
much attention to "Vietnamization" and the inability of
Vietnamese forces to operate effectively without American
firepower.

908. Michael, Stanley J., Jr. "Vietnam: Failure to Follow
the Principles of War." Marine Corps Gazette 61 (August
1977):56-62. Critiques both the American and communist
efforts in Vietnam. Michael asserts that the United States
lost because of its poor strategy.

909. Moore, William C. "History, Vietnam, and the Concept
of Deterrence." Air University Review 20 (September-October
1969):58-63. Suggests that the United States should have
left the nature of its military actions in Indochina
ambiguous, in order to heighten their deterrent effect.
Moore strongly supports the American commitment in Vietnam,
nevertheless.

910. Palmer, George E. "The Strategy of Unconventional
Warfare." Military Review 56 (August 1976):58-62.
Recommends that more attention be given to the study of
unconventional warfare. Palmer argues that Vietnam was
primarily an unconventional conflict and briefly reviews
the many successes the communists enjoyed in Vietnam
because of their tactics.

911. Pappas, Nicholas J. "The Academic Strategists and the
Vietnam War." Naval War College Review 36 (July-August
1983):32-37. Asserts that the conduct of the Vietnam
conflict from the American side was guided ultimately by
strategists outside the military or even the federal
government. Their approach was overly theoretical,
providing bad advice for those who made the decisions.

912. Pike, Douglas. "The Other Side." Wilson Quarterly 7
(Summer 1983):114-124. Examines strategic thinking in
North Vietnam from 1965 to 1975, when the North Vietnamese
succeeded in overthrowing the Saigon regime.

913. Rostow, Walter W. "The Strategic Significance of
Vietnam and Southeast Asia." In Vietnam in Remission,
edited by James F. Veninga and Harry A. Wilmer, 33-53.
College Station: Texas A&M University Press, 1985. Reviews
American policy toward Southeast Asia from 1941 to the

1980's, emphasizing continuity between administrations. Rostow also examines other powers' strategic view of the area.

914.   Rostow, Walt W.   "Vietnam and Southeast Asia: the Neglected Issue."   Parameters 13 (March 1983):2-14. Examines the geopolitical aspects of Vietnam and the surrounding region. Rostow believes that both the American public and many governmental leaders failed to recognize Vietnam's importance.

915.   Shultz, Richard.   "Strategy Lessons from an Unconventional War: The U.S. Experience in Vietnam." In Nonnuclear Conflicts in the Nuclear Age, edited by Sam C. Sarkesian, 138-184. New York: Praeger Publishers, 1980. Sees Vietnam as having been fought first through pacification, then through a more militarized strategy, and finally through Vietnamization. Shultz examines the rationale for, the execution of, and the problems of each strategy.

916.   Sights, A.P., Jr.   "Graduated Pressure in Theory and Practice." United States Naval Institute Proceedings 96 (July 1970):40-45.   Criticizes the policy of escalating American military moves in reaction to North Vietnamese operations. Hard, sudden blows can cause shocks that can bring favorable changes in the military situation. This approach was not used in Vietnam.

917.   Summers, Harry G.   "A Strategic Perception of the Vietnam War."   Parameters 13 (June 1983):41-46.   Attacks what Summers views as the American over-emphasis on counter-insurgency. Vietnam was ultimately a conventional war. Summers also decries the failure of the United States to establish objectives for the war.

918.   Trager, Frank N.   "Vietnam: The Military Requirements for Victory." Orbis 8 (Fall 1964):563-583.   Discusses the various kinds of conflict that exist within the Vietnam war.   Several strategies are needed to cope with the different challenges offered by the communists.

The Air War

Official Policy Statements

919.   Johnson, Lyndon B.   "Statement by the President Announcing Resumption of Air Strikes on North Vietnam. January 31, 1966." In Public Papers of the Presidents of the United States: Lyndon B. Johnson 1966, I, 114-116. Washington, D.C.: Government Printing Office, 1967. Reports that a 37-day respite from air attacks has not induced the North Vietnamese to negotiate for an end to the war.   Johnson states that his key advisers have warned against giving North Vietnam "continued immunity" and affirms that despite renewed bombing, further steps are

being taken by the United States to achieve peace.

920.   Johnson, Lyndon B.   "The President's Address to the
Nation Upon Announcing His Decision to Halt the Bombing of
North Vietnam.   October 31, 1968." In Public Papers of the
Presidents of the United States: Lyndon B. Johnson 1968-69,
II,   1099-1103.   Washington,   D.C.:   Government   Printing
Office, 1970.   Notes that bombing of most of North Vietnam
had   ended   in   the   spring   of   1968.   Bombing   has   only
continued because of North Vietnamese actions.   Negotia-
tions are now going well enough to justify the complete
cessation of the air attacks.

Bibliography

921.   Smith, Myron J., Jr.   Air War Southeast Asia 1961-
1973:   An   Annotated   Bibliography   and   16mm   Film   Guide.
Metuchen, New Jersey: Scarecrow Press, Inc., 1979.   298p.
Seemingly   comprehensive   for   the   years   until   the
bibliography   was   issued.   Smith's   bibliography   includes
books, articles, dissertations, and studies at the Air War
College and Air Command and Staff College, among other
materials.   Entries are very briefly annotated, and there
is a short subject index.

Books

922.   Cecil, Paul Frederick.   Herbicidal Warfare: the Ranch
Hand Project in Vietnam.   Westport, Connecticut: Greenwood
Press,   Inc.,   1986.   Reviews   the   defoliation   campaign   in
Indochina.   Cecil examines criticisms of the program and
analyzes the Agent Orange controversy.   He challenges some
of the views of defoliation presented by the media.

923.   Littauer, Ralph and Norman Uphoff, editors.   The Air
War in Vietnam.   Boston: Beacon Press, 1973. 189p. Presents
a detailed description, including an extensive compilation
of   statistics,   on   air   operations   in   Vietnam,   Laos,   and
Cambodia.   Major air weapons, including aircraft and bombs,
are also discussed.

924.   Momyer, William W.   Air Power in Three Wars (World
War II, Korea, Vietnam).   Washington,   D.C.:   Government
Printing Office, 1977?   358p. SOD D301.2:A;7/30.   Despite
the title, Momyer emphasizes Vietnam.   At the same time,
this is a genuinely comparative study, stressing tactical
air operations.

Periodical Articles

925.   Buckingham, William A., Jr.   "Operation Ranch Hand:
Herbicides in Southeast Asia." Air University Review 34
(July-August 1983):42-53.   Defends American employment of
herbicides and discounts possible ill effects on American
personnel.

926.   Cagle, Malcolm W.   "Task Force 77 in Action Off
Vietnam."   United States Naval Institute Proceedings 98
(May 1972):66-109.   Examines operations between 1964 and
1968.   Cagle discusses all aspects of the navy's air
attacks on North Vietnam and concludes that the bombing
brought North Vietnam to the point of negotiating.

927.   Eade, George J.   "Reflections on Air Power in the
Vietnam War." Air University Review 25 (November-December
1973):2-9.   Compares the air bombardments of 1965-1968 and
1972 in Vietnam with the Allied air offensive in World War
II.   Eade points to the presence of political
considerations that limited the effectiveness of bombing in
the 1960's and 1970's.

928.   Gilster, Herman L.   "Air Interdiction in Protracted
War: An Economic Evaluation." Air University Review 28
(May-June 1977):2-18.   Focuses on Laos (Operation Commando
Hunt), although Gilster briefly examines American
experiences in World War II and Korea.   Gilster concludes
that air interdiction works best when combined with active
ground attacks and that in Vietnam and in other limited
wars its value was, at best, unclear.

929.   Gilster, Herman L.   "The Commando Hunt V Interdiction
Campaign: A Study in Constrained Optimization." Air
University Review 29 (January-February 1978):21-37.
Detailed statistical analysis of efforts to reduce enemy
mobility in Vietnam and Cambodia.   Gilster concludes that
air power was used effectively.

930.   Gilster, Herman L.   "On War, Time, and the Principle
of Substitution." Air University Review 30 (September-
October 1979):2-19.   Compares the air offensive against
North Vietnam with the Allied bombing of Germany in World
War II.   In both cases, the enemy was given time to adjust
to the gradual escalation of attacks.   Future United States
strategy should emphasize blitzkrieg blows that would not
allow this to occur.

931.   Hampe, D.E.   "Tactics and the Helicopter." Military
Review 46 (March 1966):60-63.   Describes the use of helicopters in Vietnam, both as support for South Vietnamese
forces and as part of such American forces as the 1st
(Airmobile) Cavalry Division.   The helicopter has a
considerable variety of military applications.

932.   Holloway, Bruce K.   "Air Superiority in Tactical Air
Warfare." Air University Review 19 (March-April 1968):1-15.
Discusses tactical air operations in Vietnam and refers to
the World War II and Korean War experiences with tactical
air units.

933.   Kipp, Robert M. "Counterinsurgency from 30,000 Feet-
The B-52 in Vietnam." Air University Review 19 (January-
February 1968):10-18.   Describes how the Strategic Air

Command (SAC) adapted its aircraft and weapons to
counterinsurgency.

934.   Luckow, Ulrik.   "Victory over Ignorance and Fear:
The U.S. Minelaying Attack on North Vietnam." Naval War
College Review 35 (January-February 1982):17-27. Applauds
the successful mining of North Vietnamese harbors in 1972
as an important thrust against the enemy. Luckow regards
the mission as a factor in reducing American fears about
triggering greater Soviet or Chinese involvement.

935.   McCutcheon, Keith B.   "Marine Aviation in Vietnam,
1962-1970." United States Naval Institute Proceedings 97
(May 1971):122-155. Provides a detailed account, including
innovations by the marines.   All aspects, including
organizational problems and construction projects, are
covered.

936.   McLaughlin, Burt W.   "Khe Sanh: Keeping An Outpost
Alive: An Appraisal." Air University Review 20 (November-
December 1968):57-77.   Analyzes the support given marines
at Khe Sanh through air supply.   The problems encountered
in this operation were finally surmounted.

937.   Menaul, S.W.B. "The Use of Air Power in Vietnam."
Journal of the Royal United Services Institute for Defence
Studies 116 (June 1971):5-15. Surveys the general role of
air operations, including movement of troops and supplies,
and ties the Vietnam experience to possible challenges to
the NATO allies.

938.   Mrozek, Donald J.   "The Limits of Innovation:
Aspects of Air Power in Vietnam." Air University Review 36
(January-February 1985):58-71.   Argues that too much
emphasis was put on technology in fighting guerrillas.
Moreover, innovations such as fixed-wing gunships were
often not employed effectively.   Mrozek also discusses the
defoliation program and use of the B-52.

939.   Parks, W. Hays. "Linebacker and the Law of War." Air
University Review 34 (January-February 1983):2-30.
Emphasizes that the strategic air bombardment of North
Vietnam in 1972 (Linebacker 1 and 2) was lawful and highly
useful for the American war effort.   Parks compares
Linebacker with air attacks in the Spanish Civil War and
World War II.

940.   Parks, W. Hays.   "Rolling Thunder and the Law of
War." Air University Review 33 (January-February 1982):2-
23.   Criticizes the limitations on air force attacks on
North Vietnam between 1965 and 1968. Parks argues that
these restrictions were not mandated by international law.

941.   Pfeiffer, E.W. "Operation Ranch Hand: The U.S.
Herbicide Program." Bulletin of the Atomic Scientists 38
(May 1982):20-24. Examines the nature of the herbicide

program, based on official sources. Pfeiffer also analyzes the successful effort to end this form of warfare.

942. Smith, Melden E., Jr. "The Strategic Bombing Debate: The Second World War and Vietnam." Journal of Contemporary History 12 (January 1977):175-191. Asserts that the success of the bombing offensive in World War II was not duplicated in Vietnam owing to political restraints on the use of air power.

943.   Stoner, John R. "The Closer the Better." Air University Review 18 (September-October 1967):29-41. Reviews the utilization of tactical air in Vietnam in support of the 1st (Airmobile) Cavalry Division.

944. Vito, A.H., Jr. "Carrier Air and Vietnam...An Assessment." United States Naval Institute Proceedings 93 (October 1967):66-75. Reviews carrier operations during the early years of the Vietnam conflict. Vito compares carriers favorably with land bases.

945. Zeybel, Henry. "Truck Count." Air University Review 33 (January-February 1983):36-45. Describes the war of fixed-wing gunships against North Vietnamese truck convoys, primarily in 1970-1971. Zeybel focuses on the problem of knowing how much damage was being inflicted.

Counterinsurgency

Books

946. Clutterbuck, Richard L. The Long, Long War: Counterinsurgency in Malaya and Vietnam. New York: Praeger Publishers, 1967. 206p. Important comparative study of the two wars by a British soldier who fought in Malaya. This analysis is quite critical of many programs undertaken by the South Vietnamese and their American allies.

947. Stanton, Shelby L. Green Berets at War: U.S. Army Special Forces in Southeast Asia, 1956-1975. Novato, California: Presidio Press, 1985. 376p. Detailed narrative of the Special Forces experience, including tactical operations and training activities, in Indochina and Thailand. Very briefly discusses the Special Forces revival during the Reagan presidency.

Periodical Articles

948.   Shultz, Richard. "Coercive Force and Military Strategy: Deterrence Logic and the Cost-Benefit Model of Counterinsurgency Warfare." Western Political Quarterly 32 (December 1979):444-466. Examines counterinsurgency in Vietnam between 1965 and 1968 in terms of both theory and implementation.

949. Weed, A.C., II "Army Special Forces and Vietnam."
Military Review 49 (August 1969):63-68. Suggests deployment of Special Forces and Civilian Irregular Defense
Groups to cities or other safe base areas. With their rear
secured, these forces could more effectively carry out
their pacification missions.

Pacification

Official Policy Statements

950. United States/Republic of Vietnam. "The Declaration
of February 8, 1966." In Public Papers of the Presidents of
the United States: Lyndon B. Johnson 1966, I, 153-155.
Washington, D.C.: Government Printing Office, 1967. Reaffirms American and Vietnamese determination to resist
communist aggression. The statement emphasizes both
governments' commitment to pacification and civic action in
order to eradicate many of the causes of the insurgency. A
Joint Statement the same day also focused on these points.

951. Chandler, Robert W. War of Ideas: The U.S.
Propaganda Campaign in Vietnam. Boulder, Colorado:
Westview Press, 1981. 320p. Analyzes the very extensive
propaganda war waged by the United States. Chandler feels
that this effort could have been much more effective if the
Americans had studied the Vietnamese more closely and had
not undercut the South Vietnamese government.

952. Colby, William and Peter Forbath. Honorable Men: My
Life in the CIA. New York: Simon and Schuster, 1978. 493p.
Several chapters deal with Colby's critical role in
Vietnam. CIA paramilitary and intelligence operations are
discussed in some detail. Colby at one time was second in
command, under Robert W. Komer, of the pacification program
in Vietnam.

953. Herrington, Stuart A. Silence was A Weapon; The
Vietnam War in the Villages; a Personal Perspective.
Novato, California: Presidio Press, 1982. 240p. Describes
Herrington's participation in Operation Phoenix, a joint
Vietnamese-American effort to destroy the Vietcong infra-
structure. Herrington's narrative incorporates his analy-
sis of the problems of fighting insurgency and of the out-
look of the Vietnamese villagers.

954. Race, Jeffrey. War Comes to Long An; Revolutionary
Conflict in A Vietnamese Province. Berkeley: University of
California Press, 1972. 299p. One of the most important
analyses of the insurgency. Most of the book focuses on
the period before large-scale American commitment occurred,
but one chapter does discuss conditions in Long An in 1970.

955. Scoville, Thomas W. Reorganizing for Pacification

Support. Washington, D.C.: Government Printing Office, 1982. 89p. SOD D114.2P11. Emphasizes the years 1966 to 1968, when the Civil Operations and Revolutionary Development Support (CORDS) program was developed and implemented. Brief, but important survey based on official records. CORDS represented a completely integrated military/civilian effort to tackle the economic and social problems of the Vietnamese countryside and thereby to weaken the power of the communist insurgents.

Periodical Articles

956.   Biggio, Charles P., Jr.   "Let's Learn from the French." Military Review 46 (October 1966):27-34. Provides a comparative analysis of the French and American commitments in Vietnam. Biggio stresses the political war waged by the Vietminh against the French.

957.   Brewer, Gary D.   "Chieu Hoi: The Surrender Program." Air University Review 18 (September-October 1967):50-60. Describes psychological warfare against the Vietcong. The article includes a good deal of information on the organizational structure of the program.

958.   Brigham, Erwin R.   "Pacification Measurement." Military Review 50 (May 1970):47-55. Describes the Hamlet Evaluation system which was used to measure the success of pacification. This is a favorable interpretation of an analytical method that later drew much criticism.

959.   Klare, Michael T.   "Operation Phoenix and the Failure of Pacification in South Vietnam." Liberation 17 (May 1973):21-27. Critizes Operation Phoenix, which Klare interprets as a brutal program of murder and intimidation.

960.   Lansdale, Edward G.   "Viet Nam: Do We Understand Revolution?" Foreign Affairs 43 (October 1964):75-86. Appraises American assistance to South Vietnam's counter-insurgency campaign. The average Vietnamese must be won over, if communism is to be defeated.

Naval Operations

961.   Baker, John W.   "Army Forces in Riverine Operations." Military Review 47 (August 1967):64-74. Provides an historical analysis of army, navy, and marine riverine campaigns and discusses contemporary operations in Vietnam.

962.   Besch, E.W.   "Amphibious Operation at Vinh." Marine Corps Gazette 66 (December 1982):54-60. Suggests that American amphibious attacks might have been employed fruitfully in response to North Vietnamese conventional attacks in 1972.

963.   Croizat, Victor. "Naval Forces in River War." United States Naval Institute Proceedings. 92 (October 1966):52-

61. Reviews current forms of river war. Croizat emphasizes
the Vietnam experience and suggests that river warfare
needs more attention.

964.   Eliot, George Fielding.   "Confidence in the Sea."
United States Naval Institute Proceedings 92 (May 1966):
64-71.   Advocates projecting American power deep into
Vietnam by means of naval vessels. Eliot believes such
a strategy would have psychological as well as military
benefits.

965.   Harllee, John.   "Patrol Guerrilla Motor Boats."
United States Naval Institute Proceedings 90 (April
1964):70-79. Points to the advantages of using small boats
to combat guerrillas.   Harllee advocates development of
such boats for Vietnam.

966.   Hayes, John D.   "Sea Power July 1966 - June 1967: A
Commentary." Naval Review 1968, 280-295. Discusses various
topics, including the Vietnam conflict and the 1967 war in
the Middle East.

967.   Hodgman, James A.   "Market Time in the Gulf of
Thailand." Naval Review 1968, 36-67.   Evaluates naval and
Coast Guard interdiction of Vietcong supplies. This is a
thorough report written by the Coast Guard officer who led
the operation.

968.   Hoiberg, Anne.   "Military Effectiveness of Navy Men
During and After Vietnam." Armed Forces & Society 6
(February 1980):232-246.   The war had limited effects on
many navy men. Compared with personnel in the early to the
mid-1970's, those serving in the 1960's were more
effective.

969.   Kendall, Lane C.   "U.S. Merchant Shipping and Vietnam." Naval Review 1968, 128-147. Discusses the vital role
of sealift in supplying American and allied forces in
Vietnam.   Kendall describes the use of formerly "moth-
balled" vessels.   He recommends strengthening the aging
American merchant marine for military contingencies.

970.   McCauley, Brian.   "Operation End Sweep." United
States Naval Institute Proceedings 100 (March 1974):18-25.
Discusses the mining of North Vietnamese harbors in 1972 by
the United States Navy.   This campaign helped interdict
North Vietnamese maritime supply lines and supplemented the
bombing offensive that brought the war to a conclusion.

971.   Middleton, W.D.   "SEABEES in Vietnam." United States
Naval Institute Proceedings 93 (August 1967):54-64.
Examines the contribution of navy construction battalions
to the war effort in Vietnam. Middleton also provides an
overview of the structure of the navy's construction
forces.

972. Mumford, Robert E., Jr. "Jackstay: New Dimensions in Amphibious Warfare." Naval Review 1968, 68-87.   Reviews Jackstay, a large amphibious landing in the delta region of Vietnam.   Mumford discusses the factors that led to success.

973.   Noble, Dennis L.   "Cutters and Sampans." United States Naval Institute Proceedings 110 (June 1984):46-53. Describes the maritime interdiction role played by the Coast Guard.   Noble provides statistical data on Coast Guard operations as well as a narrative.

974. Peatross, O.F. "Application of Doctrine: Victory at Van Tuong Village." Naval Review 1967, 2-13.   Studies a joint assault on a North Vietnamese position and discusses the role of amphibious doctrine in the operation.

975.   Schreadley, Richard L.   "The Naval War in Vietnam, 1950-1970." United States Naval Institute Proceedings 97 (May 1971):180-209.   Surveys naval assistance from the middle of the First Indochina War to the beginning of Vietnamization under Nixon.   The navy's commitment was quite limited until 1961.

976.   Schreadley, Richard L.   "Sea Lords." United States Naval Institute Proceedings 96 (August 1970):22-31.   Describes an operation designed to interdict Vietcong infiltration.   Schreadley assesses the coastal and riverine patrols and attacks as highly successful both in terms of immediate military benefits and in terms of bolstering the South Vietnamese.

977.   Wells, W.C.   "The Riverine Force in Action, 1966-1967." Naval Review 1969, 46-83. Despite its title, the article deals with the years 1965 to 1967. Wells argues that the navy is the key to securing the Mekong Delta.

The War in Laos, Cambodia, and on the Borders of Thailand

Books

978.   Caldwell, Malcolm and Lek Tan.   Cambodia in the Southeast Asian War. New York: Monthly Review Press, 1973. 446p.   Presents a critique of American involvement in Cambodian affairs that is highly sympathetic to neutralist leader Norodom Sihanouk.

979.   Kirk, Donald. Wider War; the Struggle for Cambodia, Thailand and Laos.   New York: Praeger Publishers, 1971. Examines relations between these nations through history, emphasizing the Indochinese war.   Kirk discusses in detail the end of the Sihanouk regime in Cambodia.

980.   Lobe, Thomas.   United States National Security Policy and Aid to the Thailand Police.   Denver: University of Denver Graduate School of International Studies, 1977.

161p. Examines United States assistance to various police
organizations in an effort to bolster internal defense and
counterinsurgency capabilities in Thailand. Lobe is
exceedingly critical of both American policies and American
and Thai performance. Contrasts sharply with Tanham's
Trial in Thailand [entry 982].

981. Shawcross, William. Sideshow: Kissinger, Nixon and
the Destruction of Cambodia. New York: Simon & Schuster,
1979. 467p. Argues that the American incursion combined
with earlier involvement of Cambodia in the Vietnam
conflict created a situation in which the radical Khmer
Rouge could take over the country.

982. Tanham, George K. Trial in Thailand. New York: Crane,
Russak & Company, Inc., 1974. 189p. Extremely detailed
analysis of communist insurgency in Thailand during the
1960's. Tanham also recounts American efforts to fight the
communists, using lessons learned in Vietnam.

Periodical Articles

983.   Alpern, Stephen I. "Insurgency in Thailand: An
Analysis of the Government Response." Military Review 55
(July 1975): 10-17. Presents a negative evaluation of the
counterinsurgency policy pursued by the Thai government,
asserting that it closely follows approaches used
unsuccessfully in Vietnam. Alpern states that the
communist insurgency movement is growing stronger. Various
organizational shortcomings are among the obstacles to an
effective attack on the insurgency.

984. Lacouture, Jean. "From the Vietnam War to an Indochina War." Foreign Affairs 48 (July 1970):617-628. Argues
that spreading the Vietnam war to Cambodia helps the
communists. Lacouture notes the problems facing a
counterrevolutionary military force operating in a former
colonial country.

985. Shaplen, Robert. "Our Involvement in Laos." Foreign
Affairs 48 (April 1970):478-493. Decries possible use of
American troops in Laos. Shaplen specifically denies that
fighting in Laos might aid in making American withdrawal
from Vietnam more rapid.

986. Smith, Russell H. "The Presidential Decision on the
Cambodian Operation." Air University Review 22 (September-
October 1971):45-53. Notes the adverse reactions to the
Cambodian incursions and traces the story of Sihanouk's
overthrow.

American Combat Performance

Books

987.   Corson, William R. The Betrayal. New York: W.W.

Norton, 1968. 317p. Severely critical of American military, especially army, performance in Vietnam. Corson also describes his experiences as a marine officer engaged in pacification.

988. Cortright, David. Soldiers in Revolt: the American Military Today. Garden City, New York: Doubleday & Company, 1975. 317p. Analyzes the unrest among American soldiers during the Vietnam conflict, which manifested itself in increased drug use, desertion, and, sometimes, outright mutiny. Cortright suggests changes needed to reduce disaffection.

989. Defense Management Study Group on Military Cohesion. Cohesion in the US Military. Washington, D.C.: National Defense University Press, 1984. 103p. SOD D5.402:M59 Discusses the nature of military cohesion in light of the frequently voiced criticism that American forces in Vietnam lacked this quality. The study is based in part on a survey of field grade officers.

990. Komer, Robert W. Bureaucracy at War: U.S. Performance in the Vietnam Conflict. Boulder, Colorado: Westview Press, 1986. 140p. Wide-ranging critique that probes not only military, but also political and economic aspects of the Vietnam war. Komer pinpoints institutional obstacles to effective American adaptation to and mastery, of the Vietnam political and military environment.

991. Oberdorfer, Don. Tet! Garden City, New York: Doubleday & Company, 1971. 159p. Analyzes the Tet offensive, its preparation, the fighting, reportage by the American media, and its impact on decision makers in Washington.

Periodical Articles

992. Admire, John H. "Understanding Limited War." Marine Corps Gazette 67 (January 1983):50-56. Criticizes limited war theory on the basis of the author's experiences in Vietnam.

993. Cardwell, Thomas A. "The Quest for Unity of Command." Air University Review 35 (May-June 1984):25-29. Examines American combined and joint operations since early in World War II, with emphasis on Vietnam. Unity of command is a desirable goal, but one which has not yet been achieved by United States forces.

994. "Commentary on Cohesion and Disintegration in the American Army." Armed Forces and Society 3 (Spring 1977): 457-490. Articles by John H. Faris, Stanford W. Gregory, Jr., Charles Cotton, and Anthony L. Wermuth discuss and attacks on American performance in Vietnam.

995. Fowler, John G., Jr. "Combat Cohesion in Vietnam."
Military Review 59 (December 1979):22-32. Fowler does not
deny that there were severe problems, most of them
reflecting strains in American society, but asserts
performance was better than often portrayed.

996. Lang, Kurt. "American Military Performance in
Vietnam: Background and Analysis." Journal of Political and
Military Sociology 8 (February 1980):269-286. Downplays
many problems of the military. Normal stresses were
heightened by racial tensions and the visible determination
of the United States to withdraw from Vietnam.

997. Livingston, George B., Jr. "Pershing II: Success Amid
Chaos." Military Review 50 (May 1970):56-60. Describes
American plans for an offensive in Vietnam which countered
the Tet attacks. Livingston considers intelligence efforts
in the pre-Tet period to have been generally successful.

998. Moskos, Charles C., Jr. "The American Combat Soldier
in Vietnam." Journal of Social Issues 31 (Fall 1975):25-37.
Discusses various factors that limited the effectiveness of
American troops. These included the single-year tours of
duty and various conflicts within the American forces.

999. Savage, Paul L. and Richard A. Gabriel. "Cohesion
and Disintegration in the American Army: An Alternative
Perspective." Armed Forces and Society 2 (Spring 1976):
340-376. Analyzes the elements in the decline of American
military performance in the late 1960's and early 1970's.
The authors compared the American experience with the
French effort in Vietnam and German problems during the
First World War.

Vietnamization

1000. Goodman, Allan E. "U.S. Development Assistance in
the Insurgency Environment: Gulliver's Coming Out." Naval
War College Review 24 (February 1972):13-23. Examines the
American experience in Vietnam and concludes that
intervention and military assistance are not effective
answers to insurgency. There are many regional conflicts
over which the major powers have little control.

1001. Johnson, Robert H. "Vietnamization: Can It Work?"
Foreign Affairs 48 (July 1970):629-647. Presents several
criticisms of the Vietnamization program and offers some
suggestions for dealing with the problems associated with
it. Nevertheless, Johnson concludes with the prediction
that Vietnam will one day be communist.

1002. Kleinman, Forrest K. "The Lost Lesson of Vietnam."
Military Review 60 (August 1980):64-71. Asserts that the
United States should have mixed Vietnamese and American
troops at squad and other lower level units. Kleinman
describes the integration of Korean troops into American

forces during the Korean War. He states that Washington considered applying "indigenous integration" in Vietnam, but failed to do so for "political reasons."

The Media and the War

Documentary Collections

1003. Vietnam, the Media, and Public Support for the War. Frederick, Maryland: University Publications of America. Compiled from various libraries and archives, this microfilm collection emphasizes relations between the Johnson administration and the media on the issue of the Vietnam war.

Books

1004. Hallin, Daniel C. The "Uncensored War"; The Media and Vietnam. New York: Oxford University Press, 1986. 320p. Concludes that the media, including the New York Times and television newscasts, were much more favorable to the war effort than usually portrayed. The media only rejected the war when other important segments of American society became critical of the commitment.

1005. Turner, Kathleen J. Lyndon Johnson's Dual War; Vietnam and the Press. Chicago: University of Chicago Press, 1985. 368p. Discusses interaction between the press and the president on the Vietnam issue, focusing on how Johnson portrayed the war in his speeches.

Periodical Articles

1006. Blanchard, Ralph. "The Newsman in Vietnam." United States Naval Institute Proceedings 95 (February 1969):50-57. Presents a balanced view of the problems of both correspondents and the military. Blanchard appears to believe that some of the military's criticism of the press is uninformed or misdirected.

1007. Delaney, Robert F. "Reflections on Political Communication and Insurgency." Naval War College Review 22 (December 1969):3-9. Discusses the role of television and public opinion concerning insurgency campaigns. The United States needs to learn how to utilize the mass media as part of its defense capability.

1008. Jacobsen, K.C. "Television and the War: The Small Picture." United States Naval Institute Proceedings 101 (March 1975):54-60. Assails the accuracy of television reporting on the war, although Jacobsen contends this bias developed from technology rather than from any conspiracy. He warns that the military must adapt to the presence of television.

1009. Lichty, Lawrence and Murray Fromson. "Comparing Notes on Television's Coverage of the War." Center Magazine 12 (September/October 1979):42-46. Asserts that the media are commonly perceived to have been more hostile to American policy in Vietnam than was the case.

1010. Mandelbaum, Michael. "Vietnam: The Television War." Parameters 13 (March 1983):89-97. Discounts television as a factor influencing American public opinion concerning the Vietnam conflict. Mandelbaum discusses news coverage of the Tet offensive as well as other topics.

1011. Sheehan, Neil. "The Press and the Pentagon Papers." Naval War College Review 24 (February 1972):8-12. Criticizes the media for having accepted administration statements about Vietnam at face value. Sheehan believes that the media should not allow itself to be manipulated by the government.

1012. Summers, Harry G. "Western Media and Recent Wars." Military Review 66 (May 1986):4-17. Assails media coverage of wars after World War II. Summers expresses alarm that the American press can be and probably is manipulated by American opponents.

1013. Venanzi, Gerald S. "Democracy and Protracted War: The Impact of Television." Air University Review 34 (January-February 1983):58-72. Declares flatly that television fostered antiwar sentiment and effectively precluded the United States from fighting the Vietnam war successfully.

1014. Watt, D.C. "American Foreign Policy and Vietnam." Political Quarterly 43 (January-March 1972):89-102. Assesses factors that brought about the American defeat in Vietnam. Watt sees the home front as the most important theater of war; the North Vietnamese clearly won the war in the United States.

Peace Negotiations

Official Policy Statements

1015. Johnson, Lyndon B. "The President's Address to the Nation Announcing Steps to Limit the War in Vietnam and Reporting his Decision Not to Seek Reelection. March 31, 1968." In Public Papers of the Presidents of the United States: Lyndon B. Johnson 1968-69, I, 469-476. Washington, D.C.: Government Printing Office, 1970. Notes the failure of the Tet offensive and asks for negotiations with North Vietnam. Johnson announces severe limits in air attacks on North Vietnam. He also discusses expansion in the South Vietnamese war effort and declares that some additional American forces, including reservists, will be sent to Vietnam.

1016. Nixon, Richard M. "Address to the Nation: 'Look to the Future.' November 2, 1972." In Public Papers of the Presidents of the United States: Richard Nixon 1972, 1084-1089. Washington, D.C.: Government Printing Office, 1974. Announces "substantial agreement on most of the terms of a settlement" in Vietnam. Nixon notes the problems that persist and vows that a final agreement will not be signed until American objectives are achieved.

Books

1017. Landau, David. Kissinger; The Uses of Power. New York: Houghton Mifflin Company, 1973. 270p. While generally approving Kissinger's policies, Landau criticizes the American disengagement in Vietnam.

Periodical Articles

1018. Cutrona, Joseph F.H. "Peace in Vietnam." Military Review 46 (November 1966):60-68. Contrasts the differing views of the United States and its allies and the communists on the resolution of the Vietnam conflict. The latter assert that they merely seek implementation of the 1954 Geneva agreements.

1019. Fall, Bernard B. "Viet Nam in the Balance." Foreign Affairs 45 (January 1966):1-18. Argues for an effort to negotiate with the National Liberation Front and to separate it from North Vietnam. The Saigon government must move in the direction of substantial reforms.

1020. Kissinger, Henry A. "The Viet Nam Negotiations." Foreign Affairs 47 (February 1969):211-234. Examines the American and North Vietnamese approaches to the war. Kissinger also discusses the impact of the Tet offensive.

Impact and Influences of the Vietnam War

Books

1021. Corson, William R. Consequences of Failure. New York: Norton, 1974. Examines the influence of the Vietnam defeat on various elements of American society, including the military establishment.

Essays and Periodical Articles

1022. Clark, John J. "Vietnam's Lesson in Defence Economics." Journal of the Royal United Services Institute for Defence Studies 116 (December 1971):36-40. Indicates relations between economics and military policy during the Vietnam war. In effect, this is an analysis of the economic aspects and consequences of limited wars.

1023. "Controversies: Vietnam as Unending Trauma." Society 21 (November-December 1983):4-33. Focuses on a presenta-

tion by Harry G. Summers, Jr., with comments from Gareth
Porter, Thomas J. Bellows, Franz Michael, and Robert A.
Scalapino.

1024.   Critchfield,   Richard.   "Lessons of Vietnam."
Annals of the American Academy of Political and Social
Science, no. 380 (November 1968):125-134. Warns that the
United States has not yet developed an effective
counterinsurgency doctrine, but that it must do so. This
doctrine must be political as well as military and needs to
provide a role for the State Department.

1025. Draper, Theodore. "Ghosts of Vietnam." Dissent 26
(Winter 1979):30-42. Examines the reasoning of Zbigniew
Brzezinski and Henry Kissinger in their defense of American
involvement in Vietnam.   Draper also discusses Guenter
Lewy's study, America in Vietnam [entry 845].

1026. Draper, Theodore. "World Politics: A New Era?"
Encounter 31 (August 1968):3-16. Asserts that limited war
theory has been demolished by the Vietnam conflict. As a
result, traditional concepts of world politics are also
changing.

1027. Durst, Jay B. "Limited Conventional War--Can It Be
Successful?" Military Review 50 (January 1970):56-63.
Discusses the impact of the Vietnam conflict on American
thinking about limited war.   Durst analyzes the various
factors inhibiting a major power that is engaging in a
conventional war.

1028. Gates, John M.   "Vietnam: The Debate Goes On."
Parameters 14 (Spring 1984):15-25.   Focuses on Harry G.
Summers' perceptions of the Vietnam war. Gates contests a
number of Summers' conclusions, including his assertions
about the nature of the conflict.

1029. Geyelin, Philip L.   "The Vietnam Syndrome." In
Vietnam in Remission, edited by James F. Veninga and Harry
A. Wilmer, 76-89.   State College: Texas A&M Press, 1985.
Suggests that the "Vietnam syndrome" embraces supporters as
well as critics of that conflict. Geyelin does not see the
Vietnam experience as totally negative and describes some
lessons from the war.

1030. Greenbacker, John E. "The Lesson of Vietnam." United
States Naval Institute Proceedings 99 (February 1973):18-
25.   Argues that the United States was over extending
itself in Vietnam.   Greenbacker's "lesson" is that the
United States should maintain its naval strength and
confine itself to a maritime strategy rather than make
large-scale military commitments ashore.

1031. Haggerty, Jerome J.   "The Perceived Lessons of
History." Army Quarterly and Defence Journal 112 (February
1982):160-165. Examines the full range of issues presented

by the Vietnam conflict and presents conclusions on the lessons of the war.

1032. Herring, George C. "Some Legacies and Lessons of Vietnam." Virginia Quarterly Review 60 (Spring 1984):210-228. Using press releases and other material Herring assesses "the major consequences of the war, its impact, its legacies."

1033. Heusinger, Adolf Ernst. "Vietnam and the U.S. Role in Europe." Atlantic Community Quarterly 3 (Winter 1965-1966):486-495. Endorses the American commitment in Vietnam and examines current security issues in Europe.

1034. Rosen, Stephen Peter. "Vietnam and the American Theory of Limited War." International Security 7 (February 1982):83-112. Stresses the need for precise objectives to be defined and for allowing the local commander flexibility within those objectives.

1035. Sarkesian, Sam C. "Revolution and the Limits of Military Power: The Haunting Specter of Vietnam." Social Science Quarterly 56 (March 1976):673-688. Discusses the problems of the United States in undertaking counter-revolutionary wars. Sarkesian warns that Vietnam created a rift between American society and the American military establishment.

1036. Staniland, Martin. "Africa, the American Intelli-gentsia, and the Shadow of Vietnam." Political Science Quarterly 98 (Winter 1983-1984):595-616. Discusses the pervasive influence of Vietnam on all participants in the debates over American policy toward Africa. Staniland argues against such extensive use of Vietnam analogies.

1037. Ulsamer, Edgar. "How USAF Prepares for Future Contingencies." Air Force Magazine 56 (June 1973):34-40. Assesses the contribution of the Vietnam experience to air force planning for conflicts which may occur elsewhere.

Chapter 6

Nixon and Ford: The Nixon Doctrine and Detente

The Nixon and Ford administrations viewed American power as much more limited than the Kennedy and Johnson administrations had; consequently, Nixon and Ford moved consciously away from the role of world policeman and took a number of steps to reduce American commitments. The Nixon Doctrine may be seen as a return to the Truman Doctrine, which emphasized assistance to countries threatened by communism.

There was a greater emphasis on Europe after many years of involvement with Asia. The perception that the Sino-Soviet rift was genuine helped make this realignment possible. The Soviets remained a threat, which was best met in Europe.

In terms of strategic weapons, a great effort was made to achieve some degree of arms control. This effort resulted eventually in SALT I and a period of considerable optimism, even about the American relationship with the Soviet Union. The reduction in American commitments and the great unpopularity of the draft led to a successful move to an all-volunteer military force.

Within the United States, Congress sought a much greater share in decision-making both in foreign relations and defense policy than had been the case during the first two or three decades of the Cold War. The Nixon Doctrine, as it applied to Indochina, failed, owing to Congressional opposition to the continuance of any American involvement in that area.

The Middle East remained an area of considerable tension, but the United States avoided any direct military commitments. By the middle of the 1970's, Africa had assumed more importance in the eyes of national security decision makers, but the Ford administration was unable to gain support for its African policies from Congress.

Decision-makers

1038. Kinnard, Douglas. "James R. Schlesinger as Secretary of Defense." Naval War College Review 32 (November--

December 1979):22-34. Discusses Schlesinger's important contributions to American defense policy.

1039. Zumwalt, Elmo R. On Watch: A Memoir. New York: Quadrangle/New York Times Book Co., 1976. 568p. Discusses strategy and other policy matters during Zumwalt's term as Chief of Naval Operations (1970-1974) and assails the Kissinger foreign policies.

Decision-making Process

General

Official Reports

1040. Blue Ribbon Defense Panel. Report to the President and Secretary of Defense on the Department of Defense. Washington, D.C.: Government Printing Office, 1970. 237p. SOD D1.2:B62/970 Proposes a radical restructuring of the defense establishment, including the placement of Deputy Secretaries between the Secretary of Defense and the armed services.

Books

1041. Licklider, Roy E. The Private Nuclear Strategists. Columbus: Ohio State University Press, 1971. 213p. Based on a survey of many nuclear specialists in the mid-1960's. Licklider examines the kinds of people who are researching and writing on national security. His study demolished many myths about this important group.

Periodical Articles

1042. Bader, William B. "Congress and National Strategy." Naval War College Review 22 (February 1970):9-18. Studies Congress' efforts to fulfill its constitutional role in foreign and military affairs. Bader also examines the increasing power of the executive in these areas.

1043. Barnds, William J. "Intelligence and Foreign Policy: Dilemmas of a Democracy." Foreign Affairs 47 (January 1969):281-295. Discusses the role of the CIA and proposals for its reorganization in the interest of increasing CIA accountability.

1044. Barrett, Raymond J. "The Role of Consultation in American Defense Policy." Air University Review 20 (May-June 1969):25-32. Examines the place the American alliance system has in defense decision-making. Barrett asserts that consultations are helpful to both the United States and to its allies.

1045. Cline, Ray S. "Policy Without Intelligence." Foreign Policy, no. 17 (Winter 1974-1975):121-135. Assails the handling of intelligence and the isolation of the State

Department during the Nixon years. Cline offers several
proposals for reorganizing the National Security Council.

1046. Davis, Vincent. "American Military Policy: Decision-
making in the Executive Branch." Naval War College Review
22 (May 1970):4-23. Focuses primarily on the Nixon administration in 1969. Davis asserts that centralization has
increased and more authority has been given to advisers
such as Henry Kissinger.

1047. Dickinson, William L. "Congress and National
Security." Air University Review 26 (March-April 1975):2-
15. Congressman Dickinson asserts that Congress will be
concerned more and more with security issues. He expresses
considerable skepticism about detente between the superpowers.

1048. Gard, Robert G., Jr. "The Military and American
Society." Foreign Affairs 49 (July, 1971):698-710. Paints
a rather dismal picture of the environment of the army
after Vietnam. An all-volunteer force will not change
morale for the better. Gard emphasizes that political
leaders profoundly influence the army environment.

1049. Kattenburg, Paul M. "Detente, Security and the
Social Sciences," Social Sciences 51 (Winter 1976):11-16.
Argues that social scientists and the knowledge they have
generated need to be incorporated much more fully into
political decision-making in the areas of national security
and superpower negotiation.

1050. Kolkowicz, Roman. "Strategic Elites and Politics of
Superpower." Journal of International Affairs 26
(1972):40-59. Discusses the various "strategic elites"
whose theorizing has been dominated by technology.
Currently, more politically oriented theorists are coming
to the forefront.

1051. Kolodziej, Edward A. "The National Security
Council: Innovations and Implications." Public
Administration Review 29 (November/December 1969):573-585.
Discusses some of the early "Innovations in procedure and
organization" effected by the Nixon administration.
Kolodziej considers the relationship of the Council to the
Secretary of State and other ramifications of the changes
described.

1052. McMahon, John F., Jr. "Revitalization of the
National Security Council System." Air University Review
21 (March-April 1970):28-36. Analyzes changes in the
National Security Council to improve its performance during
the Nixon administration. Much of the article deals with
the role of Henry Kissinger as Special Assistant for
National Security Affairs.

1053.   Vornbrock, Walter G.   "DOD Resource Management."
Air University Review 20 (July-August 1969):70-77.
Describes efforts being made to improve management in
response to public criticism of rising military costs.

The Joint Chiefs of Staff

1054.   Ballagh, Robert S., Jr. "The JCS Challenge." Military Review 51 (April 1971):25-34. Reviews the history of
the Joint Chiefs of Staff. Much of the focus is on
proposals for changes in the Joint Chiefs.

1055.   McMahon, John F., Jr.   "Streamlining the Joint
Chiefs of Staff." Military Review 49 (January 1969):36-46.
Assails the current role and functioning of the Joint
Chiefs. McMahon is concerned that "logrolling" among the
services has undermined the Joint Chiefs and has encouraged
the President and Secretary of Defense to find advisers
other than the Joint Chiefs.

1056.   Simons, William E.   "Military Professionals as
Policy Advisers." Air University Review 20 (March-April
1969): 2-10. Rejects traditional objections to military
participation in national policy making. Simons warns
against too much reliance on civilian strategists who may
promise more than they can deliver. Several pages examine
the role of the Joint Chiefs of Staff.

Military Role in the Decision-making Process

Books

1057.   Bletz, Donald F.   The Role of the Military
Professional in U.S. Foreign Policy. New York: Praeger
Publishers, 1972. 320p.   Recommends teaching military
leaders to consider political factors in determining
courses of action in the area of national security. The
study included survey research at the National War College.

Periodical Articles

1058.   Benson, Robert S.   "The Military on Capitol Hill:
Prospects in the Quest for Funds." Annals of the American
Academy of Political and Social Science, no. 406 (March
1973):48-58.   Surveys military-legislative relations,
emphasizing the limited changes Congress has been able to
effect.   Public opinion, as well, has only a little
influence on military spending.

1059.   Cagle, Malcolm W.   "The Most Silent Service."
United States Naval Institute Proceedings 95 (August
1969):37-41.   Deplores what Cagle regards as the rigid
restrictions on the freedom of officers to speak out on

controversial issues. These curbs have grown stricter as civilians have taken greater control of the Defense Department.

1060. Edelstein, Daniel N. "Worlds Apart?" United States Naval Institute Proceedings 99 (February 1973):18-25. Warns that military officers should be encouraged to work against the isolation of the military from American society that seems to be increasing.

1061. Flint, Roy K. "Army Professionalism for the Future." Military Review 51 (April 1971):3-11. Warns that the military must avoid becoming alienated from civilians because of their criticism of the armed forces. World War II and the early decades after that war marked a period of unusual esteem for the American military, which could not last.

1062. Halperin, Morton H. "The President and the Military." Foreign Affairs 50 (January 1972):310-324. Surveys the period from the Roosevelt to the Nixon administrations. Halperin discusses the methods each President has used in dealing with the services and proposes further changes.

1063. Hanks, Robert J. "Against All Enemies." United States Naval Institute Proceedings 96 (March 1970):22-29. Criticizes the Vietnam-inspired anti-defense movement in the United States. Hanks discusses the role of the professional military in the face of this attack on their activities.

1064. Hyman, Sidney. "The Governance of the Military." Annals of the American Academy of Political and Social Science, no. 406 (March 1973):38-47. Surveys the great changes in relations between the civilian government and the military since 1945. Hyman emphasizes the weakening of Congressional powers.

1065. Larson, Arthur D. "Military Professionalism and Civil Control: A Comparative Analysis of Two Interpretations." JPMS: Journal of Political & Military Sociology 2 (Spring 1974):57-72. Analyzes Samuel P. Huntington's and Morris Janowitz's theories of military professionalism. Larson generally favors Janowitz's approach, but warns that the military must not become too involved with politics.

1066. Madigan, John J. III. and Pat C. Hoy, Jr. "The Dialectical Imperative: Civil-Military Confrontation." Military Review 53 (November 1973):41-54. Discusses the responses of professional officers to media criticisms of the military.

1067. Preston, Adrian. "The 'New' Civil-Military

Relations: Retrospect and Prospect." _Air University Review_ 24 (March-April 1973):51-53. Briefly surveys the impact of potential nuclear warfare and of actual low-intensity conflict. Preston proposes changes in relationships to enhance effective governance of the armed services.

1068. Sage, H.J. "The Military and Politics." _United States Naval Institute Proceedings_ 100 (October 1974):47-55. Prescribes approaches for the services as they find themselves increasingly in the political arena. These include minimizing secrecy and educating their own members about politics.

1069. Sarkesian, Sam C. "Political Soldiers: Perspectives on Professionalism in the U.S. Military." _Midwest Journal of Political Science_ 16 (May 1972):239-258. Emphasizes the increasing need for the services to develop more political sensitivity.

1070. Werner, Roy A. "Down the Road to Armageddon?" _Military Review_ 55 (July 1975):30-40. Discusses changes in American youth that are reducing the ability of the United States to respond to foreign challenges. Werner argues against the use of Vietnam analogies that paralyze action. He feels the United States has to avoid both isolation and militarization.

1071. Yarmolinsky, Adam. "The Military Influence within the Executive Branch." _Foreign Service Journal_ 48 (January 1971):34-38, 44. Traces the gradual growth of military influence in the executive branch during the 20th century and the decline of the State Department.

The Role of Public Opinion

1072. Bletz, Donald F. "AFTER VIETNAM: A Professional Challenge." _Military Review_ 51 (August 1971):11-15. As the American commitment in Vietnam was reduced, Bletz assesses trends in public opinion that may impact on American military power and the military professional.

1073. Clotfelter, James. "Vacillation and Stability in American Public Opinion Toward Military and Foreign Policy." _Naval War College Review_ 23 (February 1971):55-61. Believes that the public has been more consistently supportive of Presidential objectives than is generally acknowledged. Clotfelter emphasizes the controversy over the American commitment to Vietnam in his discussion of the relationship between the President and the public.

1074. Free, Lloyd A. "The Impact of American International Attitudes on the U.S. Military." _Air University Review_ 25 (July-August 1974):17-26. Reviews academic writing on American public opinion concerning defense and foreign policy. Free then examines current opinion based on a poll Free and William Watts took for their book, State of the Nation. Views on foreign policy and defense issues are compared for 1964, 1966, and 1972.

1075. Gelb, Leslie H. "Domestic Change and National Security Policy." In The Next Phase in Foreign Policy, edited by Henry Owen, 249-280. Washington, D.C.: Brookings Institution, 1973. Analyzes changes in public opinion about United States commitments abroad and relationships between public opinion and Congressional views. Much of the discussion deals with Congressional activism in the field of national security.

1076. Kastl, Joseph W. "Antimilitarism in the Age of Aquarius." Air University Review 23 (November-December 1971):32-38. After analyzing contemporary American antimilitarism, Kastl proposes some ways to improve younger age groups' views of the armed services.

1077. Ranney, J. Austin. "Popular Pressures on Government." Naval War College Review 22 (December 1969):10-16. Discusses public opinion and security policy in the United States. Ranney considers the role of interest groups and the varying sizes of concerned publics which, in turn, depend upon the salience of the issue being debated.

Military Policy

Official Policy Statements

1078. Nixon Richard. "Informal Remarks in Guam with Newsmen. July 25, 1969." In Public Papers of the Presidents of the United States: Richard Nixon 1969, 544-556. Washington, D.C.: Government Printing Office, 1970. Enunciates the Nixon Doctrine, which limited American commitments in land conflicts in Asia. Nixon warns against allowing Asians to become overly dependent upon the Americans, although they can expect aid if nuclear attack is a possibility.

1079. Nixon, Richard. "First Annual Report to the Congress on United States Foreign Policy for the 1970's. February 18, 1970." In Public Papers of the Presidents of the United States: Richard Nixon 1970, 116-190. Washington, D.C.: Government Printing Office, 1971. Fundamental statement of the Nixon administration's foreign and military policies. Nixon notes the end of the "monolithic Communist world" and many other changes in world politics. He describes the Nixon Doctrine and discusses the National Security Council, our alliance system, and current policy regarding Vietnam.

1080. Nixon, Richard. "Address at Graduation Exercises of the Naval Officer Candidate School, Newport, Rhode Island.

March 12, 1971.   In <u>Public Papers of the Presidents of the</u>
<u>United States: Richard Nixon 1971</u>, 427-431.   Washington,
D.C.: Government Printing Office, 1972.   Stresses the need
for military and naval preparedness, which Nixon terms "the
peace forces".   Nixon warns Americans against giving way to
the seductions of isolationism and devoting too much
federal money to domestic programs and not enough to
defense.

1081.   Nixon, Richard.   "Address to the Nation About
Vietnam and Domestic Problems.   March 29, 1973."   In <u>Public</u>
<u>Papers of the Presidents of the United States: Richard</u>
<u>Nixon 1973</u>, 234-238.   Washington, D.C.: Government Printing
Office, 1975.   Reviews negotiations on termination of the
Vietnam conflict and discusses post-Vietnam defense needs.
The defense budget is lower in terms of percentage of the
gross national product than for two decades and should not
be reduced further.   According to Nixon, "we would not have
made the progress toward lasting peace that we have made
this past year unless we had had the military strength that
commanded respect."

1082.   Nixon, Richard.   "Letter to Senate Leaders About
Proposed Reductions in the Defense Budget.   September 22,
1973."   In <u>Public Papers of the Presidents of the United</u>
<u>States: Richard Nixon 1973</u>, 819-821.   Washington, D.C.:
Government Printing Office, 1975.   Makes a detailed statement on the serious repercussions of proposed cuts in
defense spending.   Disarmament negotiations, the
maintenance of the NATO alliance, and further weapons
development would be seriously impacted by slashes in
funding.   Nixon warns that an "adequate defense must not
become a partisan issue."

1083.   Ford, Gerald R.   "Remarks at a Briefing for Representatives of Military Organizations on Defense and Foreign
Policy.   February 10, 1976."   In <u>Public Papers of the</u>
<u>Presidents of the United States: Gerald R. Ford 1976-77</u>, I,
246-247.   Washington, D.C.: Government Printing Office,
1979.   Reviews the current defense budget very briefly.
Ford asserts that in the "protracted struggle with the
enemies of freedom" victory will result from "peace through
strength" rather than "by warming over the old rhetoric of
the cold war."   He adds that his administration tried to
stop communist intervention in Angola, but could not do so
because of Congressional opposition.

Books

1084.   Canan, James W.   <u>The Superwarriors; the Fantastic</u>
<u>World of Pentagon Superweapons</u>.   New York: Weybright and
Talley, 1975.   Examines not only the weapons themselves,
but the continued drive for more sophisticated military
systems and the organizational forces associated with
military technology.

1085.   Litwak,   Robert.   Detente and the Nixon Doctrine: American Foreign Policy and the Pursuit of Stability, 1969-1976. Cambridge, England: Cambridge University Press, 1984. 240p.   Systematic study of American foreign policy during the Nixon-Kissinger period.   Litwak notes the relationship between the Vietnam experience and the Nixon Doctrine, but discusses the Doctrine's applications in other contexts as well.

1086.   Middleton, Drew.   Can America Win the Next War? New York: Scribner, 1975.   Explores both the military services and political factors such as American public opinion. Middleton offers many comparisons between the United States and the USSR.

1087.   Paul,   Roland A.   American Military Commitments Abroad.   New Brunswick, New Jersey: Rutgers University Press, 1973.   Discusses the American alliance system. Paul's book, in effect, summarizes hearings by the Senate Foreign Relations Committee's Subcommittee on U.S. Security Agreements Abroad.

1088.   Taylor, Maxwell Davenport.   Precarious Security. New York: Norton, 1974. 203p.   Outlines proposals for a revised military policy in the post-Vietnam era.   Among other changes,   Taylor   asks   for   a   larger   National   Security Council, which would coordinate security affairs to a much greater extent than it currently does.

1089.   Wong-Fraser, Agatha S.Y.   Symmetry and Selectivity in U.S. Defense Policy: A Grand Design or a Major Mistake? Latham, Maryland: University Press of America, Inc., 1980. 164p.   Discusses the "Schlesinger Doctrine" regarding nuclear   strategy.   Wong-Fraser   puts   Schlesinger's initiative into the perspective of the post-World War II American defense doctrine.   She sees both McNamara and Schlesinger   as   seeking   greater   flexibility   in   American strategy.

Essays and Periodical Articles

1090.   Allison,   Graham   and   others.   "Limits   to Intervention."   Foreign Affairs 48 (January 1970):245-261. Proposals for implementing Nixon's new policy of limiting military intervention.   The authors discuss the Nixon initiative in light of American disillusionment about the Vietnam venture.

1091.   Allison, Graham T.   "Military Capabilities and American Foreign Policy."   Annals of the American Academy of Political and Social Science, no. 406 (March 1973):17-37.   Probes the impact of rapid deployment force capability on decision-making and briefly describes various episodes such as Laos and the Bay of Pigs.

1092.   Barber, James Alden, Jr.   "Military Force and Nonmilitary Threats." Military Review 55 (February 1975):3-13. Discusses the limitations of military force in dealing with political problems. Barber concludes that the armed services retain much of their usefulness, but this is realized primarily in their potential, rather than their actual employment.

1093.   Barrett, Raymond J.   "UN Peacekeeping and U.S. National Security." Air University Review 24 (March-April 1973):28-40.   Advocates greater American commitment to supporting United Nations peacekeeping efforts. Barrett reviews United Nations experience in this area.

1094.   Battreall, Raymond R., Jr. "Thesis: Massive Retaliation Antithesis: Flexible Response Synthesis: Nixon Doctrine." Military Review 55 (January 1975):65-74. Stresses the general continuity of American military strategy in the post-World War II years. Battreall argues that American planners must concentrate on specific military goals that can be achieved quickly.   By implication, the article advocates hard, fast blows as opposed to becoming involved in protracted wars which serve communist ends.

1095. Brzezinski, Zbigniew. "Peace and Power." Military Review 49 (July 1969):31-43. Warns that conflict between the United States and the Soviet Union is likely to increase. Brzezinski discusses ways in which it can be reduced.

1096.   Chapman, John W.   "Political Forecasting and Strategic Planning." International Studies Quarterly 15 (September 1971):317-357. Warns that planning can be done effectively only for two years at most.   Therefore, flexibility is probably the most important element in planning.

1097. Clark, John J. "The Encircling Sea." United States Naval Institute Proceedings 95 (March 1969):26-35. Analyzes forces that make a nation powerful and suggests what the United States needs to do in order to develop a "national strategy."   Clark also discusses specific naval strategies.

1098. Elliott, John D. "A New Thinking Plateau." Military Review 50 (October 1970):68-73. Recommends more attention to short-range planning. Elliott is quite critical of the military's emphasis on conformity, feeling that there needs to be greater freedom of expression in the army.

1099. Frank, Lewis A.   "The Decision to Respond: What Forces Do We Need in a Crisis?" Air University Review 26 (March-April 1975):16-26. Examines the kinds of forces needed in light of SALT and the United States acceptance of Soviet equality in nuclear weapons. This is sophisticated analysis of the military demands of a crisis.

1100. Gleason, Robert L. "Quo Vadis?--The Nixon Doctrine and Air Power." Air University Review 23 (July-August 1972):45-56. Discusses the relationship between the Vietman war and the Nixon Doctrine. Gleason sees little alternative to something like the Nixon Doctrine. He analyzes at length the potential of air force special warfare units to implement the Nixon Doctrine.

1101. Hamburg, Roger. "Massive Retaliation Revisited." Military Affairs 38 (February 1974):17-23. Views the Nixon Doctrine as pointing the way to commitment of the United States to policies similar to the "massive retaliation" stance of the 1950's.

1102. Hosmer, Craig. "The New Geopolitics." United States Naval Institute Proceedings 99 (August 1973):18-23. Asserts that the United States may be able to reduce defense expenditures somewhat because the USSR is preoccupied with the Peoples Republic of China, but reductions can only be carried so far.

1103. Huntington, Samuel P. "After Containment: The Functions of the Military Establishment." Annals of the American Academy of Political and Social Science, no. 406 (March 1973):1-16. Stresses the need for a reassessment of the objectives and roles of the armed forces in the now multi-polar world. Huntington advocates that greater intervention capability be developed.

1104. Jefferies, Chris L. "Defense Policy in a World of Limited Resources: A look at the Possibilities." Air University Review 26 (July-August 1975):29-37. Warns that the military may have to compete more with civilians for resources, using the dispute in 1973 over the allocation of aviation gasoline in the United States as an example. Jefferies notes the possibility that defense costs may grow while the gross national product does not, thereby creating serious economic problems.

1105. Kost, John G. "Diplomacy and Defense Planning." Naval War College Review 27 (November-December 1974):53-66. Praises the Nixon Doctrine and reviews the problems of supporting and implementing his strategy that must be overcome by the armed services.

1106. Laird, Melvin R. "A Strong Start in a Difficult Decade: Defense Policy in the Nixon-Ford Years." International Security 10 (Fall 1985):5-26. Vigorous defense of the Nixon-Ford military policies. Laird discusses the basic plans and objectives, "strategic forces and arms control," the North Atlantic Treaty Organization, and military assistance during the early to mid-1970's.

1107. Pfaltzgraff, Robert L., Jr. "National Security in a Decade of Transition." Air University Review 25 (July--August 1974):2-8. Discusses American relationships with China, the USSR, Europe, and Japan. Pfaltzgraff stresses the importance of the Middle East.

1108. Rosenberg, Douglas H. "Arms and the American Way: The Ideological Dimension of Military Growth." In Military Force and American Society, edited by Bruce M. Russett and Alfred Stepan, 143-195. New York: Harper & Row, Publishers, 1973. Analyzes what Rosenberg views as the ideological-mythic bases of American national security thinking and discusses the increasing criticism of military power in the United States.

1109. Rostow, Walt W. "Will We Snatch Defeat from the Jaws of Victory?" Naval War College Review 24 (September 1971):3-18. Suggests that there is a real opportunity for peace and progress for the world, but this chance must not be lost through an American retreat into isolationism.

1110. Simpson, Benjamin M. "Current Strategic Theories." Naval War College Review 24 (May 1972):76-85. Focuses on theories of deterrence, limited war, and revolutionary insurgency wars. Simpson recommends the reanalysis of American strategic theories in the post-Vietnam era.

1111. Smith, Edward C. "New Directions for National Defense." Military Review 50 (March 1970):3-10. Generally applauds the United States military establishment, including the so-called military-industrial complex, which Smith sees as making important contributions in nonmilitary as well as in defense fields.

1112. Staley, H.A. "The Nixon Doctrine--A New Era in Foreign Policy?" Air University Review 24 (September-October 1973):89-92. Contrasts Nixon's and Kennedy's approaches to defense. Staley sees the Nixon Doctrine as accurately reflecting changes in world politics and American domestic public opinion.

1113. Swarztrauber, S.A. "On Hugging Bear, Take Care." United States Naval Institute Proceedings 100 (July 1974): 18-22. Emphasizes the need for a strong defense posture from which detente and other policies can be undertaken safely. Swarztrauber implies that the public must be educated about defense needs.

1114. Wheeler, Edd D. "U.S. Military Strategy: Paradoxes in Perspectives." Air University Review 24 (July-August 1973):2-12. General survey of American strategy and the factors such as public opinion that influence it. Wheeler also discusses the impact of SALT.

Defense Costs

1115. Bingham, Jonathan B. "Can Military Spending be
Controlled?" Foreign Affairs 48 (October 1969):51-66.
Discusses structural elements of the federal government
that promote great increases in defense expenditures.
Bingham suggests that Congress is in a position to exercise
more oversight in the defense field.

1116. Blechman, Barry M. and Edward R. Fried. "Controlling
the Defense Budget." Foreign Affairs 54 (January 1976):
233-249. Argues that while the current level of military
spending is justified, further increases implemented
without reducing waste would be counterproductive.

1117. Du Boff, Richard B. "Converting Military Spending
to Social Welfare: The Real Obstacles." Quarterly Review of
Economics and Business 12 (Spring 1972):7-22. Attributes
relative levels of spending for defense and welfare to
current social and economic stratification in the United
States. Major changes in spending patterns are not
practical without extreme changes in American society.

1118. Hogan, Jerry H. "National Objectives into
Specific Programs." Military Review 55 (January 1975):35-
39. Seeks to explain rather than to criticize or evaluate
the PPBS system. Hogan examines the major documents in the
cycle of relating military goals to budgetary constraints.

1119. Jennings, Richard M. "Running the Qualitative Race
(and Not Losing)." Military Review 55 (October 1975):58-68.
Analyzes military spending by the United States and the
USSR during the post-World War II years. The present arms
race differs from earlier events for several reasons and
has become in fact "a series of quantitative subraces."
Jennings presents a number of prescriptions for American
participation in the increasingly sophisticated military
competition with the Soviet Union.

1120. Moot, Robert C. "Defense Spending: Myths and
Realities." Naval War College Review 23 (December 1970):4-
10. Moot, Assistant Secretary of Defense, argues that
critics of defense spending exaggerate the level of
expenditures. He discusses the full span of governmental
spending, including state and local, to put military
expenses into perspective.

1121. Odeen, Philip. "In Defense of the Defense Budget."
Foreign Policy, no. 16 (Fall 1974):93-108. Argues that the
defense establishment should generate savings which could
be used for critical programs. This is preferable to
reducing defense spending.

1122. Schultze, Charles L. "Reexamining the Military

Budget." Public Interest 18 (Winter 1970):3-24. Projects
defense expenditures into the mid-1970's, correctly
forecasting a withdrawal from Vietnam. Schultze recommends
that the Defense Department present a five-year projected
budget each year for action by Congress.

1123. Stellini, Edward. "Defense Dollars for Deterrence: A
Matter of Priorities." Air University Review 23 (September-
October 1972):24-37. Analyzes the deterrence concept and
suggests that defense funds are not as plentiful as they
once were. Stellini suggests principles for assessing the
deterrence value of weapon systems and other elements of
military power.

Military-Industrial Complex Issues

Books

1124. Agapos, A.M. Government-Industry and Defense:
Economics and Administration. University: University of
Alabama Press, 1975. 184p. Presents an overview of defense
contracting and propounds some theories of defense spending
and defense procurement that aroused criticism because of
their departures from generally accepted approaches to
these issues.

Periodical Articles

1125. Clotfelter, James. "Senate Voting and Constituency
Stake in Defense Spending." Journal of Politics 32
(November 1970):979-983. Focuses on voting in the Senate
in 1969. Clotfelter's evidence seems to minimize the
influence of the military-industrial complex. At least, it
does not seem to influence Senate voting directly.

1126. Gottlieb, Sanford. "A State Within a State: What Is
the Military-Industrial Complex?" Dissent 18 (October
1971): 492-502. Criticizes the military-industrial
complex for diverting funds from non-military programs and
advocates basic changes in public policies within the
United States.

1127. Yale, Wesley W. "The Military-Industrial Complex."
Military Review 50 (September 1970):45-50. Answers attacks
on the military-industrial complex. While problems exist,
they are not the result of actions of the military.

General Strategy

1128. Bletz, Donald F. "How Much Force to Defend Against
What?" Military Review 54 (January 1974):3-12. Assesses
the impact of the Nixon Doctrine and of changes in world
politics on the armed forces, especially the army. Bletz
offers no precise answers to the questions posed in the
title of the article, but does analyze the factors that

will influence the answers to them.

1129. Clark, Wesley K.   "Gradualism and American Military Strategy." Military Review 55 (September 1975):3-13. Discusses "gradualism" in the Vietnam conflict, after briefly outlining post-World War II American strategy. Clark examines conflicts between military and political goals and stresses that "gradualism" is an element of "flexible response."

1130. Delaney, Robert F.   "The Psychological Dimension in National Security Planning." Naval War College Review 25 (January-February 1973):53-59.   Given the increasing complexity of the media and their rising impact, Delaney advocates further emphasis on American publicity and public information activities.

1131. Donovan, James. "The Military Continues to Prepare for World War II." Washington Monthly 3 (December 1971): 28-36. Discusses military policy making after Vietnam. The emphasis is on older strategies; Vietnam and its lessons are receiving little attention.

1132. Eccles, Henry E. "Strategy: The Essence of Professionalism." Naval War College Review 24 (December 1971):43-51. Presents a detailed theoretical analysis of strategy. Eccles discusses relationships between strategy and other military concepts.

1133. Haidler, William H.   "Energy Resources: An Element of National Power." Air University Review 23 (January--February 1972):2-13. Discusses the availability of energy resources to the United States and analyzes the political and military problems associated with them.

1134. Helms, Robert F. II.   "A New Strategy for the US Army." Military Review 55 (August 1975):49-55. Presents a strategy for the period 1975-1990, which takes account of the decline of bipolarity and the increased American need for foreign resources. Helms notes the goals of preserving a "conventional deterrence force in Europe, capability for protecting US interests abroad, and defending the continental United States."   Interestingly, he advocates restricting reserve forces to continental defense.

1135. Janowitz, Morris.   "Stabilizing Military Systems: An Emerging Strategic Concept." Military Review 55 (June 1975):3-10. Suggests that the army is becoming more and more of a "force in being" like the air force and the navy. The armed services are developing into institutions for avoiding or limiting conflict. There must be a renewed emphasis on relating military power to political goals and strategies.

1136. Kurtz, Howard G. and Harriet B. Kurtz.   "The

Collapse of U.S. Global Strategy." Military Review 49 (May 1969):43-52. Presents a variety of proposals to rebuild United States strategy in the wake of American inaction during and after the Soviet invasion of Czechoslovakia.

1137.   Mayer, Laurel A. and Ronald J. Stupak.   "The Evolution of Flexible Response in the Post-Vietnam Era; Adjustment or Transformation?" Air University Review 27 (November-December 1975):11-21.   Discusses the various post-World War II theories of deterrence.   The authors believe that the United States continues to be totally preoccupied with superpower rivalry, virtually ignoring the problem of low-intensity conflict.

1138.   Osgood, Robert E. "Introduction: The Nixon Doctrine and Strategy." In Retreat from Empire? The First Nixon Administration, edited by Robert E. Osgood and others, 1-27.   Baltimore: Johns Hopkins University Press, 1973. Describes the "Nixon Strategy" rather than the "Nixon Doctrine" of 1969.   Osgood finds much continuity with the policies of earlier post-World War II administrations, but also detects changes in emphasis. He summarizes Nixon's approach as "military retrenchment without political disengagement."

1139.   Wolk, Herman S. "Formulating a National Strategy for the 1970's."   Air University Review 21 (November-December 1970):45-50.   Examines Nixon's approach to defense, which he compares to those of Eisenhower, Kennedy, and Johnson. Wolk asserts that Nixon's policies reflect the influence of and the experience of the Eisenhower years.

1140.   Zock, Richard.   "Resource Management, Economic Analysis, and Discounting in the Department of Defense." Air University Review 24 (January-February 1973):32-36. Examines the increasing impact of economic thinking on defense planning, especially in light of cuts in defense expenditures.   Zock also discusses "discounting" as an analytical tool in the Department of Defense.

Nuclear Strategy

Books

1141. Quanbeck,   Alton H.   and Barry M.   Blechman. Strategic Forces: Issues for the Mid-Seventies; a Staff Paper. Washington, D.C.: Brookings Institution, 1973. 94p. Focuses on nuclear forces, comparing American and Soviet strength.   The various delivery systems such as bombers are discussed.   The study provides valuable data, but avoids prescriptive recommendations.

1142.   Tsipis, Kosta.   The Future of the Sea-Based Deterrent.   Cambridge, Massachusetts: MIT Press, 1973.

266p. Deals with the maintenance of missiles aboard submarines as part of the nuclear triad. Several essays discuss the closely related topic of antisubmarine warfare.

Essays and Periodical Articles

1143. Backus, Paul H. "The Vulnerable Homelands." United States Naval Institute Proceedings 96 (December 1970):18-22. Argues that bombers and ICBMs should be eliminated. Deterrence would be left to maritime weapons such as the POLARIS submarines. Satellites would assist in verifying compliance with disarmament agreements.

1144. Barnett, A. Doak. "A Nuclear China and U.S. Arms Policy." Foreign Affairs 48 (April 1970):427-442. Analyzes relations between the United States, the Peoples Republic of China, and the USSR regarding nuclear arms. Barnett believes that the United States and the USSR must avoid the appearance of working together against the interests of China.

1145. Beaumont, Roger A. "Prospects for Nuclear Nullification." Military Review 49 (October 1969):29-35. Presents a scenario of events if nuclear weapons disappeared as a strategic factor. Beaumont warns that military power would continue to have a major role in world politics.

1146. Blunt, Raymond S. and Thomas O. Cason. "Realistic Doctrine: Basic Thinking Today." Air University Review 24 (May-June 1971):21-33. Reviews Secretary of Defense Laird's fiscal year 1972 budget message and AFM 1-1, United States Air Force Basic Doctrine. Blunt asserts that there are significant gaps between "national policy" in the field of national defense and the "basic doctrine" of the air force.

1147. Burke, Gerald K. "The Metaphysics of Power Realities and Nuclear Armaments." Military Review 55 (September 1975): 14-24. Analyzes the debate over the concept of "overkill." Burke discusses the various American strategic weapons systems and the possible effects of a Soviet strategy that focuses attacks on American missiles and aircraft. He believes that the fact that there is "overkill" capability is important even though it may be a psychological rather than a purely military factor.

1148. Cohen, S.T. "U.S. Strategic Nuclear Weapons Policy-- Do We Have One? Should There Be One?" Air University Review 26 (January-February 1975):12-25. Examines changes in nuclear weapons policy under Nixon, specifically the switch to selective targeting. Cohen questions whether the United States really has such a policy and whether one is needed. He proposes development of highly mobile, widely dispersed missiles with warheads stored separately.

1149. Gallois, Pierre M.   "U.S. Foreign Policy: A Study in
Military Strength and Diplomatic Weakness."   Orbis 9
(Summer 1965):338-357.   Reviews nuclear diplomacy as
practiced by the United States.   Gallois also examines
relations with the allies of the United States such as NATO
partners and the Republic of Vietnam.

1150.   Giddings, Ralph L., Jr. "Battle Management for
Strategic Weapons Systems." United States Naval Institute
Proceedings 97 (January 1971):49-52. Discusses the role of
nuclear weapons and the decisions to be taken on their use.
There are conflicts between military and civilian leaders
in the United States, and much more attention needs to be
given to these questions.

1151.   Gray, Colin S.   "Strategic 'Superiority' in Superpower Relations." Military Review 51 (December 1971):8-21.
Defines the concept of superiority and discusses the impact
of the USSR's increasing strength.

1152.   Mahley, Donald A.   "The New 'Nuclear Options' in
Military Strategy." Military Review 56 (December 1976):3-7.
Reviews nuclear strategy as stated by Secretary of Defense
Schlesinger.   Mahley examines the various "levels of
nuclear deterrence" and the recent elaboration of nuclear
strategy as the "controlled use of nuclear weapons." Mahley
asserts that the real problem is how to end a nuclear war
once it has begun.

1153. Martin, Laurence W.   "Military Issues: Strategic
Parity and Its Implications." In Retreat from Empire? The
First Nixon Administration, edited by Robert E. Osgood and
others, 137-171.   Baltimore: Johns Hopkins University
Press, 1973. Focuses on the increasing nuclear strength of
the USSR, symbolized by the Strategic Arms Limitation
Agreements in 1972.   Martin also usefully compares the
approaches of McNamara and of the Nixon administration to
strategic weapons strategy.

1154. Moll, Kenneth L.   "Realistic Deterrence and New
Strategy."   Air University Review 23 (November-December
1971):2-12. Analyzes the impact of the Nixon Doctrine on
the armed services. Various factors are important in the
maintenance of "realistic deterrence."

1155. Nichols, David L. "Who Needs Nuclear TACAIR?" Air
University Review 27 (March-April 1976):15-25. Argues that
tactical air forces with nuclear capability add to the
flexibility of NATO forces.   Nichols believes that new
doctrine has to be developed for tactical air to make it
more effective.

1156.   Nitze, Paul H.   "Assuring Strategic Stability in an

Era of Detente." Foreign Affairs 54 (January 1976): 207-
232. Argues that despite SALT, the United States must
maintain its ability to present a credible deterrence.

1157. Nusbaum, Keith C. "Conventional Versus Nuclear
Firepower." Military Review 41 (May 1961):91-96. Treats
tactical nuclear weapons as part of normal munitions
available to the military. Nusbaum suggests that
commanders will be cautious about using nuclear fire in
order to apply it only when it will be effective.

1158. O'Ballance, Edgar. "The Megatonnage and Missile
Gaps." Military Review 49 (March 1969):65-70. Expresses
alarm over increasing Soviet strength in very destructive
nuclear weapons. O'Ballance also sketches nuclear weapons
development generally.

1159. Paolucci, Dominic A. "The Development of Navy
Strategic Offensive and Defensive Systems." United States
Naval Institute Proceedings 96 (May 1970):204-223. Ad-
vocates primary dependence on sea-based nuclear weapons.
Paolucci describes the impact of MIRV (Multiple
Independently Targeted Reentry Vehicle), which makes
seaborne missiles all the more necessary.

1160. Pinckney, Thomas C. "Overkill and Underthought." Air
University Review. 15 (July-August 1964):37-48. Contrasts
advocates of "overkill," who feel the threat of massive
nuclear attacks is an appropriate and sufficient deterrent
with those who favor counterforce strategy, which involves
concentrating attacks on military targets. Pinckney is
highly critical of "overkill" strategy.

1161. Reed, Robert H. "On Deterrence: A Broadened
Perspective." Air University Review 26 (May-June 1975):2-
17. Examines the vast changes in American attitudes on
foreign policy and the much greater complexity of world
politics. Reed sees much more emphasis being given to
deterrence by the United States and its allies. He looks at
various types of possible conflicts and the ways to deter
them.

1162. Reinhardt, George C. "The Doctrinal Gap." United
States Naval Institute Proceedings 92 (August 1966):61-69.
Pinpoints the need for doctrine covering the use of
tactical nuclear weapons. Reinhardt asserts that the
employment of nuclear weapons should be considered in
limited wars because they might have a very potent
deterrent effect.

1163. Russett, Bruce M. "Assured Destruction Of What? A
Countercombatant Alternative to Nuclear MADness." Public
Policy 22 (Spring 1974):121-138. Argues that military
installations should be the primary targets for nuclear
attacks.

1164. Strauch, Ralph E. "Winners and Losers: A Conceptual Barrier in Our Strategic Thinking." <u>Air University Review</u> 23 (July-August 1972):33-44. Argues that the concept of "winners" and "losers" is not applicable in a world where competitors can destroy each other. Strauch sees a future nuclear war "as a process of bargaining" in which use of nuclear weapons would be minimized as much as possible.

1165. Sullivan, Robert R. "ABM, MIRV, SALT and the Balance of Power." <u>Midwest Quarterly</u> 13 (October 1971):11-36. Discusses political aspects of weapons systems such as MIRV. Sullivan asserts that the United States should use these systems not only for restoring its nuclear supremacy but also for furthering its goals in various parts of the world.

1166. Thompson, Roy L. "The Triad and Beyond: The Future of Strategic Deterrence." <u>Air University Review</u> 25 (July-August 1974):9-16. Describes new weapons within the American Triad and proposes ways to make the Triad more effective. Thompson favors more systems thinking and warns that "weak links" in the American defenses must be guarded against.

1167. Ullman, Richard H. "No First Use of Nuclear Weapons."
<u>Foreign Affairs</u> 50 (July 1972):669-683. Recommends that the United States make a "no first use" declaration and discusses the various processes and instruments that might be used to enunciate such a policy.

1168. Van Cleave, William R. and Harold W. Rood. "Spread of Nuclear Weapons." <u>Military Review</u> 46 (December 1966):3-10. Reviews the development of nuclear weapons by additional nations. Van Cleave and Rood present the reasons why a given nation wants to equip itself with such weapons.

1169. Winne, Clinton H., Jr. "Salt and the Blue-Water Strategy." <u>Air University Review</u> 25 (September-October 1974):25-35. Discusses the significance of basing ICBMs at sea, but ultimately argues for a balanced force of submarines and manned bombers for delivery of these weapons.

Air Strategy

General

1170. Deitchman, S.J. "The Implications of Modern Technological Developments for Tactical Air Tactics and Doctrine." <u>Air University Review</u> 29 (November-December 1975):23-45. Stresses the continuing importance of tactical air. Deitchman refers to many military situations from World War II through Vietnam and describes the vast technological changes affecting tactical air.

1171. Stellini, Edward. "The Threat, Foreign Policy, and Cost Control: Parameters for Force Planning." Air University Review 24 (September-October 1973):2-15. Discusses proposals for cuts in defense spending and relates them to changes in foreign policy. Stellini focuses on tactical air force levels.

1172. Stiles, Dennis W. "Air Power: A New Look from an Old Rooftop." Air University Review 27 (November-December 1975): 49-59. Traces the development of air force doctrine since World War II and analyzes the role of the air force in the context of the total defense force. In part, Stiles seeks to assimilate the Vietnam experience.

1173. Stodder, Joseph H. "Aspects of Air Force Strategy Today." Air University Review 27 (November-December 1975): 38-48. Discusses air force limited and general war strategy and the effects of recent technological changes. Stodder concludes with an assessment of the impact of SALT.

1174. Vander Els, Theodore. "The Irresistible Weapon." Military Review 51 (August 1971):80-90. Seeks to deflate the exaggerated reputation of strategic air bombardment. Much of its importance lies in appearance rather than in practice.

Missiles

1175. Brennan, Donald G. "The Case for Missile Defense." Foreign Affairs 47 (April 1969):433-448. Favors a ballistic missile defense system instead of an offensive system. Brennan critiques the McNamara offensive missile strategy.

1176. Davis, Lynn Etheridge and Warner R. Schilling. "All You Ever Wanted to Know about MIRV and ICBM Calculations But were Not Cleared to Ask." Journal of Conflict Resolution 17 (June 1973):207-242. Assesses the vulnerability of American and Soviet intercontinental ballistic missiles to MIRV attacks.

1177. Geiger, George J. "Air Defense Missiles for the Army." Military Review 49 (December 1969):39-49. Examines a number of weapons, including the Hawk, and discusses their potentiality for protecting ground forces.

1178. Wildavsky, Aaron. "The Politics of ABM." Commentary 48 (November 1969):55-63. Reviews the debate over anti-ballistic missiles. Wildavsky feels that it has not been helpful and that the decision to implement ABM should have been taken.

Military Airlift

1179. Carlton, Paul K. "Strategic Airlift: A Cargo Capability Shortfall." Air University Review 27 (November-December 1975):2-10. Warns that the United States must have more airlift capability, which can be developed, in part, by encouraging the design of civilian aircraft for emergency military use.

Ground Strategy

Composition of Forces

1180. Gelb, Leslie H. and Arnold M. Kuzmack. "General Purpose Forces." In The Next Phase in Foreign Policy, edited by Henry Owen, 203-224. Washington, D.C.: Brookings Institution, 1973. Investigates the foreign and domestic considerations influencing the size and deployment of general purpose (conventional) forces. The authors also explore the Nixon administration's move to a "1-1/2 war" strategy as opposed to the "2-1/2 war" stance of the 1960's.

1181. Gibson, James M. "A Case for Mechanized Infantry." Military Review 50 (September 1970):56-70. Argues for use of infantry forces smaller than traditional divisions. New forms of organization are needed partly because of pending reductions in force levels.

1182. Karemaa, Aadu. "The Airmobile Armored Division." Military Review 50 (September 1970):3-8. Describes the organization and operation of an airmobile armored division. Karemaa sees many useful features in such a division.

1183. McWilliams, Keith E. "Divisions or Brigades for the Army National Guard." Military Review 51 (January 1971): 35-42. Reviews army and army national guard decisions to replace divisions with brigades. McWilliams examines the strengths and weaknesses of such a policy.

1184. Webb, George S., Jr. "More Cavalry for the Infantry Division." Military Review 49 (January 1969):14-21. Proposes changing some infantry battalions into armored cavalry forces. This would have the effect of further maximizing personnel utilization in Vietnam.

Limited War

1185. Beavers, Roy. "A Doctrine for Limited War." United States Naval Institute Proceedings 96 (October 1970):26-34. Emphasizes that the United States must maintain a limited war capability. Beavers discusses the nature of limited war, which he feels must focus on specific objectives if it is to be fought successfully.

1186.   Brown, Harold.   "Air Power in Limited War." Air University Review 20 (May-June 1969):2-15.   Reviews the role of air power in the Vietnam conflict and forecasts its utility in similar future wars. Brown sees little merit in various criticisms of aviation in Vietnam; on the contrary, the air force was highly effective. Brown warns against dwelling too much on Vietnam when planning for the future, however.

1187. Deitchman, Seymour J.   "Limited War."   Military Review 51 (July 1971):3-16. During limited wars national objectives change with the degree of military succcess or failure.

1188. LeGro, William E. "The WHY and HOW of Limited War." Military Review 50 (July 1970):32-39.   Analyzes various concepts of limited war.   LeGro discusses Robert E. Osgood's Limited War (1957) [see entry 377] at length.

1189. Murry, William V. "Clausewitz and Limited Nuclear War." Military Review 55 (April 1975):15-28. Argues that the Principles of War have not led to suitable American limited nuclear war doctrine.   Murry reviews the applicability of these principles, only three of which seem fully usable in the nuclear context.

1190.   Parnell, Charles L.   "Victory in Limited war." United States Naval Institute Proceedings 95 (June 1969):26-31. Speaks against the concept of limited war and argues for a total commitment to military victory in any conflict. Limited war theory and practice puts the United States at a disadvantage.

Naval Strategy

General

1191. Barber, James A., Jr. "Is There a Generation Gap in the Naval Officer Corps?" Naval War College Review 22 (May 1970):24-40. Compares students in officer candidate school and at the Naval War College. Some differences in attitude were detected, but there were many similarities as well.

1192. Barber, James A., Jr. "The Nixon Doctrine and the Navy." Naval War College Review 23 (June 1971):5-15. Suggests that the implications of the Nixon Doctrine will enhance the role of maritime strategy and, thereby, increase the importance of naval forces.

1193. Bathurst, Robert B.   "The Lemming Complex: Ritual Death in the Norwegian Sea." Naval War College Review 26 (May-June 1974):35-42. Uses recent naval maneuvers to warn that the United States Navy looks back to World War II, while the Soviet Navy is better attuned to current conditions.

1194. Bathurst, Robert B. "The Patterns of Naval Analysis." Naval War College Review 27 (November-December 1974):16-27. Argues that the United States must consider more carefully political factors in developing a naval strategy.

1195. Behrens, William W., Jr. "Environmental Considerations in Naval Operations." Naval War College Review 24 (September 1971):70-77. Explains the mission and work of the navy's Oceanographic Office. Behrens includes an historical survey.

1196. Burke, Arleigh A. "Role of Naval Forces." Naval War College Review 22 (March 1970):5-11. In an examination of naval forces and foreign affairs, Burke observes that the United States is unlikely to undertake major operations without the consent of its allies. He also looks at the increasing strength of the Soviet navy.

1197. Caldwell, Robert C. "The Role of the Tracked Amphibian in Modern Amphibious Warfare." Naval War College Review 22 (January 1970):68-99. After examining the history of amphibious landing vehicles, Caldwell discusses current American needs for such vehicles.

1198. Case, Frank B. "Constriction of the Free Sea." Military Review 46 (March 1966):3-12. Discusses legal aspects of access to seaways. Case believes that the United States must protect its rights.

1199. Clift, A. Denis. "Of Diplomats and Ocean Politics." United States Naval Institute Proceedings 96 (July 1970): 31-39. Examines United Nations activity on the law of the sea and related issues. Clift also discusses the increasing interest of the United States in these matters.

1200. Cohen, Paul. "The Erosion of Surface Naval Power." Foreign Affairs 49 (January 1971):330-341. Asserts that surface vessels are so open to attack that submarines may have to assume transport as well as weapons-carrying roles.

1201. Greenbacker, John E. "Where Do We Go From Here?" United States Naval Institute Proceedings 102 (June 1976): 18-24. Reaffirms the need to preserve a strong navy in the face of Soviet threats.

1202. Herrington, Arthur C. "U.S. Navy Policy." Naval War College Review 22 (September 1969):4-13. Advocates a kind of geopolitical approach to structuring naval forces. Attention to land masses important to American foreign policy would replace the more general goal of sea control.

1203. Holloway, James L. III.   "The US Navy: A Bicentennial
Appraisal." United States Naval Institute Proceedings 102
(July 1976):18-24.   Chief of Naval Operations laments the
diminution of American naval strength.   Holloway warns that
the Soviets may well surpass the United States at sea.

1204. Kendall, Lane C.   "Capable of Serving as a Naval and
Military Auxiliary." United States Naval Institute Proceedings 97 (May 1971):210-227.   Traces the decline in the
American merchant marine as an effective adjunct to the
armed forces.   There is less and less interest in the
military applications of cargo vessels and tankers.

1205.   Klare, Michael T.   "Superpower Rivalry at Sea."
Foreign Policy, no. 21 (Winter 1975-1976):86-96, 161-167.
Plays down Soviet capabilities for maritime operations and
argues that the United States does not have to build up its
navy against a Soviet threat.

1206. Koburger, Charles W., Jr.   "Seapower: The Lower
Spectrum." Military Review 51 (June 1971):62-68.   Discusses
the services the navy can and does provide in short of war
and other politico-military situations.   Koburger compares
these services with the operations of the Royal Navy in
support of British goals.

1207. Lowe, George E.   "The Only Option?"   United States
Naval Institute Proceedings 97 (April 1971):18-26.   Argues
that the United States Navy is the service best suited to
implement the Nixon Doctrine.   Lowe describes navy needs
and possible contributions.   He asserts that manned bombers
flying from land bases are obsolete.

1208. McClintock, Robert. "An American Oceanic Doctrine."
United States Naval Institute Proceedings 96 (February
1970):46-57.   Emphasizes the need for both a strong navy
and a vigorous merchant marine.   McClintock also focuses
attention on legal issues connected with the use of the
sea.

1209.   McDevitt, Joseph B.   "Current International Law
Problems of the Navy." Naval War College Review 22 (May
1970):41-49.   Examines various international legal issues,
the most important of which seems to be the definition of
territorial waters which influences naval operations.

1210.   McFarlane, Robert C.   "At Sea: Where We Belong."
United States Naval Institute Proceedings 97 (November
1971):36-42.   Recommends a huge expansion of the navy to
provide more flexible readiness forces.   McFarlane argues
that this would be cheaper than relying on land bases in
sensitive areas.

1211. Murphy, Frank B. "Ocean Surveillance: New Weapons
of Naval Warfare." United States Naval Institute Pro-

ceedings 97 (February 1971):38-41. Discusses various types
of sensors and other surveillance devices. Murphy argues
that the navy should be given complete control of ocean
surveillance.

1212.   Sherman, James R.   "Forcible Entry: A Lost Art?"
Military Review 56 (September 1976):14-20. Asserts that the
United States may be losing its ability to make seaborne
attacks.   There are problems because of the weakness of the
American merchant marine and because much military cargo
consists of vehicles and other non-containerized goods,
which cannot be carried on newer types of merchant ships.

1213.   Shreckengost, Raymond C. "Science, Technology, and
Change: Implications for the Navy." Naval War College
Review 24 (November 1971):1-16.   Assesses the implications
of current technological developments on the navy and its
missions and its structure.

The Marines and Rapid Deployment

1214.   Amme,   Carl   H.,   Jr.   "The   Need   for   Assault
Capabilities." Military Review 50 (November 1970):12-22.
Discusses naval and air assault forces.   Amme expresses
concern that American capability for both types of assaults
will be reduced in the near future.

1215. Bowden, James A.   "The RDJTF and Doctrine." Military
Review 62 (November 1982) :50-64.   Emphasizes that the
rapid deployment force is a logical outgrowth of post-World
War II American military responsibilities.

1216. Millett, Allan R.   "The U.S. Marine Corps: Adaptation
in the Post-Vietnam Era." Armed Forces and Society 9
(Spring 1983):363-392.   Suggests that the marines have
benefitted from current strategic perceptions.   The marine
corps is revising its structure to maintain its role in the
defense establishment.

1217.   United States Marine Corps. Marine Corps Concepts
and Issues. Washington, D.C.: Headquarters, United States
Marine Corps. 1986? SOD D214.27:985.   Outlines the role of
the marine corps in national defense and discusses at
length weapons and communications systems of the corps.
Personnel issues are reviewed briefly.

Military Assistance

Official Policy Statements

1218. Nixon, Richard.   "Special Message to the Congress
Proposing Reform of the Foreign Assistance Program.   April
21, 1971." In Public Papers of the Presidents of the United
States: Richard Nixon 1971, 564-578.   Washington, D.C.:

Government Printing Office, 1972. Presents a plan to "enable security assistance to play more effectively its critical role in supporting the Nixon Doctrine," to differentiate security and other types of funding, and to make other appropriate changes. A lengthy section of the message discusses administrative restructuring of the program and the respective roles of security assistance and arms sales.

Books

1219. Sorley, Lewis. Arms Transfers under Nixon: A Policy Analysis. Lexington: University Press of Kentucky, 1983. 248p. Detailed study of military assistance under the Nixon Doctrine which stipulated more aid and less American military presence. Most chapters examine particular countries or regions.

Periodical Articles

1220. Baines, John M. "U.S. Military Assistance to Latin America: An Assessment." Journal of Inter-American Studies and World Affairs 14 (November 1972):469-487. Discusses various facets of assistance and reviews the assertions that have been made about its role and its value.

1221. Barrett, Raymond J. "Arms Dilemma for the Developing World." Military Review 50 (April 1970):28-35. Noting that there is a greater need for economic than for military assistance in the Third World, Barrett assesses the records of the United States and the Soviet Union in providing appropriate kinds of aid.

1222. Barrett, Raymond J. "The Changing Role of the Military Advisor." Military Review 54 (September 1974):25-30. Explores the role of the Military Assistance Program (MAP) in the environment created by the Nixon Doctrine. Barrett discusses the demands on contemporary military advisers and the characteristics they must display to be effective. The last section of the article deals with the increasing trend from gifts of military equipment to sales.

1223. Blake, Donald F. "A Realistic Look at USAF Military Assistance and Foreign Military Sales." Air University Review 22 (November-December 1970):35-44. Reviews air force efforts in these areas and warns that assistance should not be allowed to undermine the economies or political systems of the countries receiving aid.

1224. Haahr, James C. "Military Assistance to Latin America." Military Review 49 (May 1969):12-21. Asserts that the military assistance program is linked with the increased willingness of the Latin American military to accept democracy. Haahr also describes the continuing need for such assistance from the United States.

1225. Kemp, Geoffrey.   "Dilemmas of the Arms Traffic."
Foreign Affairs 48 (January 1970):274-284.   Discusses
various aspects of American sales and gifts of military
material.   Sales have risen as military assistance has
declined.

1226.   Kent, Irvin M.   "Political Warfare for Internal
Defense."   Military Review 50 (August 1970):66-69.
Emphasizes American military assistance to the Republic of
China (Taiwan).   Kent examines the political implications
of such assistance.

1227. Lansdale, Edward G.   "The Opposite Number."   Air
University Review 23 (July-August 1972):22-32.   Warns that
American opponents are likely to be professional
revolutionaries rather than professional soldiers and that
American military leaders need to be ready.   Lansdale
emphasizes eliminating shortcomings in American allies that
give the revolutionaries an opportunity to foster
dissension.

1228. Meyer, Charles A.   "U.S. Military Activities in Latin
America."   Inter-American Economic Affairs 23 (Autumn
1969):89-94.   Assistant Secretary of State for Inter-
American Affairs asserts that the United States is sending
less military aid to Latin America and denies that aid
promotes dictatorships or excessive defense spending.

1229. Pierson, Earl F. "The United States Role in Counterinsurgency." Naval War College Review 25 (January-February
1973):88-99. Warns that counterinsurgency doctrine is still
needed as a part of American defense planning.   Pierson
stresses assistance to countries threatened by insurgency,
leaving American military intervention as a last resort.

1230. Tippin, Garold L.   "The Army as a Nationbuilder."
Military Review 50 (October 1970):11-19.   Predicts that
provision of military and other forms of assistance will
continue to be a major army mission for some time to come.
Tippin cites American military assistance experience in
Vietnam.

1231. Victor, A.H., Jr.   "Military Aid and Comfort to
Dictatorships." United States Naval Institute Proceedings
95 (March 1969):42-47.   Examines the various types of
American aid that may help non-communist authoritarian
regimes.   Victor suggests that criticism is currently
directed at assistance to certain Latin American countries.
Victor argues that authoritarian regimes such as the Shah
of Iran's can improve economic conditions and may evolve
into democratic systems.

Disarmament and Arms Control

Official Policy Statements

1232. Nixon, Richard. "Remarks at a Ceremony Marking the Ratification and Entry Into Force of the Treaty on the Non-Proliferation of Nuclear Weapons. March 5, 1970." In Public Papers of the Presidents of the United States: Richard Nixon 1970, 241-242. Washington, D.C.: Government Printing Office, 1971. Stresses the bipartisan commitment to nonproliferation, citing the efforts of the Kennedy and Johnson administrations. Nixon expresses the hope that strategic weapons will soon be limited.

1233. Nixon, Richard. "Message to the Senate Transmitting the Geneva Protocol of 1925 on Chemical and Bacteriological Methods of Warfare. August 19, 1970." In Public Papers of the Presidents of the United States: Richard Nixon 1970, 677-678. Washington, D.C.: Government Printing Office, 1971. In asking the Senate to ratify the Protocol, Nixon states that the United States will not make "first-use of lethal and incapacitating chemical weapons," will not use "biological and toxin weapons" at all, and will promote further progress on disarmament in these fields.

1234. Nixon, Richard. "Remarks at the Signing Ceremony of the Seabed Arms Control Treaty. February 11, 1971." In Public Papers of the Presidents of the United States: Richard Nixon 1971, 150-151. Washington, D.C.: Government Printing Office, 1972. Sees the treaty as "only one step toward . . . the control of nuclear weapons." Nixon emphasizes that the treaty is an important innovation and expresses considerable optimism about further progress in disarmament.

1235. Nixon, Richard "Address to a Joint Session of the Congress on Return From Austria, the Soviet Union, Iran, and Poland. June 1, 1972." In Public Papers of the Presidents of the United States: Richard Nixon 1972, 660-666. Washington, D.C.: Government Printing Office, 1974. Portrays SALT I and the ABM Treaty as a new beginning in Soviet-American relations. Nixon explains the ABM Treaty briefly and asserts "that this is an agreement in the interest of both countries."

Periodical Articles

1236. Barrett, Raymond J. "The Hard Realities of Arms Control." Air Force Magazine. 55 (February 1972):47-49. Argues that while arms control is important, defense expenditures may not be materially reduced even if significant agreements are reached.

1237. Beavers, Roy L., Jr. "SALT I." United States Naval Institute Proceedings 100 (May 1974):204-219. Emphasizes

the limitations of SALT I, which neither reduced superpower
friction nor prevented a continued arms race.

1238. Bills, Ray W. "What Should Be the United States'
Position on Chemical Warfare Disarmament?" Military Review
55 (May 1975):12-23. Reviews Nixon's efforts to promote
chemical disarmament and the current negotiations on this
matter. Bills summarizes earlier attempts to bar the use
of chemical weapons by treaty. Much of the article
describes opposition within the United States to the
chemical warfare program.

1239. Brindel, Charles L. "The Implications of SALT Agreements in the 1970s." Military Review 55 (June 1975):39-48.
Briefly tabulates the course of arms control negotiations
from 1959 onward and then surveys prospects for further
progress. Brindel takes a generally favorable view of
developments and asserts that "[n]one of the previous
agreements, including those signed in 1974, present a
security risk to the United States."

1240. Brown, Harold. "Security Through Limitation."
Foreign Affairs 47 (April 1969):422-432. Expresses optimism
concerning the possibility of strategic arms limitations.
Brown analyzes weapons developments that would undermine
"second-strike" capability, which would in turn diminish
the chances for arms reductions.

1241. Burt, Richard. "SALT II and Offensive Force Levels."
Orbis 18 (Summer 1974):465-481. Reviews SALT II and
compares Soviet and American nuclear weapons arsenals.

1242. Clark, Donald L. "What's an MBFR?" Air University
Review 27 (July-August 1976):51-64. Comments on negotiations on Mutual and Balanced Force Reductions (MBFR) in the
1970's. Clark explains the complicated process and
advocates continued talks. Results may stave off unilateral
American force reductions in Europe.

1243. Clarke, Duncan L. "The Arms Control and Disarmament
Agency: Effective?" Foreign Service Journal 52 (December
1975):12-14, 28-30. Asseses the Agency's success in
reducing the possibility of nuclear war.

1244. Dougherty, James E. "The Status of the Arms Negotiations." Orbis 9 (Spring 1965):49-97. Vigorously advocates
further pursuit of disarmament agreements, despite the
apparent lessening of superpower competition in the arms
field. Dougherty is much in favor of preventing further
proliferation of nuclear weapons.

1245. Feld, Bernard T. "The Charade of Piecemeal Arms
Limitation." Bulletin of the Atomic Scientists 31 (January
1975):8-16. Reviews American agreements with the Soviets,
including efforts to end nuclear testing.

1246. Foster, William C. "Prospects for Arms Control." Foreign Affairs 47 (April 1969):413-421. Notes technological developments that are reducing the value of "second-strike" capability. Foster concludes that progress is being made toward an arms control agreement between the superpowers.

1247 Giddings, Ralph L., Jr. "Arms Control: No Simple Answers." United States Naval Institute Proceedings 96 (February 1970):41-45. Argues that the military must be involved in formulating arms control policy. Giddings expresses faith in the concept of arms control negotiations.

1248. Gray, Colin S. "Of Bargaining Chips and Building Blocks: Arms Control and Defense Policy." International Journal 28 (Spring 1973):266-296. Studies relationships between American military policies and the continuing negotiations with the USSR for disarmament.

1249. Gray, Colin S. "A Problem Guide to SALT II." Military Review 56 (April 1976):82-89. Analyzes the problems still to be negotiated for an effective SALT II agreement. Much of the article deals with cruise missiles and their relationships to arms control. Gray also discusses the potential political impact of repeated accusations that one side or the other is violating SALT I.

1250. Hanks, Robert J. "The Paper Torpedo." United States Naval Institute Proceedings 95 (May 1969):26-34. Warns the navy and American leaders that disarmament and demilitarization are dangerous to the United States. Hanks expresses concern in particular about proposals concerning the seabed which are being considered by the United Nations.

1251. Hayden, Eric W. "Soviet-American Arms Negotiations-1960-1968: A Prelude for SALT." Naval War College Review 24 (January 1972):65-82. Discusses the very limited arms related agreements of the early to mid-1960's such as the Nonproliferation Treaty. Hayden notes that the SALT talks were the first serious disarmament discussions concerning nuclear weapons.

1252. Korb, Lawrence J. "The Issues and Costs of the New United States Nuclear Policy." Naval War College Review 27 (November-December 1974):28-41. Analyzes the complexities of weapons technology that make disarmament negotiations so difficult.

1253. Menos, Dennis. "Beyond SALT." Military Review 50 (June 1970):91-97. Stresses the significance of the SALT talks, but warns that not all nuclear weapons challenges will be met by implementing the agreements. Menos proposes a treaty to protect cities from Soviet or American nuclear attack.

1254. Schneider, Mark B.   "Safeguard, Sufficiency, and SALT." Military Review 51 (May 1971):24-33. There must be balance between national security and negotiating success during the SALT talks. Schneider emphasizes the Safeguard antimissile missiles in his proposals.

1255. Schneider, Mark B.   "Strategic Arms Limitation." Military Review 50 (March 1970):20-28.   Discusses the obstacles to effective agreement.   Schneider recommends that the United States move very slowly and carefully in seeking a treaty.

1256. Scoville, Herbert, Jr. "Beyond Salt One." Foreign Affairs 50 (April 1972):488-500. Predicts that SALT One will diminish the number of anti-ballistic missiles. Scoville foresees that an agreement on strategic offensive weapons will be more difficult to achieve.

1257. Sherman, Michael E. "Nixon and Arms Control." International Journal 24 (Spring 1969):327-338. Predicts that there will be little movement toward disarmament during Nixon's presidency, although some limited accords may be reached.

1258. Smith, Gerald C. "SALT After Vladivostok," Journal of International Affairs 29 (Spring 1975):7-18. Discusses the Vladivostok Accord and the anti-ballistic missile treaty. Smith also examines continuing problems related to these agreements.

1259. Stone, Jeremy J. "When and How to Use 'Salt.'" Foreign Affairs 48 (January 1970):262-273. Analyzes relationships between arms policies and internal political factors in the United States and the USSR. Even without a treaty, the arms race needs to be and can be curbed.

1260. Watt, D.C. "Balanced Force Reductions: The American Withdrawal from Germany." Royal United Service Institute Journal 115 (June 1970):42-44. Examines the possible removal of American troops. Watt asserts that the West must negotiate further with the Soviets to allay their fears of Germany.

1261. Youngflesh, Richard D. "What's This Essential Equivalence Bit?" Air University Review 26 (September-October 1975):15-20. Examines the Vladivostok agreement of November, 1974. Youngflesh warns that "equivalence" is an unappealing goal and may lead the Soviets to consider a first strike.

Military Personnel

Official Policy Statements

1262. Nixon, Richard. "Special Message to the Congress on Draft Reform. April 23, 1970." In Public Papers of the Presidents of the United States: Richard Nixon 1970, 394-98. Washington, D.C.: Government Printing Office, 1971. Proposes transition to a volunteer system for the armed services and changes in the interim selective service system such as the elimination of many deferment categories. Nixon refers to the Gates Commission report [entry 1263] and endorses its findings.

1263. U.S. President's Commission on an All-Volunteer Armed Force. The Report of the President's Commission on an All-Volunteer Force. London: Collier Books/Macmillan Company, 1970. Gates Commission recommends unanimously that conscription be ended. The report discusses all phases of conscription, including the "doctor draft," and possible alternative policies.

1264. Nixon, Richard. "Special Message to the Congress About Draft Reform. January 28, 1971." In Public Papers of the Presidents of the United States: Richard Nixon 1971, 75-78. Washington, D.C.: Government Printing Office, 1972. Summarizes Nixon's efforts to move toward an all-volunteer force, thereby ending the draft. Nixon reviews a number of legislative proposals he is making in order to improve the ability of the armed services to attract volunteers and to make the draft system fairer.

1265. Nixon, Richard "Statement About Progress Toward Establishment of an All-Volunteer Armed Force. August 28, 1972." In Public Papers of the Presidents of the United States: Richard Nixon 1972, 825-826. Washington, D.C.: Government Printing Office, 1974. Reviews developments in reducing the number of men drafted and the establishment of an interim lottery system as a substitute for the earlier structure with its many deferments. Nixon predicts an end to the draft by July 1973.

Periodical Articles

1266. Abramowitz, Benjamin L. "Can the Reserve Component Make It?" Military Review 56 (May 1976):58-64. Notes that reserve units have not in the past received enough appropriate training to be used in combat immediately. Abramowitz argues that the army needs to develop more realistic expectations. Only some reserve forces need be combat ready immediately; the army could not effectively utilize all the reserve troops at once, even if they were ready.

1267. Carson, Ray M. "Improved Command and Control for the

United States Army Reserve." <u>Military Review</u> 55 (July 1975):83-94. Focuses primarily on the Army Reserve Command level and the efforts made to improve reserve readiness. Carson sees significant problems arising from limited personnel in the ARCOMs, which frustrates their ability to control reserve units. National Guard Headquarters, on the other hand, have substantially larger staffs.

1268. Cerchione, Angelo J. "A Case for Continuity." <u>Air University Review</u> 20 (March-April 1969):33-41. Discusses problems incurred by the frequent transfer of personnel. Cerchione sees a special problem in relationships between air force installations overseas and the local foreign communities.

1269. Ebel, Wilfred L. "Guard and Reserve Forces: America's Maginot Line?" <u>Military Review</u> 54 (March 1974):21-24. To support the Nixon Doctrine, the reserve and guard forces must be capable of being mobilized as fully effective elements in the armed services, and there must be a willingness on the part of political leaders to mobilize them when necessary. Ebel discusses the work of the Total Force Study Group, which is examining the posture of the reserve and guard for the years 1975-1982.

1270. Evans, Robert, Jr. "The Military Draft as a Slave System: An Economic View." <u>Social Science Quarterly</u> 50 (December 1969):535-543. Compares military service with slavery in the United States and with forced labor in totalitarian states. Evans describes four major elements that these systems have in common.

1271. Fisher, Franklin M. and Anton S. Morton. "Reenlist-ments in the U.S. Navy: A Cost Effectiveness Study." <u>American Economic Review</u> 57 (May 1967):32-38. Examines various incentives for reenlistment, finding that the existing system was quite effective except for electronics personnel.

1272. Ford, William Freithaler and Robert Tollison. "Notes on the Color of the Volunteer Army." <u>Social Science Quarterly</u> 50 (December 1969):544-547. Suggests that as the army becomes more technical in orientation, the overrepre-sentation of blacks will probably disappear. The authors mention other factors working against a heavily black army.

1273. Gray, George H. "What Are US Reserve Forces Really For?" <u>Military Review</u> 55 (June 1975):82-91. Briefly surveys the contribution of reserve and National Guard forces in the 20th century before Vietnam. Gray explores the possible reasons for not calling up reserve and guard forces during the Vietnam conflict and argues that the decision not to do so was the biggest error of the war.

1274. Janowitz, Morris. "Volunteer Armed Forces and

Military Purpose." <u>Foreign Affairs</u> 50 (April 1972):427-443. Proposes the reduction of American forces in Europe and asserts that American negotiating strategy viz-a-viz the Soviet Union must include the recognition that troop levels need to be lowered.

1275. Joulwan, George A.   "ROTC: An Academic Focus." <u>Military Review</u> 51 (January 1971):43-47. Reviews changes in ROTC, highlighting a new program at Loyola University of Chicago. Joulwan suggests that there can be more fruitful participation in college programs by ROTC instructors.

1276. Katauskas, Philip J. "Last Muster for the Citizens' Army?" <u>United States Naval Institute Proceedings</u> 98 (February 1972):61-67. Analyzes the movement toward an all volunteer force that developed as a result of the Vietnam conflict. Katauskas also discusses ways to avoid too much separation American society from its armed forces.

1277. Palmer, Bruce Jr. and Curtis W. Tarr.   "A Careful Look at Defense Manpower." <u>Military Review</u> 56 (September 1976): 3-13. Reviews the work of the Defense Manpower Commission. The authors make a number of forthright criticisms of personnel procurement, although they note that the army has made a successful conversion to an all-volunteer basis.

1278. Scott, Joseph W.   "ROTC Retreat." <u>Trans-action</u> 6 (September 1969):47-52. Examines the impact of campus unrest during the 1960's on ROTC and the changes that have been made in the program. There is a real danger that ROTC effectiveness will be sharply reduced by the elimination of programs at many prestige colleges and universities.

1279.   Sorensen, Neal G.   "Implications of a Volunteer Force." <u>Air University Review</u> 22 (March-April 1971):45-52. Suggests that there may be changes in the civilian-military relationship and in the pattern of officer procurement. These changes need not necessarily threaten the American system of government, however.

1280. Stockstill, Louis R.   "The All-Volunteer Force: Its Cloudy Pros and Cons." <u>Air Force and Space Digest</u> 53 (June 1970):67-76. Reviews the recommendations of the Gates Commission and comments that a volunteer force is likely to be attempted. Stockstill is skeptical about the Gates Commission's [see entry 1263] responses to many of the problems of a volunteer force.

1281. Toner, Richard J. "The Total Force Concept: An Air Force View." <u>Air University Review</u> 24 (November-December 1972):2-9. Toner discusses the efforts to achieve total integration of active and reserve forces and personnel and asserts that the air force has been applying the "total force" concept for some time.

Latin America

1282.   Barrett, Raymond J. "The United States and the
Caribbean." <u>Air University Review</u> 22 (May-June 1971):44-51.
Notes the continuing concern of the United States with
political changes and tensions in the Caribbean. Barrett
also discusses economic development in the area and
examines the possibility that United States military
operations may be needed in some circumstances.

1283.   Bissell, Richard E.   "New Waves in the South
Atlantic: A Strategy Needed?" <u>Air University Review</u> 26
(March-April 1975):38-44. Notes that the United States was
not much concerned about Latin America and Africa until
about 1960. This has changed with the independence of many
African nations, further economic and political development
in Latin America, and Soviet and Chinese entrance into
Africa.

1284.   Corbett, Charles D. "Toward a US Defense Policy:
Latin America." <u>Military Review</u> 55 (June 1975):11-18.
Warns that Latin America may be given short shrift in a
period when military resources are becoming more limited.
Corbett outlines some of the challenges facing the United
States in Latin America, not all of them the result of
Soviet activities. He favors more emphasis on collective
security in the Western Hemisphere.

North Atlantic Treaty Organization

Official Policy Statements

1285. Nixon, Richard M. "The Time to Save NATO." <u>Atlantic
Community Quarterly</u> 6 (Winter 1968/1969):479-484. Radio
address, October 13, 1968, proposes much more of an
American commitment to NATO. Nixon also discusses NATO and
its contemporary role and problems.

1286. Nixon, Richard.   "Statement About United States
Military Forces in Europe. May 15, 1971." In <u>Public Papers
of the Presidents of the United States: Richard Nixon 1971</u>,
635-636.   Washington, D.C.: Government Printing Office,
1972. Assails efforts to reduce United States military
commitments in Europe such as Senator Mike Mansfield's
proposal to cut troop strength in half. Notes following
the statement refer to support Nixon received from
Presidents Johnson and Truman.

Books

1287. Newhouse, John and others. <u>U.S. Troops in Europe:
Issues, Costs, and Choices</u>. Washington, D.C.: Brookings
Institution, 1971.   177p. Examines Soviet policy and the
role of nuclear weapons, but most of the emphasis is on

economic problems associated with the maintenance of large numbers of American troops in Europe.

1288. Schilling, Warner R. and others. <u>American Arms and a Changing Europe: Dilemmas of Deterrence and Disarmament</u>. New York: Columbia University Press, 1973. An in-depth survey of the impact of current weapons technology on European security. It offers policy prescriptions for Americans. The book rests on research done for the United States Arms Control and Disarmament Agency.

Periodical Articles

1289. Borden, Donald F. "Inflexibility in NATO's Flexible Response." <u>Military Review</u> 56 (January 1976):24-41. Examines the meaning and background of "flexible response" in Europe. It began in the Kennedy administration and was eventually accepted by NATO, except for France, which left the alliance. Borden discusses a number of alternatives NATO may consider in its efforts to counter Warsaw Pact strength.

1290. Brennan, Donald G. "Some Fundamental Problems of Arms Control and National Security." <u>Orbis</u> 15 (Spring 1971):218-231. Advocates a European force with nuclear weapons and a reduction of the American commitment to Europe. Brennan is highly critical of the mutual assured destruction theory.

1291. Case, Frank B. "The Continuing Need for NATO." <u>Military Review</u> 45 (October 1965):61-67. Discusses the elements in an effective alliance that must be maintained. Although conditions in the 1960's are different from those in the 1950's, NATO is still necessary.

1292. Clarkson, Albert G. "United States NATO Force Levels." <u>Military Review</u> 50 (August 1970):38-44. Recommends reductions in American troop commitments, but discusses the complexities of American force levels in light of the French departure from NATO. Other considerations might also limit reductions or even cause increases.

1293. Enthoven, Alain C. and K. Wayne Smith. "What Forces for NATO? And From Whom?" <u>Foreign Affairs</u> 48 (October 1969):80-96. Improvements can be made in NATO without large additional inputs of money or personnel. American costs for NATO have to be balanced with other defense demands.

1294. Hahn, Walter F. "Nuclear Balance in Europe." <u>Foreign Affairs</u> 50 (April 1972):501-516. Asserts that Europe is becoming disillusioned about American commitments to nuclear deterrence of Soviet attack. Hahn offers a number of suggestions for mending the NATO alliance.

1295. Harrison, Stanley L. "Defense of the Atlantic Community." United States Naval Institute Proceedings 95 (October 1969):44-49. Reviews debates over NATO strategy during the 1960's and the persistence of discord between the European members of NATO and the United States. Harrison proposes reductions in American forces in Europe and a greater emphasis on missiles based on submarines to bolster deterrence.

1296. Harrison, Stanley L. "Revival for NATO is Needed Now." Air University Review 21 (March-April 1970):60-67. Reviews the political development of NATO and discusses the sources of current dissension within the alliance.

1297. Kaplan, Lawrence S. "NATO and the Nixon Doctrine: Ten Years Later." Orbis 24 (Spring 1980):149-164. Records the gradual increase in NATO power as a result of Nixon's emphasis on a European orientation in his defense policy.

1298. Kilmarx, Robert A. "Challenge of the Mediterranean: Crossroads of United States-Soviet Relations." Military Review 50 (November 1970):81-89. Emphasizes the importance of the Mediteranean for NATO and warns against increased Soviet activity.

1299. Kochenour, Robert W. "The United States, NATO and the Decade Ahead." Military Review 56 (July 1976):14-24. Acclaims the achievements of NATO and asserts that the alliance is basically healthy. Kochenour vigorously advocates maintaining present troop levels.

1300. Komer, Robert W. "Treating NATO's Self-Inflicted Wound." Foreign Policy, no. 13 (Winter 1973-74):34-48. Criticizes NATO's inadequate conventional posture. Komer believes that not enough is being done to defend against armored attacks; he notes problems resulting from higher costs and differing American and European approaches to the defense of Europe.

1301. Lang, Walter P., Jr. and John N. Taylor. "The Best Defense Is . . ." Military Review 56 (August 1976):12-22. Scenario for a limited Soviet attack on West Germany. The authors advocate developing a strategy which would not include use of tactical (or strategic) nuclear weapons to counter such a move, but would rely on a "defensive zone" in West Germany that might deter the Soviets.

1302. Partlow, Frank A., Jr. "Deterrence in NATO--The Role of the Military Committee." Military Review 54 (December 1974):3-8. Argues that the Military Committee can and should focus attention on maintaining a military posture for effective deterrence. It should also promote strengthening of the alliance through research, increasing industrial capacity, and other measures.

1303.   Pierre, Andrew J.   "Nuclear Diplomacy: Britain,
France, and America." Foreign Affairs 49 (January 1971):
283-301. Argues for more European participation in nuclear
defense decisions.   Pierre's position is influenced by
possible changes in relations between the United States and
NATO as a result of the SALT negotiations.

1304. Polk, James H.   "The New Short War Strategy."
Military Review 56 (March 1976):58-64. This strategy for
Europe puts more emphasis on combat strength that can be
employed rapidly for a short time.   In part, this approach
reflects the lessons of the Middle East campaign in 1973.
Polk analyzes the possible dangers of this change.

1305. Record, Jeffrey.   "To Nuke or Not to Nuke: A Critique
of Rationales for a Tactical Nuclear Defense of Europe."
Military Review 54 (October 1974):3-13.   Examines and rejects each of the rationales advanced for a strategy of
primary dependence on tactical nuclear weapons for the
defense of Europe.   A fundamental obstacle is the unlike-
lihood of the Soviets respecting a "firebreak" between
tactical and strategic nuclear weapons.

1306. Santilli, Joseph F., Jr.   "NATO Strategy Updated."
Military Review 54 (March 1974):3-20.   Discusses the
maintenance of NATO security in a period of detente.
Santilli asserts that a Soviet attack on Western Europe is
unlikely, although threats of force may be used to bolster
Soviet negotiating positions.   To enhance NATO's power,
there is a continuing need for nuclear weapons, including a
"first use," if need be.

1307. Wettern, Desmond.   "NATO's Northern Flank." United
States Naval Institute Proceedings 95 (July 1969):52-59.
Assesses the military strength of Norway and other NATO
components in Northern Europe.   Wettern notes Soviet moves
in the North and the resulting Norwegian concern about
avoiding friction with the Soviets.

1308. Wheeler, Edd D.   "Dove in the Cockpit: Peace in
Today's Europe." Air University Review 27 (January-February
1976):36-44. Discusses factors limiting NATO's effectiveness, including reduced defense budgets and lack of
standardization in many technical fields.

Asia

General

1309.   Cameron, Allan W.   "The Strategic Significance of
the Pacific Islands." Orbis 19 (Fall 1975 Special
Issue):1012-1036. Focuses on Micronesia. After a review
of World War II campaigns, Cameron discusses the influence
of the Vietnam conflict which directed attention to the

American-held islands. The article is a thorough
examination of this area in terms of its potentiality for
American defense installations.

1310. Cannon, Sammy J. "A CENTO for the 1970s." Military
Review 55 (March 1975):36-42. Discusses the current role
of the Central Treaty Organization (CENTO) formed by Iran,
Pakistan, Turkey, and the United Kingdom, with the aid and
encouragement of the United States. Its military role is
quite limited; most of the alliance's effort is directed
toward nonmilitary problems. Cannon recommends that the
United States try to convert CENTO into an alliance similar
to NATO.

1311. Kennedy, William V. "East is No Longer Least."
Military Review 52 (March 1972):52-56. Discusses the
increasing importance of Asia to the United States. Kennedy
stresses the need to defend Alaska to protect oil supplies
for Japan.

1312. Magnus, Ralph H. "U.S. Political-Strategic Interests
in the Middle East." Military Review 49 (March 1969):47-55.
Emphasizes the importance of Greece in Europe; and Iran,
Pakistan, and Turkey in the Middle East. Magnus proposes
various strategies for dealing with the problems of the
Middle East.

1313. Nuechterlein, Donald E. "Future Security Arrangements for Southeast Asia." Military Review 49 (March
1969):79-83. Recommends that the Association of Southeast
Asian Nations (ASEAN), with American participation, prepare
to fill the gap left by the end of British military commitments in the area. Nuechterlein prefers a multinational
approach over total reliance on American power.

1314. Ravenal, Earl C. "The Nixon Doctrine and Our Asian
Commitments." Foreign Affairs 49 (January 1971):201-217.
Discusses the paradox that the Nixon administration is
trying to maintain a strong American role in Asia while
reducing military forces there. Ravenal believes that
continued indecision will sharply erode American influence
in Asia.

1315. Scalapino, Robert A. "The United States and Asia:
The Formulation of American Policy in a Revolutionary Era."
Air University Review 21 (March-April 1970):37-51.
Counsels careful policy development and the avoidance of
extremes such as isolationism. Scalapino emphasizes
Vietnam and the need to achieve peace in all of Southeast
Asia.

Japanese-American Relations

1316. Elster, James M. "The United States-Japan Alliance."
Naval War College Review 22 (January 1970):19-39. Assesses

tensions in the alliance, stressing the effects of the Vietnam conflict. Elster makes some prognostications on such issues as the Ryukyu Islands.

1317. Langdon, Frank. "Strains in Current Japanese-American Defense Cooperation." Asian Survey 9 (September 1969):703-721. Among the tensions were the use of Okinawa as a base for air raids on North Vietnam and the issue of nuclear armaments. Langdon feels that such tensions have been building for some time.

1318. Wilhelm, Alfred D., Jr. "The Nixon Shocks and Japan." Military Review 54 (November 1974):70-77. Reviews Japanese-American relations since World War II and examines the effects of Nixon's advances toward the Peoples Republic of China on the relationship. Wilhelm suggests that Nixon has persuaded Japan to assume more responsibility for its own security and to take a more active role in international relations.

Thai-American Relations

1319. Caswell, John D. "The Changing Thai-United States Alliance: Implications for the Nixon Doctrine in Asia." Naval War College Review 24 (October 1971):59-75. Reviews Thai diplomatic strategy during the 19th and 20th centuries. The Thais are now pursuing a somewhat more conciliatory policy toward the USSR, North Vietnam, and China as a result of the Nixon Doctrine.

1320. Darling, Frank C. "A New American Policy in Thailand." Air University Review 21 (July-August 1970):58-64. Suggests various policies and proposes one option which would build on past commitments and make the necessary changes in the United States-Thailand relationship.

Crises and Force Projection

War Powers Controversy

Official Policy Statements

1321. Nixon, Richard. "Veto of the War Powers Resolution. October 24, 1973." In Public Papers of the Presidents of the United States: Richard Nixon 1973, 893-895. Washington, D.C.: Government Printing Office, 1975. Argues that foreign relations decisions have to result from cooperation between the executive and legislative branches, "not through rigidly codified procedures." Nixon asserts that this legislation is unconstitutional and highly unwise. He states that relations between government branches should be studied by a special commission.

1322. Nixon, Richard. "White House Statement About House

Action Overriding the War Powers Resolution Veto. November
7, 1973." In Public Papers of the Presidents of the United
States: Richard Nixon 1973, 915. Washington, D.C.: Government Printing Office, 1975. Expresses Nixon's grave misgivings about passage of the War Powers Resolution and
predicts serious problems that may well arise from this
legislation.

Periodical Articles

1323. Harrison, Stanley L. "The War Powers Wrangle."
Military Review 54 (July 1974):40-49. Early analysis of
the War Powers Resolution and its strategic and legal
implications. Harrison discusses the increase in executive
power in foreign relations and defense matters and summarizes the provisions and legislative history of the War
Powers Resolution.

Termination of the Indochina Commitment

1324. Nixon, Richard. "Statement About the Situation in
Laos. March 6, 1970." In Public Papers of the Presidents
of the United States: Richard Nixon 1970, 244-249.
Washington, D.C.: Government Printing Office, 1971.
Reviews North Vietnamese military penetration of Laos since
the agreement in 1962 to neutralize the country and notes
the effort to use Laos to channel supplies to the
communists in South Vietnam. Nixon outlines his policy of
air attacks within Laos, without ground operations.

1325. Nixon, Richard. "Joint Statement Following
Discussions With President Thieu of the Republic of
Vietnam. April 3, 1973." In Public Papers of the Presidents
of the United States: Richard Nixon 1973, 251-254.
Washington, D.C.: Government Printing Office, 1975.
Sketches the events of the conference between Nixon and
Thieu. Nixon describes the application of the Nixon
Doctrine to Vietnam, including the continued provision of
military aid to South Vietnam.

1326. Nixon, Richard. "Letter to the Speaker of the
House and the Majority Leader of the Senate About the End
of United States Bombing in Cambodia. August 3, 1973." In
Public Papers of the Presidents of the United States:
Richard Nixon 1973, 686-687. Washington, D.C.: Government
Printing Office, 1975. Criticizes the insistence of
Congress on ending bombing in Cambodia and predicts
possible dire consequences. Allies such as Thailand may
lose confidence, and the North Vietnamese may be encouraged
to invade various parts of Indochina. Nixon warns the
North Vietnamese not to assume that they can act aggres-
sively without a vigorous American response.

1327. Ford, Gerald R. "Statement Following Evacuation of
United States Personnel From the Republic of Vietnam.

April 29, 1975." In Public Papers of the Presidents of the United States: Gerald R. Ford 1975, I, 605. Washington, D.C.: Government Printing Office, 1977. Announces the evacuation of American personnel and refers to the fall of Saigon. Ford advises "all Americans to close ranks, to avoid recrimination about the past" and look to the future.

The Middle East Crisis, 1973

1328. Nixon, Richard. "Remarks About United States Diplomatic Actions Following the Outbreak of Fighting in the Middle East. October 8, 1973." In Public Papers of the Presidents of the United States: Richard Nixon 1973, 848-849. Washington, D.C.: Government Printing Office, 1975. Notes discussions between Nixon and Kissinger. Nixon indicates that the United States will not make "a grandstand play . . . unilaterally." Both Nixon and Kissinger make it clear that the United States is committed to ending the fighting through diplomatic efforts alone.

Mayaguez Crisis, 1975

Official Policy Statements

1329. Ford, Gerald R. "Letter to the Speaker of the House and the President Pro Tempore of the Senate Reporting on United States Action in the Recovery of the SS Mayaguez. May 15, 1975." In Public Papers of the Presidents of the United States: Gerald R. Ford 1975, I, 669-670. Washington, D.C.: Government Printing Office, 1977. Recounts briefly the events of the Mayaguez seizure and the decisions Ford made during the crisis. The report was submitted in accordance with the War Powers Resolution of 1973.

Periodical Articles

1330. Carlile, Donald E. "The Mayaguez Incident Management." Military Review 56 (October 1976):3-14. Presents a generally favorable analysis of the crisis and its resolution. Carlile believes the decisive American actions restored some of the prestige the United States lost when the Vietnam conflict ended with the capture of Saigon.

1331. Kelly, Peter A. "Raids and National Command: Mutually Exclusive!" Military Review 60 (April 1980):19-26. Examines the Mayaguez crisis and the effort to free American prisoners of war in the Sontay mission. Kelly feels that commanders on the scene should be given more leeway during crises and points to the Mayaguez episode as an example of over-control by national decision-makers.

1332. Lamb, Chris. "Belief Systems and Decision Making in the Mayaguez Crisis." Political Science Quarterly 99

(Winter 1984-1985):681-702.   Analyzes   the   motives   of
American decision-makers during the crisis. Lamb believes
American actions were dictated almost solely by the desire
to show that the United States was not impotent, despite
reverses in Indochina.

Chapter 7

Carter and National Security: Continued Detente, Human Rights, and Rearmament

During roughly half his administration Carter followed and expanded the Nixon and Ford policies. He narrowed definitions of American interest in various parts of the world. It was planned, for example, to eliminate the American ground force commitment in South Korea. He actively pursued arms control negotiations and championed the SALT II agreement, which was not ratified by the Senate.

The B-1 bomber program was cancelled, and in other ways defense received less emphasis that had once been the case. Carter was much more critical than previous presidents of human rights violations said to have been committed by American allies and endeavored to use American assistance to curb abuses. The fall of the Somosa regime in Nicaragua, therefore, was not unwelcome in Washington.

The second half of the Carter administration brought significant changes because of challenges by the Soviets, the Iranians, and by terrorists. The Soviet invasion of Afghanistan undermined detente and spurred the United States to look to its defenses in a way that Soviet involvement in Africa had not done. The upheaval in the Persion Gulf area aroused American concern, and more emphasis was given to the Rapid Deployment Force, which could intervene in the Middle East, if necessary.

Anti-terriorist units were developed, and other special operations assumed more importance. An elaborate plan for rescuing the American hostages in Iran failed because of technical problems.

Decision-making Process

1333.   Davis, Vincent. "The President and the National Security Apparatus." In Defense Policy and the Presidency: Carter's First Years, edited by Sam C. Sarkesian, 53-110. Boulder, Colorado: Westview Press, 1979. Suggests that Carter failed to use the National Security Council effectively and did not develop useful alternatives.

Highly critical of Carter's style and his inability to deal with foreign policy and defense problems. Davis includes a lengthy discussion of research on foreign policy and defense bureaucracies.

1334.   Hale, Russell D. and Leland G. Jordan.   "New Congressional Budgeting Procedures: An Initial Analysis of Effects on the Department of Defense." In The Changing World of the American Military, edited by Franklin D. Margiotta, 119-128.   Boulder, Colorado: Westview Press, 1978.   Discusses the impact of the Congressional Budget and Impoundment Control Act of 1974, using fiscal years 1976 and 1977 as examples.   The authors predict more effective Congressional budget control.

1335.   Hoeber, Francis P.   "Myths About the Defense Budget." Air University Review 29 (September-October 1978):2-17.   Analyzes current criticisms of defense spending and their appeal in the political arena.   Hoeber dismisses them as largely myths after examining six primary criticisms.

1336.   Hogan, James J.   "Increasing Executive and Congressional Staff Capabilities in the National Security Arena." In The Changing World of the American Military, edited by Franklin D. Margiotta, 103-118.   Boulder, Colorado: Westview Press, 1978.   Discusses Congress' effort to provide the support staff needed to facilitate and implement its enhanced role in foreign and military policy.   Hogan documents the growth in staff and the qualitative improvements in organizing and utilizing staff efforts.

1337.   Korb, Lawrence J.   "National Security Organization and Process in the Carter Administration." In Defense Policy and the Presidency: Carter's First Years, edited by Sam C. Sarkesian, 111-137.   Boulder, Colorado: Westview Press, 1979.   Examines changes in the National Security Council during Carter's administration.   Korb makes many comparisons with the Nixon/Kissinger period during which some improvements were made.

1338.   Korb, Lawrence J.   "The Process and Problems of Linking Policy and Force Structure through the Defense Budget Process." In American Security Policy and Policy-Making, edited by Robert Harkavy and Edward A. Kolodziej, 181-192.   Lexington, Massachusetts: Lexington Books, 1980. Discusses Department of Defense efforts to coordinate defense policy and defense posture and the obstacles, such as sunk costs, to its doing so more effectively.

1339.   Odeen, Philip, "National Security Policy Integration." In Defense Planning and Arms Control: Proceedings of a Special NSAI Conference 12-14 June 1980 National Defense University, 23-50.   Washington, D.C.:   National Security

Affairs Institute, 1980. SOD D5.402:D36. Discusses
structures and institutions associated with defense and
arms control as well as processes such as the defense
budget. Odeen briefly examines planning issues and
proposes a number of specific actions that need to be taken
by various levels of the executive branch.

1340. Picard, Louis A. "The SALT I Negotiations: The
Utility of a Game Theory Paradigm." In American Security
Policy and Policy-Making, edited by Robert Harkavy and
Edward A. Kolodziej, 239-254. Lexington, Massachusetts:
Lexington Books, 1980. Specifically uses the "prisoner's
dilemma" theory, which is based on distrust, to examine
SALT I. Picard suggests that judicious use of game theory
can be useful in conducting negotiations.

1341. Smernoff, Barry J. "Strategic and Arms Control
Implications of Laser Weapons." Air University Review 29
(January-February 1978):38-50. Examines funding levels and
the organization of the American military and naval laser
research effort. Smernoff also discusses lasers as space
weapons and the impact of SALT on further laser
development.

1342. Sorley, Lewis S. "Nonmilitary Instruments of Defense
Policy." In Nonnuclear Conflicts in the Nuclear Age, edited
by Sam C. Sarkesian, 99-121. New York: Praeger
Publishers, 1980. Examines relationships between military
and nonmilitary elements of power, the usefulness of such
nonmilitary factors, and the failure of the United States
to utilize nonmilitary strengths effectively. Sorley
outlines ways to improve American capabilities in this
area.

1343. Toner, James H. "National Security Policy: The Un-
spoken Assumptions." Air University Review 28 (July-August
1977):36-43. These assumptions include the view that the
United States is threatened and has the ability to preserve
its security. Toner posits three "objectives of defense
policy."

1344. Trice, Robert H. "The Impact of Domestic Policies
on U.S. National Security Policies." In The Changing World
of the American Military, edited by Franklin D. Margiotta,
89-101. Boulder, Colorado: Westview Press, 1978.
Discusses the decline of the power of the executive over
foreign and military policy. Congress and interest groups
have become far more active than they once were.

1345. Williams, Phil. "Carter's Defence Policy." In The
Carter Years: The President and Policy Making, edited by M.
Glenn Abernathy and others, 84-105. New York: St.
Martin's Press, 1984. Sees three phases in Carter's
national security policy, as he committed himself to
strengthening American defense. Williams examines each of

Carter's defense budgets and the debate over SALT II in detail. He also discusses the conflicts within the Carter administration over foreign policy and defense issues.

1346. Wood, Robert S. "Structure and Process in Forming National Security Policy." In <u>Toward Cooperation, Stability and Balance Proceedings of the National Security Affairs Conference July 18-20, 1977 National Defense University</u>, 199-213. Washington, D.C.: National Defense University, 1977. SOD D5.412:Se2/977. Begins with a general consideration of the "separation of powers" concept in American political theory and then examines assertions about the nature of executive power and some court decisions on the subject. A longer section deals with other court decisions on presidential and Congressional powers in the field of foreign relations.

1347. Yarmolinsky, Adam. "Inter-Sector Cooperation and Competition: Where Do We Go From Here?" In <u>Toward Coopera-tion, Stability and Balance Proceedings of the National Security Affairs Conference July 18-20, 1977 National Defense University</u>, 215-221. Washington, D.C.: National Defense University, 1977. SOD D5.412:Se2/977. Notes that national security policy changes quite slowly in most periods and contends that there have been few "national debates" about major policies; one of these few was the civil defense controversy early in the Kennedy admini-stration. Yarmolinsky identifies the wide range of factors that may impact on decisions in the security sphere and asserts that there is a need for more informed public participation to avoid domination of the process by special interests.

The Role of Public Opinion

1348. Hofstetter, C. Richard and David W. Moore. "Watching TV News and Supporting the Military: A Surprising Impact of the News Media." <u>Armed Forces and Society</u> 5 (Winter 1979): 261-269. Asserts that coverage was much more supportive of the military than generally assumed. The more people saw of the Vietnam war on television, the more they supported American policies.

1349. Kriesberg, Louis and Ross Klein. "Changes in Public Support for U.S. Military Spending." <u>Journal of Conflict Resolution</u> 24 (March 1980):79-111. Analyzes forty years of public opinion polls from the late 1930's through the late 1970's. The authors see a partial distancing from the Vietnam syndrome.

1350. Russett, Bruce and Miroslav Nincic. "American Opinion on the Use of Military Force Abroad." In <u>The Changing World of the American Military</u>, edited by Franklin D. Margiotta, 129-151. Boulder, Colorado: Westview Press, 1978. Uses the results of public opinion polls to assess sentiments toward the issue noted in the title. The major factor seems to be the proximity to the United States of a country threatened by attack. Support for use of armed force is low; it seems to be comparable to the pre-World War II period of isolationism.

Military Policy

Official Policy Statements

1351. Carter, Jimmy. "University of Notre Dame. Address at Commencement Exercises at the University. May 22, 1977." In Public Papers of the Presidents of the United States: Jimmy Carter 1978, I, 954-962. Washington, D.C.:Government Printing Office, 1977. Advocates using American power "for humane purposes." Carter criticizes some recent American policy makers for having, in effect, borrowed strategies and tactics from the communists. Carter pledges further efforts to reach arms control and other agreements with the Soviet Union, expresses support for detente, and advocates reducing the world's arms trade.

1352. Carter, Jimmy. "Winston-Salem, North Carolina. Address at Wake Forest University. March 17, 1978." In Public Papers of the Presidents of the United States: Jimmy Carter 1978, I, 529-535. Washington, D.C.: Government Printing Office, 1979. Refers to America's military tradi- tion and the services of the Carter family in the armed forces. Carter asserts that the United States is not "pulling back from protecting its interests and its friends around the world." He describes the Soviet military buildup, and efforts at military modernization the United States is undertaking, and the status of current arms control negotiations.

1353. Carter, Jimmy. "American Legion: Remarks at the Legion's Annual Conference. February 19, 1980." In Public Papers of the Presidents of the United States: Jimmy Carter 1980-81, I, 344-349. Washington, D.C.: Government Printing Office, 1981. Asserts that "from the very start, my administration . . . has been engaged in a substantial and carefully planned strengthening of our military forces." Carter notes a decline in defense spending during the Nixon and Ford administrations and Congressional reductions in his own defense budgets, but declares there is now a national consensus that our defense capabilities have to be further developed.

1354. Carter, Jimmy. "The State of the Union: Annual Message to the Congress. January 16, 1981." In Public Papers of the Presidents of the United States: Jimmy Carter 1980-81, III, 2931-2997. Washington, D.C.: Government Printing Office, 1982. Discusses primary objectives of American foreign policy and the damage that the Soviet invasion of Afghanistan has done to Soviet-American relations. Carter pledges "a sustained growth of 3 percent in real terms" for defense and stresses deterrence and "the primacy of our Atlantic relationship." There is also a description of "rapid deployment forces."

Books

1355.   Barnet, Richard J.   Real Security; Restoring American Power in A Dangerous Decade. New York: Simon & Schuster, 1981.   127p. Examines American policies of the 1970's and criticizes Carter's return to a cold war stance. He stresses the need for disarmament and discusses the limits of military force as exercised by the two superpowers.

1356. Shepherd, William G. in association with Theodora B. Shepherd. The Ultimate Deterrent: Foundations of US-USSR Security Under Stable Competititon.   New York:Praeger Publishers, 1986. 137p. Applies economic approaches to defining the concept of "national interest" and suggests that the conflict between the superpowers is really much more limited than generally supposed. The Shepherds deal in part with the regions of primary concern to the superpowers. They also deny that one superpower can really threaten the other.

Essays and Periodical Articles

1357.   Fedder, Edwin.   "Policy Proposals: U.S. Political and Military Response."   In Nonnuclear Conflicts in the Nuclear Age, edited by Sam C. Sarkesian, 126-137.   New York: Praeger Publishers, 1980.   Emphasizes the uncertain results produced by intervention and takes a skeptical view of many American positions in the Cold War such as the Truman Doctrine.   Several pages deal with American relations with the allies of the United States.

1358. Foster, James L. "Essential Equivalence: What Is It and How Should It Be Measured?"   In Equivalence, Sufficiency, and the International Balance: Proceedings of the Fifth National Security Affairs Conference July 17-19, 1978, 23-51. Washington, D.C.: Government Printing Office, 1978.   SOD D5.412:978. Reviews both definitions and statistical measures of equivalence in weapons strength between the United States and the USSR. Foster states that all measurements are rather inexact.

1359. Gray, Colin S. and Jeffrey G. Barlow.   "Inexcusable Restraint: The Decline of American Military Power in the 1970's."   International Security 10 (Fall 1985):27-69. Presents a critique of the Carter administration's defense policy, which the author believes greatly weakened the United States.

1360. Grinter, Lawrence. "The United States: Military and

Political Perspectives." In <u>Nonnuclear Conflicts in the Nuclear Age</u>, edited by Sam C. Sarkesian, 61-98. New York: Praeger Publishers, 1980. Warns that the United States does little long-range political or military planning. Grinter analyzes the breakdown of superpower bipolarity and the current posture of American conventional forces. He makes a plea for keeping some forces ready for low-intensity operations in the Third World.

1361. Head, Richard G. "Technology and the Military Balance." <u>Foreign Affairs</u> 56 (April 1978):544-563. Argues that the United States has made great advances in military technology during the 1960's and 1970's. Head compares American and Soviet approaches to military research and development and outlines further responses that the United States and NATO need to make.

1362. Kastl, Joseph W. "Detente and an Adequate American Defense." <u>Air University Review</u> 30 (September-October 1979):20-25. Discuss the nature of detente and the Soviet commitment to it. Kastl counsels a relatively cautious American approach to detente.

1363. Komer, Robert W. "What 'Decade of Neglect?'" <u>International Security</u> 10 (Fall 1985):70-83. Takes issue with Gray and Barlow ("Inexcusable Restraint", entry 1359). Komer attributes changes in the rate of defense expenditures to the ending of the Vietnam conflict, not failures on the part of the Nixon, Ford, and Carter administrations.

1364. Korb, Lawrence J. "The Policy Impacts of the Carter Defense Program." In <u>Defense Policy and the Presidency: Carter's First Years</u>, edited by Sam C. Sarkesian, 138-199. Boulder, Colorado: Westview Press, 1979. Compares Carter's and Ford's defense budgets and discusses the effects of Carter's changes on military posture and readiness. Korb notes that Carter's gradually more assertive stand on foreign affairs was not matched by greater defense spending.

1365. Lind, William S. "Military Doctrine, Force Structure, and the Defense Department Decision-Making Process." <u>Air University Review</u> 30 (May-June 1979):21-27. Warns that instead of "force structure" developing from "military doctrine," the reverse often occurs with damaging effects on American defense. Lind discusses maneuver strategy and deplores the influence of groups of officers who are so wedded to a particular weapon such as submarines that they compose distorted strategies.

1366. Rostow, Walt W. "Competing for Resources in A Two Trillion Dollar Economy." In <u>Equivalence, Sufficiency, and the International Balance: Proceedings of the Fifth National Security Affairs Conference July 17-19, 1978</u>,

235-247. Washington, D.C.: Government Printing Office, 1978. SOD D5.412:978. Discusses the economic problems that inhibit increases in defense expenditures. Rostow advocates some increases, but feels that basic economic problems must be dealt with to achieve the level of growth that would readily support larger defense expenditures.

General Strategy

1367. Baker, John D., Jr. "Detente: Myth and Reality." Military Review 57 (December 1977):41-50. Interprets the Soviets as viewing detente as simply a time of reduced world tensions, not a fundamental change in the relationship between the superpowers. Baker cites increases in Soviet military power that suggest detente is reducing the American ability to counter the Soviets.

1368. Blechman, Barry M. "The Balance of Conventional Forces and the US Role in Assuring Regional Stability." In Toward Cooperation, Stability and Balance Proceedings of the National Security Affairs Conference July 18-20, 1977 National Defense University, 55-67. Washington, D.C.: National Defense University, 1977. D5.412:Se2/977. Discusses the increasing strength of Soviet conventional forces and
nuclear weapons and how the United States may meet this challenge. Blechman provides much data on the Soviet build-up in an analysis of the American-Soviet balance in Europe, the Middle East, especially the Mediterranean area, and the Far East. He recommends concentrating our forces in the first two regions.

1369. Bloomfield, Lincoln P. and Harland Cleveland. "Strategy for the United States." International Security 2 (Spring 1978):32-55. Asserts that a strategy is needed to meet the challenge presented by the Special Sessions on Disarmament of the United Nations General Assembly. The authors analyze the United Nations as a forum for disarmament discussions and the changes in the disarmament debate that the United States might foster.

1370. Braestrup, Peter. "The Changing Outlook." Wilson Quarterly 3 (Spring 1979):124-130. Traces Carter's military policy from an initial commitment to reducing defense expenditures to his proposal for a substantial increase in 1978.

1371. Collins, John M. "Principle of Deterrence." Air University Review 31 (November-December 1979):17-26. Argues that, recently, relatively little attention has been given to the theory of deterrence. Collins proposes a number of principles of deterrence, relating not only to general war but also to limited wars, low-intensity conflicts and to "nonmilitary conflicts."

1372. Critchley, W. Harriet. "Defining Strategic Value:
Problems of Conceptual Clarity and Valid Threat
Assessments." In American Security Policy and Policy-
Making, edited by Robert Harkavy and Edward A. Kolodziej,
45-65. Lexington, Masschusetts: Lexington Books, 1980.
Assails what Critchley regards as "delusions" in American
strategic thinking. She also describes "strategic value,"
using petroleum as an example.

1373. Elliott, A.L. "The Calculus of Surprise Attack." Air
University Review 30 (March-April 1979):56-67. Examines
American and Soviet views of surprise in military
operations.

1374. Gray, Colin S. "The Military Requirements of US
Strategy." Military Review 59 (September 1979):2-13.
Argues that American planners need to concentrate on
fighting effectively and to put less emphasis on
deterrence. Gray sees the United States as relatively
"passive." It waits for challenges and crises. He offers a
number of prescriptions for defeating the enemy in Europe.

1375. Gray, Colin S. "Strategic Stability Reconsidered."
Daedalus 109 (Fall 1980):135-154. Argues that the concept
of strategic stability needs to be rethought in order to
improve United States military capabilities.

1376. Grinter, Lawrence E. "Avoiding the Burden: The
Carter Doctrine in Perspective." Air University Review 33
(January-February 1983):73-82. Reviews Carter's foreign
and military policies and compares Carter's public
statements with Soviet actions in 1978 and 1979. Grinter
is severely critical of Carter's handling of the Iranian
crisis.

1377. Kemp, Geoffrey and Harlan K. Ullman. "US Global
Strategy: The Future of the Half-War Planning Contingency--
Problems and Prospects for Global Security." In Toward
Cooperation, Stability and Balance Proceedings of the
National Security Affairs Conference July 18-20, 1977
National Defense University, 69-77. Washington, D.C.:
National Defense University, 1977. D5.412:Se2/977. Sees the
key to American strategy as the maintenance of "some form
of access to overseas resources, military basing
facilities, and if need be, areas in which force must be
projected." The American capability for waging less than
general conflicts is declining. The primary focus of the
essay lies in the Persian Gulf and the Far East.

1378. Kolodziej, Edward A. "Living with the Long Cycle:
New Assumptions to Guide the Use and Control of Military
Force." In American Security Policy and Policy-Making,
edited by Robert Harkavy and Edward A. Kolodziej, 21-43.
Lexington, Massachusetts: Lexington Books, 1980. Reviews
American strategic assumptions during the post-World War II

Cold War and the great optimism about American power that underlay them. Kolodziej goes on to examine these assumptions in the light of more contemporary views of world politics and the political situation in the United States.

1379. Nelson, C.R. "The Dimensions of Current US Military Strategy." _Military Review_ 56 (August 1976):88-92. Reviews Secretary of Defense Rumsfeld's initial report, for fiscal year 1977, and analyzes the strategy set forth. Nelson emphasizes the need to maintain a balance between American political commitments and military capabilities.

1380. Oseth, John M. "FM 100-5 Revisited: A Need for Better 'Foundation Concepts'?" _Military Review_ 60 (March 1980):13-19. Reviews the debate over Field Manual FM 100-5 because of its emphasis on a European war. Oseth asserts that the manual is really defective because it is based on faulty political assumptions and because the military is most comfortable with planning for a large-scale war in Europe, not Third World contingencies.

1381. Pfaltzgraff, Robert L., Jr. "Emerging Major Power Relationships: Implications for the U.S. Military in the Late Twentieth Century." In _The Changing World of the American Military_, edited by Franklin D. Margiotta, 71-87. Boulder, Colorado: Westview Press, 1978. Discusses the Sino-Soviet conflict, but gives primary attention to the development of regional powers with significant military strength. The most serious challenges to the United States are the arming of regional powers with nuclear weapons and the increasing projection of Soviet power all over the world.

1382. Posen, Barry R. and Stephen W. Van Evera. "Overarming and Underwhelming." _Foreign Policy_, no. 40 (Fall 1980):99-118. Asserts that the belief that the USSR is growing stronger than the United States is not well founded and warns that without changes in the American military establishment, increasing defense spending may actually weaken the United States.

1383. Quester, George H. "Defining Strategic Issues: How to Avoid Isometric Exercises." In _American Security Policy and Policy-Making_, edited by Robert Harkavy and Edward A. Kolodziej, 195-207. Lexington, Massachusetts: Lexington Books, 1980. Warns that the West especially the United States, may focus too much attention on Soviet military capabilities, thereby assisting the Soviets to make political and diplomatic capital out of their strength. Quester counsels more self-confidence in this country.

1384. Sarkesian, Sam C. "Introduction." In _Defense Policy and the Presidency: Carter's First Years_, edited by Sam C. Sarkesian, 1-27. Boulder, Colorado: Westview Press,

1979.   Reviews the decision-making structure for national
security questions and the varying perspectives on the very
meaning of "national security." Sarkesian also discusses
criticisms of Carter's approach to defense problems.

1385.   Smernoff, Barry J.   "Science, Technology, and the
US-Soviet Competition." In Rethinking US Security Policy
for the 1980s Proceedings of the Seventh National Security
Affairs Conference 21-23 July 1980, 265-291.   Washington,
D.C.:   National   Defense   University   Press,   1980.   SOD
D5.412:980. Asserts that both Japan and the USSR are
beginning to reduce the technology gap between themselves
and the United States.   Smernoff outlines the status of
American and Soviet weapons and other military systems.   He
analyzes   the   shortcomings   of   Soviet   research   and
development and the American policy of "offsetting" high
quality American technology for the larger military forces
mustered by the Soviets.

Nuclear Strategy

1386.   Adelman, Kenneth.   "Beyond MAD-ness." Policy Review
(Summer   1981):77-85.   Focuses   primarily   on   Carter's
Presidential Directive 59 (PD 59), which changed American
military targeting plans.   Adelman argues that the Soviets
do not now and never have accepted the concept of "mutual
assured destruction."

1387.   Burke, G.K.   "The MX and Strategic Deterrence in the
1980s." Air University Review 30 (May-June 1979):28-38.
Compares the potential of the MX to other American weapons
systems.   Burke discusses Soviet civil defense measures and
foresees other factors that reduce the nuclear strength of
the United States.   Therefore, the MX is much needed.

1388.   Burt, Richard.   "Reassessing the Strategic Balance."
International Security 5 (Summer 1980):37-52.   Analyzes the
effects of SALT I and SALT II on American security.   The
Soviets greatly expanded their nuclear arsenal during the
1970's.   Burt warns against basing American strategy on
SALT.

1389.   Charles,   William   M.,   Jr.   "Rethinking   the
Unthinkable: Limited Strategic Nuclear Options--Credible
or Dangerous?" Air University Review 28 (May-June 1977):60-
71.   Analyzes the advent of "flexible response" and the
continuing   debate   over   the   concept,   and   over   "mutual
assured   destruction." After   a   thorough   review   of   the
arguments, Charles concludes that flexibility is needed to
counter the Soviets.

1390.   Giller, Edward B.   "Nuclear Technology in Support of
Our Strategic Options." Air University Review 28 (November-
December 1976):26-34.   Asserts that the USSR is greatly
improving   and   expanding   its   nuclear   weapons   arsenal.

Giller argues that the United States must preserve its military technology lead and discusses some weapons that are being developed.

1391. Slater, Jerome. "Population Defense Reconsidered: Is the ABM Really Inconsistent with Stability?" In American Security Policy and Policy-Making, edited by Robert Harkavy and Edward A. Kolodziej, 101-114. Lexington, Massachusetts: Lexington Books, 1980. Analyzes the theory of mutual assured destruction and proposes changes to deal with less than allout nuclear attacks, by terrorist groups, for example. Slater favors anti-ballistic missiles and civil defense on a limited basis as safeguards.

Nonproliferation

Official Policy Statements

1392. Carter, Jimmy. "Nuclear Non-Proliferation Act of 1978." In Public Papers of the Presidents of the United States: Jimmy Carter 1978, I, 498-502. Washington, D.C.: Government Printing Office, 1979. Includes a set of remarks and a formal statement on the legislation, which Carter sees as "clarifying our own Nation's policy." It is designed to make possible nuclear technology transfer from the United States to other countries without creating the risk of further proliferation of nuclear weapons.

Periodical Articles

1393. Clark, Donald L. "Could We Be Wrong?" Air University Review 29 (September-October 1978):28-37. Discusses the strategy of nonproliferation. Clark argues that controlled proliferation may be more feasible and much more effective than trying to impose nonproliferation.

1394. Dunn, Lewis A. "U.S. Strategic Force Requirements in a Nuclear-Proliferated World." Air University Review 31 (July-August 1980):26-33. Predicts a significant increase in the number of nuclear powers, a development with substantial implications for American security policy. One section discusses possible Soviet responses to Japanese or German nuclear capability.

1395. Morawitz, Wayne L. "Nuclear Proliferation and U.S. Security." Air University Review 28 (January-February 1977):19-28. Concentrates on short-range projections of proliferation. Morawitz argues that the countries most likely to develop nuclear weapons are allies of the United States or at least not unfriendly powers.

Air Strategy

General

1396.   Erhard, Robert C. "Some Thoughts on Air Force
Doctrine." Air University Review 31 (March-April 1980): 29-
38. Argues that "doctrine" is used in too broad a sense and
proposes a more limited use of the concept. Ehrhart warns
of limitations to air power and discusses the need to take
account of the other services in developing air force
doctrine.

1397.   Pauly, John W.   "The Thread of Doctrine."   Air
University Review 27 (May-June 1976):2-10.   Discusses air
force doctrine from the 1920's through the 1970's.   Pauly
generally views doctrinal development in the air force
favorably, asserting that it has reflected national and air
force needs.

1398. Quester, George H.   "The Impact of Strategic Air
Warfare." Armed Forces and Society 4 (Winter 1978):179-206.
Examines American perceptions of the efficacy of bombing
and presents an objective assessment of its usefulness in
achieving military goals.   Quester argues that Americans
have taken a moralistic attitude toward air bombardment of
civilians. Bombing is sometimes effective, sometimes not.

1399. Stiles, Dennis W. "Air Power: A New Look from an Old
Rooftop." Air University Review 27 (November-December
1975):49-59.   Discusses the development of air force
doctrine since World War II and analyzes the role of the
air force in the context of the total defense force.   In
part, Stiles seeks to assimilate the Vietnam experience.

1400. Wolk, Herman S. "Roots of Strategic Deterrence."
Aerospace Historian 19 (Fall, September 1972):137-144.
Examines American commitment to strategic air warfare since
World War II.

Missiles

1401. Snow, Donald M. "The MX-Basing Mode Muddle." Air
University Review 31 (July-August 1980):11-25.   Reviews the
pros and cons of the MX in detail. Snow generally takes a
cautious view of MX, feeling that the arguments for it are
not as strong as the Carter administration asserts.

Bombers

1402. Burke, G.K.   "A Case for the Manned Penetrating
Bomber." Air University Review 28 (July-August 1977):2-14.
Argues that bombers give needed flexibility nuclear Triad.
They would be useful for hitting moving targets after a
nuclear war began and can be used to threaten convincingly
without having to attack.   Burke, therefore, favors

development of the B-1 Bomber.

1403.   Kohout, John J.   "A Post-B-1 Look at the Manned
Strategic Bomber." Air University Review 30 (July-August
1979):27-51. Reviews various efforts to develop a replacement for the B-52.   After reviewing the B-50 and B-36,
Kohout discusses criteria for a successor to the B-52.

1404. Martin, Abner B.   "The B-1; Strategic Deterrence into
the Twenty-First Century." Air University Review 27
(March-April 1976):2-14.   Discusses reasons for a new
bomber to replace the B-52 and the characteristics of a
satisfactory new bomber.   Martin describes fully the B-1
program as it existed in 1975.

1405. Wheeler, Edd D.   "Prospects for the Manned Bomber:
High Noon or Sunset?" Air University Review 30 (January-
February 1979):2-15.   Discusses the question in light of
the Carter administration's decision to cancel further
development of the B-1.   Wheeler sees a more limited role
for bombers in the future and discusses their weaknesses in
contemporary conflicts.

Ground Strategy

General

1406. Deitchman, Seymour J.   New Technology and Military
Power: General Purpose Military Forces for the 1980s and
Beyond. rev. ed. Boulder, Colorado: Westview Press, 1979.
278p. Examines tactical weapons, including nuclear devices,
for land, naval, and air forces.   The second section
analyzes the problems of defending Europe.

Low-Intensity Conflict

1407. Graber, Doris A.   "Intervention Policies of the
Carter Administration: Political and Military Dimensions."
In Defense Policy and the Presidency: Carter's First Years,
edited by Sam C. Sarkesian, 200-235.   Boulder, Colorado:
Westview Press, 1979. In an historical review, Graber sees
the Eisenhower and Nixon Doctrines as limiting the geographical scope of the Truman Doctrine. She discusses the
decline in popular support for intervention and reviews
intervention issues that arose during 1977 and 1978.

1408.   Holton, William J.   "The TAC Role in Special
Operations." Air University Review 28 (November-December
1976):54-68.   Reviews the post-Vietnam role of special
operations forces and tactical air missions.   Holton
discusses psychological warfare, counterinsurgency, and
other topics.

1409. Janowitz, Morris and Ellen P. Stern. "The Limits of

Military Intervention: A Propositional Inventory." <u>Military Review</u> 58 (March 1978):11-21. Discusses ten factors militating against American intervention. These include a less effective military establishment because of the end of the draft and legislative-executive conflicts. The authors warn that proponents of intervention must offer plans which consider these limits to military action.

1410.   Johnson, Thomas M. and Raymond T. Barrett. "The Rapid Deployment Joint Task Force." <u>United States Naval Institute Proceedings</u> 106 (November 1980):95-98. Examines the reasons for the Task Force, and its organization. Initiatives to improve American airlift and sealift capabilities and other actions to enhance the Task Force are also noted.

1411.   Sabrosky, Allan Ned. "Political Constraints on Presidential Wars," In <u>Nonnuclear Conflicts in the Nuclear Age</u>, edited by Sam C. Sarkesian, 209-246. New York: Praeger Publishers, 1980. Discusses the collapse of the post-World War II foreign policy consensus in the United States and analyzes the various "constraints" on a limited or low-intensity war waged by the United States executive branch. These include structual factors such as fixed presidential terms, Congressional militancy, public opinion, and public ignorance.

1412. Snyder, William P. and Roger A. Beaumont. "Military Intervention Forces." In <u>Nonnuclear Conflicts in the Nuclear Age</u>, edited by Sam C. Sarkesian, 185-208. Warns that planning for intervention is extremely difficult and that detailed planning is practically impossible. The authors also examine the many limitations of the American armed forces in terms of intervention capability.

1413.   Tarr, David W. "The Strategic Environment, U.S. National Security, and the Nature of Low Intensity Conflict." In <u>Nonnuclear Conflicts in the Nuclear Age</u>, edited by Sam C. Sarkesian, 41-60. New York: Praeger Publishers, 1980. Discusses the increasing complexity of world politics and changes in military relations that influence American involvement in low-intensity conflicts. Tarr reviews the weakening American defense posture and argues that American forces are not prepared for low-intensity conflict.

Naval Strategy

1414.   Haynes, Fred. "The Marines Through 1999." <u>United States Naval Institute Proceedings</u> 104 (September 1978): 24-33. Reviews recent studies of the marine corps and its missions. Various alternatives have been proposed, including giving the marines more armor in order to fight in Europe. Haynes recommends that the corps retain its ability to operate in a variety of high or low-intensity combat environments.

1415. Kemp, Geoffrey and Harlan K. Ullman. "Towards a New Order of U.S. Maritime Policy." Naval War College Review 30 (Summer 1977):98-114. Argues that the United States must develop a strategy for utilizing the oceans to further its policies. Mahan's dicta on the effectiveness of sea power are still valid, despite changes in the application of his principles.

1416. Krepon, Michael. "A Navy to Match National Purposes." Foreign Affairs 55 (February 1977):355-367. Criticizes large aircraft carriers for presenting highly vulnerable targets. Krepon argues that other weapons such as small carriers and land-based aviation are more appropriate means for force projection than the large aircraft carriers.

1417. Polmar, Norman and D.A. Paolucci. "Sea-Based 'Strategic' Weapons for the 1980s and Beyond." United States Naval Institute Proceedings 104 (May 1978):98-113. American nuclear weapons are increasingly based on submarines, but Soviet capabilities in this area are outstripping those of the United States. The authors review the Trident and Poseidon programs and suggest that surface ships be added to the American missile-bearing fleet.

1418. Salzer, Robert S. "The Navy's Clouded Amphibious Mission." United States Naval Institute Proceedings 104 (February 1978):24-33. After World War II, amphibious capability came to center on small "amphibious ready groups" rather than larger task forces. Due to changes in technology and more armaments in the Third World countries, these groups may be increasingly vulnerable and less effective. Salzer advocates refocusing amphibious commitments to the more traditional role of supporting sea control in general war situations.

1419. Siuru, William D. "SLBM--The Navy's Contribution to the Triad." Air University Review 28 (September-October 1977):17-29. Discusses the special characteristics of submarine launched ballistic missiles that make them an important part of the American strategic nuclear force. Siuru briefly describes the missiles in use and those that are being developed.

1420. Zakheim, Dov S. "Maritime Presence, Projection and the Constraints of Parity." In Equivalence, Sufficiency, and the International Balance: Proceedings of the Fifth National Security Affairs Conference July 17-19, 1978, 101-118. Washington, D.C.: Government Printing Office, 1978. SOD D5.412:978. Suggests that force projection can involve more than a naval presence. Ground forces and tactical aircraft can be a part of a presence which can considerably enlarge the American impact. Ships smaller than aircraft carriers may be useful in replying to Soviet moves.

Disarmament and Arms Control

Official Policy Statements

1421. Carter, Jimmy. "SALT Negotiations With the Soviet Union: Remarks and a Question-and-Answer Session with Reporters. March 30, 1977." In Public Papers of the Presidents of the United States: Jimmy Carter 1977, I, 538-544. Washington, D.C.: Government Printing Office, 1977. Summarizes current American proposals on arms control and refers to negotiations on related topics such as an end to nuclear weapons testing. Much of the discussion concerns cruise missiles and their deployment. Carter asserts that he would not trade his insistence on the maintenance of human rights for progress in the arms control sphere.

1422. Carter, Jimmy. "United States Naval Academy. Address at the Commencement Exercises. June 7, 1978." In Public Papers of the Presidents of the United States: Jimmy Carter 1978, I, 1052-1057. Washington, D.C.: Government Printing Office, 1979. Warns that the United States and the Soviet Union will be competing "for a very long time." Carter describes the conditions needed for detente. Much of the address focuses on SALT II negotiations, which Carter believes will be successful. He expresses profound concern about Soviet and Cuban "involvement" in Africa, however.

1423. Carter, Jimmy. "Atlanta, Georgia. Remarks at a Special Convocation of the Georgia Institute of Technology. February 20, 1979." In Public Papers of the Presidents of the United States: Jimmy Carter 1979, I, 300-306. Washington, D.C.: Government Printing Office, 1980. Stresses that the United States is in "a world of danger" and that there are distinct limits to the American ability to manage change. Carter argues that the "United States cannot control events within other nations." About half the address expresses faith in SALT II and warns of the serious problems that will emerge if SALT II is rejected by Congress.

1424. Carter, Jimmy. "New York, New York. Remarks at the Annual Convention of the American Newspaper Publishers Convention. April 25, 1979." In Public Papers of the Presidents of the United States: Jimmy Carter 1979, I, 693-699. Washington, D.C.: Government Printing Office, 1980. Focuses on SALT II and the need for ratifying the agreement. Carter stresses American military and economic strength and the need to seek peace. He describes the course of the SALT II negotiations, noting that Soviet and American "strategic forces" are "essentially equivalent." SALT II will help the United States maintain parity with the Soviet Union and avoid an intensified arms race.

1425. Carter, Jimmy. "Vienna Summit Meeting. Address
Delivered Before a Joint Session of the Congress. June 18,
1979." In <u>Public Papers of the Presidents of the United
States: Jimmy Carter 1979</u>, I, 1087-1092. Washington, D.C.:
Goverment Printing Office, 1980. Describes the
difficulties encountered in reaching an agreement and calls
SALT II "The most detailed, far-reaching, comprehensive
treaty in the history of arms control." Carter pledges
improvements in American "strategic forces" even with the
conclusion and implementation of SALT II.

Books

1426. Graham, Daniel Orrin. <u>Shall America be Defended? SALT
II and Beyond</u>. New Rochelle, New York: Arlington House,
1979. 267p. Assails the SALT II concept and warns that the
Soviet Union is approaching the place where it can defend
itself effectively against nuclear attack. Graham became a
major proponent of the Strategic Defense Initiative.

1427. Myrdal, Alva. <u>The Game of Disarmament; How the United
States and Russia Run the Arms Race</u>. New York: Pantheon
Books, 1977. 397p. Scores the superpowers for having
failed to work decisively toward disarmament and presents
policy proposals for disarmament. Myrdal emphasizes the
obstacles to this goal and expresses fears that Europe may
become the site of a limited war.

Essays and Periodical Articles

1428. Burt, Richard. "Defense Policy and Arms Control."
In <u>Continuity and Change in the Eighties and Beyond: Sixth
National Security Affairs Conference 1979 Proceedings 23-25
July 1979 National Defense University</u>, 13-27. SOD
D5.412.979. Washington, D.C.: National Defense University,
1979. Reviews arms control negotiations of the 1970's and
the disillusionment that has arisen about arms control.
Burt analyzes the disjuncture between military strategy and
arms control policy. He contends that arms control must be
viewed realistically, as being "primarily useful for
registering and codifying an existing balance of forces."

1429. Butterworth, Robert Lyle. "The Arms Control Impact
Statement: Program and Logic." In <u>American Security Policy
and Policy-Making</u>, edited by Robert Harkavy and Edward A.
Kolodziej, 149-164. Lexington, Massachusetts: Lexington
Books, 1980. Examines the Arms Control Impact Statements
required by Congress beginning in 1975. Butterworth
discusses the obstacles to making effective statements and
proposes a way to improve the process.

1430. Coffey, Joseph I. "Arms, Arms Control, and Alliance
Relationships: The Case of the Cruise Missile." In <u>American
Security Policy and Policy-Making</u>, edited by Robert Harkavy

and Edward A. Kolodziej, 69-84. Lexington, Massachusetts: Lexington Books, 1980. Examines the characteristics and potentiality of the cruise missile. The focus is on the implications of the cruise missile for the military balance in Europe.

1431. Collins, John M. "A Structured Framework for SALT Decision-Making." Air University Review 31 (January-February 1980):22-26. Discusses the presumed effects of SALT II on United States, allied, and Soviet weapons systems. Collins favors SALT II after reviewing the interplay of strategy and the treaty's requirements.

1432. Dougherty, James. "Arms Control in the 1980s: Retrospect, Contrast, Prospect." In Defense Planning and Arms Control: Proceedings of a Special NSAI Conference 12-14 June 1980 National Defense University, 87-119. Washington, D.C.: National Security Affairs Institute, 1980. SOD D5.402:D36. Compares the atmosphere surrounding the origins of SALT I and the problems of SALT II. Dougherty notes the rising tensions of the 1970's and examines negotiations as of 1980.

1433. Gray, Colin S. "SALT II: the Real Debate." Policy Review (Fall 1979):7-22. SALT II reflects the decline of American power during the 1970's. Gray feels that SALT II is fundamentally flawed; its critics should not focus on merely "technical" objections to it.

1434. Harkavy, Robert. "Harmonizing Policies across Arms Control Domains: Dilemmas and Contradictions." In American Security Policy and Policy-Making, edited by Robert Harkavy and Edward A. Kolodziej, 129-147. Lexington, Massachusetts: Lexington Books, 1980. Discusses the many arms control initiatives and analyzes disharmonies and conflicts between many of them. Sophisticated treatment of a large range of issues and theories, which also relates these topics to American security planning.

1435. Legvold, Robert. "Strategic 'Doctrine' and SALT: Soviet and American Views." Survival 21 (January-February 1979): 8-13. Examines the varying views of deterrence taken by the Soviets and Americans. The Soviets consider American theories such as "flexible response" as vague notions that may actually promote utilization of nuclear weapons. Legvold includes a detailed discussion of Soviet and American negotiating strategies in arms control talks.

1436. Nacht, Michael. "The Role of Arms Control in Defense Planning: Integration, Subordination, or Obliteration?" In Defense Planning and Arms Control: Proceedings of a Special NSAI Conference 12-14 June 1980 National Defense University, 9-21. Washington, D.C.: National Security Affairs Institute, 1980. SOD D5.402:D36. Reviews the slackening support for arms control in the United States and the problems created by SALT. Nacht emphatically recommends "integration" of arms control planning and national security planning. He also discusses arms control and specific weapons systems such as the B-1 bomber.

1437. Reppy, Judith. "Military Research and Development: Institutions, Output, and Arms Control." In American Security Policy and Policy-Making, edited by Robert Harkavy and Edward A. Kolodziej, 165-180. Lexington, Massachusetts: Lexington Books, 1980. Reviews recent military research and development activities in the United States, including managerial aspects. Reppy goes on to discuss the often destabilizing effects of research and development on arms control efforts.

Military Assistance

1438. Carter, Jimmy. "Conventional Arms Transfer Policy Statement by the President. May 19, 1977." In Public Papers of the Presidents of the United States: Jimmy Carter 1977, I, 931-932. Washington, D.C.: Government Printing Office, 1977. Points to the danger represented by the growing arms traffic. Carter states that the United States will follow "a policy of arms restraint" and sets forth a number of steps that will be taken to reduce arms shipments from the United States. He also will pursue negotiations with the Soviets to secure their cooperation in reducing the world arms traffic.

Military Personnel

Books

1439. Bachman, Jerald G. and others. The All-Volunteer Force: A Study of Ideology in the Military. Ann Arbor: University of Michigan Press, 1977. 210p. Early analysis of the AVF based on a survey administered to civilians and army and navy personnel in the early to mid-1970's. The authors found much support for the AVF concept. They warn against thinking of military service as simply another form of employment.

Essays and Periodical Articles

1440. Janowitz, Morris. "The Citizen Soldier and National Service." Air University Review 31 (November-December 1979): 2-16. Asserts that the "citizen soldier" plays a vital role even in the absence of conscription because many soldiers serve only a single enlistment. Janowitz also presents arguments for a national service program.

1441. King, William R. "Men, Women, and the Crisis In Military Force Levels." In Equivalence, Sufficiency, and the International Balance: Proceedings of the Fifth

National   Security Affairs Conference July 17-19, 1978,
249-261.   Washington,   D.C.: Government Printing Office,
1978.   SOD D5.412:978. Warns that it will be difficult to
maintain   force   levels   because   of   the   relatively   few
potential servicemen and women and competition for them
from the private sector.   King briefly reviews studies of
the all-volunteer force in the 1960's and 1970's and
examines problems facing it in the 1980's.

1442.   Moskos, Charles C.   "How to Save the All-Volunteer
Force." Public Interest 61 (Fall 1980):74-89.   Delineates
the problems encountered by the all-volunteer force in
terms of the mental groups and educational levels, racial
composition,   number   of   women,   and   marital   status   of
recruits.   Treating military service as just another
occupation has also caused problems.   Moskos explains why
he thinks the force can meet American military manpower
needs through various benefits and a two-track system for
short-term and long-term servicemen and women.

1443. Tarr, Curtis W.   "Managing the Human Resources of the
Total Force." Air University Review 28 (January-February
1977):2-11.   Examines military personnel issues in light of
the Defense Manpower Commission's study.   Requirements for
numbers   of   servicemen   and   women,   recruiting,   and
compensation are discussed.

North Atlantic Treaty Organization

Official Policy Statements

1444. Carter,   Jimmy.   "Brussels,   Belgium.   Text   of
Remarks at a Meeting of the North Atlantic Council.
January 6, 1978." In Public Papers of the Presidents of the
United States: Jimmy Carter 1978, I, 36-38.   Washington,
D.C.: Government Printing Office, 1979.   Discusses long and
shortterm plans for NATO, a study of the Warsaw Pact, and
more "cooperation in defense procurement" among the NATO
partners.   Carter asserts that his defense budget will add
significantly to American strength, thereby benefitting the
alliance.   Changes will include more United States troops
in Europe and enhanced "reinforcement capability" for NATO
forces   from   the   United   States.   He   pledges   full
consultation with the European allies on SALT II.

1445. Carter, Jimmy.   "North Atlantic Alliance Summit.
Text of Remarks on NATO Defense Policy. May 31, 1978." In
Public Papers of the Presidents of the United States:
Jimmy Carter 1978, I, 1019-1021. Washington, D.C.: Government Printing Office, 1979.   Discusses Carter's decision to
stress the defense of Europe, "especially the conventional
defenses needed in the initial stages of a conflict." Most
of the address describes NATO's Long-Term Defense Program.

Essays and Periodical Articles

1446.   Armstrong, Alan P.   "Nuclear Weapons and NATO."
Military Review 60 (May 1980):11-17.   Discusses competing
theories of NATO: as a tripwire to initiate American use of
strategic nuclear weapons or a war-fighting alliance able
to conduct a conventional military campaign.   Armstrong
advocates helping the United Kingdom and France to establish their own nuclear deterrence force and the withdrawal
or conversion of "theater nuclear weapons."

1447.   Beard, Robin L.   "U.S. NATO Policy: The Challenge
and the Opportunity." United States Naval Institute
Proceedings 104 (November 1978):52-61.   Warns of the
increasing strength of the Soviets in Europe and advocates
increases in NATO conventional forces. Much of the article
deals with the standardization issue within NATO and the
industrial aspects of defense.

1448.   Burney, John C., Jr.   "Nuclear Sharing in NATO."
Military Review 49 (June 1969):62-68. Examines efforts to
promote multilateral approaches to nuclear weapons policy
within NATO.

1449.   Canby, Steven L.   "NATO Defense: The Problem is Not
More Money." In American Security Policy and Policy-Making,
edited by Robert Harkavy and Edward A. Kolodziej, 85-99.
Lexington, Massachusetts: Lexington Books, 1980.   Proposes
ways for expanding NATO's conventional forces.   Canby
especially favors borrowing Dutch methods for integrating
regulars and reservists.

1450.   Canby, Steven L.   "NATO Strategy: Political-Military
Problems of Divergent Interests and Operational Concepts."
Military Review 59 (April 1979):50-58.   Analyzes American
and European perspectives on NATO strategy, especially the
role of nuclear weapons and deterrence theory.   Canby sees
American planning as oriented toward firepower, while
Soviet strategy emphasizes maneuver.

1451. Cimbala, Stephen J.   "Flexible Targeting, Escalation
Control, and War in Europe." Armed Forces and Society 12
(Spring 1986):383-400.   Compares American and European
views of deterrence and defense.   Cimbala emphasizes the
likely impact of political considerations on American
military action in Europe.

1452. Cimbala, Stephen J.   "Theater Nuclear and Conventional Force Improvements." Armed Forces & Society 11 (Fall
1984):115-129.   Examines NATO force modernization. Cimbala
notes that Europeans are generally more in favor of nuclear
deterrence and less interested in building up conventional
forces than are American decision makers.

1453.   Clark, John J.   "Is the NATO Alliance Structure

Appropriate for the 1980s?" Military Review 59 (April
1979):25-34. Discusses various economic and social trends
impacting on NATO and American national power. Clark
examines various hypotheses that are often used to justify
defense expenditures such as the view that any European war
will become a nuclear exchange. Clark goes on to question
the reliability of the NATO allies. He would like NATO to
be converted into "a truly global alliance."

1454. Higgins, Michael and Christopher Makins. "Theater
Nuclear Forces and 'Gray Area' Arms Control." In
Continuity and Changes in the Eighties and Beyond:
Proceedings of the National Security Affairs Conference
23-25 July 1979 National Defense University, 29-48.
Washington, D.C.: National Defense University Press, 1979.
SOD D5.412:979. Argues for the development of specific
doctrine for theater nuclear forces. The authors view the
maintenance of "cohesion" within NATO and the acceptance of
theater nuclear weapons as legitimate by the European
members of NATO as the primary goals for American policy.

1455. Megill, William K. "The Deployment of Pershing II to
Europe--Some Implications." Military Review 60 (December
1980):58-66. Examines the importance of Pershing II in
giving NATO forces in Europe a nuclear deterrent that can
reach Soviet targets. Their presence in Europe brings with
it some ambiguity; the Soviets will necessarily fear that
Western European countries can use the weapons, although
they are currently under American control.

1456. Rasmussen, Robert D. "The A-10 in Central Europe."
Air University Review 30 (November-December 1978):26-44.
Offers recommendations for making the most of the A-10
aircraft in ground air support. Rasmussen notes problems
such as frequent adverse weather conditions in Europe and
discusses basing strategy extensively.

1457. Rasmussen, Robert D. "The Central European Battlefield: Doctrinal Implications for Counterair-Interdiction."
Air University Review 29 (July-August 1978):2-20. Discusses
the impact of suface-to-air defense systems on interdiction. Rasmussen is especially concerned about Soviet
surface-to-air missiles in Europe, which he describes.

1458. Samuel, Wolfgang W.E. "The Impossible Task--Defense
Without Relevant Strategy." Air University Review 31
(March-April 1980):15-28. Argues that NATO is more powerful than often realized, but NATO strategy must be
improved. Samuel criticizes the concepts of "flexible
response" and "forward deployment," comparing current
deployments with the Allied posture against the Germans in
1940.

1459. Stachurski, Richard J. "The Nunn-Bartlett Report: A
Realistic Prescription for NATO?" Air University Review 29

(July-August 1978):21-25. Examines <u>NATO and the New Soviet Threat</u>, issued by the Senate Armed Services Committee in 1977. Stachurski favors "a mobile defense in depth" rather than too much emphasis on forward deployment of NATO Forces.

1460. Staudenmaier, William O. "Some Strategic Implications of Fighting Outnumbered on the NATO Battlefield." <u>Military Review</u> 60 (May 1980):38-50. Anticipates that if there is a Soviet attack in Europe, it will be "a short, violent campaign," with the object of preventing NATO from bringing its great potential strength to bear. Staudenmaier examines the theories that have developed to interpret the relative strength of NATO and the Warsaw Pact.

Asia

1461. Carter, Jimmy. "Withdrawal of United States Ground Forces from the Republic of Korea. Statement by the President. April 21, 1978." In <u>Public Papers of the Presidents of the United States: Jimmy Carter 1978</u>, I, 768. Washington, D.C.: Government Printing Office, 1979. Reiterates that the withdrawal of ground forces will be balanced by improvements in the South Korean defense forces and increased United States Air Force commitments in South Korea. Carter recommends that Congress approve additional military assistance to the Republic of Korea to support current American policy.

Sino-American Relations

1462. Hartmann, Frederick H. "The Strategic Triangle: China, Russia, and the United States." In <u>Rethinking US Security Policy for the 1980s: Proceedings of the Seventh National Security Affairs Conference 21-23 July 1980</u> 11-20. Washington, D.C.: National Defense University Press, 1980. SOD D5.412:980. Discusses the limitations of the "bipolar" approach to analyzing world politics. Much of the article focuses on Soviet foreign policies, particularly in regard to China.   There are shorter sections on Chinese and American views of the "triangle."

1463. Pfaltzgraff, Robert L., Jr. "Sino-Soviet-American Relationships: Prospects for the 1980s." In <u>Rethinking US Security Policy for the 1980s: Proceedings of the Seventh National Security Affairs Conference 21-23 July 1980</u>, 21-36. Washington, D.C.: National Defense University Press, 1980. SOD D5.412:980. Reviews American efforts to counter Soviet expansionism by developing friendler relations with the Peoples Republic of China, which in large measure failed.   The Soviets were growing so much stronger than either China or the United States that there seemed little the United States could do to assist China in balancing the Soviets.

Africa

1464. Murdock, Clark A.   "Political and Military Dimensions
of the African Problem, 1980-2000.   In <u>Continuity and
Change in the Eighties and Beyond: Sixth National Security
Affairs Conference 1979 Proceedings 23-25 July 1979 National Defense University</u>, 77-95.   Washington, D.C.: National Defense University, 1979.   SOD D5.412:979. Notes the
diversity of current American opinion concerning security
developments in Africa.   Murdock views the USSR as an
aggressive element in Africa which should be prevented from
damaging the significant interests of the United States.
The most suitable strategy for the United States in
Southern Africa is to conciliate the black-ruled states in
exchange for their not venting hostility on the United
States for its inability to change the situation in the
Republic of South Africa.

The Middle East

1465. Cameron, Juan.   "What If?   US Military Strategy for
the Middle East." <u>Military Review</u> 59 (November 1979):8-17.
Focuses on threats to Western oil supplies, a contingency
for which the United States seems to lack a strategy.
Cameron discusses the severe political and climatic
challenges which would face American operations in the
Persian Gulf area.

1466.   Christman, Daniel W. and Wesley K. Clark. "Foreign
Energy Sources and Military Power." <u>Military Review</u> 58
(February 1978):3-14.   Asserts that military force is
unlikely to be very effective for dealing with future
American resources crises, judging by the experience of the
Arab oil embargo in 1973-1974.

1467. Crowe, William J. "The Persian Gulf: Central or
Peripheral to United States Strategy?" <u>United States Naval
Institute Proceedings</u> 104 (March 1978):184-209.   Surveys
the countries of the Persian Gulf and adjacent areas in
terms of their recent political history and geopolitical
importance.   A lengthy section compares the American and
Soviet military postures in or near the Persian Gulf
region.   Crowe warns that the Soviets might well intervene
in the Middle East without there being a concurrent war in
Western Europe.

1468. Kemp, Geoffrey.   "Contingency Planning and Persian
Gulf Options."   In <u>Continuity and Change in the Eighties
and Beyond: Proceedings of the National Security Affairs
Conference 23-25 July 1979 National Defense University</u>, 61-
76.   Washington, D.C.: National Defense University, 1979.
SOD D5.412L979. Sees a general need for contingency forces
beyond defense of Western interests in the Persian Gulf
area.   Kemp reviews American thinking about the military

role of Iran during and after the Second World War. Most of the article focuses on possible contemporary threats in the Persian Gulf.

1469. Ulin, Robert R. "US National Security and Middle Eastern Oil." <u>Military Review</u> 59 (May 1979):39-49. Describes the vital nature of energy resources to the maintenance of American security. Ulin reviews the development of a common front by the major Arab oil producing nations and the course of the 1973 embargo. He asserts that the United States must depend upon diplomacy rather than military intervention to keep oil flowing.

The Iranian Rescue Mission

Official Policy Statements

1470. Carter, Jimmy. "Rescue Attempt for American Hostages in Iran: Letter to the Speaker of the House and the President Pro Tempore of the Senate Reporting on the Operation. April 26, 1980." In <u>Public Papers of the Presidents of the United States: Jimmy Carter 1980-81</u>, I, 777-779. Washington, D.C.: Government Printing Office, 1981. Report to Congress under the provisions of the War Powers Resolution of 1973. Carter describes the mishaps that thwarted the rescue mission. He states that the initial outlook for the attempt was "excellent," and he defends the right of the United States to have tried to free its nationals. His interpretation of the operation is that it was "a humanitarian mission."

1471. Carter, Jimmy. "United States-Iran Agreement on Release of the American Hostages. Message to the Congress. January 19, 1981." In <u>Public Papers of the Presidents of the United States: Jimmy Carter 1980-81</u>, III, 3040-3043. Washington, D.C.: Government Printing Office, 1982. Describes the agreement reached with Iran. Much of the message discusses unblocking of Iranian assets in the United States. Carter summarizes each of the Executive Orders he intends to issue when the hostages are freed.

Books

1472. Beckwith, Charlie A. and Donald Knox. <u>Delta Force</u>. New York: Harcourt Brace Jovanovich Publishers, 1983. 310p. Presents the events of the Iran hostage rescue effort as seen by the commander of the mission. It is an extremely detailed account, naturally defending Beckwith's conduct of the expedition.

Periodical Articles

1473. "Iranian Rescue Mission." Parts 1, 2, 3. <u>Aviation Week & Space Technology</u>. 113 (September 15, 22, 29, 1980): 61-63, 65-71; 140-144; 84-85, 88-91. Text of the report on the Iran hostage mission by the Special Operations Review Group. It examines in detail the technical and organizational problems that prevented the American rescue attempt from being successful.

The Soviet Invasion of Afghanistan

1474. Carter, Jimmy.   "Soviet Invasion of Afghanistan. Address to the Nation. January 4, 1980." In Public Papers of the Presidents of the United States: Jimmy Carter 1980-81, I, 21-24.   Washington, D.C.: Government Printing Office, 1981.   Begins with a denunciation of the Iranian seizure of American hostages, but most of the speech states retaliatory actions Carter is taking because of the Soviet invasion of Afghanistan. These include asking Congress to postpone debate on SALT II, a grain embargo, and American abstention from the 1980 Olympics.   He also promises military and other aid to Pakistan which is threatened by the USSR.

Chapter 8

Reagan: Reassertion and Rearmament

In some respects, the electoral victory and early defense initiatives of Ronald Reagan resembled those of John F. Kennedy two decades earlier. Like Kennedy, Reagan campaigned in part with charges that the incumbent president had permitted American military strength to run down. As in the early 1960's, the United States under Reagan moved to improve American military capabilities at all levels. More missiles were constructed and deployed in innovative ways, efforts were made to expand the navy, and there was a renewed emphasis on military forces to carry out special operations such as anti-terrorist actions and counterinsurgency. The Central Intelligence Agency was once again directed to provide paramilitary training.

The environment of the 1980's was far different from that of the 1960's, however. Vietnam and the problems associated with that war were very much in the minds of executive branch officers, members of Congress, private citizens, and media personnel. Despite much concern with Soviet activities in Afghanistan, Africa, and the Western Hemisphere, the Reagan administration often found it difficult, if not impossible, to muster needed support for its policies. The Soviet Union was stronger than it had been in the Kennedy era; one of the most striking changes was the new Soviet fleet that lent itself to force projection on a scale impossible earlier.

Notwithstanding anti-Soviet rhetoric and its emphasis on rearmament, the Reagan administration demonstrated a continuing commitment to arms control negotiations. Sino-American relations continued to improve, but it was apparent that a friendlier China was not an ally in the NATO sense, and, therefore, this relationship would not permit the United States to reduce its defense commitments by relying on Chinese aid.

Decision-making

Books

1475. Blechman, Barry M. and William J. Lynn, editors. <u>Toward A More Effective Defense: Report of the Defense Organization Project</u>. Cambridge, Massachusetts: Ballinger

Publishing Company, 1985. 247p. Contributors include Robert
J. Art, Morton Halperin, and Philip A. Odeen. The
proposals seek to improve American defense capability in a
period when the costs of defense are again being
questioned. The report comes from the Center for Strategic
and International Studies at Georgetown University.

1476. Feld, Werner J. and John K. Wildgen. Congress and
National Defense: The Politics of the Unthinkable. New
York: Praeger Publishers, 1985. 126p. Investigates the
involvement of Congress with nuclear weapons. The authors
discuss individual Congressional decision-makers in the
defense field and their views on nuclear defense.

1477. Hoxie, R. Gordon with others. The Presidency and
National Security Policy. New York: Center for the Study
of the Presidency, 1984. 463p. Contributors include Caspar
W. Weinberger, George P. Shultz, and Robert C. McFarlane.
Among the topics examined are the place of public opinion
in debates over national security, structures such as the
National Security Council and the Joint Chiefs of Staff,
and processes for making policy in the security field.

1478. Luttwak, Edward N. The Pentagon and the Art of War:
The Question of Military Reform. New York: Simon &
Schuster, 1985. 333p. Highly critical account of the shortcomings of the American military. Luttwak suggests that an
interservice general staff would solve many problems and
improve performance.

1479. Sims, Robert B. The Pentagon Reporters. Washington,
D.C.: National Defense University Press, 1983. 177p. SOD
D5. 402:R29. Profiles the reporters from all forms of
media, including broadcasting networks, newspapers, wire
services, and both general and technical periodicals. Sims
also examines the audiences for which these reporters are
writing.

1480. Stubbing, Richard A. with Richard A. Mendel. The
Defense Game: An Insider Explores the Astonishing Realities
of America's Defense Establishment. New York: Harper &
Row, Publishers, 1986. 448p. Examines all phases of policy-
making in the field of national security, including the
role of Congress and budgetary aspects. Stubbing also
studies the role of the Secretaries of Defense since
McNamara's long tenure.

Essays and Periodical Articles

1481. Barrett, Archie D. "Department of Defense
Organization: Planning for Planning." In Planning U.S.
Strategy, edited by Philip S. Kronenberg, 111-138.
Washington, D.C.: National Defense University Press, 1981.
SOD D5.402:Se2/3/980-81. Scores heavily the continued

independence of the services. Barrett advocates strengthening the roles of the service secretaries.

1482. Barrett, Archie D. "Impediments to Department of Defense Reorganization." In Understanding U.S. Strategy: A Reader, edited by Terry L. Heyns, 247-306. Washington, D.C.: National Defense University Press, 1983. SOD D5.402:St8/3. Reviews proposals for change made in 1982 by various military leaders and analyzes the clashing interests within the defense establishment which prevent fundamental changes in structure.

1483. Cancian, Mark F. "PPBS: Rude Awakening." United States Naval Institute Proceedings 110 (November 1984):44-52. Notes that program budgeting has had few advantages and a great many disadvantages insofar as it has been implemented in the field of national defense.

1484. Clark, Asa,A. IV "Interservice Rivalry and Military Reform." In The Defense Reform Debate: Issues and Analysis, edited by Asa A. Clark IV and others, 250-271. Baltimore: Johns Hopkins University Press, 1984. Asserts that the army and marines are the most concerned about reform, the air force somewhat interested, and the navy the least enthusiastic. Clark explores the reasons for their varying perspectives.

1485. Clark, Asa A.IV. "The Outlook [for the Defense Reform Movement]" In The Defense Reform Debate: Issues and Analysis, edited by Asa A. Clark IV and others, 346-359. Baltimore: Johns Hopkins University Press, 1984. Asserts that the military reform movement will persist, but also discusses factors that retard change.

1486. Cyr, Arthur. "How Important is National Security Structure to National Security Policy?" World Affairs 146 (Fall 1983):127-147. Discusses the basic bilateral structure (State Department and National Security Council). Cyr examines the ways in which presidents have operated to maintain an equilibrium between the two agencies.

1487. Fox, J. Ronald. "Revamping the Business of National Defense." Harvard Business Review 62 (September-October 1984):62-70. Analyzes flaws in American defense procurement. Fox, a leading expert in the field, looks at the management of the programs by testing how well the budget is spent. He examines overruns and suggests improvements to prevent or reduce them.

1488. Hall, David L. "War Powers By the Clock." United States Naval Institute Proceedings 113 (September 1987):36-40. Argues that the War Powers Resolution does not hamper anti-terrorist responses because they are generally rapid, not sustained operations. Hall discusses the War Powers Resolution and the Sidra Strait episode in 1986 and current problems in the Persian Gulf.

1489. Komer, Robert W.   "Strategymaking in the Pentagon."
In Reorganizing America's Defense: Leadership in War and
Peace, edited by Robert J. Art and others, 207-229.
Washington, D.C.: Pergamon-Brassey's, 1985.   Argues that
conventional strategy has received little attention in
the United States during the post-World War II period. He
also believes some changes can be made in the machinery for
making strategy despite the salience of politics in defense
debates.

1490. Korb, Lawrence J. "On Making the System Work."   In
Planning U.S. Strategy, edited by Philip S. Kronenberg,
139145.   Washington, D.C.: National Defense University
Press, 1981.   SOD D5.402:Se2/3/980-81.   Points to
governmental "fragmentation" which produces bureaucratic,
rather than strategic decisions.   Korb proposes a group
like the Hoover Commission to investigate defense
organization.

1491. Kronenberg, Philip S. "National Security Planning:
Images and Issues."   In Planning U.S. Strategy, edited by
Philip S. Kronenberg, 73-110.   Washington, D.C.: National
Defense University Press, 1981.   SOD D5.402:Se2/3/980-81.
Usefully puts military planning into the broader context of
planning theory and compares military and business
planning.   Kronenberg suggests ways to improve decision-
making despite the many obstacles.

1492. Lind, William S. "Defense Reform: A Reappraisal." In
The Defense Reform Debate: Issues and Analysis, edited by
Asa A. Clark IV and others, 327-333. Baltimore: Johns
Hopkins University Press, 1984.   Assesses the military
reform movement and predicts that it will receive greater
attention in the future.   Lind argues that the reformers
hope to make the services initiate further changes on their
own.

1493.   Lovell, John P.   "From Defense Policy to National
Security Policy: The Tortuous Adjustment for American Military Professionals." Air University Review 32 (May-June
1981):42-54.   Traces the impact of technology on military
decision-making and various other changes that make policy
making more and more complex.

1494. Lovell, John P. "The Idiom of National Security."
JPMS: Journal of Political & Military Sociology 11 (Spring
1983):35-51. Analyzes the role of language in debates over
security, including weapons systems.   The discussions are
transformed as issues reach wider audiences.

1495. Lupfer, Timothy S.   "The Challenge of Military
Reform." In The Defense Reform Debate: Issues and Analysis,
edited by Asa A. Clark IV and others, 23-32.   Baltimore:

Johns Hopkins University Press, 1984. Focuses on the need
to develop a strategy for effecting changes in the military
establishment. Lupfer distinguishes between "military
critics" and "military reformers," the latter being in a
position to bring about change.

1496. Nuechterlein, Donald E. "National Interests and
National Strategy: The Need for Priority." In Understanding
U.S. Strategy: A Reader, edited by Terry L. Heyns, 35-63.
Washington, D.C.: National Defense University Press, 1983.
SOD D5.402:St8/3. Assesses the strategic significance of
various areas of the world to American policy goals.
Nuechterlein warns that the United States should not try to
pursue as many objectives as it is currently trying to do.

1497. Odeen, Philip. "A Critique of the PPB System." In
Reorganizing America's Defense, edited by Robert J. Art,
375-380. Washington, D.C.: Pergamon-Brassey's, 1985. Very
briefly outlines the development of PPB in the Kennedy
administration and reviews current problems. Odeen defends
the concept, while admitting that it has significant
shortcomings.

1498. Oliver, James K. and James A. Nathan. "The American
Environment for Security Planning." In Planning U.S.
Strategy, edited by Philip S. Kronenberg, 31-54. Washing-
ton, D.C.: National University Press, 1981. SOD D5.402:
D36/2/977-80. Analyzes internal, primarily constitutional,
structural, and popular influences on security planning.
Other essays in the volume tend to emphasize executive-
legislative relations.

1499. Puritano, Vincent. "Resource Allocation in the
Pentagon." In Reorganizing America's Defense: Leadership in
War and Peace, edited by Robert J. Art and others, 359-374.
Washington, D.C.: Pergamon-Brassey's, 1985. Reviews
defense budget-making procedure, and then discusses the
Reagan administration's effort to make changes in the
process. Puritano complains of Congressional intrusion
into Defense Department activities.

1500. Reed, James W. "Congress and the Politics of Defense
Reform." In The Defense Reform Debate: Issues and Analysis,
edited by Asa A. Clark IV and others, 230-249. Baltimore:
Johns Hopkins University Press, 1984. Discusses the
Military Reform Caucus and other manifestations of the
increasing involvement of Congress in national security
policy. Congress has not made any major changes, but Reed
takes a generally positive view of its activity.

1501. Schlesinger, James. "The Office of the Secretary of
Defense." In Reorganizing America's Defense: Leadership in
War and Peace, edited by Robert J. Art and others, 255-274.
Washington, D.C.: Pergamon-Brassey's, 1985. Emphasizes the
divided power in the American political system and

discusses the problems of the Secretary of Defense, relying in part on Schlesinger's experience in that post. Schlesinger also discusses the Joint Chiefs of Staff, generally aligning himself with proposals made by David Jones [entries 1508-1509].

1502. Smith, William Y. "The U.S. Military Command-Present and Future." In Reorganizing America's Defense: Leadership in War and Peace, edited by Robert J. Art and others, 292-329. Washington, D.C.: Pergamon-Brassey's, 1985. Discusses the weakness of unified commanders. Smith also warns that tinkering with the Joint Chiefs of Staff and changes in the chain of command are only partial solutions of American defense problems. Followed by comments from David C. Jones, Edward C. Meyer III, and Thor Hanson, 330-343.

1503. Stupak, Ronald J. "Military Professionals and Civilian Careerists in the Department of Defense." Air University Review 32 (July-August 1981):68-75. Deals with day-to-day relationships below the highest levels of decision-making in the government. Stupak sees the Civil Service Reform Act of 1978, which created the Senior Executive Service, as having a potentially very beneficial effect on the Department of Defense.

1504. Tilford, Earl H., Jr. "Military Leadership in a Changing Service." Air University Review 34 (September-October 1983):29-37. Stresses the need for appropriate leaders. Tilford very briefly sketches the contributions to the air force of such leaders as Mitchell and LeMay, and notes the characteristics of effective leaders at lower levels.

The Joint Chiefs of Staff

1505. Davis, Vincent. "The Evolution of Central U.S. Defense Management." In Reorganizing America's Defense: Leadership in War and Peace, edited by Robert J. Art and others, 149-167. Washington, D.C.: Pergamon-Brassey's, 1985. Provides a brief historical survey of defense organization up to the 1960's and then focuses on contemporary debates. Davis asserts that little has changed; interservice conflicts continue, despite repeated efforts at centralization.

1506. Gorman, Paul F. "Toward a Stronger Defense Establishment." In The Defense Reform Debate: Issues and Analysis, edited by Asa A. Clark IV and others, 287-297. Baltimore: Johns Hopkins University Press, 1984. Examines the question of why significant changes have not been made in the Joint Chiefs of Staff. Gorman reviews in some detail 20th century efforts to improve service coordination.

1507. Hall, David K. "An Assessment of the JCS as an Advisory and Decisionmaking Institution." Naval War College Review 38 (September-October 1985):37-54. Asserts that the Joint Chiefs of Staff has improved materially, partly as the result of the attention it has received from the media. Hall argues against a major enhancement of the role of the Chairman of the Joint Chiefs of Staff.

1508. Jones, David C. "What's Wrong with the Defense Establishment?" In The Defense Reform Debate: Issues and Analysis, edited by Asa A. Clark IV and others, 272-286. Baltimore: Johns Hopkins University Press, 1984. Analyzes the need to free decision makers in the defense field from too much dependence on earlier decisions. Jones also reviews the history of the Joint Chiefs of Staff and proposes ways to improve defense budgeting.

1509. Jones, David C. "Why the Joint Chiefs of Staff Must Change." In Understanding U.S. Strategy: A Reader, edited by Terry L. Heyns, 307-325. Washington, D.C.: National Defense University Press, 1983. SOD D5.402:St8/3. Former Chairman of the Joint Chiefs of Staff presents an important critique. While recording some progress, Jones scores the ineffective committee system embodied by the Joint Chiefs of Staff. This essay is a powerful argument for strengthening the authority of the Chairman of the Joint Chiefs of Staff.

1510. Lynn, William J. "The Wars Within: The Joint Military Structure and Its Critics." In Reorganizing America's Defense: Leadership in War and Peace, edited by Robert J. Art and others, 168-204. Washington, D.C.: Pergamon-Brassey's, 1985. Discusses the development of the Joint Chiefs of Staff, dealing at some length with changes in the system during the Eisenhower administrations. Lynn then examines various options for reforming the Joint Chiefs of Staff, although he sees little prospect for major changes.

1511. Meyer, Edward C. "The JCS--How Much Reform is Needed?" In Understanding U.S. Strategy: A Reader, edited by Terry L. Heyns, 327-346. Washington, D.C.: National Defense University Press, 1983. SOD D5.402:St8/3. Reviews and critiques the growth of decision-making structures for defense. Meyer emphasizes the importance of the unified commands and proposes a military council to assess their needs and to make recommendations unhampered by direct ties to the services.

1512. Odeen, Philip A. "JCS Reform: A Commentary " In The Defense Reform Debate: Issues and Analysis, edited by Asa A. Clark IV and others, 298-304. Baltimore: Johns Hopkins University Press, 1984. Argues that a "general staff" is needed rather than simply improvements in the Joint Chiefs of Staff. Odeen takes a pessimistic view of the prospects for change of any kind.

Military Policy

Official Policy Statements

1513. Reagan, Ronald. "Statement on Signing the Department
of Defense Appropriation Act, 1982. December 29, 1982." In
Public Papers of the Presidents of the United States:
Ronald Reagan 1981, 1204. Washington, D.C.: Government
Printing Office, 1982. Terms the law "a significant step"
in rebuilding American defenses and notes the "bipartisan
support" for the program in Congress.

1514. Reagan, Ronald. "Radio Address to the Nation on
Defense Spending. February 19, 1983." In Public papers of
the Presidents of the United States: Ronald Reagan 1983, I,
257-259. Washington, D.C.: Government Printing Office,
1984. Citing the pre-World War II rise of Nazism, Reagan
argues that national defense must not be neglected in
peacetime. Reagan discusses the Soviet buildup and the
attack on Afghanistan. He asserts that defense expenditures have to be expanded to meet possible crises in
the short-term and also to make up for previous deficiencies.

1515. Reagan, Ronald. "Remarks at the Annual Washington
Conference of the American Legion. February 22, 1983." In
Public Papers of the Presidents of the United States:
Ronald Reagan 1983, I, 264-271. Washington, D.C.:
Government Printing Office, 1984. Assails the record of
recent administrations for weakening American defenses and
playing a primarily reactive role in foreign relations.
Reagan outlines his principal arms control policies and
reviews relations with various countries and regions of the
world.

1516. Reagan, Ronald. "Statement on United States Defense
Policy. March 9, 1983." In Public Papers of the Presidents
of the United States: Ronald Reagan 1983, I, 367-368.
Washington, D.C.: Government Printing Office, 1984.
Emphasizes the wholly defensive nature of American military
policy and posture and cites the extensive, ongoing military program of the Soviets. A strong American defense is
"a real incentive" to the Soviets to negotiate arms
reductions.

1517. Reagan, Ronald. "Remarks at the National Leadership
Forum of the Center for International and Strategic Studies
of Georgetown University. April 6, 1984." In Public Papers
of the Presidents of the United States: Ronald Reagan
1984, I, 477-485. Washington, D.C.: Government Printing
Office, 1986. Terms the 1970's a "decade of neglect"
during which American defenses declined, thereby inviting
Soviet expansionism. Reagan sees the United States as once
again pursuing an effective policy of deterrence. He

reviews arms control negotiations and emphasizes his willingness to reduce nuclear weapons. In an examination of Central American problems, he asserts that both military and economic assistance are needed.

Books

1518. Bender, David L., editor. The American Military: Opposing Viewpoints. St. Paul, Minnesota: Greenhaven Press, 1983. 228p. Consists of readings from many sources, presenting many points of view. The bibliography is highly useful.

1519. Berkowitz, Bruce D. American Security: Dilemmas for a Modern Democracy. New Haven: Yale University Press, 1986. 276p. Useful current survey. Much of the focus is on nuclear weapons and strategy and on the defense of Europe. One chapter deals with Persian Gulf security.

1520. Blechman, Barry M. U.S. Security in the Twenty-First Century. Boulder, Colorado: Westview Press, 1987. 173p. Suggests four scenarios for developments in world politics that would influence American defense planning. Blechman interviewed many security specialists and uses a variety of data, economic and demographic, as well as military, in this study.

1521. Degrasse, Robert W. Military Expansion, Economic Decline; the Impact of Military Spending on U.S. Economic Performance. New York: M.E. Sharpe, 1983.260p. Constitutes an enlarged version of Degrasse and others' report for the Council on Economic Priorities. The book includes material on historical Cold War spending trends, noting the impact on the American economy. The emphasis is on expenditures under Reagan.

1522. Etzold, Thomas H. Defense or Delusion? America's Military in the 1980's. New York: Harper & Row, 1982. 259p. Examines weapons, strategy, and personnel issues among other topics. Etzold discusses recent military failures such as the Iran hostage rescue attempt.

1523. Fallows, James M. National Defense. New York: Random House, 1981. 204p. Examines all phases of the American defense posture and the theories surrounding it. Fallows assails the Defense Department and the military for tying themselves to increasingly cumbersome weapons systems and criticizes various factors which he believes stem from the McNamara era.

1524. Komer, Robert W. Maritime Strategy or Coalition Defense? Cambridge, Massachusetts: Abt Books, 1984. 116p. Emphasizes that the United States cannot depend upon sea-power to the detriment of its commitments to the defense of Europe and Asia and advocates working within our alliance system rather than "going it alone."

1525. Poole, Robert W., Jr., editor. Defending A Free
Society. Lexington, Massachusetts: Lexington Books, 1984.
364p. Proposes considerable change in American defense
policy. Writing from a libertarian perspective, the authors
of the essays recommend more emphasis on the defense of the
United States, free trade, and an end to intervention
abroad.

1526. Record, Jeffrey. Revising U.S. Military Strategy:
Tailoring Ends to Means. Washington, D.C.: Pergamon-
Brassey's, 1984. 113p. Stresses that American military
assets are too limited to sustain the broad political
commitments that have been made. Record recommends taking
measures to reduce the gap between American political goals
and military capabilities and pressing the American allies
to undertake more of the common defense burden. This is
also an important summary of American strategy since 1945.

1527. Ricci, Fred J. and Daniel Schutzer. U.S. Military
Communications: A C^3 I Force Multiplier. Rockville,
Maryland: Computer Science Press, 1986. 263p. Thorough
overview of American and NATO military communications.
Includes a useful review of the requirements imposed on
communications systems by combat environments.

1528. Spinney, Franklin C. Defense Facts of Life: The
Plans/Reality Mismatch, edited by James Clay Thompson.
Boulder,Colorado: Westview Press, 1985. 260p. Focuses on
the process of making decisions about national security.
Spinney sees fundamental problems that need to be resolved
if there is to be real growth in American military power.
He uses tactical air as an example to illustrate the
problems he identifies.

1529. Van Cleave, William R. and Scott W. Thompson,
editors. Strategic Options for the Early Eighties: What
can be Done?
New Brunswick, New Jersey: Transaction Books, 1979. 200p.
Consists of papers read at a conference sponsored by the
National Strategy Information Commission and aerospace
specialists. Highly technical studies by major figures
such as Paul Nitze. Includes much material on the mutual
assured destruction strategy and SALT.

Essays and Periodical Articles

1530. Cordesman, Anthony H. "The Reagan Administration: Its
Past and Future Impact on Western Defense." Journal of the
Royal United Services Institute for Defense Studies 131
(January 1986):36-44. Reviews defense spending under
Reagan, noting that the United States has not surpassed the
Soviet Union in armaments. Cuts may be necessary in the
future in order to reduce the federal deficit.

1531. Davis, Vincent. "The Reagan Defense Program: Decision Making, Decision Makers, and Some of othe Results." In The Reagan Defense Program: An Interim Assesment, edited by Stephen J. Cimbala, 23-62. Wilmington, Delaware: Scholarly Resources, Inc., 1986. Emphasizes the role of the Department of Defense. In a generally critical survey, Davis discusses Reagan's major appointments in the national security sphere and the decisions and actions of these people, including the rivalries between Weinberger and Haig and between Weinberger and Shultz.

1532. Komer, Robert W. "Strategy and Military Reform." In The Defense Reform Debate: Issues and Analysis, edited by Asa A. Clark IV and others, 5-15. Baltimore: Johns Hopkins University Press, 1984. Argues that most military reformers emphasize rather limited objectives instead of concentrating on the improvement of strategy. There is a need to analyze the institutional machinery for generating strategy.

1533. Korb, Lawrence J. and Linda P. Brady. "Rearming America: The Reagan Administration Defense Program." International Security 9 (Winter 1984-85):3-18. Examines three criticisms that have been leveled at the defense buildup under Reagan and points to the fundamental flaw in each criticism. The critics state (1) now is not the right time; (2) money is spent without solving problems; and (3) in rearming, the United States is neglecting readiness and sustainability.

1534. Kronenberg, Philip S. "Planning and Defense in the Eighties." In Planning U.S. Strategy, edited by Philip S. Kronenberg, 147-192. Washington, D.C.: National Defense University Press, 1981. SOD D5.402:Se2/3/980-81. Synthesizes "major themes" in the other papers in this book. Contributors emphasize the complex governmental structure, lack of national consensus, and the need for a kind of a planning attitude rather than further restructuring of the government and of defense planning processes.

1535. Oliver, James K. and James A. Nathan. "The Reagan Defense Program: Concepts, Continuity, and Change." In The Reagan Defense Program: An Interim Assessment, edited by Stephen J. Cimbala, 1-21. Wilmington, Delaware: Scholarly Resources, Inc., 1986. Sees numerous changes from earlier administrations' defense policies, notably SDI. In many aspects, however, the Reagan program does not constitute a break with the Carter approach. The effects of Reagan's changes will not, in any case, be evident for some time.

1536. Oseth, John M. "An Overview of the Reform Debate." In The Defense Reform Debate: Issues and Analysis, edited by Asa A. Clark IV and others, 44-61. Baltimore: Johns Hopkins

University Press, 1984. The fundamental criticism offered by the reformers is that Americans must move away from attritional warfare. They also focus on the ability of military leaders in the United States.

1537. Posen, Barry R. and Stephen Van Evera. "Defense Policy and the Reagan Administration: Departure from Containment." International Security 8 (Summer 1983):3-45. Stresses that a defense policy cannot be properly formulated unless national strategy and national military capabilities are first determined. These elements are examined in terms of the containment policy. The authors are critical of the Reagan defense strategy because it makes excessive, unrealistic demands on American capabilities.

1538. Quester, George H. "National Security and National Purpose." Air University Review 33 (March-April 1982):18-32. Uses scenarios of world politics and internal developments in the United States, the USSR, and the Peoples Republic of China to analyze American security needs and policy responses. Quester sees the USSR as relatively self-confident, perhaps more than the United States and the PRC.

1539. Record, Jeffrey. "Implications of a Global Strategy for U.S. Forces." In The Defense Reform Debate: Issues and Analysis, edited by Asa A. Clark IV and others, 147-165. Baltimore: Johns Hopkins University Press, 1984. Recommends more emphasis on a maritime strategy, with fewer resources for the army in Europe and more for the navy and marines outside Europe. Record also favors smaller ships in larger numbers to meet new requirements. He is quite critical of the Rapid Deployment Force concept.

1540. Rosenau, James N. "Fragmegrative Challenges to National Security." In Understanding U.S. Strategy: A Reader, edited by Terry L. Heyns, 65-82. Washington, D.C.: National Defense University Press, 1983. SOD D5.402:St8/3. Questions whether formulation of a "national strategy" is possible and introduces the concept of "fragmegration" (fragmentation and integration) to show why such a strategy is so difficult to achieve.

1541. Sanders, Ralph. "Integrating Technology, Military Strategy, and Operational Concepts." In Technology, Strategy and National Security, edited by Frank Margiotta and Ralph Sanders, 157-190. Washington, D.C.: National Defense University Press, 1985. SOD D5.402:T22. Reviews critiques that assert the elements in the essay's title are not effectively coordinated in the United States. Sanders believes that such criticisms exaggerate current problems.

1542. Sprey, Pierre. "The Case for Better and Cheaper Weapons." In The Defense Reform Debate: Issues and Analysis, edited by Asa A. Clark IV and others, 193-208.

Baltimore: Johns Hopkins University Press, 1984. Argues that American weapons are unnecessarily complex and expensive, making the numbers of weapons produced for American forces decline. Sprey examines various weapons from World War II to the present to prove his case against costly, complicated approaches.

1543. Stubbing, Richard. "The Defense Program: Buildup or Binge?" Foreign Affairs 63 (Spring 1985):848-872. Blasts the increase in defense spending initiated by President Reagan. Compares American and Soviet military capabilities and cites evidence of poor leadership and management in the United States defense establishment.

1544. Stuckey, John D. "Echelons Above Corps." Parameters 13 (December 1983):39-47. Discusses the impact of the decision in the 1970's not to develop doctrine for army and army group levels.

1545. Tragakis, Christopher J. and John M. Weinstein. "The Moral Dimension of National Security." Military Review 63 (August 1983):2-13. Discusses the moral aspects of deterrence and of American military involvement in such countries as El Salvador. The authors strongly defend American policies.

1546. Waller, Forrest E., Jr. "Paradox and False Economy: Military Reform and High Technology." Air University Review 34 (May-June 1983):11-23. Asserts that many military reformers, who criticize over-dependence on technology, are not analyzing weapons systems correctly and make invalid comparisons between old and new systems. Their efforts are useful in making the military more sensitive to the problems of technology.

1547. Wass de Czege, Huba. "Army Doctrinal Reform." In The Defense Reform Debate: Issues and Analysis, edited by Asa A. Clark IV and others, 101-120. Baltimore: Johns Hopkins University Press, 1984. Argues that it is unrealistic to juxtapose "maneuver" versus "attrition" warfare. The author generally praises the army concept of AirLand Battle.

1548. Wendzel, Robert L. and James L. True. "Selective Involvement: A National Security Policy for a Changing World." Air University Review 33 (March-April 1983):2-16. Projects a proposed strategy through the end of the 20th century. The authors discuss many changes in world politics such as the emergence of more independent power centers. A strategy of "selective involvement" will require more flexibility on the part of the United States armed forces.

1549. Wilkerson, Lawrence B. "The Military in the Post Vietnam Era: A Search for Relevance." Naval War College Review 36 (May-June 1983):72-85. Discusses tensions between American traditions and the armed forces.

1550.   Woolsey, R. James. "The Politics of Vulnerability: 1980-83." Foreign Affairs 62 (Spring 1984):805-819. Presents a general review of Reagan's efforts to upgrade American military capabilities.

Technology and Strategy

1551. Benson, Sumner.   "The Impact of Technology Transfer on the Military Balance." Air University Review 36 (November-December 1984):4-15.   Discusses the USSR's consistent efforts to borrow technology from foreign countries and surveys the results of recent successful Soviet transactions.   The United States Air Force has an especially important stake in preventing Western enhancement of Soviet military capabilities.

1552. Duff, Karl M. "Eating Our Seed Corn." United States Naval Institute Proceedings 110 (July 1984):86-93. Criticizes the size of research and development funding, which Duff feels promotes waste and lost opportunities for innovation.

1553. Gansler, Jacques. "The US Technology Base: Problems and Prospects."   In Technology, Strategy and National Security, edited by Frank Margiotta and Ralph Sanders, 105-138. Washington, D.C.: National Defense University Press, 1985.   SOD D5.402:T22. Discusses defense expenditures and research and development in the United States.   Gansler reviews the weapons acquisitions process and examines remedies for problems in procurement such as multiyear budgets.

1554. Gingrich, Newt and James W. Reed.   "Guiding the Reform Impulse." In The Defense Reform Debate: Issues and Analysis, edited by Asa A. Clark and others, 33-43. Baltimore: Johns Hopkins University Press, 1984. Warns that too much emphasis on technology may obscure the need for more military resources. The authors argue that the United States must make basic choices about its military posture. They argue against a maritime strategy and present an extremely ambitious land strategy, involving much larger expenditures and a compulsory military service system.

Defense Costs

Books

1555. Adams, Gordon.   The Iron Triangle: the Politics of Defense Contracting.   New York: Council on Economic Priorities, 1981. 465p. Analyzes the eight major defense contractors and their relationships with Congress, the Department of Defense, and the services.   Adams proposes some reforms in defense procurement.

1556. Tobias, Sheila and others.   What Kinds of Guns are They Buying for Your Butter? A Beginner's Guide to Defense, Weaponry, and Military Spending.   New York: W. Morrow, 1982. 428p. Popular, but solid introduction to the topic. The authors take no particular stance, but offer information of use to people with varied perspectives on defense policy.

Essays and Periodical Articles

1557. Evans, David.   "The Ten Commandments of Defense Spending." Parameters 15 (Winter 1985):76-81. Assails many poor practices of both the public and private sectors in terms of defense spending. Lack of interservice cooperation is one of the factors that leads directly to unnecessary expenditures.

1558. Gansler, Jacques S. "How to Improve the Acquisition of Weapons." In Reorganizing America's Defense: Leadership in War and Peace, edited by Robert J. Art and others, 381-404.   Washington, D.C.: Pergamon-Brassey's, 1985. Generally defends the Department of Defense and the weapons it has fielded.   Gansler does offer some proposals for reform such as long-term budgeting and improvements in the defense industry.

1559. Nadiri, M. Ishaq.   "Increase in Defense Expenditure and Its Impact on the U.S. Economy." In Constraints on Strategy: The Economics of Western Security, edited by David B.H. Denoon, 27-58.   Washington, D.C.: Pergamon Brassey's International Defense Publishers, Inc., 1986. Examines Reagan's plans for increasing American defenses, the views of some of his critics, and the influence on the American economy of projected military spending.   Nadiri asserts that the buildup has not done damage to the economy, but there can be problems in the future.

General Strategy

Official Policy Statements

1560.   Reagan, Ronald.   "Statement on United States Strategic Policy.   October 21, 1981." In Public Papers of the Presidents of the United States: Ronald Reagan 1981, 979.   Washington, D.C.: Government Printing Office, 1982. Replies to "several propaganda statements" of the USSR by reaffirming the policy of "flexible response."   Reagan denies that the United States would contemplate "fighting a nuclear war at Europe's expense."

1561. Reagan, Ronald. "Address at Commencement Exercises at Eureka College in Illinois. May 9, 1982." In Public Papers of the Presidents of the United States: Ronald Reagan 1982, I, 580-586. Washington, D.C.: Government Printing Office,

1983. Sets forth a policy for dealing with the USSR, stating that it "consists of five points: miliary balance, economic security, regional stability, arms reductions, and dialog." Toward the end of the address, he indicates that an approach has been made to the Soviets to begin negotiations on START, the reduction of strategic weapons.

1562. United States. Joint Chiefs of Staff. Unified Action Armed Forces (UNAAF). Washington, D.C.: Joint Chiefs of Staff, 1987. (Joint Chiefs of Staff Publication 2) 194p. SOD D5.12:2/986. Establishes doctrine and policies for interservice cooperation. It also describes the structure of the Department of Defense and of the services. Chapter 4 discusses interservice cooperation in various sorts of operations.

Books

1563. Blechman, Barry M. and Edward N. Luttwak, editors. Global Security: A Review of Strategic and Economic Issues. Boulder, Colorado: Westview Press, 1987. 258p. Essays deal with such topics as the balance between the East and West, the health of NATO in the Mediterranean area, and relationships between American national security and the world economy.

1564. Brzezinski, Zbigniew K. Game Plan: A Geostrategic Framework for the Conduct of the U.S.-Soviet Contest. Boston: Atlantic Monthly Press, 1986 288p. Sets forth an ambitious total strategy for the United States to weaken the Soviet Union and to defend itself. Brzezinski suggests, among other options, reducing troop commitments in Western Europe and strengthening American rapid deployment capabilities for dealing with Third World emergencies.

1565. Cimbala, Stephen J. and Keith A. Dunn, editors. Conflict Termination and Military Strategy: Coercion, Persuasion, and War. Boulder, Colorado: Westview Press, 1987. 196p. Arguing that the United States needs to include the concept of conflict termination in its strategic thinking, the authors of the essays explore the complexities of ending a war short of complete victory; a concept that eventually had been quite unpopular as the theory of "limited war."

1566. Ra'anan, Uri and Robert L. Pfaltzgraff, Jr., editors. Security Commitments and Capabilities: Elements of an American Global Strategy. Hamden, Connecticut: Archon Books, 1985. 204p. Essays examine the obstacles to developing an appropriate strategy for the remainder of this century. They deal with the maintenance of alliances and comparisons between the United States and the Soviet Union, among other topics.

Essays and Periodical Articles

1567. Betts, Richard K. "Dubious Reform: Strategism versus Managerialism." In The Defense Reform Debate: Issues and Analysis, edited by Asa A. Clark IV and others, 62-82. Baltimore: Johns Hopkins University Press, 1984. Discusses the problems of measuring relative military and naval strength and examines the contributions to the defense reform debate by various scholars. Betts presents a measured criticism of those who assail the systems analysis/budgeting approach to defense study.

1568. Brown, Harold L. "Keynote Address: Evolving Strategies for a Changing World." In Understanding U.S. Strategy: A Reader, edited by Terry L. Heyns, 15-25. Washington, D.C.: National Defense University Press, 1983. SOD D5.402:St8/3. Emphasizes that a variety of nonmilitary factors, including both national and international economic problems, have to be viewed as parts of a national strategy.

1569. Cheney, Richard P. "Strategic Underpinings of a Future Force." Military Review 66 (October 1986):4-13. Criticizes much military thought for concentrating on strategies understandable to Congress. The author sketches the kinds of forces needed for the future and stresses the importance of technology.

1570. Clark, Asa A. IV and Thomas W. Fagan. "Trends in Defense Budgeting: Mortgaging the Future." In The Defense Reform Debate: Issues and Analysis, edited by Asa A. Clark IV and others, 214-229. Baltimore: Johns Hopkins University Press, 1984. Deplores the practice of changing defense expenditures without considering the policy implications. Personnel issues may be slighted, for example, because manning costs are somewhat more flexible than weapons systems in terms of expenditures.

1571. Cohen, Eliot A. "When Policy Outstrips Power--American Strategy and Statecraft." 75 Public Interest (Spring 1984):3-19. Discusses critiques that emphasize diplomacy and deemphasize military power in the conduct of American foreign relations. Cohen echoes Kissinger's observations about the lack of American military and strategic planning.

1572. Denoon, David B.H. "The Context." In Constraints on Strategy: The Economics of Western Security, edited by David B.H. Denoon, 1-26. Washington, D.C.: Pergamon-Brassey's International Defense Publishers, Inc., 1986. Reviews briefly the new strategic environment created by increasing Soviet strength, and notes the analyses made of the situation by military specialists. Much of the chapter examines the American alliance system and the economic problems underlying it.

1573. Dilworth, Robert L.   "An Emerging Triad of Power."
Military Review 61 (March 1981):62-65.   Analyzes the
increasing complexity of world politics, which makes the
theory of "bipolarity" and the associated American
concentration on communist enemies obsolete.   Friendly
relations between the United States, China, and Japan may
offset the Soviets' expanding influence in many Third World
countries.

1574. Downing, Wayne A.   "US Army Operations Doctrine."
Military Review 61 (January 1981):64-73.   Severely critical
of contemporary army doctrine regarding conflict in Europe.
Downing discusses the greatly strengthened position of the
Soviets which makes American planning unrealistic.   He
would put the emphasis on maneuver warfare, which would
capitalize on American capabilities.

1575. Fallows, James. "Public Perception, Political Action
and Public Policy." In The Defense Reform Debate: Issues
and Analysis, edited by Asa A. Clark IV and others, 334-
345.   Baltimore: Johns Hopkins University Press, 1984.
Criticizes damaging variations in defense expenditures. To
remedy these up and down movements in support, Fallows
advocates involving the public in discussions of defense
issues to a much greater degree than now occurs.

1576. Gray, Colin S.   "International Order and American
Power." Air University Review 35 (September-October 1984):
26-34.   Presents the Soviet Union as an aggressive, but
cautious imperialist nation that is fundamentally in-
tolerant of non-Communist elements.   Gray asserts that
American military power must support and be adequate to
American political commitments abroad.

1577. Haseman, John B.   "The United States, Interdependence
and National Security." Military Review 61 (April 1981):9-
15.   Discusses the more complex challenge to American
strategists in the 1980's as a variety of threats emerge.
Haseman asserts that the United States must be ready for
conflict in the Third World, including maintenance of an
adequate rapid deployment force.

1578. Hulett, Louisa S.   "Containment Revisited: U.S.
Soviet Relations in the 1980s." Parameters 14 (Autumn
1984):51-63.   Compares Reagan's stance toward the USSR with
that of Harry Truman.   Hulett states that American
assertiveness will persuade the Soviets to follow a more
conciliatory course.

1579. Kiernan, Bernard P.   "The Myth of Peace Through
Strength." Virginia Quarterly Review 57 (Spring 1981):193-
209.   Argues that Reagan's effort to strengthen American
security will be counterproductive.   Kiernan asserts that
there is a fundamental contradiction between superpower
competition and superpower assertions that they view

stability in world affairs as a desirable goal.

1580. Kolodziej, Edward A. "Implications of Security Patterns Among Developing States." Air University Review 33 (September-October 1982):2-22. Notes the increasing number of smaller, developing nations with significant military strength and the increasing conflicts within the Third World. Kolodziej argues against over emphasizing East-West and North-South divisions; the world is more complex than that.

1581. Kross, Walter. "High/Low Technology, Tactical Air Forces, and National Strategies." In Technology, Strategy and National Security, edited by Franklin D. Margiotta and Ralph Sanders, 43-76. Washington, D.C.: National Defense University Press, 1985. SOD D5.402:T22. Discusses efforts of certain "Military Reformers" to persuade the military establishment to become less dependent upon highly complex weapons systems. Kross discusses the relationships between their approach and tactical air warfare.

1582. Luttwak, Edward N. "On the Need to Reform American Strategy." In Planning U.S. Strategy, edited by Philip S. Kronenberg, 13-29. Washington, D.C. : National Defense University Press, 1981. SOD D5.402:Se2/3/980-81. Asserts that American planners have not linked strategy with military policy. Luttwak is particularly critical of systems analysis, which diverts attention from policy issues to budgeting methods.

1583. Nacht, Michael. "Toward an American Conception of Regional Security." Daedalus 110 (Winter 1981):1-22. Briefly discusses global regions and the varying American interest in them. Nacht favors a naval strategy, selective support for some regional powers, and in some situations, American military action that would "prempt" the Soviets.

1584. Ravenal, Earl C. "A Strategy of Restraint for the United States." In Alternative Military Strategies for the Future, edited by Keith A. Dunn and William O. Staudenmaier, 177-207. Boulder, Colorado: Westview Press, 1985. Stresses the importance of the American political system for determining American strategy and analyzes Reagan's choices in terms of defense spending. Ravenal asserts that missions and resulting force structure determine defense costs; he outlines an alternative strategy that could reduce military expenditures considerably.

1585. Wildrick, Craig D. "Bernard Brodie: Pioneer of the Strategy of Deterrence." Military Review 63 (October 1983):39-45. Reviews Brodie's writing and assesses his influence. Wildrick argues that Brodie's theorizing is highly relevant today.

Nuclear Strategy

Official Policy Statements

1586.   Reagan, Ronald.   "Remarks Endorsing the Recommendations in the Report of the President's Commission on
Strategic Forces. April 19, 1983." In Public Papers of the
Presidents of the United States: Ronald Reagan 1983, I,
555-557. Washington, D.C.: Government Printing Office,
1984. Summarizes the recommendations of the Commission,
also known as the Scowcroft Commission, after its Chairman,
Brent Scowcroft. Reagan stresses again and again that only
the prospect of the United States arming brings the Soviets
to the negotiating table for arms control talks.

1587. Reagan, Ronald.   "Statement on the Final Report of
the President's Commission on Strategic Forces.   April 9,
1984." In Public Papers of the Presidents of the United
States: Ronald Reagan 1984, I, 495-496. Washington, D.C.:
Government Printing Office, 1986. Stresses the consensus
on the proposals of the Commission (also known as the
Scowcroft Commission), which had presented a report in 1983
recommending modernization of the strategic force.   The
final report deals with arms control. It emphasizes the
avoidance of false hopes about arms control and the
importance of verification.

Books

1588.   Beres, Louis. Mimicking Sisyphus: America's Countervailing Nuclear Strategy.   Lexington, Massachusetts:
Lexington Books, 1983. 142p. Important statement of the
thesis that a more flexible approach to nuclear warfare may
move the world closer to total nuclear war. Other aspects
of United States doctrine are also examined. This is, in
effect, a defense of the mutual assured destruction
strategy.

1589. Cimbala, Stephen J. Nuclear War and Nuclear Strategy:
Unfinished Business.   Westport, Connecticut: Greenwood
Press, 1987. 276p. Proposes a strategy to induce the
Soviets to cooperate with the Western allies to reduce
armaments.   This would involve movement away from
deterrence along the line of mutual assured destruction.

1590. Cohen, S.T. The Truth about the Neutron Bomb: The
Inventor of the Bomb Speaks Out. New York:W. Morrow, 1983.
226p. Vehement defense of the neutron bomb, and criticism
of a great number of public figures for their opposition to
it.

1591. Garvey, Gerald.   Strategy and the Defense Dilemma:
Nuclear Policies and Alliance Politics. Lexington,
Massachusetts: Lexington Books, 1984. 136p. Proposes many
fundamental changes in American nuclear strategy. Garvey

recommends developing a "first use" policy for the United States.

1592. Hart, Gary with William S. Lind. America Can Win: The Case for Military Reform. Bethesda, Maryland: Adler & Adler, 1986. 301p. Begins with a discussion of the military reform movement. Parts One and Two discuss current problems in the defense establishment, and Part Three proposes various changes.

1593. Jones, Rodney W., editor. Small Nuclear Forces and U.S. Security Policy: Threats and Potential Conflicts in the Middle East and South Asia. Lexington, Massachusetts: Lexington Books, 1984. 304p. Examines the impact of the emergence of regional nuclear powers such as Pakistan. Chapters by Stephen M. Meyer and Anthony H. Cordesman deal directly with American policy toward potential nuclear powers.

1594. Lifton, Robert Jay and Richard Falk. Indefensible Weapons: the Political and Military Case Against Nuclearism. New York: Basic Books, 1982. 301p. Vigorous criticisms of American military nuclear policies. The authors compare Soviet and American positions in the arms race. Much of the emphasis is on psychological damage done by the fear of nuclear warfare.

1595. McNamara, Robert S. Blundering Into Disaster: Surviving the First Century of the Nuclear Age. New York: Pantheon Books, 1986. 212p. Tightly argued plea for greater efforts at detente and arms control. Running through the book is criticism of the foreign and military policies of the Reagan administration.

1596. Martel, William C. and Paul L. Savage. Strategic Nuclear War: What the Superpowers Target and Why. New York: Greenwood Press, Inc., 1986. 249p. Detailed study of Soviet and American nuclear strategies, including the counterforce doctrines of the two nations. The authors provide detailed scenarios for possible nuclear conflicts.

1597. Seiler, George J. Strategic Nuclear Force Requirements and Issues. Maxwell Air Force Base, Alabama: Air University Press, 1983. (Research Report No. Au-ARI-82-1, Revised Edition). 5 volumes in 1.SOD D.301.26/6:N88. Sophisticated examination of American nuclear forces and of issues related to modernization. The first section discusses a means for measuring relative American and Soviet strength.

1598. Smoke, Richard. National Security and the Nuclear Dilemma: An Introduction to the American Experience. Reading, Massachusetts: Addison-Wesley Publishing Company, 1984. 288p. Reviews the development of American nuclear weapons strategy and American efforts to achieve arms control or disarmament. This is a very useful, nontechnical introduction. Smoke feels there is no prospect for an end to the nuclear arms race, especially after the introduction of the cruise missile. Includes an essay, "National Security as a Field of Study."

1599. Snow, Donald. <u>Nuclear Strategy in a Dynamic World;</u> <u>American Policy in the 1980s</u>. University: University of Alabama Press, 1981. 284p. Examines both Soviet and American doctrines and, despite the title, provides an historical survey of developments from the Eisenhower administrations to the late 1970's. Snow includes a chapter on arms control.

Essays and Periodical Articles

1600. Adelman, Jonathan P. "American Strategic Nuclear Modernization and the Soviet Succession Crisis." <u>Air</u> <u>University Review</u> 35 (November-December 1983):15-29. Examines the Soviet achievement of nuclear parity with the United States, a factor which gave the Soviets considerable leverage in world politics during the 1970's. Adelman analyzes Soviet views of the Reagan defense buildup and speculates about its effects on succession in the USSR.

1601. Beres, Louis Rene. "Tilting Toward Thanatos: America's 'Countervailing' Nuclear Strategy." <u>World</u> <u>Politics</u> 34 (October 1981):25-46. Favors the development of varied responses to enemy nuclear threats. The present plan calls for a counterforce capability over and above that needed for mutual assured destruction.

1602. Betts, Richard K. "Strategic Equivalence: What Is It How Do We Get It?" <u>Air University Review</u> 33 (November-December 1981):20-28. Emphasizes the need to clarify the concept of "strategic equivalence," which seems to be the most feasible goal for the United States in the 1980's. Betts reviews its changing meaning through the 1970's.

1603. Cimbala, Stephen, J. "The Reagan Strategic Offensive Modernization Program." In <u>The Reagan Defense Program: An</u> <u>Interim Assessment</u>, edited by Stephen J. Cimbala, 187-202. Wilmington, Delaware: Scholarly Resources, Inc., 1986. Describes the nature of strategic modernization and its relationship to the Strategic Defense Initiative. Cimbala also discusses the impact of British and French strategic modernization on arms control negotiations.

1604. Douglass, Joseph D., Jr. "Strategic Planning and Nuclear Insecurity." <u>Orbis</u> 27 (Fall 1983):667-694. Compares Soviet and American nuclear strategy. Douglass argues that the United States needs to revise its strategy significantly in order to counter the offensive stance and detailed planning of the Soviets.

1605. Douglass, Joseph D., Jr. "What Happens If Deterrence Fails?" Air University Review 34 (November-December 1982):2-17. Discusses the development of selective targeting during the 1970's. Douglass doubts whether the Soviets will accept such a strategy and may indeed be encouraged to make a mass attack. He compares American and Soviet nuclear strategies.

1606. Fritz, Nicholas H. "Clausewitz and U.S. Nuclear Weapons Policy." Air University Review 34 (November-December 1982):18-28. Presents an outline of Clausewitz's On War and analyzes its relation to nuclear strategy. The final section puts Fritz into Clausewitz's role by discussing ways to make American policy conform to the principles of On War.

1607. Iklé, Fred Charles. "Nuclear Strategy: Can There be a Happy Ending?" Foreign Affairs 63 (Spring 1985):810-826. Explains that it is highly improbable that a stable equilibrium of vulnerability between the United States and the Soviet Union can be achieved. Therefore, the United States must seek technological changes to make defense systems more effective, thereby leading to a "safer nuclear strategy."

1608. Keegan, John. "The Human Face of Deterrence." International Security 6 (Summer 1981):136-151. Presents an analysis of the ability of military personnel to continue their missions in the aftermath of nuclear exchanges. Keegan also discusses defusing some contemporary crises in the new Cold War.

1609. Kugler, Jacek. "Terror Without Deterrence: Reassessing the Role of Nuclear Weapons." Journal of Conflict Resolution 28 (September 1984):470-506. Argues that deterrence theory is not really a good guide to the way nations behave in crises. Kugler asserts that deterrence really contributed to stabilizing relations between the superpowers.

1610. McNamara, Robert S. "The Military Role of Nuclear Weapons: Perceptions and Misperceptions." Foreign Affairs 62 (Fall 1983):59-80. Advocates a much greater commitment to conventional forces in Europe and less reliance on nuclear weapons. McNamara discounts the possibility of limited nuclear war.

1611. Nacht, Michael. "The Future Unlike the Past: Nuclear Proliferation and American Security Policy." International Organization 35 (Winter 1981):193-212. Proliferation does not seem to be changing either relations between the United States and the new nuclear powers or the defense posture of the United States.

1612. Payne, Keith B. "Strategic Defense and Stability."

258 Reagan: Reassertion and Rearmament

Orbis 28 (Summer 1984):215-227. Recommends concentrating American defense strategy on defending the population of the United States and nuclear strike forces. Payne examines the problems associated with such a change in course.

1613. Potter, William C. "Nuclear Proliferation: U.S.-Soviet Cooperation." Washington Quarterly 8 (Winter 1985):141-154. Reviews the continuing and rather extensive cooperation between the superpowers. This collaboration has survived various crises and superpower tensions in other spheres.

1614. Ravenal, Earl C. "No First Use: A View from the United States." Parameters 13 (June 1983):81-87. Argues that the promise of a "no first use" of nuclear weapons against Soviet forces invading Europe promotes the possibility of war.

1615. Smernoff, Barry J. "Images of the Nuclear Future." Air University Review 34 (May-June 1983):2-10. Two apparent paths into the nuclear future are extensive disarmament or incremental additions to the nuclear arsenals of the world. Smernoff advocates moving away from both mutual assured destruction and impractical disarmament schemes to some form of defensive systems for both superpowers.

1616. Snow, Donald M. "Levels of Strategy and American Strategic Nuclear Policy." Air University Review 35 (November-December 1983):63-73. Examines the debate in the United States over countering the Soviet military challenge. Snow distinguishes three levels of nuclear strategy: public pronouncements, technological development, and the use of weapons.

1617. Thomas, Raymond E. "Maritime Theater Nuclear Warfare: Matching Strategy and Capability." In Essays on Strategy: Selections from the 1984 Joint Chiefs of Staff Essay Competition, 39-51. Washington, D.C.:National Defense University Press, 1985. SOD D5.402:St 8/7. Reviews Soviet naval strategy and discusses the difficult task facing the United States Navy, which must formulate a nuclear strategy. Thomas proposes ways of increasing American maritime nuclear strength; the United States already has a conventional naval superiority over the Soviet Union.

1618. Thornton, Richard C. and William H. Lewis. "Arms Control and Heavy Missiles." Naval War College Review 37 (January-February 1984):93-107. Reviews Soviet and American nuclear policy after 1969. The authors argue that the Soviets are trying to increase their power to pursue destructive political goals.

1619. Tucker, Robert W. "The Nuclear Debate." Foreign Affairs 63 (Fall 1984):1-32. Deals with what Tucker sees as the clouding of the deterrence concept. Tucker indicates the steps that must be taken to allow the United States to utilize deterrence effectively.

Nonproliferation

Official Policy Statements

1620. Reagan, Ronald. "Statement on United States Nuclear Nonproliferation Policy. July 16, 1981." In Public Papers of the Presidents of the United States: Ronald Reagan 1981, 630-631. Washington, D.C.: Government Printing Office, 1982. Reaffirms the American commitment to nonproliferation. Reagan sets the policies the United States will follow in pursuit of nonproliferation. The United States is equally concerned with developing peaceful uses of nuclear energy and will cooperate fully with other nations on appropriate projects.

1621. Reagan, Ronald. "Statement on the 15th Anniversary of the Signing of the Treaty on the Non-Proliferation of Nuclear Weapons. July 1, 1983." In Public Papers of the Presidents of the United States: Ronald Reagan 1983, I, 960-961. Washington, D.C.: Government Printing Office, 1984. Outlines the significance of the treaty and hails the fact that one hundred and nineteen nations have adhered to it. Reagan refers to current American policy established in 1981 to promote "nuclear assistance," with safeguards to ensure that nuclear materials are used only for nonmilitary purposes.

Books

1622. Brito, Dagobert L. and others, editors. Strategies for Managing Nuclear Proliferation: Economic and Political Issues. Lexington, Massachusetts: Lexington Books, 1983. 311p. These essays argue that proliferation needs to be managed, not prevented. They present economic and political analyses rather than technological assessments of proliferation and its course.

1623. Snyder, Jed C. and Samuel F. Wells, Jr., editors. Limiting Nuclear Proliferation. Cambridge, Massachusetts: Ballinger Publishing Company, 1985. 363p. Contributors include George H. Quester, Richard P. Cronin, and Lawrence Scheinman. Essays discuss all aspects of the nonproliferation issue and the system for maintaining the nonproliferation stance.

Periodical Articles

1624. Kennedy, Richard T. "Nonproliferation: Where We Are and Where We're Going." Department of State Bulletin 83 (December 1983):52-57. Outlines efforts the United States has made to prevent proliferation of nuclear weapons internationally. This is the text of a statement by Richard

T. Kennedy to Senate Committees on September 30, 1983.

1625. Spector, Leonard S. "Proliferation: The Silent Spread." Foreign Policy, no. 58 (1985):53-78. Questions American commitment to enforcing nonproliferation. Spector argues that enforcement by the United States has been highly selective.

Air Strategy

1626. Brown, Michael E. "The Strategic Bomber Debate Today." Orbis 28 (Summer 1984):365-388. Presents a detailed examination of issues surrounding bomber policies. Brown indicates his enthusiasm for the B-1 and B-1A.

1627. Cole, James L. "Air Power in the Western Hemisphere." Air University Review 34 (July-August 1983):2-11. Favors expanding assistance to friendly states in the Americas, especially in the Caribbean area.

1628. Hall, R. Cargill. "The B-58 Bomber: Requiem for a Welterweight." Air University Review 33 (November-December 1981):44-56. Describes the origin and development of the B-58 in considerable detail.

1629. Johnson, Herbert W. "Air Force Fighters: Simple or Complex?" Air University Review 34 (May-June, 1983):24-35. Describes simple and complex fighters and the theories associated with them. Johnson argues that sophisticated aircraft can do more. Future fighters will need improved all-weather and night capabilities.

1630. Krieger, Clifford R. "USAF Doctrine: An Enduring Challenge." Air University Review 35 (September-October 1984):16-25. Analyzes Basic Aerospace Doctrine of the United States Air Force (1984) and World War II air force experience. Krieger emphasizes that doctrines change continuously.

Missiles

Official Policy Statements

1631. Reagan, Ronald. "Statement on Deployment of the MX Missile. November 22, 1982." In Public Papers of the Presidents of the United States: Ronald Reagan 1982, II, 1502-1503. Washington, D.C.: Government Printing Office, 1983. Reviews the deliberations that preceded the decision to deploy MX missiles and states that former presidents Nixon, Ford, and Carter support this move. Reagan asserts that he has no intention of disrupting the Anti-Ballistic Missile Treaty, provided that the USSR complies with it.

1632. Reagan, Ronald "Statement on Senate Action on Production of the MX Missile and Announcing the Formation of a Bipartisan Commission to Study Basing Options. December 17, 1982." In Public Papers of the Presidents of the United States: Ronald Reagan 1982, II, 1617. Washington, D.C.: Government Printing Office, 1983. Praises Congress for its action regarding the MX. Reagan also announces establishment of a commission to study strategic weapons, which later became known as the Scowcroft Commission, after its chair.

1633. Reagan, Ronald. "Remarks at a White House Briefing for Chief Executive Officers of Trade Associations and Corporations on Deployment of the MX Missile. May 16, 1983." In Public Papers of the Presidents of the United States: Ronald Reagan 1983, I, 714-715. Washington, D.C.: Government Printing Office, 1984. Emphasizes the need for bipartisan consensus on MX missile deployment. Reagan refers several times to the Scowcroft Commission recommendations regarding strategic arms and points to the increasing strength of the Soviet missile force.

Periodical Articles

1634. Arkin, William M. "Sleight of Hand with Trident II." Bulletin of the Atomic Scientists 40 (December 1984):5-6. Discusses the potential impact of the deployment of thousands of Trident IIs by the United States Navy. Arkin indicates that this would mark a major change in the configuration of American nuclear forces.

1635. Cockburn, Andrew and Alexander Cockburn. "The Myth of Missile Accuracy." Parameters 11 (June 1981):83-89. Expresses concern over the general thesis that missiles are certain to hit their targets. Missiles' unreliability tends to undermine the theory that a nuclear exchange limited to attacks on military objectives would be possible. Article reprinted from the New York Review of Books, 1980.

1636. Korb, Lawrence J. "The Case for the MX." Air University Review 31 (July-August 1980):2-10. Discusses the development of the MX concept and the progress of the MX program. Korb defends the cost effectiveness of MX and examines the possible effects of Soviet countermeasures.

1637. Lodal, Jan M. "Deterrence and Nuclear Strategy." Daedalus 109 (Fall 1980):155-175. Argues that the American ability to pursue deterrence is being undermined by increased Soviet armaments. Lodal strongly advocates more emphasis being given to the ABM (anti-ballistic missile) program.

1638. Werrell, Kenneth P. "The Cruise Missile: Precursors and Problems." Air University Review 32 (January-February 1981):36-50. Describes the development of the cruise missile system, including its forerunners which date back to the world wars.

Military Airlift

1639. Boston, Ronald G. "Doctrine by Default: The Historical Origins of Tactical Airlift." Air University Review 34 (May-June 1983):64-75. Examines the Military Airlift Command and its antecedents. Several pages deal with Vietnam.

1640. Gropman, Alan L. "The Compelling Requirement for Combat Airlift." Air University Review 33 (July-August 1982):2-15. Renewed American assertiveness after Reagan's election makes improved airlift a necessity. Gropman discusses a large number of post-World War II instances when airlift was used very effectively to further American goals.

1641. Liggett, William R. "Long-Range Combat Aircraft and Rapid Deployment Forces." Air University Review 33 (July-August 1982):72-81. Discusses the nature of rapid deployment force operations and the contribution of long-range combat aircraft such as the B-52. Liggett sees the Rapid Deployment Force as having "deterrence," "force projection," and "war-fighting" capabilities.

Space Operations

Books

1642. Durch, William J., editor. National Interests and the Military Use of Space. Cambridge, Massachusetts: Ballinger Publishing Company, 1984. 286p. Essays present much information and varying points of view on the military use of space.

1643. Karas, Thomas H. The New High Ground; Systems and Weapons of Space Age War. New York: Simon & Schuster, 1983. 224p. Examines the potential for space warfare and space weapons development. Karas describes the growing commitment to space weaponry, a trend he regards with disquiet.

1644. Ra'anan, Uri and Robert L. Pfaltzgraff, Jr., editors. International Security Dimensions of Space. Hamden, Connecticut: Archon Books, 1984. 324p. Essays examine legal, political, and military aspects of space and the Soviet and American space efforts. The appendices help make this a reference book for the subject.

Essays and Periodical Articles

1645. Cady, Steven E. "Beam Weapons in Space." Air University Review 33 (May-June 1982):33-39. Recommends an extensive beam weapon program to counter Soviet progress in this field. Cady identifies a number of factors producing too much confidence in American strategic nuclear weapons.

1646. Lorenzini, Dino A. "Space Power Doctrine." Air University Review 33 (July-August 1982):16-21. Argues for developing space theory separate from air power doctrine. Lorenzini discusses what he sees as bureaucratic obstacles to more effective military utilization of space by the United States.

1647. Smernoff, Barry, "A Bold Two-Track Strategy for Space: Entering the Second Quarter-Century." In Technology, Strategy and National Security, edited by Frank Margiotta and Ralph Sanders, 139-156. Washington, D.C.:National Defense University Press, 1985. SOD D5.402:T22. Reviews five possible space strategies and asserts that space must be made a part of general military and disarmament policy. Smernoff argues that the United States must develop national objectives for space.

1648. Smernoff, Barry J. "The Strategic Value of Space-Based Laser Weapons." Air University Review 33 (March-April 1982):2-17. Discusses air force experiments with laser weapons and their possible value. Initial systems will have quite limited capability, but later generation weapons will be powerful defenses against ICBMs.

1649. Stoehrmann, Kenneth C. "Aerospace Strategy in the Post Nuclear Age." Air University Review 34 (November-December 1982):76-81. Argues that the potential movement of warfare into outer space is as revolutionary as the development of military aviation and the coming of nuclear arms. Stoehrmann outlines some components of an aerospace strategy.

Strategic Defense Initiative

Official Policy Statements

1650. Reagan, Ronald. "Address to the Nation on Defense and National Security. March 23, 1983." In Public Papers of the Presidents of the United States: Ronald Reagan 1983, I, 437-443. Washington, D.C.: Government Printing Office, 1984. Defends the Reagan administration's current defense budget and sharply attacks efforts to reduce defense spending by some specific amount of money. Reagan applauds the "strategy of deterrence." After reviewing the massive Soviet military buildup and his administration's response, he briefly describes a system to "intercept and destroy strategic ballistic missiles" fired by the Soviets. This was the Strategic Defense Initiative, or Star Wars Plan.

Bibliographies

1651. Lawrence, Robert M. and Sallay M. Reynolds. SDI: Bibliography and Research Guide. Boulder, Colorado: West view Press, 1986. 125p. Convenient guide to the debate, which includes bibliographic sections on both sides, as well as a more technically oriented segment. These bibliographies are accompanied by essays which help to put into perspective the publications, including journal articles, which are listed and annotated.

1652. Petitmermet, Jane and Ann Cook. Strategic Defense Initiative: A Selected Bibliography. Washington, D.C.: National Defense University Library, 1986. 99p. Very extensive, unannotated listing of government documents, books, periodical and newspaper articles, and research reports. The bibliography covers all aspects of SDI, including technical and economic facets and the relation of this defense effort to arms control.

Books

1653. Bova, Ben. Assured Survival: Putting the Star Wars Defense in Perspective. Boston: Houghton Mifflin, 1984. 343p. Surveys the history of nuclear weapons development and analyzes many of the problems associated with the Strategic Defense Initiative. Bova also examines the circumstances under which nuclear might occur.

1654. Brauch, Hans Guenter, ed. Star Wars and European Defence: Implications: Perceptions and Assessments. New York: St. Martin's Press, 1987. 599p. Essays examine the Strategic Defense Initiative and responses to it within NATO and the Warsaw Treaty Organization. Among the topics discussed are possible conflicts between SDI and other defense measures and between SDI and the Anti-Ballistic Missile Treaty of 1972. There is a lengthy bibliography.

1655. Dallmeyer, Dorinda, editor, in association with Daniel S. Papp. The Strategic Defense Initiative: New Perspectives on Deterrence. Boulder, Colorado: Westview Press, 1986. 112p. Essays explore all aspects of SDI, presenting a number of points of view on the major issues associated with it.   Several chapters examine the relationship between SDI and American obligations under the ABM Treaty. Other sections deal with political/diplomatic and technical/scientific facets.

1656. Drell, Sidney D., and others. The Reagan Strategic Defense Initiative: A Technical, Political, and Arms Control Assessment. Cambridge, Massachusetts: Ballinger Publishing Company, 1985. 168p. Detailed examination of the Strategic Defense Initiative in the perspective of the strategic balance between the superpowers.

1657. Garthoff, Raymond L. Policy versus the Law: The Reinterpretation of the ABM Treaty. Washington, D.C.: Brookings Institution, 1987. 117p. Assails American arguments that the Strategic Defense Initiative is not

prohibited by the Anti-Ballistic Missile Treaty of 1972.
Garthoff participated in the making of the ABM treaty.

1658. Guerrier, Steven W. and Wayne C. Thompson, editors.
Perspectives on Strategic Defense. Boulder, Colorado:
Westview Press, 1987. 358p. Extensive collection of essays
covers virtually all facets of the controversial Strategic
Defense Initiative. Among the many topics examined are the
impact of SDI on relations between the United States and
Soviet Union and the views of the NATO allies concerning
SDI.

1659. Pressler, Larry. Star Wars: The Strategic Defense
Initiative Debates in Congress. New York: Praeger
Publishers, 1986. 179p. Detailed examination of the
Strategic Defense Initiative program and its pros and cons.
In addition to studying the debate, Pressler provides a
great deal of data about the technology associated with
SDI. The book also includes some consideration of treaties
which limit the militarization of space.

1660. Vlahos, Michael. Strategic Defense and the American
Ethos: Can the Nuclear World be Changed? Boulder, Colorado:
Westview Press, 1986. 119p. Praises the Strategic Defense
Initiative as a realistic response to the changing balance
of power and to new trends in American public opinion about
defense and the continued stockpiling of nuclear weapons.

1661. Waldman, Harry. The Dictionary of SDI. Wilmington,
Delaware: Scholarly Resources, Inc., 1988. 182p. Designed
primarily for the layman, this reference source includes a
large number of dictionary entries and illustrations. The
dictionary also reprints the 1972 ABM Treaty and President
Reagan's address on the Strategic Defense Initiative, March
23, 1983 [entry 1650].

1662. Waller, Douglas C. and others. The Strategic Defense
Initiative, Progress and Challenges: A Guide to Issues and
References. Claremont, California: Regina Books, 1987.
172p. Useful introduction to the Strategic Defense
Initiative debate. It provides guidance on discussing the
issue without trying to present definitive answers.

1663. Wells, Samuel F., Jr. and Robert S. Litwak, editors.
Strategic Defenses and Soviet-American Relations. Cambridge
Massachusetts: Ballinger Publishing Co., 1987. 216p.
Balanced collection of essays which is generally supportive
of the Strategic Defense Initiative. The book provides for
considering SDI in the perspective of earlier developments
in missile attack and defense.

Essays and Periodical Articles

1664. Black, Edwin F. "The Unsellable Dream?" United States
Naval Institute Proceedings 110 (September 1984):38-42.

Asserts that public opinion is generally supportive of antiballistic missile defenses. Black suggests that President Reagan might find an advisory council on the Strategic Defense Initiative (SDI) useful.

1665. Bryden, James F. "The Emerging BMD Debate: Deja Vu or Not?" Air University Review 36 (November-December 1984):42-51. Compares the debate over earlier plans for ballistic missile defense, especially Safeguard, with current discussions of the Strategic Defense Initiative (SDI). Bryden notes major factors to consider in evaluating any ballistic missile defense system.

1666. Gray, Colin S. "Deterrence, Arms Control, and the Defense Transition." Orbis 28 (Summer 1984):227-240. Warns that the Strategic Defense Initiative must be implemented fairly quickly, if the commitment is made, to avoid various possible Soviet moves. Gray also discusses SDI in relation to disarmament and other topics.

1667. Jones, Rodney W. and Steven A. Hildreth. "Star Wars: Down to Earth, or Gleam in the Sky?" Washington Quarterly 7 (Fall 1984):104-111. Early survey of the Strategic Defense Initiative controversy. Examines both the Reagan administration's commitment and the comments of the scientific community on planning for this ambitious new approach to defend the United States against nuclear attack.

1668. Lawyer, John E. "Beyond Deterrence: The Strategic Defense Option." Air University Review 36 (November-December 1984):32-41. Emphasizes the major change in strategy implied by the Strategic Defense Initiative. Lawyer projects the possible future debates and negotiations over SDI. He compares SDI with British air defense efforts in the 1930's based on radar.

1669. Snow, Donald M. "Ballistic Missile Defense: The Strategic Defense Initiative." In The Reagan Defense Program: An Interim Assessment, edited by Stephen J. Cimbala, 145-159. Wilmington, Delaware: Scholarly Resources, Inc., 1986. Examines the debate over Ballistic Missile Defense (BMD) during the 1960's and 1970's and traces the development of the Reagan administration's position on the issue. Snow reviews the arguments for and against the Strategic Defense Initiative and compares the SDI and ABM debates.

Ground Strategy

General

Books

1670. Kupperman, Robert H. and William J. Taylor, Jr.,

editors. Strategic Requirements for the Army to the Year
2000. Lexington, Massachusetts: Lexington Books, 1984.
539p. The essays in this collection assert that the United
States will be faced increasingly by low-intensity
conflicts and proposes changes in the army to meet these
challenges.

1671. Perkins, Stuart L. Global Demands, Limited Forces: US
Army Deployment. Washington, D.C.: National Defense
University Press, 1984. 123p. SOD D5.402:G51. The heart of
the study is a section describing possible strategic
options for the United States. A lengthy section deals with
airlift/sealift capabilities and the contributions of
American allies.

Essays and Periodical Articles

1672. Crawford, Dorn. "The Operational Level of
Deterrence." Military Review 67 (January 1987): 14-22.
Analyzes the nature of deterrence in the face of possible
military threats to the United States. Crawford focuses on
deterrence through conventional forces.

1673. Holder, L.D. "Operational Art in the US Army: New
Vigor." In Essays on Strategy III: Selections from the 1985
Joint Chiefs of Staff Essay Competition, 111-133.
Washington, D.C.: National Defense University Press, 1986.
SOD D5.402:St/8/5/985. Discusses the "operational art" as
a connection between strategy and tactics for a given
theater of war. Holder states that operations have not been
studied in the United States since before World War II. The
author expresses concern about the ability of the army to
move quickly and to keep itself adequately supplied.

1674. Lind, William S. "The Case for Maneuver Doctrine." In
The Defense Reform Debate: Issues and Analysis, edited by
Asa A. Clark IV and others, 88-100. Baltimore: Johns
Hopkins University Press, 1984. Reviews the history of
maneuver warfare such as blitzkrieg. Lind sees maneuver war
as a way of thinking that the army needs to adopt.

1675. Lind, William S. "Conventional Forces: Framing the
Issues." In Alternative Military Strategies for the Future,
edited by Keith A. Dunn and William O. Staudenmaier, 133-
146. Boulder, Colorado: Westview Press, 1985. Summarizes
the most basic criticism made by the military reformers,
emphasizing the need for competent combat leaders and
deflating claims often made for advanced military
technology.

1676. Mayer, John D., Jr. "Heavy versus Light Forces: A
Question of Balance." In The Defense Reform Debate: Issues
and Analysis, edited by Asa A. Clark IV and others, 166-
176. Baltimore: Johns Hopkins University Press, 1984.
Warns that the army has gone too far in putting resources

into light divisions for possible use outside Europe. Some
light divisions need to be converted to heavy divisions to
match Soviet strength.

1677. Mitchell, Rodney B. "Enhancing Unit Cohesion."
Military Review 61 (May 1981):30-43. Emphasizes the need
for developing a high degree of unit cohesion in
preparation for possible combat operations. Mitchell
proposes a plan for reorganizing combat forces and
reworking tours of duty to minimize overseas service and
maximize cohesion.

1678. Perry, William J. "Defense Reform and the Quantity-
Quality Quandary." In The Defense Reform Debate: Issues and
Analysis, edited by Asa A. Clark IV and others, 182-192.
Baltimore: Johns Hopkins University Press, 1984. Argues
that American conventional forces must match Soviet
capabilities. Very specific uses of technology, among other
measures, are needed to improve the American posture. Perry
believes stating the problem as one of quantity versus
quality is profoundly misleading.

AirLand Battle

1679. Aubin, Stephen P. and Robert E. Kells, Jr. "Airland
Battle Doctrine: Soviet Strategy Revisited." Military
Review 65 (October 1985):42-53. Scores AirLand Battle for
trailing Soviet military thought by decades. This is a
detailed comparison of American and Soviet strategies.

1680. Hanne, William G. "Doctrine, Not Dogma." Military
Review 63 (June 1983):11-25. Examines the development of
the "extended battlefield" concept and its articulation in
AirLand Battle. Hanne reviews American commentaries on
AirLand Battle and current Soviet strategy; his conclusion
is that American planners should not focus exclusively on
attacking second-line Soviet forces.

1681. Machos, James A. "Air-Land Battle or AirLand Battle?"
Military Review 63 (July 1983):33-40. Describes efforts the
air force must make in order to adapt to the army's AirLand
Battle doctrine. Machos discusses both tactical air and
interdiction missions and the role of ground and air
components in these spheres. He focuses primarily on
interservice cooperation and coordination.

1682. Machos James A. "TACair Support for Airland Battle."
Air University Review 35 (May-June 1984):16-24. Reminds
readers that the air force has not committed itself
completely to the army's AirLand Battle concept. Machos
offers a "stratified responsibilities" plan for
distinguishing and meshing army and air force functions.

1683. Powell, Jon S. "AirLand Battle: The Wrong Doctrine
for the Wrong Reason." Air University Review 36 (May-June

1985): 15-22. Criticizes assumptions about Soviet
deployment and war-fighting that underlie the AirLand
Battle concept. Powell also notes air force deficiencies
that limit its ability to fight an AirLand Battle.

1684. Richey, Stephen W. "The Philosophical Basis of the
AirLand Battle." Military Review 63 (May 1983):48-53. Seeks
the origins of AirLand Battle doctrine in German military
doctrine from late in World War I through World War II.
Richey describes, generally, German military operations and
makes recommendations on how American military leaders can
use German principles.

1685. Romjue, John L. "The Evolution of the AirLand Battle
Concept." Air University Review 35 (May-June 1984):4-15.
AirLand Battle had its origins in army efforts to upgrade
its technology after the Vietnam war. Romjue emphasizes the
theory of the "extended battlefield" to embrace attacks on
reserves approaching the combat zone.

Special Operations

Books

1686. Dean, David J. The Air Force Role in Low-Intensity
Conflict. Maxwell Air Force Base, Alabama: Air University
Press, 1986. 127p. SOD D301.26/6:C76/2. About half the book
recounts American assistance to Morocco in its recent
counterinsurgency campaigns. Several chapters deal with the
air force's experience in counterinsurgency, although the
Vietnam phase is not discussed in any detail.

1687. Maurer, John H. and Richard H. Porth, editors.
Military Intervention in the Third World: Threats,
Constraints, and Options. New York: Praeger Publishers,
1984. 239p. Deals with both Soviet and American
intervention in a collection of highly sophisticated
essays. Many authors warn of the increasing likelihood of
American forces encountering Soviet troops in Third World
crises. This is a valuable collection of essays; they are
not listed and annotated individually in this bibliography
because of their relatively specialized nature.

1688. Sarkesian, Sam C. The New Battlefield: The United
States and Unconventional Conflicts. Westport, Connecticut:
Greenwood Press, 1986. 349p. Examines guerrilla, terrorist,
and unconventional strategies and their impact on American
goals. Sarkesian analyzes American efforts to meet these
challenges and strongly recommends still greater emphasis
on improving the American posture for unconventional
warfare.

1689. Woodward, Bob. Veil: The Secret Wars of the CIA,
1981-1987. New York: Simon & Schuster, 1987. 543p.

Controversial, undocumented study of CIA operations during the Reagan years. Woodward argues that the CIA assumed a very large role in American foreign relations under Reagan and CIA Director William Casey.

Essays and Periodical Articles

1690. Baratto, David J. "Special Forces in the 1980s: A Strategic Reorientation." Military Review 63 (March 1981): 2-14. Reviews the history of Special Forces and its predecessors, emphasizing the Vietnam experience. Baratto also summarizes and analyzes current doctrinal works on counterinsurgency and special operations.

1691. Cohen, Eliot A. "Constraints on America's Conduct of Small Wars." International Security 9 (Fall 1984):151-181. Examines the many factors that work against the United States' developing an effective response to small wars in which it becomes involved.

1692. Dean, David J. "The USAF in Low-Intensity Conflict: The Special Air Warfare Center." Air University Review 36 (January-February 1985):45-57. Reviews the Center's activities during the 1960's. Dean asserts that the Center's experience is a valuable precedent for future air force special operations, especially counterinsurgency.

1693. Dubik, James M. "FM 100-5 and Counter-insurgency Warfare." Military Review 63 (November 1983):41-48. Seeks to apply the principles in Field Manual FM 100-5 to counterinsurgency, which is not discussed at length in this manual. Successful counterinsurgency must focus on winning the people from the insurgents. Dubik examines the ways in which this can be accomplished.

1694. Gorman, Paul F. "Military Instruments of Containment." In Containment: Concept and Policy, edited by Terry L. Deibel and John Lewis Gaddis, 217-238. Washington, D.C.: National Defense University Press, 1986. SOD D5.402:C76/2 v. 1. Discusses the military elements of "counterforce" used to deter Soviet expansionism and warns that by no means enough is being done to prepare for low-intensity conflict. Most intelligence efforts, for example, are aimed at the Soviets, not Third World contingencies.

1695. Kriesel, Melvin E. "Psychological Operations: A Strategic View." In Essays on Strategy: Selections from the 1984 Joint Chiefs of Staff Essay Competition, 53-94. Washington, D.C.: National Defense University Press, 1985. SOD D5.402:St8/7. Argues for the full inclusion of psychological elements in American national strategy and suggests organizational steps to be taken for implementing this proposal. Kriesel notes efforts made to improve American capability in psychological warfare during the

Reagan administration and very briefly discusses
psychological operations in Grenada.

1696. Kuster, Thomas J. "Dealing with the Insurgency
Spectre." Military Review 67 (February 1987):20-29.
Discusses the usefulness of insurgency for achieving Soviet
goals and warns that the United States must not allow the
Vietnam experience to deter it from maintaining an
effective counterinsurgency capability.

1697. Linn, Thomas C. "Military Power Short of War." United
States Naval Institute Proceedings 112 (November 1986):73-
77. Warns against underestimating the effectiveness of
guerrilla warfare and terrorism. Linn argues for
coordinated efforts by the United States to combat enemies
in low-intensity conflicts.

1698. Little, Wendell E. "Covert Operations: A Needed
Alternative." Air University Review 33 (September-October
1982):65-70. Reviews Soviet strategy and covert activity,
as well as American covert operations after World War II.
Little argues that the United States should build up its
covert capability.

1699. Livingston, Neil C. "Fighting Terrorism and 'Dirty
Little Wars.'" Air University Review 35 (March-April 1984):
4-16. Discusses the sources of conflict and terrorism that
lend themselves to Soviet manipulation. The United States
is concentrating on preparation for a possible general war
and is ignoring the need to develop low-intensity
capabilities.

1700. Morelli, Donald R. and Michael M. Ferguson. "Low-
Intensity Conflict: An Operational Perspective." Military
Review 64 (November 1984):2-16. Warns that the army will
necessarily be involved in low-intensity conflict, indeed
that it is already so engaged. While some useful steps have
been taken, the army needs to do much more to prepare for
low-intensity conflict.

1701. Rylander, R. Lynn. "The Future of the Marines in
Small Wars." Naval War College Review 40 (Autumn 1987):64-
75. Recommends a vigorous response to Soviet sponsored
low-intensity conflicts, which should include extensive
nonmilitary assistance to nations that are threatened and
aid for guerrillas trying to undermine Soviet supported
regimes. Rylander summarizes marine corps efforts to
maintain readiness for low-intensity conflicts, notably the
development of Marine Amphibious Units.

1702. Sarkesian, Sam C. "Low-Intensity Conflict: Concepts,
Principles and Policy Guidelines." Air University Review 36
(January-February 1985):4-23. Examines current American
thinking on the subject of low-intensity conflict.
Sarkesian warns it involves great challenges because of the

limited ability of the United States to shape events.

1703. Sarkesian, Sam C. "Special Operations Forces in the 1980s." In The Reagan Defense Program: An Interim Assessment, edited by Stephen J. Cimbala, 93-117. Wilmington, Delaware: Scholarly Resources, Inc., 1986. Reviews counterinsurgency developments under Kennedy and the effect of Vietnam on the American commitment to counterinsurgency. For the 1970's and 1980's, Sarkesian focuses on the problems faced by the United States during encounters with insurgency forces in the Third World.

1704. Staudenmaier, William O. and Alan N. Sabrosky. "A Strategy of Counterrevolutionary War." Military Review 65 (February 1985):2-15. Analyzes the nature of counterrevoluntary (counterinsurgency) warfare, emphasizing the political nature of revolutionary war. Indeed, the authors assert that in such contests "the military play an important, but subsidiary role." In the military sphere, sanctuaries are essential for a guerrilla movement to win, at least in most cases.

1705. Wasielewski, Philip G. "Sea Power and Counterinsurgency." United States Naval Institute Proceedings 112 (December 1986):62-66. Focuses on contemporary Southwest Asia. Wasielewski argues for a navy/marine approach to counterinsurgency without the kind of large-scale military intrusion that occurred in Vietnam.

Naval Strategy

1706. Barnett, Roger W. "The Maritime-Continental Debate Isn't Over." United States Naval Institute Proceedings 113 (June 1987):28-34. Summarizes the "continental" and "maritime" theories of American strategy. Barnett warns that both theories have limitations; the U.S.S.R., for example, seems less vulnerable to attack from the sea than the United States.

1707. Brooks, Linton F. "The Nuclear Maritime Strategy." United States Naval Institute Proceedings 113 (April 1987):33-39. Warns that the maritime strategy must not be frozen by tying it to assumptions that may not be realized in a Soviet-American war. Planning for the possibility that nuclear weapons may be used at sea in such a conflict must be a fundamental component of the maritime strategy.

1708. Bunn, George. "Satellites for the Navy: Shielded by Arms Control?" Naval War College Review 38 (September-October 1985):55-69. Notes the importance of communication and other satellites to the navy and suggsts limiting Soviet and American testing of anti-satellite weapons to lower altitudes.

1709. Komer, Robert W. "Maritime Strategy vs. Coalition

Defense." <u>Foreign Affairs</u> 60 (Summer 1982):1124-1144. The alternatives are to seek domination of the seas, yielding military dominance of the Eurasian landmass to the Soviets or to rely on a coalition defense effort for high priority areas such as Western Europe, Northeast Asia, and the Persian Gulf. The Reagan administration is trying to follow both courses, but economic constraints may force a choice. Komer believes the coalition approach is vital because the United States could not survive if the Soviets had control of the economic resources of Eurasia.

1710. Lehman, John. "Utility of Maritime Power: The Restoration of US Naval Strength." <u>Journal of the Royal United Services Institute for Defence Studies</u> 128 (September 1983):13-18. Financial limits prevented the NATO countries from achieving the naval superiority they would prefer. Increased reliance on technology makes it all the more necessary to protect this technology from the Soviets.

1711. Maiorano, Alan. "A Fresh Look at the Sixth Fleet." <u>United States Naval Institute Proceedings</u> 110 (February 1984):52-58. Argues that the United States needs to concentrate more of its naval strength outside the Mediterranean Sea, especially in the Atlantic. Maiorano offers suggestions for effective use of the NATO naval forces that would remain in the Mediterranean.

1712. O'Neil, W.D. "Executing the Maritime Strategy." <u>United States Naval Institute Proceedings</u> 112 (December 1986):39-41. Concludes that the navy is successfully keeping the Soviets on the defensive at sea. O'Neil stresses the role of technology, especially in antisubmarine warfare.

1713. Serig, Howard W., Jr. "Stretching the Fleet into the 1990s." <u>United States Naval Institute Proceedings</u> 110 (May 1984):164-179. Discusses efforts to modernize navy ships to keep the fleet at needed strength levels. A controversial aspect of this program is its emphasis on aircraft carriers and associated naval units.

1714. Williams, John Allen. "The U.S. and Soviet Navies: Missions and Forces." <u>Armed Forces & Society</u> 10 (Summer 1984):507-528. Compares American and Soviet naval strategies. The United States Navy is still stronger and in the event of war would act aggressively against Soviet targets. The Soviets would very likely confine themselves to a defensive role.

Mobilization

1715. Merritt, Hardy L. and Luther F. Carter, editors. <u>Mobilization and the National Defense</u>. Washington, D.C.: National Defense University, 1985. 186p. SOD D5.402:M71/2. These essays discuss all aspects of mobilization, but

emphasize industrial mobilization. One essay examines the
Defense Production Act. Other essays deal with reserve
forces and military retirees as a resource.

1716. Mobilization--What Should Be Done? What Can Be Done?
Proceedings Based on the Fourth Annual Mobilization
Conference. May 16-17, 1985. Washington, D.C.: Government
Printing Office, 1985. 356p. SOD D5.402:M 71/3. Essays and
accompanying discussions reflect the great complexity of
economic mobilization. Among the topics considered are
medical resources, the army reserve, and electrical power
for defense industries.

Intelligence

Official Policy Statements

1717. Reagan, Ronald. "Statement on United States
Intelligence Activities. December 4, 1981." In Public
Papers of the Presidents of the United States: Ronald
Reagan 1981, 1126-1139. Washington, D.C.: Government
Printing Office, 1982. Most of the statement is taken up
by two Executive Orders on intelligence matters. While
asserting a need "to maintain the legal protection of all
American citizens," Reagan stresses the need to take a more
positive view of intelligence and the operations needed to
gather it.

Books

1718. Godson, Roy, editor. Intelligence Requirements for
the 1980's: Intelligence and Policy. Lexington,
Massachusetts: Lexington Books, 1985. 208p. Explores the
problems of the American intelligence establishment.
Contributors include both executive and legislative branch
personnel and, very importantly, figures from the
intelligence community. This is a significant source for
understanding the intelligence function and the
controversies that surround it in the United States.

Essays and Periodical Articles

1719. Bobrow, Davis B. "Security Futures: INTELLIGENCE and
Intelligence." In Planning U.S. Strategy, edited by Philip
S. Kronenberg, 55-71. Washington, D.C.: National Defense
University Press, 1981. SOD D5.402:Se2/3/980-81. Deals
with agencies such as the CIA and "intelligence" structures
such as research organizations. Bobrow faults the tendency
to limit forecasting to weapons systems, downgrading
political and economic intelligence.

1720. Goodman, Allan E. "Dateline Langley: Fixing the
Intelligence Mess." Foreign Policy, no. 59 (Winter 1984-
1985):160-179. Reviews efforts during the Nixon and Carter

administrations to make changes in the CIA. Goodman argues, seemingly somewhat paradoxically, for both more centralization and more tolerance for differing opinions within the CIA.

Civil Defense

Books

1721. Scheer, Robert. With Enough Shovels: Reagan, Bush and Nuclear War. New York: Random House, 1982. 285p. Harshly criticizes the apparent assumptions of the Reagan administration concerning nuclear war and civil defense. Scheer's research included interviews with President Reagan, Vice President Bush, Paul H. Nitze, and others.

Periodical Articles

1722. Beres, Louis Rene. "Surviving Nuclear War: U.S. Plans for Crisis Relocation." Armed Forces & Society 12 (Fall 1985):75-94. Criticizes the Reagan administration's civil defense plans, which Beres asserts may make nuclear war more likely.

1723. Troxell, John F. "Soviet Civil Defense and the American Response." Military Review 63 (January 1983):36-46. Describes the Soviet civil defense program and the increased American concern about it during the Carter and Reagan administrations. The Soviets have developed plans to protect both people and industrial operations. Measures by the United States are discussed briefly.

Arms Control and Disarmament

Official Policy Statements

1724. Reagan, Ronald. "Remarks to Members of the National Press Club on Arms Reduction and Nuclear Weapons. November 18, 1981." In Public Papers of the Presidents of the United States: Ronald Reagan 1981, 1062-1067. Washington, D.C.: Government Printing Office, 1982. Quotes extensively from his letter to Soviet President Brezhnev concerning arms control. Reagan points to reductions in nuclear armaments and conventional forces by NATO and the lack of an appropriate response by the Soviets. Reagan summarizes current American arms control proposals and christens the present effort START, or Strategic Arms Reduction Talks.

1725. Reagan, Ronald. "The President's News Conference. May 13, 1982." In Public Papers of the Presidents of the United States: Ronald Reagan 1982, I, 618-626. Washington, D.C.: Government Printing Office, 1983. Reviews current American disarmament efforts, which Reagan sees as linked "with our efforts to restore a credible national defense." Reagan describes American objectives in terms of reducing numbers of nuclear weapons and criticizes SALT because "it simply legitimizes an arms race."

1726. Reagan, Ronald. "Address to the Nation on Strategic Arms Reduction and Nuclear Deterrence. November 22, 1982." In Public Papers of the Presidents of the United States: Ronald Reagan 1982, II, 1505-1510. Washington, D.C.: Government Printing Office, 1983. Describes the nature of nuclear deterrence and traces the growth of Soviet nuclear forces in detail. Reagan summarizes new arms control proposals being made by the United States to the USSR and scores the Soviets for their unwillingness to undertake serious negotiations.

1727. Reagan, Ronald. "Remarks and A Question-and-Answer Session with Reporters on Strategic Arms Reduction and Military Deterrence. January 14, 1983." In Public Papers of the Presidents of the United States: Ronald Reagan 1983, I, 50-54. Washington, D.C.: Government Printing Office, 1984. Asserts that America's strategic nuclear forces have now been modernized; so that the Soviets are encouraged to enter into serious arms reduction talks. In response to a question, Reagan reviews his criticism of Carter's MX plan.

1728. Reagan, Ronald. "Remarks at the Annual Convention of the National Association of Evangelicals in Orlando, Florida. March 8, 1983." In Public Papers of the Presidents of the United States: Ronald Reagan 1983, I, 359-364. Washington, D.C.: Government Printing Office, 1985. Much of the address deals with the abortion issue and relations between religion and public life. Reagan refers to the Soviet Union as "an evil empire" and assails "the so-called nuclear freeze solutions," but calls on the Soviets to agree to large bilateral cuts in nuclear weapons.

1729. Reagan, Ronald. "Remarks Announcing a Proposed Interim Intermediate-Range Nuclear Force Reduction Agreement. March 30, 1983." In Public Papers of the Presidents of the United States: Ronald Reagan 1983, I, 473-474. Washington, D.C.: Government Printing Office, 1984. Citing the Soviet deployment of many SS-20 missiles, Reagan discusses American efforts to have intermediate-range missiles eliminated entirely. He accuses the Soviets of having failed to make any useful counter proposals. Throughout his address, Reagan emphasizes the complete involvement of the NATO allies in current deliberations.

1730. Reagan, Ronald. "Statement on Action by the House of Representatives on the Nuclear Arms Freeze Resolution. May 5, 1983." In Public Papers of the Presidents of the United States: Ronald Reagan 1983, I, 644-645. Washington, D.C.: Government Printing Office, 1984. Expresses some satisfaction that the original proposal for a nuclear freeze has been substantially modified to include a call for maintaining the strategic nuclear balance, but states that it is still "not an answer to arms control that I can responsibly support."

1731. Reagan, Ronald. "Remarks Announcing Changes in the United States Position at the Strategic Arms Reduction Talks. June 8, 1983." In Public Papers of the Presidents of the United States: Ronald Reagan 1983, I, 831-833. Washington, D.C.: Government Printing Office, 1984. Discusses the impact of the Scowcroft Commission recommendations on United States arms control negotiating policy. The thrust of the remarks is that Reagan has instructed the American arms control negotiators to assume a somewhat more flexible stance.

1732. Reagan, Ronald. "Radio Address to the American People on Nuclear Weapons. October 29, 1983." In Public Papers of the Presidents of the United States: Ronald Reagan 1983, II, 1524-1525. Washington, D.C.: Government Printing Office, 1985. Applauds the decision made by NATO to reduce further the number of missiles based in Europe. Reagan notes that an earlier reduction was carried out in 1980. He criticizes the Soviet Union for adding to its missile force and briefly refers to current negotiations with the Soviets.

1733. Reagan, Ronald. "Address to the Nation and Other Countries on United States-Soviet Relations. January 16, 1984." In Public Papers of the Presidents of the United States: Ronald Reagan 1984, I, 40-44. Washington, D.C.: Government Printing Office, 1986. On the eve of the Stockholm disarmament conference, Reagan asserts that there is a good chance for worthwhile agreements, in part because of increased American strength which is an inducement to the Soviets to negotiate on arms control issues. Reagan endorses a strategy of "credible deterrence, peaceful competition and constructive cooperation." He outlines current American arms control proposals and expresses confidence in the ability of the superpowers to negotiate effectively.

1734. Reagan, Ronald. "Message to the Congress Transmitting a Report and a Fact Sheet on Soviet Noncompliance with Arms Control Agreements. January 23, 1984." In Public Papers of the Presidents of the United States: Ronald Reagan 1984, I, 72-76. Washington, D.C.: Government Printing Office, 1986. Briefly discusses the need for adherence to the arms control agreements and stresses the need for cooperation between the executive and legislative branches of government to ensure that such agreements are complied with by all the nations concerned. The "Fact Sheet" examines seven areas "of serious concern," ranging from chemical, biological, and toxin weapons to tests of nuclear weapons and intercontinental ballistic missiles.

Books

1735.   Einhorn, Robert J. Negotiating from Strength:
Leverage in U.S.-Soviet Arms Control Negotiation. New York:
Praeger Publishers, 1985. 120p. Examines both American and
Soviet disarmament strategies in terms of their efforts to
"negotiate from strength."

1736. Halloran, Bernard F., editor. Essays on Arms Control
and National Security. Washington, D.C.:   Government
Printing Office, 1986. 395p. SOD AC1.2:Es7. Collection of
essays to note the 25th anniversary of the Arms Control and
Disarmament Agency. Contributors include Robert S.
McNamara, James R. Schlesinger, and Kenneth L. Adelman.

1737. Krepon, Michael. Strategic Stalemate: Nuclear Weapons
and Arms Control in American Politics. New York: St.
Martin's Press, 1984. 191p. The "stalemate" Krepon
discusses is not on the international level, but rather the
conflict in the United States between disarmament advocates
and those deeply concerned about Soviet advances.   This
survey of the arms control controversy considers the
varying perspectives in the Reagan administration.

1738. Potter, William C., editor. Verification and Arms
Control. Lexington, Massachusetts: Lexington Books, 1985.
288p. Essays examine verification in regard to all major
types of arms, including chemical and biological weapons,
bombers and missiles, and antisatellite devices. The
authors of the essays present a generally pessimistic view
of arms control insofar as verification is concerned.

1739. Rowell, William F. Arms Control Verification: A Guide
to Policy Issues for the 1980s. Cambridge, Massachusetts:
Ballinger Publishing Company, 1986. 192p. Thorough
discussion of the problems of verification, including both
technical and political aspects. Rowell examines a number
of ways to approach arms control verification.

1740. Scott, Robert Travis, editor. The Race for Security:
Arms and Arms Control in the Nuclear Age. Lexington,
Massachusetts: Lexington Books,1985. 297p. Essays examine a
great variety of topics relating to defense and arms
control. A number of weapons and weapons systems are
covered, as is the nuclear strategy of the Reagan administration. A current survey of national defense and
disarmament policy and the part played in both by public
opinion complete the study.

1741. Van Cleave, William R. and S.T. Cohen. Nuclear
Weapons, Policies, and the Test Ban Issue. New York:
Praeger Publishers, 1987. 118p. Advocates further
development of nuclear weapons and expresses skepticism
about making sharp distinctions between the use of
conventional and nuclear weapons. The authors also view

arms control efforts as often harmful to American interests.

1742. Waller, Douglas C. Congress and the Nuclear Freeze: An Inside Look at the Politics of a Mass Movement. Amherst: University of Massachusetts Press, 1987. Traces efforts during the 1980's to induce Congress to legislate a nuclear freeze. Waller was a participant in the movement and is highly critical of the Reagan administration for its stance on disarmament.

Essays and Periodical Articles

1743. Adelman, Kenneth L. "Arms Control with and Without Agreements." Foreign Affairs 63 (Winter 1984-1985):240-263. Argues that there are various ways of achieving arms control in addition to formal agreements. These techniques are described in some detail.

1744. Blechman, Barry M. and James E. Nolan. "Reorganizing for More Effective Arms Negotiations." Foreign Affairs 61 (Summer 1983):1157-1162. Assails the Arms Control and Disarmament Agency and argues that it should be abolished. The authors also suggest how to realign for better negotiations from the American perspective.

1745. Borawski, John. "Theater Nuclear Arms Control and Forward-Based Systems." Air University Review 33 (May-June 1982):11-19. Describes "forward-based systems" such as aircraft and intermediate range missiles and their role in SALT negotiations. After reviewing verification problems associated with these weapons, Borawski warns that the United States must be prepared to negotiate effectively on this subject.

1746. Clarke, Duncan L. "Arms Control and Foreign Policy Under Reagan." Bulletin of the Atomic Scientists 37 (November 1981):12-19. Discusses the Arms Control and Disarmament Agency, especially as it operated at the beginning of Reagan's first term.

1747. Dean, Jonathan. "MBFR: From Apathy to Accord." International Security 7 (Spring 1983):116-139. Advocates further effort to achieve a Mutual and Balanced Force Reduction (MBFR) to help preserve peace in Europe. MBFR involves conventional forces rather than nuclear weapons.

1748. Drell, Sidney D. and others. "Preserving the ABM Treaty: A Critique of the Reagan Strategic Defense Initiative." International Security 9 (Fall 1984):51-91. Provides historical background on nuclear weapons competition and disusses the Strategic Defense Initiative and the antiballistic missile agreement.

1749. Durel, F.M. "Tantalus Revisited: The Banning of

Chemical Weapons." In Essays on Strategy: The 1983 Joint Chiefs of Staff Essay Competition, 13-27. Washington, D.C.: National Defense University Press, 1984. SOD D5.402:St 8/5. Reviews American efforts to abolish chemical warfare. Durel emphasizes the problem of verification that dominates current discussions of chemical disarmament. He argues that without chemical weapons the United States might have to retaliate with nuclear weapons against chemical attacks.

1750. Estes, Howell M., Jr. "Strategic Arms Limitation and the Air Force." Air University Review 34 (November-December 1982):46-53. Criticizes the air force for giving too little attention to the issues associated wth strategic arms limitations. Estes feels that it is a useful policy option for the United States, and presents reasons why the air force must be informed about and interested in this topic.

1751. Fascell, Dante B. "Congress and Arms Control." Foreign Affairs 65 (Spring 1987):730-749. Criticizes what Fascell views as the Reagan administration's movement away from the cooperation between the executive and legislative branches on arms control that developed in the 1960's and 1970's. Fascell examines and rejects the view that Congress has only a relatively limited role to play in this field. Most of the article deals with Congressional activism in 1986.

1752. Flowerree, Charles C. "The Politics of Arms Control Treaties: A Case Study." Journal of International Affairs 37 (Winter 1984):269-282. Reviews disarmament efforts, including those directed against chemical warfare.

1753. Gellner, Charles R. with Jeanette Voas. "Arms Control: An Evolving Record of Hope." In The Reagan Defense Program: An Interim Assessment, edited by Stephen J. Cimbala, 161-185. Wilmington, Delaware: Scholarly Resources Inc., 1986. Briefly reviews Reagan's attitude toward the USSR insofar as disarmament is concerned and arms control negotiations during Reagan's first term. About half the chapter deals with the impact of the Strategic Defense Initiative proposal.

1754. George, James L. "INNF" United States Naval Institute Proceedings 113 (June 1987):35-39. Suggests that an agreement eliminating INF weapons in Europe enhances the role of naval forces because they must provide a substitute deterrent. George describes the appropriate naval weapons (carrier aviation and submarine launched missiles, especially the Tomahawk cruise missiles).

1755. Gray, Colin S. "Moscow is Cheating." Foreign Policy. no. 56 (Fall 1984):141-152. Accuses the USSR of extensive violations of disarmament agreements. These violations relate to chemical, biological and radiological weapons generally, not just nuclear devices.

1756. Hirschfield, Thomas J. "Reducing Short-Range Nuclear Systems in Europe: An Opportunity for Stability in the Eighties." Annals of the American Academy of Political and Social Science, no. 469 (1983):77-90. Europe fears Soviet attack less than it once did, for a number of reasons that are discussed in the article. Nevertheless, there seems to be little chance for significant arms reduction.

1757. Horelick, Arnold. "U.S.-Soviet Relations: The Return of Arms Control." Foreign Affairs 63 (Special Issue 1985):511-537. Reviews arms control talks and related events between 1983 and 1985. Horelick asserts that the Soviets would be well advised to negotiate seriously.

1758. Hulett, Louisa S. "START, Stops, and Nuclear Strategy." Journal of Strategic Studies 7 (June 1984):154-168. Discusses the Reagan administration's disarmament policies and its effort to continue strategic deterrence despite problems with NATO and domestic controversies over defense policy.

1759. Johnson, Arthur and Douglas Norton. "SALT on the Back Burner: Some Considerations for US Defense Policy." In Defense Planning and Arms Control: Proceedings of a Special NSAI Conference 12-14 June 1980 National Defense University, 121-147. Washington, D.C.:National Security Affairs Institute, 1980. SOD D5.402:D36. Discusses deterrence both in a non-SALT II and a SALT II situation, general characteristics of American efforts to achieve arms control agreements, and decisions related to SALT II and non-SALT II scenarios which need to be taken. The authors also examine various alternative policies which should be considered.

1760. Krepon, Michael. "Both Sides are Hedging". Foreign Policy, no. 56 (Fall 1984):153-172. Sets forth a possible American strategy for conducting arms control negotiations. Krepon feels that American interests have not been harmed by existing agreements.

1761. McKitrick, Jeffrey S. "Arms Control and the Joint Chiefs of Staff." Parameters 14 (Autumn 1984):64-74. The Joint Chiefs of Staff has had little impact on disarmament negotiations. McKitrick describes the reasons for its failure to influence this important part of national security planning.

1762. Millett, Stephen M. "Forward-Based Nuclear Weapons and SALT I." Political Science Quarterly 98 (Spring 1983):79-97. Surveys SALT I negotiations on various types of forward-based nuclear weapons, including both missiles and bombers.

1763. Petraeus, David H. "What is Wrong with a Nuclear

Freeze." <u>Military Review</u> 63 (November 1983):49-64. Discusses the freeze movement and its appeals. Petraeus points to advantages to the Soviets deriving from a freeze. It would also have drastic effects on NATO. The article is a thorough rebuttal of the arguments of freeze proponents.

1764. Rowny, Edward. "Integrating Defense Planning." In <u>Defense Planning and Arms Control: Proceedings of a Special NSAI Conference 12-14 June 1980 National Defense University</u>, 51-57. Washington, D.C.: National Security Affairs Institute, 1980. SOD D5.402:D36. Argues strongly for subordinating arms control initiatives to the overriding need to maintain the "common defense."

1765. Schelling, Thomas C. "What Went Wrong with Arms Control." <u>Foreign Affairs</u> 64 (Winter 1985-86):219-233. Detailed review of American negotiating stances between the Nixon and Reagan administrations. Schelling discusses the course of negotiations and concludes with an examination of the Strategic Defense Initiative.

1766. Snow, Donald M. "ICBM Vulnerability, Mobility, and Arms Control." <u>Air University Review</u> 32 (March-April 1981):32-42. Emphasizes the complexity of theorizing about ICBM vulnerability. Snow asserts that vulnerability will increase sharply in the near future. Arms control will also be more difficult to attain.

1767. Starr, Richard F. "The MBFR Process and Its Prospects." <u>Orbis</u> 27 (Winter 1984):999-1009. Reviews East-West negotiations between 1973 and 1983 on Mutual and Balanced Force Reductions. Starr does not believe the Soviets are seriously interested in reaching an agreement.

Military Assistance

Official Policy Statements

1768. Reagan, Ronald. "Announcement Concerning a Presidential Directive on United States Conventional Arms Transfer Policy. July 9, 1981." In <u>Public Papers of the Presidents of the United States: Ronald Reagan 1981</u>, 615-617. Washington, D.C.:Government Printing Office, 1982. Marks a change in policy from Carter's 1977 Presidential Directive 13. Reagan's announcement discusses the importance of arms transfers and their contribution to American defense. Reagan spells out in detail how foreign requests for arms will be evaluated. Citing lack of Soviet interest in making an agreement to limit such transfers, the United States "will deal with the world as it is, rather than as it would like it to be."

1769. Shultz, George P. "Foreign Aid and U.S. Policy Objectives." <u>Department of State Bulletin</u> 84 (May 1984):17-

22. Amplifies the conclusions of the National Bipartisan Commission for Central America, headed by Henry A. Kissinger, as well as the Commission on Security and Economic Assistance, headed by Frank C. Carlucci, which reviewed the American foreign assistance programs. Shultz discusses, region by region, the importance to the United States of these programs.

Books

1770. Gervasi, Tom. Arsenal of Democracy II: American Military Power in the 1980s and the Origins of the New Cold War with a Survey of American Weapons and Arms Exports. New York: Grove Press, 1981 272p. Concentrates on defense expenditures and the role of the Unites States in the world's arms traffic. Includes a long and useful bibliography.

1771. Hough, Richard L. Economic Assistance and Security: Rethinking US Policy. Washington, D.C.:National Defense University Press, 1982. 129p. SOD D5.402:Ec7. Focuses exclusively on nonmilitary types of assistance. Hough describes current programs and proposes various changes, including more of a role for nongovernmental elements.

1772. Klare, Michael T. and Cynthia Arnson. Supplying Repression: U.S. Support for Authoritarian Regimes Abroad. Washington, D.C.: Institute for Policy Studies, 1981. 165p. Emphasizes assistance to foreign police forces, although one chapter discusses military assistance and arms sales. The book also describes weapons and other equipment supplied by the United States. Appendices contain extensive statistics.

1773. Louscher, David J. and Michael D. Salomone. Technology Transfer and U.S. Security Assistance. Boulder, Colorado: Westview Press, 1986. 192p. Deals with American technological assistance to allies and other friendly states, which wish to acquire the latest military assets. Problems arising from American policies need to be examined for their possible harmful effects on the American military posture.

1774. McKinlay, R.D. and A. Mughan. Aid and Arms to the Third World: An Analysis of the Distribution and Impact of US Official Transfers. New York: St. Martin's Press, 1984. 282p. Highly sophisticated statistical analysis. The emphasis is on the United States, but there is some information on other non-Soviet bloc countries. The authors are very critical of the containment policy.

1775. Neuman, Stefanie G. Military Assistance in Recent Wars: The Dominance of the Superpowers. New York: Praeger Publishers, 1986. 199p. Studies the involvement of the superpowers in eight Third World wars and the search for arms by the smaller nations. The political and economic, as well as the purely military, aspects of arms transfers are analyzed. This is an important comparative work.

Periodical Articles

1776.   Graves, Ernest.   "U.S. Security Assistance in the 1980's." Washington Quarterly 7 (Winter 1984):145-155. Reviews the use of military assistance by the United States from the late 1950's through the early 1980's.

1777.   Marcella, Gabriel.   "Security Assistance Revisited: How to Win Friends and Not Lose Influence." Parameters 12 (December 1982):43-52.   Emphasizes that security assistance may in some cases give the receiving nation power over the provider of assistance.   The United States has not derived much influence from the provision of arms to various Latin American countries, for example.

Military Personnel

Official Policy Statements

1778.   Reagan, Ronald.   "Statement on America's All-Volunteer Force. November 17, 1981." In Public Papers of the Presidents of the United States: Ronald Reagan 1981, 1055. Washington, D.C.:Government Printing Office, 1982. Asserts that the all-volunteer force concept is working better than ever in 1981 and that it is "the best way to meet our manpower requirements in the times of peace." Reagan points to increased benefits and more "patriotism" as factors in the improving level of recruits.

Books

1779.   Binkin, Martin. America's Volunteer Military: Progress and Prospects.   Washington, D.C.:Brookings Institution, 1984. 63p. Warns that although economic and demographic trends have made volunteer armed forces exceptionally successful, these conditions can change.   If force levels remain stable and if the forces do not acquire more complicated technology, the all-volunteer force concept seems viable.

1780.   Binkin, Martin. Military Technology and Defense Manpower.   Washington, D.C.:Brookings Institution, 1986. 143p. Focuses specifically on the problem of recruiting personnel for the armed forces with the ability to utilize current technology.   Binkin illuminates the problem through a discussion of the technological changes being introduced in the military services.

1781.   Danzig, Richard and Peter Szanton, National Service: What Would It Mean? Lexington, Massachusetts: Lexington

Books, 1986. 207p. Provides a detailed analysis of the various options for a national service program. This is an important overview of the whole issue.

1782.   Foster, Gregory D. and others, editors. The Strategic Dimension of Military Manpower.   Cambridge, Massachusetts: Ballinger Publishing Company, 1987. 240p. Essays by Irving Louis Horowitz, Jeffrey Record, Sam C. Sarkesian and others examine manpower issues in light of economic and social trends, the military reform movement, and other factors.

Essays and Periodical Articles

1783.   Baldwin, Robert H. and Thomas V. Daula.   "The Cost of High-Quality Recruits." Armed Forces & Society 11 (Fall 1984):96-114. Discusses efforts to attract adaptable and intelligent recruits. The authors note that it is difficult to determine how much superior recruits are worth in terms of their usefulness and their cost.

1784.   Burk, James. "Patriotism and the All-Volunteer Force." JPMS: Journal of Political & Military Sociology 12 (Fall 1984):229-241.   Suggests that patriotism is a neglected factor in analyses of personnel procurement for the armed forces in the post-draft era.

1785.   Dale, Charles and Curtis Gilroy.   "Determinants of Enlistments: A Macroeconomic Time-Series   View." Armed Forces & Society 10 (Winter 1984):192-210.   Discusses the significance of economic incentives in attracting recruits. Unemployment rates are important, but they are not a totally decisive element.

1786.   Faris, John H. "Economic and Noneconomic Factors of Personnel Recruitment and Retention in the AVF." Armed Forces & Society 10 (Winter 1984):251-275.   Discusses the perceived success of the volunteer concept, including the impact of noneconomic factors such as family influences.

1787.   Jacobs, James B. and Dennis McNamara. "Selective Service Without a Draft." Armed Forces & Society 10 (Spring 1984):361-379.   Warns that vigorous enforcement would be required to compel compliance with selective service in today's society.   The authors weigh the factors related to a decision to return to the draft.

1788.   Korb, Lawrence J. "Defense Manpower and the Reagan Record." In The Reagan Defense Program: An Interim Assessment, edited by Stephen J. Cimbala, 63-92. Wilmington, Delaware: Scholarly Resources, Inc., 1986. Examines the problems of the all-volunteer force when Reagan took office and the marked success of the Reagan administration in increasing the number and quality of servicemen and women and rates of retention.

1789.   Margiotta, Franklin D. and Michael Maccoby. "Future
Challenge to Military Leadership: Adjusting to the Human
Implications of Advanced Technology." In Technology,
Strategy and National Security, edited by Franklin D.
Margiotta and Ralph Sanders, 77-103. Washington, D.C.:
National Defense University Press, 1985. SOD D5.402:T22.
Focuses on problems in attracting and retaining technicians
for the armed forces.   About half the essay examines
technology in the air force.

1790.   Moskos, Charles C. "Making the All-Volunteer Force
Work: A National Service Approach." Foreign Affairs 60
(Fall 1981):17-34. Advocates not placing complete reliance
on the all-volunteer force or on compulsory military
service.   Moskos suggests that a combination of national
service, more benefits, such as the GI Bill for servicemen
and women, and a two-track structure for paying members of
the armed forces would be feasible under current conditions
and would not cost a great deal more than the present
system.

1791.   Puscheck, Herbert C. "Selective Service
Registration: Success or Failure?" Armed Forces & Society
10 (Fall 1983):5-25. Discusses Carter's program for draft
registration and compares it with earlier American efforts.
Puscheck notes that most men subject to registration
requirements have obeyed the law.

1792.   Quester, Aline O. and James S. Thomason. "Keeping
the Force: Retaining Military Careerists." Armed Forces &
Society 11 (Fall 1984):85-95.   Warns of approaching
problems in maintaining appropriate force strength,
particularly specialized personnel. This is an analysis of
competition for people between the military and civilian
sectors.

1793.   Rimland, Bernard and Gerald E. Larson. "The Manpower
Quality Decline: An Ecological Perspective." Armed Forces &
Society 8 (Fall 1981):21-78. Discusses what the authors
regard as a decline in recruit quality. They seek to
identify the causes of this decline.

1794.   Snyder, William P. "Officer Recruitment for the All-
Volunteer Force: Trends and Prospects." Armed Forces &
Society 10 (Spring 1984):401-425. Assesses the impact of
changes and projected changes in ROTC on officer procurement. The program has functioned well and seems firmly
established after the controversies of the 1960's.

Reserve Forces

Books

1795.   Wilson, Bennie J. III. The Guard and Reserve in the
Total Force: The First Decade, 1973-1983.   Washington,
D.C.: National Defense University Press, 1985. 340p. SOD
D5.402.G93/973-83.   Extensive   collection   of   journal
articles, original papers, and other materials that discuss
the strengths and shortcomings of reserve and National
Guard and Air National Guard forces. Five parts deal with
reserve   history,   "image   and   attitudes,"   personnel,
equipment, and mobilization capability.

1796.   Zurcher, Louis A. and others, editors. Citizen-
Sailors in a Changing Society.   Westport, Connecticut:
Greenwood Press, 1986. 290p. Essays deal with recruitment
and retention problems and other aspects of maintaining an
effective naval reserve as far as personnel is concerned.
The subject is analyzed from a variety of points of view
and with a number of different social science techniques.

Essays and Periodical Articles

1797.   Beaumont, Roger A. "Constabulary or Fire Brigade?
The Army National Guard." Parameters 12 (March 1982):62-69.
Discusses   the   Guard's   conventional   military   and   civic
action/police   duties.   In part, Beaumont examines the
Guard's role in the total force concept.

1798.   Gould, James L. "The Guard and Reserve: Towards
Fuller   Realization   of   the   Total   Force   Potential."   In
Mobilization and the National Defense, edited by Hardy L.
Merritt   and   Luther   F.   Carter,   111-131.   Washington,
D.C.:National   Defense   University   Press,   1985.   SOD
D5.402:M71/2. Discusses development of reserve forces, the
total force concept, and the enhanced readiness of reserve
forces. The total force approach is discussed in some
detail.

1799.   Kempf, Cecil J. "The Status of the Naval Reserve."
United States Naval Institute Proceedings 110 (October
1984):58-64.   Describes   the   development   of   the   naval
reserve. Kempf details the numbers of ships and aircraft
that are the responsibility of reserve forces.

1800.   Sharp, Benjamin F. and Donald B. Skipper. "The
Reserve Component Dilemma: Mission Versus Time." Military
Review 64 (November 1984):62-79. Discusses the problem of
the reserve forces: they lack sufficient time in a given
year to execute their training missions.   The authors
review the development of reserve forces after the coming
of   the   all-volunteer   force   and   examine   the   problems
associated with increasing training time.

Terrorism

Official Policy Statement

1801.   Reagan,   Ronald.   "Message   to   the   Congress
Transmitting Proposed Legislation to Combat International
Terrorism.   April   26,   1984."   In   Public Papers of the
Presidents of the United States: Ronald Reagan 1984,   I,
575-577.   Washington,   D.C.:   Government   Printing   Office,
1986.   Reviews   some   of   the   major   incidents   involving
terrorism during the early 1980's.   Reagan summarizes the
four bills to combat terrorism he favors.   These prohibit
various types of terrorist activity and provide rewards for
useful evidence.

Documentary Resources

1802.   Terrorism: Special Studies, 1975-1985.   Frederick,
Maryland: University   Publications   of   America,   Inc.   This
collection   consists   of   studies   by   governmental   agencies
such   as   the   National   Defense   University   and   by   private
sector research groups and universities.   All the research
was conducted for the federal government. Nuclear as well
as conventional terrorism is analyzed.

Books

1803.   Livingstone,   Neil   C.   The War Against Terrorism.
Lexington,   Massachusetts: Lexington   Books,   1982.   304p.
Discusses   terrorist   strategies   and   tactics   and   countermeasures.   Livingstone   examines   the   antiterrorist   stances
and   policies   of   the   Carter   and   early   Reagan years.   The
study   is   based   in   part   on   extensive   interviews   with
concerned specialists.

Alliances

Books

1804.   Boyd,   Gavin,   editor.   Regionalism   and   Global
Security.   Lexington, Massachusetts: Lexington Books, 1984.
194p.   Proposes   the   development   of   a   series   of   economic
groups somewhat similar to the European Economic Community.
Essays   suggest   the   economic   and   social   challenges   facing
the   Third   World   can   be   best   solved   by   creating   new
international structures.

1805.   Sabrosky,   Alan   Ned,   editor.   Alliances   in   U.S.
Foreign Policy: Issues in the Quest for Collective Defense.
Boulder,   Colorado: Westview   Press,   1986.   225p.   Stresses
NATO,   in a study of the problems inherent in any alliance
relationship.   The   essays   in   this   collection   examine   a
variety of issues, including political and economic as well
as military topics.

Periodical Articles

1806. Morris, Robert King. "Clientism Unbound: America and
the Tactics of Third World Security." Naval War College
Review 34 (May-June 1981):75-82. Defends the American
record in dealing with its smaller allies, but proposes
changes in the approaches used toward such countries.

1807. Ott, George. "Geopolitics for an Uncertain Era." Air
University Review 33 (September-October 1982):29-35. Warns
that the United States must provide contingency plans
because of the decline in its alliance system. Ott is
relatively optimistic about the military security and
economic stability of the Western Hemisphere. He asserts
that the NATO partners, Japan, and the Peoples Republic of
China could contain the USSR, even without the United
States.

1808. Sutter, Thomas C. "Base Rights Agreements." Air
University Review 34 (July-August 1983):32-41. Summarizes
American basing rights abroad and suggests ways to
negotiate such rights which will create a favorable
atmosphere in the countries which grant such privileges.

Latin America

Books

1809. Schultz, Lars. National Security and United States
Policy Toward Latin America. Princeton: Princeton
University Press, 1987. 377p. Examines the political and
military importance of Central America to the United
States. Schultz's study is based heavily on several hundred
interviews with American political and governmental
leaders.

Periodical Articles

1810. Haley, P. Edward. "Cuba and United States Strategy."
Air University Review 35 (November-December 1983):82-93.
Warns that the United States is militarily weak in the
Caribbean. Haley compares American forces that could be
used to invade Cuba with the forces used to take Okinawa
and British forces used in the Falkland Islands war.

1811. Kirkpatrick, Jeane. "U.S. Security & Latin America."
Commentary 71 (January 1981):29-40. Deplores the American
movement away from the Monroe Doctrine in the face of
increasing Soviet pressure in the Western Hemisphere.

1812. Nuechterlein, Donald E. "North America: Our
Neglected Heartland." Parameters 15 (Autumn 1985):58-65.
Discusses post-World War II American security policy
regarding the Western Hemisphere. Nuechterlein argues that

Latin America was neglected for some time.

1813. Ronfeldt, David F. "Rethinking the Monroe Doctrine."
Orbis 28 (Winter 1985):684-696. Reviews the relationship
between the Monroe Doctrine and American strategy.
Ronfeldt argues for a somewhat less assertive American
stance in the Caribbean area.

North Atlantic Treaty Organization

Books

1814. Brady, Linda P. and Joyce P. Kaufman, editors. NATO
in the 1980s: Challenges and Responses. New York: Praeger
Publishers, 1985. 286p. Essays deal with virtually all
major facets of the alliance, including arms control issues
and the role of NATO outside Europe, specifically in the
Persian Gulf.   The place of the United States in the
alliance is also discussed.

1815.   Charles, Daniel. Nuclear Planning in NATO.
Cambridge, Massachusetts: Ballinger Publishing Company,
1987. 176p. Discusses the employment of nuclear weapons in
Europe. Charles examines the issue of control of nuclear
weapons in a war and the factors involved in deciding
whether or not to use them against the Soviets. He sees a
discrepancy between political and military planning within
NATO concerning nuclear weapons.

1816.   Daalder, Ivo H. The SDI Challenge to Europe.
Cambridge, Massachusetts: Ballinger Publishing Company,
1987. 185p. Examines the possible implications for European
defense of the American commitment to the Strategic Defense
Initiative. Various possibilities include a reduced
American assurance to Europe in case of Soviet attack.

1817. Killibrew, Robert B. Conventional Defense and Total
Deterrence: Assessing NATO's Strategic Options.
Wilmington, Delaware: Scholarly Resources Inc., 1986. 176p.
Speaks strongly in favor of an improved conventional
capability. Killibrew also supplies a good deal of
information on current NATO and Warsaw Pact planning.

1818. Olive, Marsha McGraw and Jeffrey D. Porro, editors.
Nuclear Weapons in Europe: Modernization and Limitation.
Lexington, Massachusetts: Lexington Books, 1983. 167p.
Essays review a number of topics related to the issue.
They examine the role of public opinion, detente, and other
matters.

1819. Schmitz, Peter N. Defending the NATO Alliance:
Global Implications. Washington, D.C.: National Defense
University Press, 1987. 178p. SOD D5.402:NB1/2 Focuses on
the question of expanding NATO's role to embrace non-
European problems. Schmitz emphasizes the need to make

NATO more of an alliance.

1820.   Sloan, Stanley R. NATO's Future: Toward a New Transatlantic Bargain. Washington D.C.:National Defense University Press, 1985. SOD D5.402:N81.   Provides a thorough review of the development of NATO. Sloan asserts that a "European Defense Community" should have been formed and that the alliance is overly dependent on nuclear deterrence.

1821.   Williams, Geoffrey Lee and Alan Williams. The European Defense Initiative: Europe's Bid for Equality. New York: St. Martin's Press, 1986. 256p. Recommends substantial changes in the NATO alliance to maintain its viability in the face of challenges by neutralists in Europe. The authors discuss current problems within the alliance. Their proposals for change include providing the Federal Republic of Germany with nuclear weapons and allowing Europeans to hold the position of Supreme Allied Commander.

Essays and Periodical Articles

1822.   Arnould, Derek C. "The Institutional Implications of NATO in a Global Milieu." In The Future of European Alliance Systems: NATO and the Warsaw Pact, edited by Arlene Idol Broadhurst, 121-129.   Boulder, Colorado: Westview Press, 1982. Analyzes the structure of NATO in light of current political and economic developments resulting from the continuing lag in the economies of East European countries and strains within the Warsaw Pact.

1823.   Art, Robert J. "The United States and the NATO Alliance: Managing the Unsolvable." In The 1980s: Decade of Confrontation? The Eighth National Security Affairs Conference 1981 Proceedings, 157-187. Washington, D.C.: National Defense University Press, 1981. SOD D5.412:981. Reviews continuing problems in NATO and proposes American approaches in dealing with the European allies. Art sees many changes in Europe and in European-American relations, but they do not alter the structure of NATO or remove the need for this alliance.

1824.   Bambini, Adrian P. "Chemical Warfare and the NATO Alliance." Military Review 61 (April 1981):27-33. Asserts that the NATO partners have not developed a common approach to chemical warfare. While Warsaw Pact nations can launch extensive chemical attacks, NATO's posture is weak, creating a dangerous gap in defense preparations.

1825.   Cimbala, Stephen J. "War-Fighting Deterrence and Alliance Cohesiveness." Air University Review 35 (September-October 1984):69-73. Examines European concerns about the possibility that the United States is lifting its deterrent umbrella over the NATO countries in Europe.

1826.   Dean, Jonathan. "Military Security in Europe."
Foreign Affairs 66 (Fall 1987):22-40. Takes an optimistic
view of the prospect for reducing tensions and arms levels
in Europe, owing to changes in Soviet policies. Dean argues
that the United States and its NATO allies need to examine
current Soviet arms control proposals seriously. He also
asserts that both NATO and Warsaw pact nations may reduce
forces unilaterally over a period of time for economic
reasons.

1827.   Denoon, David B.H. "Conclusions: Economic
Constraints and U.S. Defense Policy in the 1980's." In
Constraints on Strategy: The Economics of Western Security,
edited by David B.H. Denoon, 195-221. Washington, D.C.:
Pergamon-Brassey's International Defense Publishers, Inc.,
1986.   Stresses the importance of Europe to American
security and examines the contributions the major European
NATO members are likely to make in the future. Several
pages discuss relationships between strategy and economics.
The key is the impact on American strategy of economic
growth (or lack of it) in Europe.

1828.   Gray, Colin S. "NATO Defense and Arms-Reduction
Proposals." Military Review 63 (October 1983):62-68.
Examines the built-in conflicts of the NATO alliance such
as the differing American and European views of deterrence.
Gray argues that "flexible response" has been rendered
obsolete by the greatly increased nuclear strength of the
Soviet Union. He sees little value in mutual and balanced-
force reduction and doubts any agreement will be reached in
this area or on theater nuclear weapons.

1829.   Howe, Geoffrey. "The European Pillar." Foreign
Affairs 63 (Winter 1984-1985):330-343.   Praises NATO for
its contemporary deterrence value. Howe urges the United
States to keep significant forces in Europe.

1830.   Hunt, Kenneth. "Atlantic Unity and European
Defence." In The Future of European Alliance Systems: NATO
and the Warsaw Pact, edited by Arlene Idol Broadhurst, 71-
86. Boulder, Colorado: Westview Press, 1982. Analyzes
changes in the NATO alliance and discusses problems such as
equality in defense expenditures, the applicability of the
alliance to non-European regions, and varying attitudes
within NATO toward the detente concept.

1831.   Hunt, Kenneth. "Crisis and Consensus in the West:
The Boundaries of Shared Interests." Naval War College
Review 37 (November-December 1984):58-70.   Discusses
tensions within NATO and how these influence NATO's
responses to crises. Hunt argues that there must be more
cooperation and consultation within NATO to improve its
responses.

1832.   Kerr, Donald M. and Steven A. Maaranen. "The Nuclear
Defense of Europe." Washington Monthly 6 (Autumn 1983):93-
110. Asserts that NATO is stronger than the Warsaw Pact
countries in terms of nuclear weapons and warns against
losing this preeminent position through disarmament.

1833.   Landry, John R. and others. "Deep Attack in Defense
of Central Europe: Implications for Strategy and Doctrine."
In Essays on Strategy: The 1983 Joint Chiefs of Staff Essay
Competition, 29-77.   Washington, D.C.: National Defense
University Press, 1984.   158p. SOD D5.402:548/5. Argues
that deep attack (preventing reinforcement of Warsaw Pact
forces) is entirely compatible with NATO's "flexible
response" strategy. The authors examine European criticisms
of deep attack theory.

1834.   McCausland, Jeff. "Dual Track or Double Paralysis?
The Politics of INF." Armed Forces & Society 12 (Spring
1986):431-452.   Analyzes tensions within NATO between the
United States and its European partners about the nature of
deterrence. Much of the article discusses the controversy
over deploying Pershing II and cruise missiles in Western
Europe.

1835.   Olson, Eric T. "NATO Burden-Sharing: A New Look
Needed." Military Review 63 (November 1983):12-20.
Predicts new tensions within the alliance over its
financial costs. Olson criticizes the measures currently
used to determine contributions and proposes changing to
what he terms "output-oriented measures."

1836.   Pfaltzgraff, Robert L., Jr., "The Atlantic Alliance:
Looking Ahead." In Defense Planning for the 1990's, edited
by William A. Buckingham, 87-108.   Washington, D.C.:
National Defense University Press, 1984. 380p. SOD
D5402:P69.   Pessimistic about the future of NATO.
Pfaltzgraff notes the desire of many Europeans for more
policy independence and the continuing debates over
allocation of resources for NATO.

1837.   Quester, George H. "The Future of the American NATO
Commitment." In Defense Planning for the 1990s, edited by
William A. Buckingham, Jr., 109-137. Washington, D.C.:
National Defense University Press, 1984. 380p. SOD
D5.402:P69.   Stresses the continuing importance of Europe
to American strategies.   Public opinion polls bolster
Quester's assertion about the primacy of Europe in American
thinking.   Quester concludes with a lengthy survey of
problems which exist or which may emerge for the alliance.

1838.   Quester, George H. "The Superpowers and the Atlantic
Alliance." Daedalus 110 (Winter 1981):23-40. Suggests that
despite the Vietnam retreat and the increasing power of the
Soviet Union, most Europeans retain their faith in American
military strength and political leadership.

1839.   Record, Jeffrey. "The Europeanization of NATO: A Restructured Commitment for the 1980s." Air University Review 33 (September-October 1982):23-28. None of the NATO partners has given the alliance enough military support; the United States is as much at fault as the European members. The United States does have non-European commitments and may therefore want to apply the Nixon Doctrine to Europe and reduce its presence in Europe.

1840.   Reinertson, John E. "The Egon Bahr Line." In Defense Planning for the 1990's, edited by William A. Buckingham, 139-156.   Washington,   D.C.:National   Defense   University Press, 1984. 380p. SOD D5.402:P69   Discusses Western European socialist advocacy of detente despite growing tension between the United States and the USSR. Reinertson examines the theories of German SPD leader Egon Bahr as an illustration of detente theory.

1841.   Remnek, Richard B. "A Possible Fallback Counter-offensive Option in a European War." Air University Review 35 (November-December 1983):52-62. Discusses the problems of mobilizing NATO fully in the face of a Soviet war threat.   If mobilization were not achieved quickly, NATO might attack East Europe from southern France or northern Italy.

1842.   Sander, Thomas F. "Project Partnership: An Aid to Cooperation between Allied Forces." Military Review 61 (February 1981):42-47. Traces efforts since 1968 to improve relations between NATO forces to prepare for coordination in wartime.   Project Partnership is important and requires more support.

1843.   Snyder, Jed C. "European Security, East-West Policy, and the INF Debate." Orbis 27 (Winter 1984):913-970. Discusses NATO strategy and the impact of United States deployment of cruise missiles in Europe. Snyder provides a detailed analysis, including Soviet efforts to prevent cruise deployment.

1844.   Thomson, James A. "The LRTNF Decision: Evolution of US Theatre Nuclear Policy, 1975-9." International Affairs 60 (Autumn 1984):601-614. Focuses on the agreement made by the NATO powers in 1979 to place intermediate-range missiles in Western Europe.   This is a detailed study of the decision and the discussion that preceded it.

1845.   Tornetta, Vincenzo. "Rethinking NATO Strategy." Washington Quarterly 7 (Summer 1984):13-20. Argues for the development of a revised general strategy for NATO.

1846.   Van Heuven, Martin. "U.S. Policy, the Press, and the Atlantic Alliance." In The Future of European Alliance Systems: NATO and the Warsaw Pact, edited by Arlene Idol Broadhurst, 113-120.   Boulder, Colorado: Westview Press,

1982. Argues that a new "political base" needs to be developed for NATO. Van Heuven then reviews the consultative structures within NATO.

1847. Wagner, Gerrit A. "Economic Impacts on the Alliance." United States Naval Institute Proceedings 110 (December 1984):6-13. Part of a "Sea Link Supplement," the article discusses economic tensions that can affect NATO. Wagner emphasizes the importance of economic stability and the significance of defending sea lanes.

1848. West, F.J., Jr. "NATO II: Common Boundaries for Common Interests." Naval War College Review 34 (January-February 1981):59-67. Looks at the geographic focus of NATO, particularly in regard to NATO naval forces. The NATO I strategy was the containment of Soviet strength to Europe. The Persian Gulf, however, is a vital region for the United States, which created the Rapid Deployment Force. West believes NATO II should be formulated by extending the boundaries of the alliance to include Japan. He examines the strategic implications of an extended NATO.

Saudi Arabia

Official Policy Statements

1849. Reagan, Ronald. "Remarks Following a Meeting with Former National Security Officials on the Sale of AWACS Plans and Other Air Defense Equipment to Saudi Arabia. October 5, 1981." In Public Papers of the Presidents of the United States: Ronald Reagan 1981, 889-890. Washington, D.C.: Government Printing Office, 1982. Notes that both Democratic and Republican national security specialists support the sale of the AWACS aircraft to Saudi Arabia. Henry Kissinger and Harold Brown also make brief statements.

Periodical Articles

1850. Peterson, J.E. "Defending Arabia: Evolution of Responsibility." Orbis 28 (Fall 1984):465-488. Compares American and British approaches to Arabian defense. The American presence so far has been more limited than the British involvement.

Asia

Official Policy Statements

1851. Reagan, Ronald. "Joint Communique Following Discussions with President Chun Doo Hwan of the Republic of Korea. February 2, 1981." In Public Papers of the Presidents of the United States: Ronald Reagan 1981, 68-70. Washington, D.C.: Government Printing Office, 1982. Affirms that "the United States has no plans to withdraw

United States ground combat forces from the Korean peninsula." The communique discusses other aspects of South Korean security and, at more length, Korean-American economic relations.

Books

1852. Webb, James H. Micronesia and U.S. Pacific Strategy: A Blueprint for the 1980s. New York: Praeger Publishers, 1974. 109p. Writing on the assumption that the United States is gradually reducing its military presence in Northwest Asia, the author examines Micronesia's role in American strategy if the United States does change its military posture.

Periodical Articles

1853. Betts, Richard K. "Washington, Tokyo, and Northeast Asian Security: A Survey." Journal of Strategic Studies 6 (December 1983):5-30.   Northeast Asia remains relatively quiet after more than twenty years of tensions, especially in Korea.   Betts examines American perceptions of United States interests in the area.

1854. Gray, Colin S. "Maritime Strategy and the Pacific: The Implications for NATO." Naval War College Review 40 (Winter 1987):8-19. Notes the land bias of much thinking about a war between the NATO and Warsaw alliances and argues for a global strategy, not simply a land or maritime strategy. Gray reviews the Soviet buildup in East Asia and suggests tactics the United States should use to counter this buildup.

1855.   Scott,   Allen.   "The South Pacific: Setting Priorities." United States Naval Institute Proceedings 113 (July 1987):50-56. Warns that the American position in the South Pacific is deteriorating, while the Soviets have improved their position in the wake of Gorbachev's 1986 Vladisvostok speech. Scott summarizes current Soviet bloc political and naval initiatives in the area and American responses.

Sino-American Relations

1856. Bullard, Monte R. "The US-China Defense Relationship." Parameters 13 (March 1983):43-50.   Emphasizes the problems in the relationship, including the limited need of the Chinese army for sophisticated American weapons.

1857. Heaton, William R. "America and China: The Coming Decade." In Defense Planning for the 1990s, edited by William A. Buckingham, Jr., 221-238.   Washington, D.C.: National Defense University Press, 1984. 380p. SOD D5.402:P69. Discusses forces that seem to have deemphasized the American relationship with the Peoples Republic of

China. Heaton recommends restraint in developing military ties with China and avoidance of clashes with it over Taiwan.

1858.   Morrison,   David   C.   "Japanese   Principles,   U.S. Policies." Bulletin of the Atomic Scientists 41 (June/July 1985):22-24.   Suggests   that   the   United   States-Japanese alliance may be affected by Japanese concern over nuclear weapons. This might limit American freedom of movement in the area near Northeast Asia.

1859. Nacht, Michael. "Will the Pacific Alliance Endure?" In Defense Planning for the 1990s, edited by William A. Buckingham,   Jr.,   255-271.   Washington,   D.C.:   National Defense University Press, 1984. 380p. SOD D5.402:P69.   The relationship between the United States and Japan is the focus of the essay.   Forecasts developments through 2000. Nacht predicts few major changes.

1860.   Tatad, Francisco S. "Keeping the Philippine Bases." Washington Quarterly 7 (Winter 1984):85-90. Describes the great significance of these bases to the American military and naval posture in the Far East. Tatad also examines the problems   connected   with   internal   conflict   in   the Philippines over the continuance of the Marcos regime.

1861.   Young, James V. "A Realistic Approach to the US-Japanese Alliance." Military Review 65 (May 1985):63-73. The United States has important reasons for maintaining close ties with Japan.   Young supports Reagan's effort to involve Japan more deeply in Pacific security.

Indian Ocean

1862.   McGuire, Kevin and others. "Australia, America, and Indian   Ocean   Security: Possibilities   for   Increased Cooperation." In Essays on Strategy: The 1983 Joint Chiefs of Staff Essay Competition, 103-143.   Washington, D.C.: National Defense University Press, 1984. SOD D5.402:S4B/5. Examines the many advantages of involving Australia more fully in Indian ocean security.   The authors feel that the United States has to be a better ally to Australia.

1863.   Rais, Rasul B. "An Appraisal of U.S. Strategy in the Indian Ocean." Asian Survey 23 (September 1983):1043-1051. Surveys the diminishing role of the United States in the area   and   notes   that   the   United   States   is   asking   for assistance from other NATO countries.

1864.   Ryan, Paul B. "Diego Garcia." United States Naval Institute   Proceedings   110   (September   1984):132-136. Describes   the   developing   American   interests   in   this British-controlled island in the Indian Ocean.   Ryan also discusses   the   influence   of   events   in   Iran   on   American efforts to build a major base at Diego Garcia.

Grenada

Official Policy Statements

1865.   Reagan, Ronald. "Address to the Nation on Events in
Lebanon and Grenada. October 27, 1983." In Public Papers of
the Presidents of the United States: Ronald Reagan 1983,
II,   1517-1522.   Washington,   D.C.:Government   Printing
Office,   1985.   Reagan   touches   briefly   on   the   events
surrounding   the   mission   to   Grenada.   Referring   to   the
American   students   and   others   in   Grenada,   he   says   that   the
"nightmare of our hostages in Iran must never be repeated."
Reagan refers to the Cuban military presence in Grenada and
the request for assistance that the United States received
from the Organization of Eastern Caribbean States.

Books

1866.   Valenta,   Jiri   and   Herbert   J.   Ellison,   editors.
Grenada   and   Soviet/Cuban   Policy: Internal   Crisis   and
U.S./OECS Intervention. Boulder, Colorado: Westview Press,
1986. 400p. Collection of essays that analyzes the Soviet
and   Cuban   documents   found   in   Grenada   and   discusses   the
challenge the United States faced in 1983.   The essays also
suggest ways for dealing with similar contingencies in the
future.

Periodical Articles

1867.   Bolger,   Daniel   P.   "Operation   Urgent   Fury   and   Its
Critics."   Military   Review   66   (July   1986):57-69.   Argues
that   the   operation   achieved   its   goals   and   that   problems
encountered have been given too much publicity.

1868.   Byron,   Michael   J.   "Fury   from   the   Sea: Marines   in
Grenada."   United   States   Naval   Institute   Proceedings   110
(May   1984):118-131.   Presents   a   general   survey   of   the
situation in Grenada and the American invasion.

1869.   Coll,   Albert   R.   "Why   Grenada   Was   Important."   Naval
War   College   Review   40   (Summer   1987):4-18.   Argues   that   the
United States must not concede large areas of the worlds in
the course of putting priorities on its national interests.
Coll   describes   the   communist   seizure   of   Grenada   and   then
examines   the   political-strategic   lessons   of   the   Grenada
episode as they concern the United States.

1870.   De   Camp,   William   T.   "Grenada: The   Spirit   and   the
Letter   of   the   Law."   Naval   War   College   Review   38   (May-June
1985):28-36.   Argues   that   the   Grenada   intervention   was
justified   by   international   law,   although   perhaps   the
intervention did infringe it formally.

1871.   Gabriel, Richard. "Scenes from an Invasion: How the

United States Stumbled to Victory in Grenada." Washington
Monthly 18 (January 1986):34-41. Severely critical account
of American military performance at Grenada. A series of
errors were perpetuated, which did not effect the ultimate
success of the operation because of the weakness of the
defending forces and the great strength of their American
opponents.

1872. Motley, James Berry. "Grenada: Low-Intensity
Conflict and the Use of U.S. Military Power." World Affairs
146 (Winter 1983-84):221-238. Asserts that the military
operations in Grenada demonstrate the effectiveness of low-
intensity warfare. Low-intensity conflicts are likely to
occur because they are in reality confrontations between
the United States and the Soviet Union. All the armed
services need the flexibility and the capability to deploy
quickly to defend American commitments.

1873. Wright, Christopher C. "U.S. Naval Operations in
1983." United States Naval Institute Proceedings 110 (May
1984):52-67, 285-295. Includes material on American naval
operations at Grenada and Lebanon. Wright also examines
naval exercises during the year and varying patterns of
naval deployment.

Lebanon

Official Policy Statements

1874. Reagan, Ronald, "Remarks to Reporters Announcing the
Deployment of United States Forces in Beirut, Lebanon.
August 20, 1982." In Public Papers of the Presidents of the
United States: Ronald Reagan 1982, II, 1062-1063.
Washington, D.C.: Government Printing Office, 1983.
Discusses the purposes of the deployment, which include
assistance in the removal of PLO elements. Reagan
summarizes recent negotiations and asserts that "my
agreement to include United States forces in a
multinational force was essential to our success."

1875. Reagan, Ronald. "Statement on the Situation in
Lebanon. February 7, 1984." In Public Papers of the
Presidents of the United States: Ronald Reagan 1984, I,
185-186. Washington, D.C.: Government Printing Office,
1986. Pointing to the continued fighting in Lebanon, Reagan
discusses the American presence in that country and
announces that air and naval gunnery support will be given
against attacks on the Multinational Force or on Beirut. He
also promises supplies and training for the Lebanese Army.
The marines are being withdrawn to American ships off the
coast, however, leaving only military advisers ashore.

Books

1876. Thakur, Ramesh. International Peacekeeping in

<u>Lebanon: United Nations Authority and Multinational Force</u>.
Boulder, Colorado: Westview Press, 1987. 356p. Generally
critical of the Multinational Force because Thakur sees a
profound contradiction between national forces supporting a
United Nations initiative and at the same time pursuing
their own nations' interests. Peacekeeping must be kept a
United Nations function in order to achieve success, Thakur
asserts.

1877. U.S. Department of Defense. <u>Report of the DoD
Commission on Beirut International Airport Terrorist Act,
October 23, 1983</u>. Washington, D.C.:   Government Printing
Office, 1983. 141p. SOD D1.2:B39. The report covers more
than the attack, although that is examined at length. It
provides a good deal of information on the political and
military situation in Lebanon at the time of the attack.

Periodical Articles

1878. Vallee, Bruce. "Within Our Reach, Beyond Our Grasp?"
<u>United States Naval Institute Proceedings</u> 111 (July 1985):
56-72. Discusses the policy problems associated with
American military intervention, using Lebanon in the 1980's
as a case in point. Goals are often not clearly set,
creating problems for the armed services.

War Powers

1879. Sullivan, John H. <u>The War Powers Resolution: A
Special, Study of the Committee on Foreign Affairs</u>.
Washington, D.C.:   Government Printing Office, 1982. 292p.
SOD Y4.F76/1:W19. Committee print presents useful
information on the origins, development and application of
the War Powers Resolution. Various sections discuss the
Resolution in relation to international crises in which the
United States was involved.

1880. Sabrosky, Alan Ned. "The War Powers Resolution:
Retrospect and Prospect." In <u>The Reagan Defense Program: An
Interim Assessment</u>, edited by Stephen J. Cimbala, 119-144.
Wilmington, Delaware: Scholarly Resources, Inc., 1986.
Reviews very briefly, experiences with the War Powers
Resolution during the Nixon, Ford, and Carter
administrations, before moving to the events of the early
1980's. Sabrosky stresses the Lebanon mission and Central
America. He predicts that "prudence will mark executive-
congressional relations in this area for the immediate
future."

Libya

Books

1881. Kaldor, Mary and Paul Anderson, editors. <u>MAD DOGS:</u>

The U.S. Raids on Libya. London: Pluto Press Ltd., 1986.
Compilation of materials on all aspects of the air attacks
in 1986. There is extensive detail not only on the
military aspects, but also on the political ramifications.
Some sections put the raid into its broader strategic
context. Highly critical of American policies.

Periodical Articles

1882. Vox Militaris. "The US Strike Against Libya:
Operation El Dorado Canyon." Army Quarterly and Defence
Journal 116 (January 1986):134-143. Highly detailed,
chronological examination of the retaliatory attack on
Libya. The author also discusses protests concerning the
American use of air bases in the United Kingdom for
mounting the attack.

Persian Gulf

Books

1883. Epstein, Joshua M. Strategy and Force Planning: The
Case of the Persian Gulf. Washington, D.C.: Brookings
Institution, 1986. 210p. Discusses possible strategies for
the United States in the Persian Gulf region. This is a
highly technical study of the feasibility of various types
of operations. Epstein favors use of a smaller American
military force than currently planned. A smaller force may
be sent to the area more quickly than a larger one.

1884. Olson, William J., editor. U.S. Strategic Interests
in the Gulf Region. Boulder, Colorado: Westview Press,
1986. 234p. Essays examine the political problems of the
area and the involvement of the Soviet Union, and then turn
to American reactions to the Gulf challenge. Force
projection, rapid deployment, and military assistance to
Gulf countries are among the topics examined.

1885. Snyder, Jed C. Defending the Fringe: NATO, the
Mediterranean, and the Persian Gulf. Boulder, Colorado:
Westview Press, 1986. 110p. Examines possible superpower
collisions outside areas protected by the NATO alliance and
proposes ways to improve United States planning for such
contingencies. Snyder also discusses the effects of the
American loss of nuclear superiority on American strategy.

Essays and Periodical Articles

1886. Betts, Richard K. "Southeast Asia and U.S. Global
Strategy: Continuing Interests and Shifting Priorities."
Orbis 29 (Summer 1985):351-385. Presents a detailed
analysis of American security interests in Southeast Asia
and the challenges that face American decision makers.

1887. Cronin, Richard P. "The United States and South Asia: India." In Defense Planning for the 1990s, edited by William A. Buckingham, Jr., 311-321. Washington, D.C.: National Defense University Press, 1984. SOD D5.402:P69. Examines United States-Indian relations primarily in terms of the problem of Pakistan. Cronin also reviews India's political scene and military policies.

1888. Ransom, David M. and others.   "Atlantic Cooperation for Persian Gulf Security." In Essays on Strategy: Selections from the 1983 Joint Chiefs of Staff Essay Competition, 79-102. Washington, D.C.: National Defense University Press, 1984. SOD 5.402:St8/5.   Analyzes the failure to build a NATO diplomatic, economic and military response to Persian Gulf problems.   The authors favor a firm NATO policy, but admit that allied unity toward the Middle East is a long way off.

1889.   Saunders, Harold H. "The Middle East and Southwest Asia: What Strategies for the US?" In The 1980s: Decade of Confrontation? Proceedings of the Eighth National Security Affairs Conference 13-15 July 1981, 65-82. Washington, D.C.: National Defense University Press, 1981. SOD D5.412.981. Sees Southwest Asia and the Middle East as the crucial area of conflict in the 1980's. Saunders presents a number of strategic options and substrategies to deal with possible crises.

1890. West, Francis J., Jr. "The United States and South Asia: India, Pakistan, Afghanistan, and Iran." In Defense Planning for the 1990s, edited by William A. Buckingham, Jr.,   323-330.   Washington,   D.C.:   National   Defense University Press, 1984. SOD D5.402.P69.   Reviews the military and economic situations of these countries and sketches their relationships with the United States. The most serious problem remains the war between Iraq and Iran.

1891. Wiley, Marshall W. "American Security Concerns in the Gulf." Orbis 28 (Fall 1984):456-464. Criticizes administration views of the war between Iraq and Iran, and offers proposals for reaching appropriate American objectives.

Central America

Official Policy Statements

1892. Reagan, Ronald. "Excerpts From an Interview with Walter Cronkite of CBS News. March 3, 1981." In Public Papers of the Presidents of the United States: Ronald Reagan 1981, 191-202.   Washington, D.C.: Government Printing Office, 1982. States that United States military advisory efforts in El Salvador are limited to training and are, therefore, quite different from the situation in Vietnam before 1965. Reagan also distinguishes between American involvement in El Salvador and the Soviet invasion

of Afghanistan. The interview includes some references by
Reagan to what action might be taken toward Cuba because of
its support for the rebels in El Salvador.

1893. Reagan, Ronald. "Message to the Congress on Proposed
Caribbean Basin Initiative Legislation. February 18, 1983."
In Public Papers of the Presidents of the United States:
Ronald Reagan 1983, I, 248-249. Washington, D.C.:
Government Printing Office, 1984. Describes the nature of
the funding he requests for the Caribbean assistance
program. It is designed to shore up the economic and,
ultimately, the political systems of those states which are
being assailed "by externally-supported minorities."

1894. Reagan, Ronald. "Remarks on Central America and El
Salvador at the Annual Meeting of the National Association
of Manufacturers. March 10, 1983." In Public Papers of the
Presidents of the United States: Ronald Reagan 1983, I,
372, 277. Washington, D.C.:   Government Printing Office,
1984. Describes the challenge of communist subversion in
the Caribbean area and affirms that the major issue in the
region "is the United States national security." Reagan
emphasizes Nicaraguan aid to communist guerrillas in El
Salvador.   He also reviews American military programs in
Central America, especially El Salvador.

1895. Reagan, Ronald. "Remarks and a Question-and-Answer
Session With Reporters on Domestic and Foreign Policy
Questions. April 14, 1983." In Public Papers of the
Presidents of the United States: Ronald Reagan 1983, I,
539-541. Washington, D.C.:   Government Printing Office,
1984. In response to questions from reporters, Reagan
states that the executive branch is complying fully with
the Boland amendment and is "simply trying to interdict"
Nicaraguan supply lines to the rebels in El Salvador. He
criticizes Nicaraguan efforts to assist the rebels.

1896. Reagan, Ronald. "Address Before a Joint Session of
the Congress on Central America. April 27, 1983." In Public
Papers of the Presidents of the United States: Ronald
Reagan 1983, I, 601-607. Washington, D.C.:   Government
Printing Office, 1984. Praises the progress El Salvador is
making toward democracy and criticizes the Nicaraguan
government for rejecting democratic development.   Reagan
quotes an address by President Truman in 1947 asking for
assistance for Greece and outlines American policy toward
Central America.

1897. Reagan, Ronald "Remarks Announcing a Proposed
Initiative for Central America. February 3, 1984." In
Public Papers of the Presidents of the United States:
Ronald Reagan 1984, I, 164-165. Washington, D.C.:
Government Printing Office, 1986. Discusses legislation
that Reagan plans to recommend to Congress for economic and
military assistance to Central American countries and for

carrying out diplomatic initiatives such as the
establishment of a Central American Development
Organization.

1898.   Reagan, Ronald. "Address to the Nation on United
States Policy in Central America. May 9, 1984." In Public
Papers of the Presidents of the United States: Ronald
Reagan 1984, I, 659-666. Washington, D.C.:   Government
Printing Office, 1986. Warns Americans of the extensive
Soviet use of "subversion... and surrogate forces" to
weaken the international position of the United States.
Reagan notes the strategic importance of the Caribbean area
and describes Nicaraguan operations in Central America,
especially support for the rebels in El Salvador. The
address includes a summary of his proposals for aiding El
Salvador and a plea for public support of his program.

Books

1899. Best, Edward. U.S. Policy and Regional Security in
Central America. New York: St. Martin's Press, 1987. 182p.
Focuses on the Reagan administration's stance toward
Central American problems. One chapter deals specifically
with American support for the Contras. Best suggests that
there are three major policy alternatives for the United
States. He favors negotiating with the Nicaraguan
government and using economic and diplomatic pressures
rather than military measures.

1900. Black, Jan Knippers. Sentinels of Empire: The United
States and Latin American Militarism. Westport,
Connecticut: Greenwood Press, 1986. 240p. Discusses
American relations with the military in various Latin
American countries during the 1960's, 1970's and 1980's.
Black is highly critical of American policies and
performance.

1901. Coleman, Kenneth M. and George C. Herring, editors.
The Central American Crisis: Sources of Conflict and the
Failure of U.S. Policy. Wilmington, Delaware: Scholarly
Resources, Inc., 1985. 224p.   A number of essays examine
the political, economic, and social aspects of the Central
American problem.   They also examine Reagan's policies,
especially regarding Nicaragua.   While the book does not
emphasize military topics, it is a useful background
source.

1902. Dixon, Marlene, editor. On Trial: Reagan's War
Against Nicaragua: Testimony of the Permanent Peoples'
Tribunal. San Francisco: Synthesis Publications, 1985.
300p. Criticizes all phases of American policy hostile to
the Sandinista government of Nicaragua. The most important
essay for the purposes of this bibliography is Rosa Pasos'
"Report on Military Aggression Against Nicaragua by U.S.
Imperialism," pages 29-51, which purports to give much

factual information on American operations in Central America.

1903. Pastor, Robert A. <u>Condemned to Reptition: The United States and Nicaragua</u>. Princeton: Princeton University Press, 1987. 392p. Extensive analysis of United States-Nicaraguan relations during the Carter administration, with a chapter on developments under Reagan. Pastor compares the relationship with the problems that developed with the United States and Cuba in the late 1950's.

1904. Saunders, John, editor. <u>Population Growth in Latin America and U.S. National Security</u>. London: Allen & Unwin, 1986. 305p. Primarily a study of economic development, this collection of essays includes recommendations for American decision makers. Emigration is also discussed. This is an important study of a problem of increasing concern in the United States.

1905. White, Richard Alan. <u>The Morass: United States Intervention in Central America</u>. New York: Harper & Row, Publishers, 1984. 319p. Highly critical account of CIA and United States military involvement. White discusses efforts to adapt lessons from Vietnam for Guatemala and El Salvador.

Periodical Articles

1906. Dickey, Christopher. "Central America: From Quadmire to Cauldron?" <u>Foreign Affairs</u> 62 (1984):659-694. Part of a special issue of <u>Foreign Affairs</u>, this article emphasizes American military assistance to El Salvador and American moves in Grenada and against Nicaragua. Reagan is able to deal more decisively with Central America and the Caribbean than with other regions of the world.

1907. O'Ballance, Edgar. "The Nicaraguan Domino." <u>Military Review</u> 63 (October 1983):2-10. Discusses the development of the Sandinista movement and traces its successful effort to overthrow the Somosa regime. O'Ballance sees the Sandinistas as Soviet allies, but is optimistic about the chances that the <u>Contras</u> will take control of Nicaragua. Several pages examine the <u>Contra</u> military effort and their training by the CIA. O'Ballance is a strong advocate of American support for the <u>Contras</u> and asserts both the <u>Contras</u> and their American allies have learned a good deal from Vietnam.

Author Index

All number references in this index refer to entries, not to pages.

Subject Index

All number references in this index refer to entries, not to pages.

About the Compiler

BENJAMIN R. BEEDE is Collection Development Librarian, Kilmer Area Library of Rutgers, the State University of New Jersey, in New Brunswick. His publications include *Politics and Government of New Jersey, 1900-1980* (1989), *Intervention and Counterinsurgency: An Annotated Bibliography of the Small Wars of the United States, 1898-1984* (1985), *Independence Documents of the Countries of the World* (1977), and *Legal Sources of Public Policy* (1977).